THE OXFORD INTERNATIONAL RELATIONS IN SOUTH ASIA SERIES

SERIES EDITORS
Sumit Ganguly and E. Sridharan

After a long period of relative isolation during the Cold War years, contemporary South Asia has grown immensely in its significance in the global political and economic order. This ascendancy has two key dimensions. First, the emergence of India as a potential economic and political power that follows its acquisition of nuclear weapons and its fitful embrace of economic liberalization. Second, the persistent instability along India's borders continues to undermine any attempts at achieving political harmony in the region: fellow nuclear-armed state Pakistan is beset with chronic domestic political upheavals; Afghanistan is paralysed and trapped with internecine warfare and weak political institutions; Sri Lanka is confronted by an uncertain future with a disenchanted Tamil minority; Nepal is caught in a vortex of political and legal uncertainty as it forges a new constitution; and Bangladesh is overwhelmed by a tumultuous political climate.

India's rising position as an important player in global economic and political affairs warrants extra-regional and international attention. The rapidly evolving strategic role and importance of South Asia in the world demands focused analyses of foreign and security policies within and towards the region. The present series addresses these concerns. It consists of original, theoretically grounded, empirically rich, timely, and topical volumes oriented towards contemporary and future developments in one of the most populous and diverse corners of the world.

Sumit Ganguly is Professor of Political Science and Rabindranath Tagore Chair in Indian Cultures and Civilizations, Indiana University, Bloomington, USA.

E. Sridharan is Academic Director, University of Pennsylvania Institute for the Advanced Study of India, New Delhi.

irsa

THE OXFORD INTERNATIONAL RELATIONS IN SOUTH ASIA SERIES

India's Military Modernization

Challenges and Prospects

Edited by
Rajesh Basrur
Ajaya Kumar Das
Manjeet S. Pardesi

OXFORD
UNIVERSITY PRESS

OXFORD
UNIVERSITY PRESS

Oxford University Press is a department of the University of Oxford.
It furthers the University's objective of excellence in research, scholarship,
and education by publishing worldwide. Oxford is a registered trademark of
Oxford University Press in the UK and in certain other countries

Published in India by
Oxford University Press
YMCA Library Building, 1 Jai Singh Road, New Delhi 110 001, India

ISBN-13: 978-0-19-809238-4
ISBN-10: 0-19-809238-5

Typeset in Adobe Jenson Pro 10.5/13
by The Graphics Solution, New Delhi 110 092
Printed in India by G.H. Prints Pvt Ltd, New Delhi 110 020

Contents

Tables and Figures

Tables

Figures

Acknowledgements

The editors are grateful to many individuals who played a vital role in helping to refine the chapters that went into this volume. Sunil Dasgupta, Anindyo Majumdar, Prakash Menon, and Deba Mohanty were specifically invited to critique the chapter drafts and provided excellent detailed critiques. Bernard Loo, Arpita Mathur, Harinder Singh, and several other participants in the authors' workshop provided valuable comments. The workshop could not have been conducted as smoothly as it was but for the able organizational assistance of Kartik Bommakanti and Eugene Tan and his team. Many thanks are due to the two anonymous reviewers who helped immeasurably to sharpen the focus of the chapters. We owe the initiation and successful outcome of this publication to the professionalism and commitment of the series editors, Sumit Ganguly and E. Sridharan. Finally, we are thankful to the team at Oxford University Press in New Delhi, for their efficiency and helpfulness through the long process of putting this volume together.

Abbreviations

AAD	area-air-defence
ABM	anti-ballistic missile
ADA	Aeronautical Development Agency
ADS	Air Defence Ship
AEC	Atomic Energy Commission
AESA	Active Electronically Scanned Array
AEW	Advanced Early Warning
AFSPA	Armed Forces (Special Powers) Act
AJT	Advanced Jet Trainer
ALH	Advanced Light Helicopter
AMCA	Advanced Medium Combat Aircraft
AR	Assam Rifles
ARF	ASEAN Regional Forum
ASR	Air Staff Requirement
ASuW	anti-surface warfare
ATGM	antitank guided missile
ATV	Advanced Technology Vessel
AWACS	Airborne Warning and Control System
BARC	Bhabha Atomic Research Centre
BBC	best of brochure claims
BDL	Bharat Dynamics Limited
BEL	Bharat Electronics Limited
BJP	Bharatiya Janata Party
BMD	ballistic missile defence
BMS	battle management systems
BSF	Border Security Force
BVR	Beyond Visual Range
C4ISR	command, control, communications, computers, intelligence, surveillance, and reconnaissance

CAPF	Central Armed Police Force
CBM	Confidence Building Measure
CCR&D	Chief Controller of Research and Development
CCS	Cabinet Committee on Security
CDS	Chief of Defence Staff
CENTO	Central Treaty Organization
CEP	Circular Error Probable
CI	counter-insurgency
CII	Confederation of Indian Industries
C-in-C	Commander-in-Chief
CISF	Central Industrial Security Force
CNO	computer network operations
COBRA	Combat Battalion for Resolute Action
COMINT	Communication Intelligence
COIN	counter-insurgency
CONOPS	Concept of Operations
COSC	Chiefs of Staff Committee
COTS	commercial off-the-shelf
CPMF	Central Para Military Force
CRPF	Central Reserve Police Force
CSIR	Council of Scientific and Industrial Research
CTBT	Comprehensive Test Ban Treaty
D&D	Design and Development
DAE	Department of Atomic Energy
DAY	dial-a-yield
DCC	Defence Committee of the Cabinet
DEAD	Destruction of Enemy Air Defences
DGP	Director General of Police
DIA	Defence Intelligence Agency
DIB	Defence Industrial Base
DMC	Defence Ministers Committee
DOFA	Defence Offset Facilitation Agency
DPP	Defence Procurement Procedures
DPSU	Defence Public Sector Undertaking
DRDO	Defence Research and Development Organization
DSV	Defence Space Vision
EADS	European Aeronautic Defense and Space Company
ECM	Electronic Counter Measures

EEZ	Exclusive Economic Zone
ELINT	Electronic Intelligence
EW	Electronic Warfare
FBW	fly-by-wire
FDI	foreign direct investment
FGFA	Fifth Generation Fighter Aircraft
FIR	First Information Report
FMS	Foreign Military Sales
GAGAN	GPS Aided GEO Augmented Navigation
GDP	Gross Domestic Product
GoM	Group of Ministers
GSQR/ QR	General Staff Qualitative Requirements
HADR	humanitarian assistance and disaster relief
HAL	Hindustan Aeronautics Limited
HE	high explosive
IA	Indian Army
IACCS	Integrated Air Command and Control System
IAEA	International Atomic Energy Agency
IAF	Indian Air Force
IAI	Israel Aircraft Industries
ICMB	Inter-Continental Ballistic Missile
IDS	Integrated Defence Staff
IDSA	Institute of Defence Studies and Analyses
IGMDP	Integrated Guided Missile Development Programme
IJT	Intermediate Jet Trainer
IN	Indian Navy
INA	Indian National Army
INCP	Interim National Command Post
INSAS	Indian Small Arms System
IONS	Indian Ocean Naval Symposium
IOR	Indian Ocean Region
IP	Industrial Participation
IPKF	Indian Peace Keeping Force
IPR	Intellectual Property Rights
IRGC	Russian Inter-Governmental Commission
ISR	Intelligence, Surveillance and Reconnaissance
ISRO	Indian Space Research Organisation
IT	information technology

ITBP	Indo-Tibetan Border Police
J&K	Jammu & Kashmir
JeM	Jaish-e-Mohammed
JIC	Joint Intelligence Committee
JWG	Joint Working Group
L&T	Larsen and Toubro
LCA	Light Combat Aircraft
LeT	Lashkar-e-Taiba
LGB	Laser Guided Bomb
LOC	Line of Control
LPD	landing platform dock
LRMP	long-range maritime patrol
LSTs	landing ships tank
LTTE	Liberation Tigers of Tamil Eelam
LWE	Left-Wing Extremist
MAD	mutually assured destruction
MBT	Main Battle Tank
MCA	Medium Combat Aircraft
MDL	Mazagon Dock Limited
MEA	Ministry of External Affairs
MHA	Ministry of Home Affairs
MIRV	multiple, independently targeted re-entry vehicles
MMRCA	Medium Multi-Role Combat Aircraft
MNF	Mizo National Front
MoD	Ministry of Defence
MPA	Maritime Patrol Aircraft
MRTA	multirole transport aircraft
MRO	Maintenance, Repair and Overhaul
MTCR	Missile Technology Control Regime
NATO	North Atlantic Treaty Organization
NCA	National Command Authority
NCP	National Command Post
NDWP	National Defence White Paper
NFU	no first use
NMD	national missile defence
NPT	Non-Proliferation Treaty
NSA	National Security Advisor
NSAB	National Security Advisory Board

NSC	National Security Council
NSG	National Security Guards
NWFP	North Western Frontier Province
NWS	Nuclear Weapon States
ODL	Operational Data Link
OEM	Original Equipment Manufacturer
OF	Ordinance Factory
OPV	offshore patrol vessel
Orbat	Order of Battle
PAF	Pakistan Air Force
PAL	permissive action link
PGM	precision guided munition
PLA	People's Liberation Army
PLAAF	People's Liberation Army Air Force
PLAN	People's Liberation Army Navy
PMO	Prime Minister's Office
PN	Pakistan Navy
POK	Pakistan Occupied Kashmir
PPRC	Policy Planning and Review Committee
PTA	pilotless target aircraft
QRSAM	Quick Reaction Surface-to-Air Missile
RAF	Royal Air Force
RUR	(*Raksha Udyog Ratnas*) Champions of Industry
SA	Scientific Advisor
SAM	Surface-to-Air Missile
SBC	Shipbuilding Centre
SEAD	Suppression of Enemy Air Defences
SEATO	Southeast Asia Treaty Organization
SFC	Strategic Forces Command
SIGINT	Signal Intelligence
SIPRI	Stockholm International Peace Research Institute
SLBM	submarine launched ballistic missile
SLOCs	Sea Lines of Communication
SNEP	Subterranean Nuclear Explosions Project
SOP	Standard Operating Procedure
SPB	Sagar Prahari Bal
SS	diesel attack submarines
SSB	Sashastra Seema Bal

SSBN	nuclear ballistic missile submarines
SSM	surface-to-surface missile
SSN	nuclear attack submarines
TMD	theatre missile defence
UAV	unmanned aerial vehicle
UCAV	unmanned combat air vehicle
UCS	Unified Command Structure
USAAF	United States Army Air Force
USAF	United States Air Force
VA/VP	Vital Area/Vital Point
WE	Weapons and Equipments

Introduction

RAJESH BASRUR, AJAYA KUMAR DAS, AND
MANJEET S. PARDESI

IN TANDEM WITH ITS RAPID economic development, India is in the
process of emerging as a major military power in Asia. In addition to
being the fourth largest global economy (when measured using purchasing
power parity) (World Bank 2011), India has the third largest armed forces
in the world (IISS 2011: 471–7). Even though India's annual defence
expenditure amounts to less than 3 per cent of its gross domestic product
(GDP), it is among the top ten defence spenders in the world.[1] A declared
nuclear weapons power, India is slowly but surely modernizing its nuclear
weapons capability and delivery systems while simultaneously working
on building missile defence systems (Tellis 2001; Ramana 2012: 33–4).
India's growing economy is expected to further improve the country's
already substantial military capabilities.[2] Consequently, it is important to
understand India's efforts to modernize its armed forces and the strategic
role that New Delhi is expected to carve for itself in Asian and world affairs.

With this overarching aim, the S. Rajaratnam School of International
Studies brought together a range of military and civilian experts from
India, the United States, and Singapore to address issues related to India's
military modernization for a workshop in Singapore in February 2011. The
nine thematic chapters in this volume were first presented at the workshop
in Singapore. The end of the Cold War era marked a watershed in India's
strategic history. It began to shift its strategic worldview from that of a
relatively weak player with a defensive outlook to that of a more confident
emerging power. However, there has been little detailed investigation
of its military forces and the ways in which they have responded to the

changing environment. Consequently, this volume aims to closely look at India's military forces and its defence policy to understand how India's armed forces are re-moulding themselves and responding to the demands of the emerging strategic setting.

Perhaps the most salient feature of India's current strategic situation is the need to foster a peaceful environment to promote the country's rapid economic development which increasingly depends on secure access to foreign sources of energy and global trade (Pardesi and Ganguly 2008). At the same time, India needs to respond to the phenomenal rise of China while ensuring the country's security vis-à-vis its increasingly unstable subcontinental rival, Pakistan, which has been resorting to a 'proxy war' (using non-state actors) against India.[3] How is the thinking and practice of India's armed forces and other organizations involved with defence policymaking evolving in the face of these and other challenges? Is the process of modernization underway in tune with the needs of the armed forces and overall strategic approach of the policymakers? What is the nature of strategic thinking and planning on military issues and how does it relate to military effectiveness?

While the rest of this volume addresses these questions in detail, it is important first to understand how India's defence and security policy has evolved since the country's independence in 1947 in order to better appreciate the challenges it currently faces. This will be the focus of the rest of this introductory chapter. The next section will briefly discuss India's defence and security policy as it emerged in the first decade-and-a-half after independence. India's policy underwent a radical change in the aftermath of its defeat in the 1962 Sino-Indian War. The change in India's worldview and its impact on the country's defence policy will be the focus of the subsequent section. During the rest of the Cold War period, the Indian approach to security evolved slowly and gradually even after India emerged as the dominant regional power in South Asia after the 1971 Bangladesh War. The penultimate section of this chapter will focus on the most important changes in India's defence and security policy after the end of the Cold War, thereby setting the stage for the rest of the essays in this volume.

Indian Defence and Security Policy, 1947–1962

India emerged from the detritus of the British Raj after the violent partition of the subcontinent in 1947 with the onerous task of integrating most of the 562 'princely states' that were tied to the British imperial administration through a system of ingeniously crafted treaties.[4] At the same time, the leadership of independent India with Prime Minister Jawaharlal Nehru in the vanguard accepted the legitimacy of India's borders inherited from the erstwhile Raj and sought to vigorously defend the territorial integrity of India (Ganguly 2010: 543–4). Even as Nehru had a personal aversion to the use of force, it had become apparent soon after independence that the military would have to play an important role in the consolidation and defence of the nascent Indian union. While most of the princely states peacefully acceded to the Indian union, Junagadh (1947) and Hyderabad (1947–8) were integrated with India only after the military was deployed.[5] Furthermore, the unusual circumstances surrounding the accession of the princely state of Kashmir with India resulted in the first war between India and Pakistan immediately after independence (1947–8) (Dasgupta 2002).

However, these problems were compounded by two major factors. The first major task was the creation and consolidation of the Indian armed forces after the partition of the British Indian military between India and Pakistan.[6] The second major problem was that the civilian leaders of India's nationalist movement were very suspicious of the military. The British Indian military had not played any significant role in the nationalist movement and had continued to remain loyal to the colonial government.[7] In fact, the military proved its nationalist credentials only in 1947–8 during the first Kashmir War. 'Overnight, so to say, the Indian army became popular with the public. During the British period, the general public had looked upon the army with suspicion … But the campaign in Kashmir changed all that' (Panikkar 1960: 36).

Given the colonial legacy of India's military and the profound impact of Mahatma Gandhi's non-violent ideology on the Indian nationalist movement (and Nehru), India sought to ensure the subordination of the military to civilian leadership and diminished the role of the military in defence policy-making after independence—policies that have continued until the present. Even before India became independent, Nehru reduced the political role of the Indian army. The Commander-in-Chief of the integrated service command had functioned as the Vice-President of the Viceroy's Executive Council under the British Raj.[8] However, after the interim government came into effect in late 1946, Nehru replaced the Commander-in-Chief with a civilian defence minister (Kavic

1967: 144). In other words, in the decision-making process that emerged after independence, India's armed forces did not have direct access to the country's top political leadership.

After 1950, the Indian Constitution ensured parliamentary control over defence issues. In theory, this meant that it was the entire parliament that controlled defence policy issues, including defence budget. However, in practice, it was the Defence Committee of the Cabinet—the apex defence policy-making body—that made the defence policy while the parliament influenced its direction 'through debates and investigations' (Thomas 1978: 67). Finally, the Indian government downgraded the administrative position of the military as well with the abolition of the position of the integrated services Commander-in-Chief in 1955. Since then, the army, the navy, and the air force have been led by their respective Chiefs of Staff (Rudolph and Rudolph 1964: 5–19).

While India's domestic policies ensured the apolitical and professional nature of the country's armed forces, India pursued a policy of refraining from entering into any global military blocs at the international level. India's nationalist leaders were very aware and critical of the role of Indian military manpower and finances in British colonial military adventures in Asia and beyond.[9] Therefore, in order to prevent India from becoming entangled in the Cold War politics, which was threatening to engulf the world around the time of its independence, India began to pursue the policy of non-alignment under Nehru's leadership (Thomas 1979: 153–71). Even before independence, Nehru had emphatically asserted that 'in no event should India be made to join any war without the consent of her own people being obtained' (Nehru 2004: 461).

In addition to its lack of material power at the time of independence, India's adoption of the policy of non-alignment to safeguard its strategic autonomy led to its marginalization in international affairs. The United States became uninterested and dismissive of India as India's quest for an independent foreign policy clashed with the United States' Cold War priorities (Kux 1993). Indo-US relations further deteriorated after the United States entered into a military alliance with Pakistan as a consequence of the 1954 mutual defence agreement. The trend continued with Pakistan's participation in US-led defence pacts in the Middle East and Southeast Asia (Kux 2001).

In the meanwhile, faced with an acute economic crisis, India cut its troops by 50,000 in 1950 (Barua 2005: 169). This reduction happened even as India was facing military crises with Pakistan (in Bengal in 1950 and in Kashmir in 1950–1) (Raghavan 2010: 149–226). It was in this strategic context that India pursued a policy of 'appeasement' towards China.[10] Nehru was confident that Tibet would continue to enjoy its autonomy under the Chinese rule if India acquiesced to Chinese sovereignty, and further believed that Tibet's forbidding terrain would limit the presence of China's People's Liberation Army (PLA)—thereby ensuring minimal Chinese military presence on India's Himalayan frontiers. Therefore, India readily accepted China's military annexation of Tibet in 1950–1 and signed an agreement with China in 1954 accepting Chinese sovereignty over it (Garver 2001: 32–109).

However, this agreement said nothing about the validity of the Tibetan (and hence Chinese) borders with India which had been agreed upon under the British Raj. So a few years later, when the Dalai Lama escaped and sought refuge in India in 1959 in the aftermath of brutal Chinese repression in Tibet, Sino-Indian relations deteriorated dramatically. Their militaries engaged in two large but localized clashes along their ill-defined borders later that year, thereby bringing their border issue to the forefront (Pardesi 2011). There was a precipitous decline in Sino-Indian relations after 1959. China's fears of Indian 'expansionism' as a result of Nehru's ill-conceived 'forward policy' along their poorly defined borders, and as a consequence of the misperception that India wanted to restore Tibet's 'buffer state' status between the two countries, resulted in a short but bitter war between India and China in 1962, in which India suffered a humiliating defeat (Garver 2006: 86–130).

The Aftermath of 1962

The Sino-Indian War had come as a huge shock to the Indian political and strategic communities, and had a drastic impact on the domestic and international bases of India's defence policy. At the domestic level, India began a programme of massive rearmament. India decided to raise ten new mountain divisions equipped and trained for high altitude warfare and to stabilize the Air Force at forty-five squadrons. At the same time, India began a massive programme to develop its defence-industrial base (Kavic 1967: 192–207). The war also had a major impact on civil-military relations in India. As a consequence of the tensions between India's civilian and military leadership that became apparent during the war, India's civilian leaders divorced themselves from operational matters by leaving them completely to the military (Raghavan 2009: 149–75). It was earlier noted that India's military leadership played no direct role in defence policy-making as a consequence of Nehru's decisions at the time of independence. With the changes in civil-military relations in India after the Sino-Indian War, the disconnect between India's civilian and military leaders on defence issues was complete—a state of affairs that persists even today.

The Sino-Indian War also had a profound impact on India's worldview as New Delhi began to realize that it needed foreign support to meet the Chinese military challenge. India sought and received (limited) military assistance from the United States (and the United Kingdom) during the 1962 Sino-Indian War. However, even this limited cooperation proved to be short-lived as India (and Pakistan) came under American military sanctions with the outbreak of the 1965 India-Pakistan War. Consequently, India came to view the United States as an unreliable strategic partner—a trend that continued for the rest of the Cold War (and continues to find resonance in certain quarters in India even today) (McMahon 1994: 272–336).

China dramatically improved its relations with India's subcontinental rival, Pakistan. The strategic implications of the Sino-Pakistani entente became apparent for New Delhi when China threatened to open a second front against India during the 1965 India-Pakistan War (Syed 1974). Sino-Indian relations became further strained after China's first nuclear test in 1964. India was unable to receive a nuclear umbrella from the United States, the Soviet Union, and the other great powers after 1964 (Noorani 1967: 490–502). Consequently, following an intense debate in the parliament, India embarked on its Subterranean Nuclear Explosions Project (SNEP) in the late 1960s (Ganguly 1983: 30–3).

The Sino-Soviet split, which had become apparent by this time, paved the way for closer Indo-Soviet relations as India continued looking for military and diplomatic help to meet the Chinese challenge. This culminated in the 1971 Treaty of Peace, Friendship, and Cooperation between India and the former Soviet Union which was signed on the eve of the Bangladesh War.[11] By this time, the United States had already reached out to China, using Pakistan as a conduit, to dramatically change the balance of power in its Cold War rivalry with the Soviet Union. During the 1971 Bangladesh War, the United States gave its tacit consent to China to attack India if New Delhi escalated the war in West Pakistan, and even threatened India militarily by sending a naval battle group to the Bay of Bengal (which was believed to be armed with nuclear weapons by Indian strategists). Although India did not escalate the war against West Pakistan, it successfully vivisected that country and created the state of Bangladesh, thereby emerging as the undisputed regional power in the subcontinent (Sisson and Rose 1990).

In 1974, India demonstrated its nuclear abilities by conducting a nuclear test that it dubbed as a 'peaceful nuclear explosion'. India had genuine security concerns which included China's nuclear capabilities, the emerging Sino-Pakistani entente, and even a perceived nuclear threat from the United States (most notably during the 1971 Bangladesh War) which ultimately led India to conduct a nuclear test. The nuclear test may also have signalled to the Soviets that India intended to maintain its foreign policy independence in spite of having signed the 1971 treaty.[12] The subcontinent enjoyed a unique period of strategic stability based on Indian predominance in the aftermath of the Bangladesh War until the Soviet invasion of Afghanistan in 1979.

India's Emergence as a Regional Power

India's bold foreign and security policy decisions (such as the military intervention in Pakistan that led to the birth of Bangladesh, and the decision to test a nuclear device in 1974) were at least in part a result of the centralization of the country's decision-making apparatus. Nehru's overwhelming dominance in the making of Indian foreign and security policy in the early independent years notwithstanding, he always tried to consult with India's small and weak opposition parties and leaders on important policy issues (Thomas 1986: 93). However, after the passing away of Nehru in 1964, 'India began moving toward the de facto presidentialization of the political system and the further centralization of the foreign policymaking process' as the Prime Minister's Office (PMO) strengthened its role in this arena (Cohen 2001: 69). The Prime Ministers that followed Nehru—Lal Bahadur Shastri, Indira Gandhi, Morarji Desai, and Rajiv Gandhi—further centralized the foreign policymaking process in the PMO and even stopped consulting opposition leaders. In fact, during Rajiv Gandhi's tenure as the Prime Minister (1984–9), the Congress Party enjoyed an overwhelming dominance in the Parliament by controlling almost 80 per cent of the seats—the highest ever—and saw no need to consult the Parliament whatsoever (Thomas 1986: 94).

In the 1980s, 'India engaged in the most significant conventional defence build-up in its history' until then (Smith 1994). Later in that decade, India initiated a number of military crises and even intervened militarily in the affairs of its neighbours. India's defence budget dramatically increased throughout the 1980s and India undertook a programme of massive arms imports (most of which were of Soviet origin). In order to test the efficacy of its newly formulated combined air-land battle plans, India's Chief of Army Staff launched two military exercises, one each along India's borders with Pakistan and China. The situation along both of these borders threatened to get out of hand and sparked fears of a major war along both of these fronts, although the actual outbreak of armed hostilities was averted in both cases (Bajpai *et al.* 1995; Natarajan 2000). The late 1980s further saw the emergence of India as a regional power with military interventions in Sri Lanka and the Maldives.[13] Later, angered by Nepal's purchase of military hardware from China, India blockaded Nepal economically to assert its regional dominance in the security affairs of the subcontinent.[14] It was widely believed by the end of the 1980s that India was transforming itself into a 'regional superpower' (Munro 1989).

The End of the Cold War and its Aftermath

In spite of its muscular diplomacy in the 1980s, India was unable to attain any of its fundamental national security goals. Its border dispute with China remained unresolved and India's mishandling of the domestic political situation in Kashmir provided an opportunity to Pakistan to convert a domestic (Indian) issue into an international issue from the late 1980s onwards by supporting elements hostile to Indian rule in Kashmir (Ganguly 1996: 76–107). Furthermore, Chinese nuclear proliferation to Pakistan from the 1970s onwards had fundamentally transformed India's strategic environment as Pakistan was widely believed to be nuclear capable by the late 1980s (Paul 2003). Moreover, as a consequence of the Sino-Soviet rapprochement in the late 1980s, it had already become apparent to New Delhi that India could no longer rely on Soviet support to meet the Chinese challenge (Garver 1991). Finally, the end of the Cold War and the implosion of India's superpower patron, the former Soviet

Union meant that the centrepiece of India's foreign policy, non-alignment, appeared to have become obsolete.[15] The implosion of the Soviet Union also meant that India lost a major source of military supplies and strategic support against China and Pakistan.

It was under these conditions that India began to draw closer to the United States. The process led to the signing of a ten-year defence agreement between India and the United States (under the governments of Prime Minister P.V. Narasimha Rao and President Bill Clinton respectively) in 1995 (Burns 1995). India also tried to improve its relations with China, and the two countries signed important military confidence-building measures in 1993 and 1996 (Sidhu and Yuan 2003: 124–6). While these were important agreements that reduced any immediate military tensions between the two countries, they did not result in any political understanding between them about their disputed and unmarked border. Nor was any progress made along other important issues that divided the two countries such as the Sino-Pakistani entente.

In 1998, a watershed event occurred—the opposition Bharatiya Janata Party (BJP) assumed power in New Delhi and conducted a series of nuclear tests in May that year, thereby ending India's policy of nuclear ambiguity.

Notwithstanding the BJP's image as a 'Hindu nationalist' party, India's decision to conduct nuclear tests had little to do with Hindu nationalism, but was the outcome of pressure from the global non-proliferation regime.[16] Preparations for the tests had begun much earlier under Prime Minister P.V. Narasimha Rao of the Congress Party. India immediately came under a host of US-led sanctions in the aftermath of its nuclear tests. However, New Delhi sought to engage Washington in talks to make the United States understand the Indian point of view. This led to a sustained dialogue between India's External Affairs Minister Jaswant Singh and the US Deputy Secretary of State Strobe Talbott.[17] Indo-US relations received a significant boost when the United States supported India's position in the 1999 Kargil War and blamed Pakistan for the crisis.[18] However, the Kargil War raised uncomfortable questions for Indian security by raising the issue of a limited conventional war in the presence of nuclear weapons.[19]

While Indo-US relations continued to improve in the aftermath of the 9/11 terrorist attacks as India offered 'unlimited support' to Washington, the terrorist threat raised even more questions for Indian defence and security policy. This clearly came to the forefront in the aftermath of the December 2001 terrorist attack on the Indian parliament by terrorist groups based in Pakistan (and believed to be supported by elements within the Pakistani military and government). India responded to this attack with its largest-ever military mobilization along the Pakistani border as an exercise in armed diplomacy in 2001–2. However, due to uncertainty about operational success amidst the presence of nuclear weapons, India did not launch military action against Pakistan (Ganguly and Kraig 2005: 290–324). While India is now searching for the strategic space to wage limited conventional military operations against Pakistan without escalating to a full-scale conventional war let alone a nuclear exchange, New Delhi has been unable to come up with a viable strategy (Ladwig 2007–8: 158–90). In fact, the search for a military option for punitive strikes against Pakistan notwithstanding, India's domestic response to terrorism also leaves much to be desired as the audacious Mumbai 2008 terror attacks (backed by elements within the Pakistani military) demonstrate (Blackwill et al. 2009).

In addition to the Pakistani challenge, Indian security planners also need to respond to the phenomenal rise of China. China's massive military modernization and infrastructure-building in Tibet has direct implications for Indian security. More importantly, China has become more assertive all along the disputed Sino-Indian border in recent years (Holslag 2010). Furthermore, the effectiveness of India's nuclear deterrent capability vis-à-vis China is questionable (Perkovich 2004.: 178–218). The Chinese threat is further exacerbated in Indian threat perceptions as a consequence of the Sino-Pakistani strategic entente. Indian strategists have noted the presence of several thousand PLA troops in Pakistan's northern areas with concern.[20] In fact, the Indian military is of the opinion that it must now prepare (in terms of doctrine, capabilities, and training) for a two-front scenario involving both Pakistan and China.[21]

Finally, India is undertaking a massive programme of weapons acquisition in order to meet its myriad security challenges. According to one estimate, India will spend US$ 80 billion on military modernization programmes by 2015 (Lombardo 2011). In recent years, Israel has emerged as India's second most important source of military systems after Russia, as India tries to diversify its military suppliers and searches for advanced weaponry (Blarel 2009). However, in as much as the dependence of military systems from foreign suppliers affects India's foreign policy options, what are the prospects for India to build an advanced defence-industrial base? And more importantly, how will the nature of civil-military relations affect the country's security policy? These and related questions are discussed in the rest of this volume.

Outline of the Volume

The Navy, the Air Force, and Nuclear Issues[22]

Given the growing centrality of the Indian Ocean in the twenty-first century, Ashok Sawhney argues that the Indian Navy should strive to establish order and stability in the Indian Ocean region in order to provide a peaceful environment for India's socio-economic growth. Sawhney believes that China's naval expansion in the Indian Ocean region and its growing partnership with Pakistan pose challenges for India's security. At the same time, Sawhney sees scope for Sino-Indian naval cooperation in the Indian Ocean region in the face of many non-traditional security threats. However, in order to maintain the credibility of its deterrence, Sawhney thinks that the Indian Navy must establish partnerships with the navies of friendly countries in the region such as the United States, Japan, Singapore, and Vietnam. Importantly, Sawhney also highlights the many domestic constraints that India faces which must be addressed before the Indian Navy can emerge as an effective force in the region. These include budgetary and indigenization limits as well as the nature of existing civil-military relations in India. He recommends that India should integrate the military in the higher national security decision-making apparatus in New Delhi. Finally, Sawhney notes that the limits of its decision-making apparatus notwithstanding, India lacks sufficient national resolve to use force proactively in a crisis.

Analogous to his army and naval counterparts, Pramod Mehra argues for a greater role of the Indian Air Force to meet the security challenges posed by Pakistan and China, and in order to support India's rising power and status. According to Mehra, India must rapidly modernize its Air Force given Chinese and Pakistani efforts to modernize their respective air forces as well the threat posed by Sino-Pakistani strategic alignment. He forcefully argues for the need for India to strive for and maintain a technological edge over its adversaries in the information age. However, Mehra identifies India's dependence on foreign suppliers as the greatest impediment to the growth of its air power. According to him, the Indian Air Force should strive for self-sufficiency. Besides addressing manpower policies, structural and training issues, Mehra feels that India should rapidly build up its defence-industrial base by involving the private sector. In the final chapter of the first section, Gurmeet Kanwal discusses India's nuclear doctrine as well as its operationalization. Kanwal notes that while India's 1974 nuclear test was a technology demonstrator, India's security concerns over China and Pakistan as well as the discriminatory nature of the global non-proliferation regimes compelled India to conduct five nuclear tests in 1998. According to Kanwal, India has based its nuclear doctrine on 'no first use' and 'credible minimum deterrence'. India's force structure is based on a triad of aircraft, mobile land-based missiles, and sea-based assets, and India is estimated to have between sixty and eighty warheads. Kanwal observes that in order to reduce the risk of accidental and inadvertent use of nuclear weapons, India has kept its warheads separate from launchers, and that the launchers are not deployed. While noting India's advocacy of universal nuclear disarmament, he emphasizes that India must modernize its nuclear warheads and delivery systems in order to respond effectively to any challenge from China or Pakistan.

Defence Industrialization

In his assessment of India's defence industries, Richard Bitzinger notes that India's quest for a self-sufficient military-industrial complex is a function of its great power aspiration and enduring lack of success will impact negatively on that ambition. However, Bitzinger notes that even as India has the second-largest defence-industrial base in the Asia-Pacific region, its performance has been unsatisfactory. According to him, India's problems are rooted in structural, financial, and cultural factors. For Bitzinger, India's Defence Research and Development Organization (DRDO) and its agenda of indigenization have been major obstacles. The DRDO has not only overestimated the technological capabilities of the local defence industry, it has also consistently low-balled production costs and timelines. Bitzinger remains somewhat skeptical that there will be any significant privatization of India's statist defence-industrial sector and concludes by noting that India's statist industry is unlikely to supply the necessary hardware to its armed forces as it continues with the mantra of self-sufficiency.

Ron Matthews and Alma Lozano explore the relevance of defence offsets in India's expanding defence industrial environment. According to them, India's policymakers view offsets as a vehicle to facilitate the enhancement of India's defence industrial capabilities. They argue that the launch of India's offset policy in 2006 was the 'easy part' but note that several difficult challenges remain, especially the task of defence indigenization through offsetting investment. They further note that Indian policymakers have failed to factor the ambivalence of defence contractors to release technology into their offsets calculus. The authors warn that India is unlikely to realize the benefits anticipated from its offset policy unless the conditions for ensuring viable and sustainable development are secured, particularly given the relative technological immaturity of India's defence economy. They emphatically argue that even as a political objective—the quest to become self-reliant in military production—was guiding India's offset policy and defence industrialization, India's policymakers have failed to realize that defence industrialization is an economic phenomenon and is heavily influenced by market forces. India must tackle the roadblocks posed by its undiversified government-owned companies, restrictions to foreign investment, and peripheral private sector participation in defence to benefit from its offsetting investment.

Domestic Politics and Internal Security

Bibhu Prasad Routray discusses the role of various Central Paramilitary Forces (CPMFs) raised by India to meet its specific national security requirements. He notes that in terms of their numerical strength, the Indian CPMFs are now the second-largest in the world. Furthermore, they have emerged as the most crucial instrument of India's counter insurgency strategy. He asks whether India is in the process creating a burgeoning population of CPMFs without actual capacities to handle the challenges they were raised for. He notes the growing demand for internal security duties as the single-most critical challenge before the paramilitary forces. According to him, two internal security developments—the Mumbai terrorist attacks and the surge in the left-wing extremist violence—have had a direct bearing on the pace and direction of the CPMF modernization process. The induction of large numbers of sufficiently fit but inadequately motivated and trained personnel into the forces is affecting their performance, promoting indiscipline, and producing an increasing number of cases of human rights violations. The modernization of state police forces needs to be given primacy over adding battalions to the CPMFs. Given the rapid expansion of India's paramilitary forces and the overlap between their duties, it makes operational sense to merge several of these organizations into a single unit. Finally, Routray notes that India needs to integrate civic action programmes with its paramilitary operations to meet internal security challenges.

Anit Mukherjee argues that civil-military relations in contemporary India are having an adverse impact on India's military effectiveness. According to him, while civilian supremacy has never been seriously questioned in India, there is an underlying fear of unrestricted military power and of the 'Man on Horseback', reinforced by the experiences of neighbouring countries. To prevent such an occurrence, the Indian military has been subjected to strong bureaucratic control. Consequently, there is a lack of civilian expertise in military affairs applicable to both political and bureaucratic elements. Mukherjee analyses India's military effectiveness by examining its four crucial determinants—weapons procurement, defence planning, integration, and human resource development. In the main, he argues, the current structure of civil-military relations has an adverse impact on the country's military effectiveness. On the other hand, this structure imbues a 'systemic stability' in India while ensuring that the armed forces remain relatively immune to politicization. Mukherjee argues that the Indian state has acknowledged these problems and has made some attempt at defence reforms. He calls for more forceful political intervention to remodel the state of civil-military relations in the country.

India and the Great Powers

In his chapter on the Indo-US defence relationship, Manjeet Pardesi analyses how this relationship has evolved since the end of the Cold War, especially after India's May 1998 nuclear tests. Pardesi argues that the United States views India's rise as a positive and benign development in the international system, and that India itself views close relations with the United States as essential to its emergence as a major power in Asia. Given that the two countries have largely overlapping grand-strategic objectives, Indo-US defence relations are slated to grow steadily in the years ahead. However, Pardesi notes that there are perceptual, structural, and institutional variables that are preventing this relationship from achieving its full potential. Even as the two countries have common grand-strategic aims, they have different policy preferences for achieving them as their disagreements over Pakistan's role in the war against terrorism indicate. Next, given the structural composition of the Indian military, the United States is unlikely to replace Russia as India's top weapons supplier even as Indo-US defence trade is on the upswing. Finally, Pardesi notes the presence of several bureaucratic-institutional hurdles on both sides that continue to limit closer Indo-US military cooperation. Nevertheless, given that there are no sources of bilateral tensions in the Indo-US relationship, he believes, this relationship will continue to grow in the years ahead and the two militaries will cooperate to hedge against unforeseen contingencies.

P. L. Dash discusses India's defence ties with Russia as they have evolved after the implosion of the former Soviet Union. He argues that, as a consequence of deep Russian entrenchment in India's defence production facilities, Russia is likely to dominate India's defence purchases in the foreseeable future. This is not to argue that Indo-Russian defence ties are entirely trouble-free, as the controversy over the purchase of the carrier Gorshkov demonstrates. However, Russia has taken note of India's growing strategic profile and views India emerging as a major military power in Asia in the years ahead. Dash argues that as a consequence of India's growing power, Russia has acknowledged India to be its geopolitical anchor in South Asia. For example, he notes that India is the only country in the world to which Russia has agreed to provide access to the military segment of the GLONASS satellite navigation system that is used for precision homing of guided missiles. Dash further notes that the Indo-Russian defence relationship is changing from a buyer-seller relationship into a strategic partnership that now includes joint production of high-end military equipment.

In a brief concluding chapter, Prakash Menon highlights the predominance of a preference for stability underlying India's military modernization. Above all, he stresses, the armed forces are guided by a political leadership that has no proclivity for the use of force. He also argues that the acquisitions of India's armed forces have not been as extensive as is often thought and must properly be viewed as meeting the need for sustaining stability.

As a whole, the diverse chapters in this volume reveal a security and defence establishment in ferment, determined to draw upon an unprecedented availability of resources to catch up with the times, not always clear as to its direction, but restrained in its attitude towards the actual utilization of its instruments. While not all readers will agree with its analyses, our aim is to give a pause to think, to underline the complexity of the process, and to provide a sound basis for discussion on how the process might be refined. If this exercise goes some way towards doing this, it will have served its purpose.

Notes

1. The SIPRI Military Expenditure Database. On the global ranking of military expenditures, see 'Chapter Ten: Country Comparisons—Commitments, Force Levels, and Economics,' *The Military Balance*. 111(1), 2011 p. 469.

2. For the classic argument that there is a correlation in the long run between economic development and military capacity, see Kennedy 1989; Cohen and Dasgupta 2010.

3. On the Sino-Indian rivalry, see Garver 2001 and Malik 2011. On the India-Pakistan conflict, see Ganguly 2001 and Basrur 2008. On Pakistan's use of terrorist organizations in its *proxy war* against India, see Byman 2005: 155–85.

4. On the partition of India and the violence and mass migration that accompanied it, see Talbot and Singh 2009. For an insider account of the integration of the *princely states* with the Indian union, see Menon 1956.

5. On this, see Raghavan 2010: 26–100.

6. On the partition of India's defence resources, see Wainwright 1994: 71–81.

7. The Indian National Army (INA) was a notable exception. However, it is noteworthy that Nehru, while applauding their patriotism, did not allow the former INA soldiers and officers to join the military of independent India as the INA was not an apolitical military force. See Kavic 1967: 142.

8. The Viceroy's Executive Council was the equivalent of the colonial state's Cabinet.

9. For example, see Metcalf 2007.

10. Appeasement, as understood in the pre-Munich sense means that 'states could accommodate the legitimate interests of their rivals without compromising their own vital interests'. See Ganguly 2004: 128.

11. See Racioppi 1994.

12. On an early view of India's 1974 nuclear test, see Marwah 1977: 96–121.

13. India intervened in the Maldives on invitation from its government. In the case of Sri Lanka, the invitation was extracted by considerable pressure from New Delhi.

14. For India's actions in Sri Lanka, Maldives, and Nepal, see Hagerty 1991: 351–63.

15. For a contrary view applied to the present day, see Khilnani *et al.* 2012.

16. On the factors that led to India's decision, see Ganguly 1999: 148–77. For the argument that there was no fundamental or substantive change

in India's foreign and security policy under the BJP, see Pardesi and Oetken 2008: 3–40.

17. For details, see Talbott 2004 and Singh 2006.

18. On the Kargil conflict, see 'Kargil: What Does It Mean?', *South Asia Monitor*, 12, 19 July 1999. Available at http://csis.org/files/media/csis/pubs/sam12.pdf.

19. On these and related issues, see Basrur 2006.

20. The presence of PLA troops was first reported in an opinion piece in *The New York Times* and was subsequently confirmed by the Indian Army. See Harrison 2010 and Gupta 2010.

21. See Unnithan 2010.

22. This volume does not include a separate paper on the Indian Army as considerable work has already been done on the subject. See, for example, Kanwal 2008 and Singh 2011: 147–68. Kanwal's paper in these pages covers the Army's nuclear weapons responsibilities.

References

Bajpai, Kanti, P.R. Chari, Pervez Iqbal Cheema, Stephen P. Cohen, and Sumit Ganguly. 1995. *Brasstacks and Beyond: Perception and Management of Crisis in South Asia*. New Delhi: Manohar Publishers.

Barua, Pradeep P. 2005. *The State at War in South Asia*. Lincoln: University of Nebraska Press.

Basrur, Rajesh M. 2008. *South Asia's Cold War: Nuclear Weapons and Conflict in Comparative Perspective*. New York: Routledge.

———. 2006. *Minimum Deterrence and India's Nuclear Security*. Stanford: Stanford University Press.

Blackwill, Robert D., Peter Chalk, Kim Cragin, C. Christine Fair, Brian A. Jackson, Brian Michael Jenkins, Seth G. Jones, Angel Rabasa, Nathaniel Shestak, and Ashley J. Tellis. 2009. 'The Lessons of Mumbai', occasional paper, Santa Monica: RAND.

Blarel, Nicolas. 2009. 'Indo-Israeli Relation: Emergence of a Strategic Partnership', in Sumit Ganguly (ed.), *India's Foreign Policy: Retrospect and Prospect*, pp. 155–74. New Delhi: Oxford University Press.

Burns, John F. 1995. 'US-India Pact on Military Cooperation', *The New York Times*, 13 January.

Byman, Daniel. 2005. *Deadly Connections: States that Sponsor Terrorism*. New York: Cambridge University Press.

Cohen, Stephen P. 2001. *India: Emerging Power*. Washington D.C.: Brookings Institution Press.

Cohen, Stephen P. and Sunil Dasgupta. 2010. *Arming without Aiming: India's Military Modernization*. Washington, DC: Brookings Institution Press.

Dasgupta, C. 2002. *War and Diplomacy in Kashmir*. New Delhi: Sage Publications.

Ganguly, Sumit. 1983. 'Why India Joined the Nuclear Club', *The Bulletin of Atomic Scientists*, April: 30–3.

———. 1996. 'Explaining the Kashmir Insurgency: Political Mobilization and Institutional Decay', *International Security*, 21 (2): 76–107.

———. 1999. 'India's Pathway to Pokhran II: The Prospects and Sources of New Delhi's Nuclear Weapons Programme', *International Security*, 23 (4): 148–77.

———. 2001. *Conflict Unending: India-Pakistan Tensions since 1947*. New York: Columbia University Press.

———. 2004. 'Border Issues, Domestic Integration, and International Security', in Francine R. Frankel and Harry Harding (eds), *The India-China Relationship: Rivalry and Engagement*. New Delhi: Oxford University Press.

———. 2010. 'Indian Defence Policy', in Niraja Gopal Jayal and Pratap Bhanu Mehta (eds), *The Oxford Companion to the Politics of India*, pp. 542–52. New Delhi: Oxford University Press.

Ganguly, Sumit and Michael R. Kraig. 2005. 'The 2001-02 Indo-Pakistani Crisis: Exposing the Limits of Coercive Diplomacy', *Security Studies*, 14 (2): 290–324.

Garver, John W. 1991. 'The Indian Factor in Recent Sino-Soviet Relations', *The China Quarterly*, 125.

———. 2001. *Protracted Contest: Sino-Indian Rivalry in the Twentieth Century*. Seattle, WA: University of Washington Press.

———. 2006. 'China's Decision for War with India in 1962', in Alastair I. Johnston and Robert S. Ross (eds), *New Directions in the Study of China's Foreign Policy*. Stanford: Stanford University Press.

Gupta, Shishir. 2010. 'Army passes intel to Govt: PLA men at pass linking PoK to China', *Indian Express*, 31 August.

Hagerty, Devin T. 1991. 'India's Regional Security Doctrine', *Asian Survey*, 31 (4): 351–63.

Harrison, Selig S. 2010. 'China's Discreet Hold on Pakistan's Northern Borderlands', *The New York Times*, 26 August.

Holslag, Jonathan. 2010. *China and India: Prospects for Peace*. New York: Columbia University Press.

International Institute for Strategic Studies (IISS). 2011. 'Chapter Ten: Country Comparisons–Commitments, Force Levels, and Economics', *The Military Balance*, 111 (1): 471–7. Available at http://www.tandfonline.com/doi/abs/10.1080/04597222.2011.559843#.UczItzvfCvM.

Kanwal, Gurmeet. 2008. *Indian Army: Vision 2020*. New Delhi: Harper Collins.

Kavic, Lorne J. 1967. *India's Quest for Security: Defence Policies, 1947–1965.* Berkeley: University of California Press.

Kennedy, Paul. 1989. *The Rise and Fall of Great Powers: Economic Change and Military Conflict from 1500 to 2000.* London: Fontana Press.

Khilnani, Sunil, Rajiv Kumar, Pratap Bhanu Mehta, Prakash Menon, Nandan Nilekani, Srinath Raghavan, Shyam Saran, and Siddharth Varadarajan. 2012. 'Nonalignment 2.0: A Foreign and Strategic Policy for India in the Twenty First Century', Centre for Policy Research, New Delhi. Available at http://www.cprindia.org/sites/default/files/NonAlignment%202.0_1.pdf (accessed 16 May 2012).

Kux, Dennis. 2001. *The United States and Pakistan, 1947-2000: Disenchanted Allies.* Washington, DC: The Johns Hopkins University Press.

———. 1993. *India and the United States: Estranged Democracies 1941–1991.* Washington, DC: National Defence University Press.

Ladwig, Walter C. 2007–8. 'A Cold Start for Hot Wars? The Indian Army's New Limited War Doctrine', *International Security,* 32 (3): 158–90.

Lombardo, Nicholas R. 2011. 'India's Defence Spending and Military Modernization', *Current Issues,* Center for Strategic and International Studies, 29 March. Available at http://csis.org/files/publication/110329_DIIG_Current_Issues_24_Indian_Defense_Spending.pdf.

Malik, Mohan. 2011. *China and India: Great Power Rivals.* Boulder, CO and London: FirstForum Press.

Marwah, Onkar. 1977. 'India's Nuclear and Space Programmes: Intent and Policy', *International Security,* 2 (2): 96–121.

McMahon, Robert J. 1994. *The Cold War on the Periphery: The United States, India, and Pakistan.* New York: Columbia University Press.

Menon, V. P. 1956. *The Story of the Integration of the Indian States.* New York: Macmillan.

Metcalf, Thomas R. 2007. *Imperial Connections: India in the Indian Ocean Arena, 1860–1920.* Berkeley: University of California Press.

Munro, Ross H. 1989. 'India: The Awakening of an Asian Power', *Time,* 3 April. Available at http://www.time.com/time/magazine/article/0,9171,957371,00.html.

Natarajan, V. 2000. 'The Sumdorong Chu Incident', *Bharat Rakshak Monitor,* 3 (3). Available at www.bharat-rakshak.com/MONITOR/ISSUE3-3/natarajan.html (accessed on 20 May 2011).

Nehru, Jawaharlal. 2004. *The Discovery of India.* New Delhi: Penguin Books.

Noorani, A.G. 1967. 'India's Quest for a Nuclear Guarantee', *Asian Survey,* 7 (7): 490–502.

Panikkar, K.M. 1960. *Problems of Indian Defence.* London: Asia Publishing House.

Pardesi, Manjeet S. 2011. 'Instability in Tibet and the Sino-Indian Strategic Rivalry: Do Domestic Politics Matter?', *Asian Rivalries: Conflict, Escalation, and Limitations on Two-level Games*, Sumit Ganguly and William R. Thompson (eds). Stanford: Stanford University Press.

Pardesi, Manjeet S. and Jennifer L. Oetken. 2008. 'Secularism, Democracy, and Hindu Nationalism in India', *Asian Security*, 4 (1): 3–40.

Pardesi, Manjeet S. and Sumit Ganguly. 2008. 'Energy Security and India's Foreign/Security Policy', in Harsh Pant (ed.), *Indian Foreign Policy in a Unipolar World*. New Delhi: Routledge.

Paul, T.V. 2003. 'The Enduring Sino-Pakistani Nuclear/Missile Relationship and the Balance of Power Logic', *Nonproliferation Review*, 10: 55–85.

Perkovich, George. 2004. 'The Nuclear and Security Balance', in Frankel and Harding, in Francine R. Frankel and Harry Harding (eds), *The India-China Relationship: Rivalry and Engagement*, pp. 178–218. New Delhi: Oxford University Press.

Racioppi, Linda. 1994. *Soviet Policy Towards South Asia since 1970*. Cambridge: Cambridge University Press.

Raghavan, Srinath. 2010. *War and Peace in Modern India: A Strategic History of the Nehru Years*. Ranikhet: Permanent Black.

———. 2009. 'Civil-Military Relations in India: The China Crisis and After', *The Journal of Strategic Studies*, 32 (1): 149–75.

Ramana, M.V. 2012. 'India', in Ray Acheson (ed.), *Assuring Destruction Forever: Nuclear Weapon Modernization around the World*, pp. 34–43. New York: Reaching Critical Will.

Rudolph, Lloyd I. and Susanne Hoeber Rudolph. 1964. 'Generals and Politicians in India', *Pacific Affairs*, 37 (1): 5–19.

Sidhu, Waheguru Pal Singh and Jing-dong Yuan. 2003. *China and India: Cooperation or Conflict?* Boulder, CO: Lynne Rienner Publishers.

Singh, Harinder. 2011. 'Assessing India's Emerging Land Warfare Doctrines and Capabilities: Prospects and Concerns', *Asian Security*, 7 (2): 147–68.

Singh, Jaswant. 2006. *In Service of Emergent India: A Call to Honor*. Bloomington: Indiana University Press.

Sisson, Richard and Leo E. Rose. 1990. *War and Secession: Pakistan, India, and the Creation of Bangladesh*. Berkeley: University of California Press.

Smith, Chris. 1994. *India's Ad Hoc Arsenal: Direction or Drift in Defence Policy?* New York: Oxford University Press.

Syed, Anwar Hussain. 1974. *China & Pakistan: Diplomacy of an Entente Cordiale*. Amherst: University of Massachusetts Press.

Talbot, Ian and Gurharpal Singh. 2009. *The Partition of India*. Cambridge: Cambridge University Press.

Talbott, Strobe. 2004. *Engaging India: Diplomacy, Democracy, And the Bomb*. Washington, DC: Brookings Institution Press.

Tellis, Ashley J. 2001. *India's Emerging Nuclear Posture: Between Recessed Deterrent and Ready Arsenal*. Santa Monica, CA: RAND.

The SIPRI Military Expenditure Database. Available at http://milexdata.sipri. org/ (accessed 20 May 2011).

Thomas, Raju G.C. 1986. *Indian Security Policy*. Princeton: Princeton University Press.

———. 1979. 'Nonalignment and Indian Security: Nehru's Rationale and Legacy', *Journal of Strategic Studies*, 2 (2): 153–71.

———. 1978. *The Defence of India: A Budgetary Perspective of Strategy and Politics*. Columbia, MI: South Asia Books.

Unnithan, Sandeep. 2010. 'The ChiPak Threat', *India Today*, 23 October. Available at http://indiatoday.intoday.in/story/the-chipak-threat/1/117399.html.

Wainwright, A. Martin. 1994. *Inheritance of Empire: Britain, India, and the Balance of Power in Asia, 1938-55*. Westport, CT: Praeger Publishers.

World Bank. 2011. 'Gross domestic product, 2009 PPP', World Development Indicators database, 14 April. Available at http://siteresources.worldbank. org/DATASTATISTICS/Resources/GDP_PPP.pdf (accessed 20 May 2011).

1   The Navy in India's Socio-Economic Growth and Development

ASHOK SAWHNEY

T HE ECONOMIC REFORMS of the 1990s ushered in an era of unprecedented growth and development in India, long overdue since independence in 1947. The 8 to 9 per cent annual growth rates of GDP achieved since 2005 have been instrumental in the government launching several additional human as well as infrastructural development schemes for the betterment of the masses. However, the Indian economy must continue to grow at this rate—if not better—for the next 20 years for the country to achieve the remaining targets of development and poverty alleviation. The core national interest of the country during this period is, therefore, continued socio-economic growth. Accordingly, the main national security objective for the Indian Armed Forces, including the Indian Navy (IN), is to ensure a peaceful, secure, and stable environment to further this interest.

The area of primary interest (Ministry of Defence 2007: 59–60) to the IN is the Indian Ocean Region (IOR), which has been the focus of the world's attention not only for its criticality vis-à-vis energy resource but also for the on-going international security challenges in Iraq, Afghanistan, Pakistan, Iran, and the rampant maritime piracy emanating from Somalia. In an increasingly globalized and economically interdependent world, there is an apparent and ongoing shift of power towards Asia. The traditional trade routes criss-crossing the Indian Ocean have been further magnified in importance by the growing economies of China, India, Japan, South Korea, and the ASEAN states. Eighty per cent of the total trade conducted over the Indian Ocean is extra-regional, with only 20 per cent being between littoral countries of the region (Indian Maritime Doctrine 2009: 58). This brings out the importance of the IOR to extra-regional powers and explains their continued presence in the region through their navies, notably the United States, the United Kingdom, and France, as well as the emerging presence of new powers like China.

This chapter aims to first establish the significance of the IOR, where the IN has been playing a proactive and responsible role towards maintaining peace and stability, in consonance with Indian maritime interests. This role has often been played in cooperation with other regional as well as extra-regional navies. The preponderant extra-regional navy in the IOR is the US Navy, with whom the IN has achieved a degree of comfort as well as interoperability over the last decade. The Chinese Navy, or the Peoples' Liberation Army Navy (PLAN), as it is called, has been making rapid strides in terms of platforms as well as capability enhancement and, since 2008, has also started making its presence felt in the IOR. This has been a cause for concern not only for India but also for other stakeholders in the region. This chapter, therefore, attempts to take a more detailed look at the reasoning and stated compulsions for this accelerated development of the PLAN, as well as its likely deployment in the IOR, before analysing the other maritime challenges and the emerging maritime balance of power in the region. Finally, the chapter examines Indian naval development in the context of naval objectives, force levels and capabilities, partnership and cooperation with other navies, and the degree to which the naval objectives towards ensuring peace, security, and stability are likely to be met. The chapter brings out that in order to fulfil the IN's primary military objective of deterrence, a strong and assertive national posture is as important as the navy's demonstrated capability and professionalism.

Significance of the Indian Ocean

Much has been written about the growing importance of the IOR in the emerging Asian century (Ministry of Defence 2007; Indian Ocean Naval Symposium 2008; Kaplan 2009: 16–32; Cordner 2010: 67–85; De Silva-Ranasinghe 2011). This section will endeavour to present some salient features that have a bearing on this chapter before discussing Indian maritime interests and challenges.

The Indian Ocean is encompassed by a land rim on three sides—west, north, and east, with maritime access to the region possible through seven established gateways or choke points. To the west, the Strait of Hormuz connects the Persian Gulf to the Indian Ocean and the busiest shipping lane passes through it. To the east, the Malacca Strait is the primary route which connects the South China Sea to the Indian Ocean and through which more than 50,000 vessels transit annually. Overall, the Indian Ocean accounts for the transportation of the highest tonnage of goods in the world, with almost 100,000 ships transiting its expanse every year, carrying two-thirds of the world's oil shipments, one-third of the bulk cargo traffic, and half the world's container shipments (Energy Information Administration 2008).

The pre-eminence of the Indian Ocean as an energy transportation corridor will further increase as global energy needs are likely to increase by 45 per cent between 2006 and 2030. Almost half of this growth in demand is likely to be from China and India. Whereas China's demand for crude oil doubled between 1995 and 2005, it is likely to double again in the following 15 years (Downs 2006: 9). More than 85 per cent of the oil and oil products bound for China cross the Indian Ocean and pass through the Strait of Malacca. India is dependent on oil for nearly 33 per cent of its energy needs, out of which it needs to import 65 per cent. With this growing demand, India is soon likely to become the world's fourth-largest energy consumer, after the United States, China, and Japan (Kaplan 2009).

Indian Maritime Interests

The maritime interests of India, outlined below, dictate that there should be free flow of trade, including import of energy and other natural resources, as well as security of coastal infrastructure from seaborne attack. As a result, in addition to be able to deter an adversary, the foremost military missions of the navy would be protection of Sea Lines of Communication (SLOCs), protection of offshore assets, and seaward defence. The areas of primary interest where the IN will be required to carry out the SLOC protection role are extensive and listed in the Indian Maritime Doctrine (Indian Maritime Doctrine 2009: 65–6). These cover almost the entire expanse of the Indian Ocean and include the entry/exit or the choke points. South China Sea and other areas of the Western Pacific are a part of the areas of secondary interest (Indian Maritime Doctrine 2009: 68).

(1) **Trade:** Like China, India's growing economy is also critically dependent on the seas for conduct of trade. More than 90 per cent of India's trade by volume and 77 per cent by value is transported over the seas (Indian Maritime Doctrine 2009: 63). For continued economic growth and with new free-trade agreements being signed, this dependence on the seas will continue to grow.

(2) **Energy:** India's domestic oil production has remained steady and, therefore, with a growing economy, oil imports have been increasing. The dependence on imported crude oil is expected to increase from more than 75 per cent in 2008–9 to nearly 95 per cent by 2024–5. The major sources of this crude oil import are in the Middle East, followed by Africa, and are not likely to change significantly in the next 15 years.

(3) **Exclusive Economic Zone (EEZ):** India's EEZ is 2,013,410 square km in area, which is equal to 66 per cent of the land mass, to which another 530,000 sq km is likely to be added as an extension to the continental shelf (Ministry of Defence 2007: 58). The country has exclusive rights over the oil, gas, minerals, and other living and non-living resources available in this area. Unlike China, which has a number of maritime boundary disputes inhibiting this resource utilization, India has demarcated her maritime boundary with the Maldives, Sri Lanka, Myanmar, Indonesia, and Thailand (Ministry of Defence 2007: 57). The problems in delimitation of the same with Pakistan and Bangladesh are being addressed (Ministry of Defence 2007: 58).

(4) **Coastal areas as economic hubs:** A substantial part of India's industrial and economic activity is located within the EEZ, along the 7,516 km long coastline. The country's 1,197 islands have further potential. India has 12 major and 187 minor ports, with a large number of new ports under development (Indian Maritime Doctrine 2009: 63). The major ports, in addition, are adjacent to large metro cities, which are regional commercial centres. The offshore oil and natural gas infrastructure is expanding on both the west and east coasts, and is a strategic national asset. The fisheries sector is an important part of India's socio-economic development, with about 15 per cent of the coastal population dependent on fishing for its livelihood (Indian Maritime Doctrine 2009: 63).

The Developing PLA Navy and its Implications

The PLAN has been growing together with China's economy, at least for the last two decades. This growth has been viewed with concern by the United States and by other maritime states of Asia, as highlighted by numerous writings that have analysed its implications.[1] Likewise, there has been a significant increase in analyses by observers in China on maritime strategy and the growth of the PLAN during the last decade. While the US establishment appears focused on the PLAN, Chinese strategists also appear focused primarily on the US Navy. Most of the analysis of the PLAN developments tends to generate alarm. On the other hand, these developments can be viewed as purely legitimate aspirations of a growing major power. This section will, therefore, first bring out the justification for the growing capabilities of the PLAN, as stated by China and as possibly perceived by a balanced, neutral observer. Thereafter, an attempt will be made to assess how these capabilities, if and when deployed in the IOR, can have a bearing on the IN.

Development Strategy

The primary strategic concept of the PLAN until the mid-1980s was one of coastal defence. In 1982, PLA Navy commander, Admiral Liu Huaqing, formulated the strategy of offshore defence, which entailed the development of the PLAN into a world-class sea power by 2040 (Kondapalli 2001: 10). The development plan chalked out by Admiral Liu almost 30 years ago appears to be in the process of being accomplished, albeit with a few changes. It did appear to be a phase of consolidation for the PLAN till the 1990s, with the newer generation of ships and submarines being commissioned only during the last 10 to 15 years. By around 2020, the PLAN is likely to attain blue-water status, as envisaged by Admiral Liu. The 1996 *Taiwan crisis* is recognized as a turning point in Chinese defence policy. The show of force by the US Navy, which sent two aircraft carrier groups to the Taiwan Strait, made it clear to China that the United States would intervene on behalf of the island state in case of an eventuality. Accordingly, Beijing began to shift focus on developing capabilities almost exclusively for a future Taiwan contingency, namely to coerce Taipei and to deter Washington.

New Vision for China's Defence Policy

Keeping in view China's expanding national interests, President Hu Jintao laid down a new vision for China's defence policy in 2004. This vision was enunciated in China's 2006 National Defence White Paper (NDWP), reaffirmed in the Chinese Communist Party's constitution in 2007, and reissued in the 2008 NDWP. The mission statement tasks the PLA to 'provide a solid security guarantee for sustaining the important period of strategic opportunity for national development, provide a strong strategic support for safeguarding national interests, and play a major role in maintaining world peace and promoting common development' (Information Office of the State Council, China's National Defense in 2008).

Naval Modernization Aims

It is clear that the aims of China's naval modernization are to develop military options with respect to Taiwan, to defend China's claims related to her maritime jurisdiction and the EEZ, to protect her SLOCs and finally, from 2004 onwards, to enhance the security and stability of the international system. The last two aims are relevant to this study, as the PLAN will need to extend its area of operations to the IOR towards their fulfilment. The primary areas of interest for the IN, till the 2025 time frame, are across the north Indian Ocean (Indian Maritime Doctrine 2009: 65–8). Let us, therefore, take a look at the capabilities of the PLAN, which will be deployable there towards the fulfilment of these aims.

(1) **Aircraft carrier**: It is apparent that China is firmly on the road to an aircraft-carrier programme (US Department of Defense 2009: 40; Office of Naval Intelligence 2009: 19; Sengupta 2009: 52–3). It is expected that the ex-Russian Navy 'Varyag', which has been undergoing renovation since 2002, is likely to become operational by 2012, and will be used to develop basic proficiencies in carrier operations. In addition, China's indigenous carrier programme includes up to six aircraft carriers, the first one to be completed in the 2015–2020 time frame (Office of Naval Intelligence 2009; O'Rourke 2009: 10).

(2) **Other surface ships**: The PLAN surface force currently consists of a mix of modern and older platforms, equipped with a variety

of weapons and sensors. During its rapid modernization drive over the last 15 years, the PLAN has imported proven and highly capable ships from Russia, while concurrently producing advanced indigenous platforms. The focus of naval procurement has shifted from large numbers of low-capacity, single-mission platforms to a smaller force with modern, more capable, multi-mission systems. The major surface fleet is comprised of 27 destroyers, 49 frigates, 55 amphibious ships, and about 50 major auxiliaries (Jane's Fighting Ships 2009–10; Office of Naval Intelligence 2009: 18).

(3) **Surface ships—enhanced capabilities:** The most notable capability enhancement in surface ships has been in area-air-defence (AAD) (Jane's Fighting Ships 2009–10; Office of Naval Intelligence 2009: 18).[2] This AAD capability will enable the PLAN surface ships to operate outside their shore-based air cover, as it makes them capable of engaging air targets outside the air-to-surface weapons range. The second major upgradation has been in anti-ship warfare capability with the induction of advanced surface-to-surface missiles (SSMs) (Jane's Fighting Ships 2009–10; Office of Naval Intelligence 2009: 18).[3] The addition of the Yuzhao-class landing platform dock (LPD) and the Fuchi-class replenishment ships indicates the emerging focus on longer-range operations. Together with some of the other auxiliaries like the Anwei-class, they can also be effectively utilized for non-traditional security roles like disaster relief and humanitarian assistance.

(4) **Newer submarines and capabilities:** Like the surface fleet, the PLAN submarine force has also seen a modernization thrust since the mid-1990s. The PLAN envisions a smaller but more lethal force, equipped with advanced weapons and sensors, and capable of sustained long-duration patrols. The submarine force currently consists of three nuclear ballistic missile submarines (SSBN), six nuclear-powered attack submarines (SSN), and 53 diesel attack submarines (SS) (Jane's Fighting Ships 2009–10; O'Rourke 2009). At current building rates, this total of 62 submarines is likely to increase to 75, by 2025 (US ONI Report 2009: 21).[4]

(5) **Asymmetric warfare capability:** China has undertaken a sweeping military modernization over the last decade that has transformed its ability to fight high-tech wars. One of the primary areas of focus of this modernization is 'information dominance', which includes the

optimum use of information by PLA forces through a fully networked architecture, while at the same time establishing control over the adversary's information flow (Krekel 2009: 6). This information dominance is viewed by Chinese military strategists as the precursor to overall success in a conflict (Krekel 2009: 6).[5] Analysis of this strategy suggests that these tools will be widely employed in the earliest phases of a conflict, and possibly pre-emptively, against an enemy's information and C4ISR systems (Krekel 2009: 7). The PLA aim appears to close the large technology/capability gap with the US military by denying it the use of its high-end capability, through information dominance.

(6) **Chinese basing facilities in the Indian Ocean**: There has been speculation about a 'string of pearls' strategy having been adopted by China to get naval footholds in the IOR. The string refers to port development activities funded by China, and being executed by Chinese companies in Pakistan, Maldives, Sri Lanka, Bangladesh, and Myanmar. However, more detailed analysis shows that most of these ventures are currently commercial in nature (Holslag 2009: 811–840; Khurana 2008: 1–39). Recent discussion in China does point towards growing interest in basing facilities in the IOR for PLAN ships. This will not only be logical but essential if the PLAN was to establish a more permanent presence in the region. As brought out in a recent analysis in India, the likely PLAN base could well be outside the perceived string, and the PLAN may well try and establish a base at Seychelles or some similar place (Agnihotri 2010). The IN will need to monitor this development closely, as it can facilitate the positioning of the growing PLAN capability much closer to home.

Overall Impact of China's Growing Maritime Power

China's maritime power has been growing with her economy as per a long-term plan and has achieved a respectable status. Continued economic growth is the foremost priority for the Communist Party to stay in power. All dimensions of this enhanced maritime power will, therefore, be used to facilitate this aim, by trying to ensure a secure and stable environment for continued growth. China's military modernization plan over the last 15 years has given the navy a range of new capabilities, deployable at longer ranges, through multi-mission platforms. The PLAN will acquire blue-water status once the indigenous aircraft carrier is operational, around 2020. Till then, groups of destroyers and frigates, supported by replenishment ships, can operate in the IOR for specific roles, as in the case of the ongoing anti-piracy mission. China is conscious of its emerging big power status and has probably decided to become a stakeholder in the international security calculus. The other cooperative deployment missions that the PLA Navy can take part in globally are counter-terrorism, humanitarian assistance, and disaster relief. The new destroyers and frigates have adequate capability and can be deployed in the SLOC protection role in the IOR. For strategic deterrence, the Jia-class SSBN will provide China with a credible, long range, second-strike capability. The SSNs can be deployed for long-range intelligence, surveillance, reconnaissance (ISR) and anti-surface warfare (ASuW) missions, whereas the conventional submarine fleet can carry out the same missions closer home. The limited Maritime Patrol Aircraft (MPA)/ Airborne Warning and Control System (AWACS) effort is likely to be deployed in the regional context. The overall focus of operations of the PLA Navy till the 2020 time frame is likely to remain in the Yellow Sea and the East and South China Seas. Though China does not want to escalate the Taiwan issue politically for the time being, militarily it remains one of the major contingencies for the PLA Navy. With the attention of all maritime states growing seawards for resources, the boundary disputes and EEZ issues are likely to gain prominence, thereby further tying the PLA Navy down to a regional focus.

Other Maritime Challenges

Let us now see the other maritime challenges that the IN is likely to encounter in the given time frame.

(1) **Pakistan:** The Pakistan Navy's (PN) major assets include nine frigates, eight submarines including three midgets, one replenishment tanker, and about five maritime patrol aircrafts (Jane's Fighting Ships 2009–10). Though numbers alone do not signify everything, their overall capability will be no match for the IN. However, taking advantage of the close proximity of the two countries, Pakistan has been indulging in asymmetric warfare through non-state actors, including terrorist groups, for the last 20 years. The normal route of this infiltration is across the land border. A seaborne terrorist attack was carried out on

the port city of Mumbai in November 2008. This exposed large gaps in the surveillance and security of the coastal areas, which had been the responsibility of a number of civil organizations, the coast guard, and the navy. In an effort to bring about greater efficiency, the navy has now been made overall responsible for maritime security, which includes coastal and offshore security (Ministry of Defence Annual Report 2008–2009; R.N. Ganesh 2009).

(2) **China-Pakistan combine:** The naval forces that China can deploy in the IOR have been discussed in the previous section. The PLAN and the PN, in collusion, can have a force-multiplier effect. Most of the new generation ships and aircrafts being inducted in the PN are of Chinese origin. Whereas this will facilitate interoperability, the availability of PN base facilities will give logistical and operational turn-around capabilities to the PLAN. The information-dominance strategy of the PLA can lead to suppression of information systems and be one of the biggest threats encountered, even before the actual outbreak of hostilities. Since China was responsible for Pakistan acquiring both nuclear weapons and missiles, thus altering the basic threshold of warfare in the sub-continent, India will need to be prepared for such a combined approach.

(3) **Non-traditional challenges:** With the growing power and mushrooming of non-state actors, threats emanating from piracy and terrorist groups are likely to grow. In addition, the increasing effects of global warming in the form of sea-level rise are likely to bring unprecedented humanitarian assistance and disaster relief (HADR) challenges in coastal areas. All this, once again, reiterates the importance of the littoral areas over the high seas, as far as the emerging challenges for the navy are concerned.

Emerging Maritime Balance of Power in the IOR

The US Navy will remain the most powerful in the IOR through 2025, the time frame of this study. It will also continue to be robustly postured in the Indian Ocean and the Western Pacific.[6] This presence will continue even beyond the time frame of the ongoing operations in Iraq and Afghanistan/Pakistan—the US naval presence in the region predates these operations by several decades. The long-term focus of the United States in the region is also brought out by the creation of a new theatre command, the US Africa Command, in 2008. In addition to deterring and winning wars, another stated objective of the US Navy is to ensure the uninterrupted flow of the global economic system over the seas.[7] The role of the US Navy as a stabilizing force in the region is likely to continue.

The PLAN views the US Navy to be capable of interfering with China's use of the maritime medium, in the eventuality of escalation of hostilities on the Taiwan issue. Since China's dependence on the maritime medium is continuing to grow in parallel with her growing economy, the security concerns have also grown even though the Taiwan issue is presently on the back-burner. China's modernization and expansion of her naval capability has been continuing with greater fervour during the last decade.

China has unresolved maritime boundary disputes with a large number of countries in the Asia Pacific region.[8] Due to the way China has conducted herself during deliberations about these disputes, often with an aggressive stance, her lack of transparency with respect to defence spending, and the nature of the political structure of the country, China's growing naval capability has raised security concerns among most of her maritime neighbours (Feuerberg 2010). This is apparent from the ongoing, very active naval capability enhancement in the region (Jane's Fighting Ships 2009–10; Eaglen and Rodeback 2010). The economic growth in the region is making these naval expansion plans viable. What remains to be seen is whether this will also make the region secure and stable, through some degree of mutual deterrence.

Indian Response to the Emerging Challenges

In this section, an attempt will be made to first briefly highlight Indian naval objectives. Thereafter, the developing IN will be discussed in terms of budgetary realities and force levels/capabilities being acquired, along with the constraints being faced by the navy. Finally, naval partnerships being forged with other navies in the region are discussed.

Indian Naval Objectives

The full range of operations which the IN may be required to participate in is vast, ranging from high intensity war-fighting at one end to HADR, at the other. These operations can be classified into four types of roles, which are termed as Military, Diplomatic, Constabulary, and Benign (Indian Maritime Doctrine 2009: 91; India's Maritime Military Strategy 2007: 71). This chapter will specifically look at the military role of the IN, in terms of its ability to safeguard security and stability in its areas of interest.

The navy's military role is characterized by the threat or use of force at and from the sea (Indian Maritime Doctrine 2009: 91). Sea Control is the central concept around which the Indian Navy is structured. As one of the most important concepts of maritime power, Sea Control denotes a condition where one is able to use a defined sea area, for a defined period of time, for one's own purposes, and at the same time deny its use to the adversary. It comprises control of the surface and sub-surface environments, the airspace above the area of control, as also the electromagnetic environment that may affect own use of the seas for the requisite duration within the area of interest. Sea Control is not an end in itself. It is a means to a higher end and very often a pre-requisite for other maritime operations and objectives, including power projection, SLOC protection, SLOC interdiction, and amphibious operations (Indian Maritime Doctrine 2009: 77). Sea denial, on the other hand, is a concept of denying the adversary use of a sea area for a certain period of time, when it is not required for own use. Submarines are often considered platforms-of-choice for the exercise of sea denial in choke points, particularly closer to enemy bases, since they are relatively less liable to detection and can be unobtrusively positioned and maintained, lowering enemy counter-measure efficacy. Sea denial can be used in an offensive manner to degrade the enemy's war waging capability, by curtailing his freedom of action and interdicting his SLOCs. It can also be used in a defensive manner by preventing the enemy from using sea areas that are not required for own use but from where own forces, capabilities, or war effort could be targeted. Sea denial and sea control are not necessarily mutually exclusive. In order to achieve sea control in a particular area, it may be necessary to exercise sea denial in another, and *vice versa* (Indian Maritime Doctrine 2009: 78). The primary military objective for the IN is to deter military adventurism against the country (Indian Maritime Doctrine 2009: 92). This chapter will focus on this objective because it is crucial to the attainment of the aim laid down for the navy. Demonstrated capability for both Sea Control and Sea Denial are essential to be able to have effective deterrence in place. As stated in the Indian Maritime Doctrine, in case deterrence fails, the navy's objective would then be to attain a decisive military victory. However, that would mean that the country would have to go to war, and so the navy would have failed to achieve its primary objective of maintaining security and stability in the region.

Deterrence

The most important task of the IN during peace and in crises is to deter war. Only attributes of conventional deterrence will be discussed in this chapter.[9] Conventional deterrence is achieved through conventional maritime forces with superiority in terms of overall strength, capability, and morale (Indian Maritime Military Strategy 2007: 76). The Indian Maritime Military Strategy document states that when dealing with a more capable adversary, deterrence can also be achieved by the formation of partnerships, thereby combining capabilities of maritime forces, or presenting a picture of solidarity. As brought out earlier, the IN does have overall superiority over the PN, but not over the PLAN. However, even the supposed deterrence vis-à-vis Pakistan has worked only in a limited manner. There has been no full scale war, but as brought out earlier, numerous incursions have been taking place from the Pakistan side, including from the sea. This aspect of only a limited deterrence against Pakistan will be discussed later under national/political posture. The IN has been going about building partnerships in a long-term planned manner. These robust partnerships, particularly the ones with the navies of the United States, Japan, Singapore, and Vietnam, should go a long way in presenting a picture of solidarity and building a credible deterrence vis-à-vis China. However, navies need to work continuously towards maintaining a credible deterrence. The first and foremost enabler towards this is to maintain a robust military capability and posture (Indian Maritime Doctrine 2009: 93).

(1) **Robust military capability:** The IN is involved in long-term planning and acquisition of modern platforms/capabilities to maintain a potent, three-dimensional force. This is clearly stated in the navy's vision statement issued in 2006 and is also discussed in this chapter under naval force levels/capabilities (see Table 1.1). It may be noted that there is a strong indigenous element in the development of surface forces, including a breakthrough in the field of weapon systems, like the *Dhanush* and *BrahMos* SSMs. This sends a positive signal with regards to the capabilities of a navy and the nation.

(2) **Military posture:** A robust military posture is best depicted by an alert navy which demonstrates its professionalism and readiness to carry out tasks, during peace time and in crises, in a proactive manner. Few operations can equal the action by IN ships in rescuing a Maldivian cabinet minister from Tamil mercenaries on board a freighter in 1988, in the aftermath of a failed coup attempt (Indian Maritime Military Strategy 2007: 22; Sakhuja 2010). The IN promptly mobilized itself in full force in the North Arabian Sea during the Kargil conflict in 1999, and together with the joint army/air force response, was able to deter Pakistan from escalating the conflict into a full-scale war.[10] The IN's large-scale response in reaching out to neighbouring countries, within hours after the *tsunami* struck Asia in 2004, is another very good example. The IN was also one of the first navies to start anti-piracy patrols off Somalia in 2008, to safeguard international merchant shipping and crew (IANS 2009). Unlike most other navies, which have been rather restrained, it even sank two pirate vessels which did not pay heed to warnings (Prakash 2009), highlighting a robust and proactive posture of the navy.

(3) **National/political posture:** India is a sovereign, democratic republic, in which the armed forces operate under the national, civil leadership. Therefore, the national posture demonstrated by the political leadership is as important as the naval posture, if not more, and is critical in establishing deterrence. India has been found wanting in this critical aspect of deterrence, which can be borne out by a few examples. In two separate incidents involving hijacking by Somali pirates, the Indian government took inordinately long to decide whether to allow the navy to intervene and secure the safety of the Indian vessels and crew (Prakash 2009).[11] Such dithering and indecision at the national level dilutes and even negates the attempts of the IN at portraying an otherwise strong, proactive posture. This happens because the armed forces are excluded from the national security decision-making apparatus (Prakash 2012: 25). Essential reforms to make the system more effective, as recommended by a group of ministers headed by the deputy Prime Minister in 2001, are still pending because of vested interests and lack of adequate political involvement in national security issues (Prakash 2012: 33; Mukherjee 2012: 72–3). At a larger, national level, it comes out

clearly that the Indian leadership does not understand this critical aspect of conveying a strong, decisive, and a rather proactive posture towards establishing credible deterrence. This is apparent from the fact that within two days of the 26/11 attack on Mumbai, the Indian government stated that war was not an option.[12] This demonstrates that lack of a national will/resolve to use military force, as and when required, to secure national interests, is probably the single major factor in deterrence not being fully effective vis-à-vis Pakistan.

Budgetary Realities

Despite a well drawn-out plan to develop a modern naval force, the IN has had to contend with budgetary realities in the actual fructification of that plan. First, the national defence budget has had very modest allocations, keeping with the requirements of a developing nation. Second, the naval share of this modest defence budget was meagre till the 1990s, and has started becoming a more respectable percentage only since 2006.

(1) **Shortfalls**: The IN had first drawn out plans for a three-carrier force in the 1950s (Sakhuja 2006: 100). However, the same has not materialized on account of budgetary realities. It is only in the 1980s that the naval share of the defence budget started increasing from the earlier 10 per cent or less. Between 1990–1 and 1995–6, the naval share was approximately 13 per cent (Roy-Chaudhury 2000: 146) and rose to an average of 15 per cent between 1996–7 and 2005–6 (Pant 2009: 279–97, 183–4), before increasing to almost 19 per cent in 2006–7. However, instead of continuing with the incremental increase, the naval share has been coming down for the last three years (Ministry of Defence Annual Reports 2006–7, 2007–8, 2008–9; Behera 2009–10). This repeated pruning of budgetary projections for the necessary acquisitions/modernization (Roy-Chaudhury 2000: 148)[13] has led to a far fewer number of naval platforms being acquired than planned (Behera 2012).

(2) **New acquisitions and inadequate capital budget**: Naval platforms have the longest gestation periods from the drawing board to actual availability, taking an average of at least five to six years for medium platforms like frigates and destroyers, and much longer for bigger/more complex platforms like aircraft carriers and submarines. Budgetary commitments for new platforms, therefore, need to be

made for a longer term and in an assured manner. The effects of any reduction to this commitment are apparent only after five to 10 years. The naval capital budget, which is the portion of the budget responsible for funding new acquisitions, has recently increased to 60 per cent of its total budget for the year 2008–9, amounting to US $2.5 billion, out of a total naval budget of about US $4 billion (Behera 2012). This is a very modest amount, which will be apparent if one compares it with some of the other naval budgets in Asia. For the same year, the naval budgets of China, Japan, and South Korea, in US$, were 32 billion, 11.6 billion, and 4.2 billion respectively (Japan Ministry of Defense 2009).

Force Levels and Capabilities

Indian naval staff did plan for a balanced, three-dimensional navy from the early years. However, in addition to the severe budgetary shortfalls brought out earlier, there was the constraint of non-availability of advanced platforms. Advanced military hardware transfer has always had strategic considerations and political strings attached. Even though almost all the IN ships had been acquired from the British till the mid-1960s, including the aircraft-carrier Vikrant, the United Kingdom refused to sell submarines to the IN. This was the period soon after the debacle with China in 1962, when India was rethinking her overall defence preparedness. As a result, a strategic partnership emerged with the USSR, and India started acquiring not only submarines, but most of her defence hardware from the erstwhile Soviet Union (Sikri 2007). This hardware was purchased at political prices and was normally about one-fourth the cost of a comparable platform in the international market.[14] The IN was, therefore, able to acquire a fairly modest capability till the 1990s despite relatively meagre budgetary provisioning. After the breakup of the USSR, an economy-conscious Russia has been continuing to provide advanced naval weapons/platforms and technology, but at international prices. This has affected naval acquisitions adversely and has also put naval budgetary constraints under sharper focus.

(1) **Indigenization:** The IN is the first armed force of India to promote indigenization of hardware. However, the production of her indigenous ships has been bogged down with time-delays and consequent cost over-runs (Jane's Fighting Ships 2009–10).[15] The

result has been that the navy is unable to maintain its force levels. The IN needs five new ships a year to maintain its strength, whereas India's defence shipyards produce at the most just three ships a year.[16] In a bid to keep pace with depleting force levels, the navy has had to resort to ordering ships from foreign shipyards, in addition to the indigenous construction.

(2) **Challenges and diversification:** The IN, therefore, is still overcoming the challenges of budgetary shortfalls, lack of a sustained, long-term budgetary commitment from the government, as well as time/cost over-runs in indigenous ship construction, affecting its efforts at maintaining and enhancing its capabilities. The breakup of the Soviet Union and Russia's shift to charging international prices has meant that naval acquisitions from overseas are now based more on capabilities and requirements, rather than the country of origin. With the strategic partnership with the United States maturing, key capabilities are now also being procured from that country. A new class of submarines is being acquired from France and two naval tankers are being built in Italy. The Talwar-class frigates are continuing to be built in Russia. With this backdrop, let us now examine the actual availability of ships, submarines, and naval aviation assets.

(3) **Aircraft carriers:** The lone aircraft carrier, Viraat, is being kept operational well beyond her originally envisaged life span, awaiting the Vikramaditya (ex-Admiral Gorshkov) from Russia, on completion of modification. The ship is likely to be delivered in 2012 (*The Hindu* 2009; Jane's Fighting Ships 2009–10). The indigenous carrier, Vikrant, being built at Kochi since 2005, is likely to be commissioned in 2015 (Jane's Fighting Ships 2009–10; Rai and Luthra 2009). Plans for another bigger carrier have been reported, which may be taken up after the launch of the Vikrant at Kochi (Jane's Fighting Ships 2009–10; Rai and Luthra 2009). This implies that the IN will be able to field a fleet of two aircraft carriers by 2015, with a third carrier probably joining by 2020.

(4) **Destroyers and frigates:** The IN currently has a total of 23 destroyers and frigates, which comprise the major, ocean-going ships. Considering the number of ships on order, the capacity of Indian shipyards and the number of ships likely to be decommissioned (Jane's Fighting Ships 2009–10; Rai and Luthra 2009), the total

number of destroyers/frigates with the IN by 2020 should be about 29, that is, only six more than the current number.

(5) **Other surface ships:** The medium-range ships comprise 24 corvettes, 21 offshore patrol vessels (OPVs), and about 10 amphibious ships, the landing ships tank (LSTs)(Jane's Fighting Ships 2009–10). One Austin-class ship, the Jalashwa, a landing transport dock (LPD), was transferred from the US Navy in 2007, and has given a boost to the amphibious capability (Jane's Fighting Ships 2009–10; *Times of India* 2007). The destroyers/frigates and the medium-range ships like corvettes, OPVs, and the LSTs with the navy, total up to about 65. In addition, the navy has an equal number of smaller crafts for seaward defence, coastal security, and minesweeping duties. In the overall context, the ship construction plans in place will barely be able to cater for replacing the ships which will need to be phased out due to ageing (Jane's Fighting Ships 2009–10; Das 2010; Rai and Luthra 2009).

(6) **Surface ships-capabilities:** The IN is, therefore, not likely to be able to field a numerically larger fleet by 2020. However, the capability of each successive platform has seen an impressive enhancement during the last 10 years. While doing this, the navy is also trying to implement standardization of weapon systems and sensors on the platforms under construction (Jane's Fighting Ships 2009–10).[17] Second, almost all weapon systems were earlier imported, giving rise to problems of non-availability of spares and maintenance facilities. This is being overcome through indigenous weapon systems like the Dhanush SSM and the joint Indo-Russian SSM BrahMos (Rai and Luthra 2009).[18]

(7) **Nuclear submarines:** The indigenous, 6,000 ton, SSN Arihant is likely to be commissioned in 2012 (Jane's Fighting Ships 2009–10; Rai and Luthra 2009). She will be armed with the indigenously developed K-15 Sagarika missile, of range 700 km (Jane's Fighting Ships 2009–10; Rai and Luthra 2009). A total of three SSNs are expected to be built. A larger, 12,000-ton Akula-II class SSN, the Nerpa, has joined the IN on lease from Russia in 2012 as INS Chakra (Rai 2011; Majumder 2012).

(8) **Conventional submarines:** The 14 conventional submarines currently with the IN consist of the four German type 209/1500 inducted in the 1980s and the 10 Russian Kilo-class inducted between 1986 and 2000. Replacement plans include six Scorpene-class submarines,

two of which are to be delivered by France and the remaining built in India, all by 2017 (Jane's Fighting Ships 2009–10).[19]

(9) **Naval aviation:** While the current aircraft carrier Viraat flies the Sea Harriers, both the new carriers being inducted, the Vikramaditya and Vikrant, will operate the MiG-29K Fulcrum (Jane's Fighting Ships 2009–10; Rai and Luthra 2009).[20] The long-range surveillance and ASW role is currently being carried out by the 13 TU-142M/IL-38 aircrafts, all procured from Russia during the 1970s–80s (Jane's Fighting Ships 2009–10; Rai and Luthra 2009).[21] With the induction of eight Boeing P-8I Poseidon long-range maritime patrol (LRMP) aircrafts commencing 2013, this particular role will get a considerable boost (Jane's Fighting Ships 2009–10; Rai and Luthra 2009).[22]

(10) **New initiatives for coastal surveillance:** In a bid to close the gaps highlighted during the 26/11 incident, a 1,000-man *Sagar Prahari Bal* (SPB) is being raised with a fleet of 80 fast, 50-knot Interceptor boats (Rai and Luthra 2009).[23] The government has also decided to double the strength of the Coast Guard, which currently has 7,000 personnel, 70 ships, and 40 aircrafts (Rai and Luthra 2009). Judicious use and a pragmatic balance of technological means like a coastal radar chain and satellite/aerial surveillance, as well as a local human surveillance and intelligence network, will be essential to bring about effective maritime domain awareness in the coastal areas.

TABLE 1.1 Naval Force Levels 2020: A Comparison

Platform	India	China	Pakistan
Aircraft carriers	2	2	–
Destroyers/Frigates	30	80	9
Nuclear submarines	3	12	–
Other submarines	14	58	5
Amphibious ships	12	60	–

Note: Numbers estimated for the year 2020 based on current known building programmes and likely induction/phasing out of ships and submarines.

Source: Jane's Fighting Ships, various publications by the US Department of Defense, Office of Naval Intelligence and Congressional Research papers, and author's assessments.

It is clear that in the overall analysis, IN will be no match for the PLA Navy numerically. Probably faced with this reality, Admiral Nirmal Verma, the Chief of Naval Staff, has stated that there has been a conceptual shift in the IN's perspective plan from 'number of platforms' to 'capabilities' (Rai and Luthra 2009). However, even in terms of capabilities, the PLAN has a definite edge in long-range strategic deterrence, with the induction of the 3,800 nautical miles Submarine Launched Ballistic Missile (SLBM) in 2010. With the induction of Chakra SSN on lease from Russia in 2012, the IN is operating a nuclear submarine for the first time after a gap of almost 20 years, and will need time to gain expertise. Similarly, the PLAN is likely to start operating an aircraft carrier for training by 2012 and operationally around 2020, and will need several years to master the nuances of carrier-borne aviation. The improved surface-to-air missile capability of the PLAN ships will provide fairly good air-defence cover to the fleet, even without an aircraft carrier. With a dedicated, indigenous, naval communication satellite likely to be launched in 2012 (Rai and Luthra 2009), there is likely to be an improvement in connectivity and network-centric warfare in the IN, enhancing effectiveness of operations. In addition, the induction of eight Boeing P-8I long-range maritime surveillance and ASW aircrafts commencing in 2013 will bring about a quantum jump in these capabilities (Rai and Luthra 2009).[24] Together, these will enhance maritime domain awareness, presently a weak area. The enhanced coastal security mission accorded to the IN is bound to affect its traditional blue-water war-fighting role.[25] As stated by Vice Admiral A.K. Singh, 'The term "balanced navy" has now acquired a different meaning altogether; a brown water or coastal force is as relevant and essential as a blue water force'.[26] It comes out rather clearly that the IN will need to forge partnerships with other navies in its areas of interest, towards accomplishing its maritime objectives.

Naval Partnerships/Cooperation

India has evolved a new paradigm of security cooperation relevant to an emerging multi-polar world, based on the premise that global threats must be met with global responses.[27] Accordingly, by 2005, India had entered into strategic partnerships with the United States, Russia, Japan, Indonesia, and the European Union, and went on to formalize strategic partnerships with Vietnam in 2007, Australia in 2009, and South Korea in 2010 (Roy Chaudhury 2009; Pasricha 2010). Taking a cue from this, the IN has been forging strong partnerships with a number of navies in the region, the more notable ones being from the United States, France, the United Kingdom, Singapore, Vietnam, Indonesia, and Japan. In addition, the IN has been successful in developing multilateral cooperation among the Asia-Pacific navies through the 'Milan' engagement at Port Blair. From four navies, which participated in 1995, the initiative has grown to include 14 navies in 2012. These include Australia, New Zealand, Bangladesh, Brunei, Indonesia, Malaysia, Mauritius, Myanmar, Philippines, Seychelles, Singapore, Sri Lanka, Thailand, and Vietnam. Another regional initiative launched by the IN was the Indian Ocean Naval Symposium (IONS) in 2008, to encourage navies of the IOR to interact with one another and find common solutions to the maritime threats and challenges that beset the region.[28]

(1) **US Navy:** The most meaningful relationship that the IN has today is with the U.S. Navy. This is because of the fact that the two navies have similar overall objectives, focusing on freedom of the seas and promotion of security and stability to ensure unhindered flow of commerce over the oceans. The navies have been exercising together annually for over a decade, gradually increasing the levels of complexity, and have achieved a degree of interoperability.[29] However, in line with the overall national posture of 'caution' while progressing with the strategic relationship with the U.S., the continued natural progression of the relationship between the two navies has also been somewhat hindered in recent years. This may change once the two countries get more deeply intertwined economically through trade and investments, including in military hardware, as also through greater and deeper societal integration, both of which have started happening (Mukherjee and Thyagraj 2012: 12–28).

(2) **Other navies:** The IN maintains a close partnership with the navies of the United Kingdom and France, which maintain a presence in the IOR. Cooperation with the Republic of Singapore Navy and the Vietnam People's Navy has also been longstanding and meaningful. Japan feels constrained because of her essential SLOCs running through the IOR without a commensurate naval presence in the region. She has, therefore, been seeking a close maritime relationship with India, including naval cooperation, which can be of mutual benefit (Prasad 2009).[30] The Japanese Maritime Self Defence Force has been

a part of the annual Indo-US naval exercise Malabar during the last two years, as a result of this strengthening relationship (Gokhale 2012). The IN has an arrangement for joint patrolling of India's maritime boundaries with Indonesia and Thailand. On the western seaboard, the IN has been actively involved in augmenting maritime security for Mauritius, Maldives, and Seychelles. The memorandum of understanding for maritime security cooperation with Oman was extended for another five years in January 2012 (Press Information Bureau 2012). These efforts enable the IN to maintain an adequate footprint, not only in the maritime neighbourhood, but also in the areas of interest beyond.

(3) **Prospects for cooperation with the PLA Navy:** With one of the foremost aims of both navies being to ensure a secure and stable environment for continued socio-economic growth, there is a definite commonality of interests. Both countries have over-stretched SLOCs in the IOR and beyond, in protection of which they can logically cooperate with each other. There are growing signs that the two countries, as well as the navies, may be moving towards such a cooperation, as demonstrated during the G20 and climate change summits, as well as bilateral defence exchanges (Yan 2010). The first IN-PLAN bilateral exercise took place off Shanghai in 2003 and the two navies have been interacting increasingly since then. The two navy chiefs discussed cooperation in anti-piracy operations in 2009 and the navies have started coordinating anti-piracy patrols since January 2012 (Suryanarayana 2009; Verma 2012; IANS 2012). In 2010, India offered to assist China in keeping vital sea lanes between the Middle East and Asia open.[31] As India's SLOCs in the Pacific Ocean become more important, China can reciprocate and there will be greater inter-dependence and mutuality of maritime security interests (Athwal 2008).[32] As an ongoing effort to improve mutual cooperation and trust, four IN ships visited Shanghai in June 2012, and even participated in exercises with PLAN ships while leaving the harbour. To give further importance to the visit during the year designated as the year of friendship and cooperation between the two countries, the head of the IN's Eastern Naval Command and his Chinese counterpart were present during the visit (Krishnan 2012). However, based upon past experiences and ongoing differences, India must remain vigilant about growing PLAN capabilities in the long term.

(4) **Concerted action vis-à-vis China:** This was demonstrated during the ASEAN Regional Forum (ARF) meeting in July 2010 in the face of growing Chinese assertiveness at sea, when 12 countries including the US countered the Chinese claim of its core national interest extending to the South China sea by stating that such claims were to the detriment of international law, freedom of navigation, maritime security, and the claims of neighbours (Thayer 2010: 4). Though China reacted strongly, it backed down from its claims and openly stated that it would respect freedom of navigation and flights on the South China Sea, as compatible with international law (Thayer 2010: 15–16). Concerted action by the US and six other nations, namely, Australia, Japan, Malaysia, Singapore, South Korea, and Vietnam, was on display at the ASEAN Defence Ministers Plus meeting in October 2010, when they together raised concerns about territorial disputes in the South China Sea. As against the known Chinese stand of resolving these disputes bilaterally, US Defence Secretary Gates stated that it is essential that 'these bilateral relationships be supplemented by strong multilateral institutions' in order to cultivate cooperation (US Department of Defense 2010).

Like-minded nations in the region with similar concerns about maritime security, amongst other issues, have started coming together to share their concerns and adopt a common approach towards seeking solutions. Relevant examples are the U.S.-Japan-India and the India-Republic of Korea-Japan trilateral meetings which have commenced in December 2011 and June 2012, respectively (*Hindustan Times* 2011; *The Economic Times* 2012). This kind of concerted political/diplomatic action could easily transform to concerted maritime action, given the growing naval capabilities in the region discussed earlier. Preparations for this are already underway and a few examples may be in order. The annual joint Indo-US naval exercise Malabar was carried out in the Bay of Bengal in 2007 with the navies of Australia, Japan, and Singapore also participating. After protests from China, only the Indian and US navies took part in the exercise in 2008 and 2009. However, Japan has again been included 2010 onwards (Gokhale 2011). Not only is the US relying heavily on the Indian Navy's stabilising role in the IOR, including the Asia Pacific (Pardesi 2011), but some ASEAN navies are also keen to cooperate with the IN to become effective in the cooperative endeavour in the shortest possible time, with Vietnam even providing base facilities at its ports (Siagian 2011; Moore and Swami 2010).

The IN should continue to build on these bilateral and multilateral partnerships. These will be of essence while encountering the non-traditional threats of piracy, terrorism, and natural disasters. Together, the combined naval power of a number of navies with similar objectives will also act as a greater deterrent against a rogue state, which may otherwise be foolhardy enough to try and upset the security and stability of the global maritime commons, for narrow, selfish interests, not tenable in international law.

***

With global power shifting to Asia, the Indian Ocean is likely to become increasingly important during the twenty-first century. This will be so not only for the economic dimensions of trade, energy, and associated security aspects but also because of the ongoing strife and emerging trouble spots being in this region, as exemplified by developments in Iraq, Afghanistan, Pakistan, Iran, and Somalia. The United States will find itself as one of a number of important actors on the world stage by 2025, though still the most powerful one, including militarily. However, other states will try and close the gap by developing asymmetric warfare capabilities whose net effect cannot yet be fathomed. Other envisaged changes, like those brought about by global warming, may change the complexion of the world in several dimensions. All major states are likely to promote stability and security in the world order for continued economic growth and will need to increasingly work together in the face of rising threats from non-state actors. Full-fledged wars between nation states are unlikely and, consequently, navies are likely to continue to be employed more in littoral areas. However, a greater naval capability is likely to be sought by more nations, commensurate with their growing economic prosperity and increasing dependence on the oceans. It is yet to be determined whether this proliferation of naval capabilities will bring about greater stability and security.

China's growing maritime power is in consequence to her growing economy and status as a major global player. China's foremost aim is likely to be to use this maritime power to ensure a stable world order for continued economic growth, at least for the next 20 years. The Yellow

Sea and the East and South China seas are likely to remain the areas of primary focus for the PLAN in this time frame. While the Taiwan issue may remain on the backburner, the maritime boundary disputes in the EEZ are likely to gain prominence and keep China preoccupied. China has taken measures to become a part of the international security framework and is expected to play an increasing role in conformity with her status. This will also mean China attaining a larger presence in the IOR where she has genuine security concerns with respect to her maritime trade and SLOCs. Not only India but also the Asia-Pacific region at large is anxious about this because of the prevailing perception with regard to China on account of a lack of transparency, manifold enhancements of defence expenditure, and an increasingly assertive attitude. While efforts are ongoing to have greater engagement with the PLAN to build trust and understanding, the developing Chinese naval capabilities need to be constantly monitored. It will be difficult for individual navies—barring the United States, with whom China is actually trying to close the gap to match these capabilities. However, in the emerging cooperative security environment predicated mainly against non-traditional threats, a collective response to the PLAN may also follow as a natural progression. This can be dictated by circumstances initiated by China, which are perceived by the international community as going against prevailing international norms and conventions. The IN has a well-thought-out engagement plan and is in partnership with other navies in the region based on common aims, objectives, and security concerns.

The IN plans to strengthen its capabilities as a three-dimensional force that comprises ships, submarines, and aircrafts to enable it to carry out the legitimate roles in fulfilling its objectives. However, there are considerable obstacles to the navy developing into an effective force in the intended time frame. Most of these emanate from the inherent inefficiencies of the defence apparatus, caused primarily by the prevailing civil-military relationship and long pending reforms. There is a way ahead to make the IN more effective. There is an urgent need for political oversight and involvement, including through legislation, in the overall national security system. Once this is achieved, it would be easier to reform the system and make it more efficient. The two areas of immediate concern for the IN to achieve its planned war fighting capability are an adequate, long-term budgetary commitment in a sustained manner and development of indigenous ship/submarine/aircraft building capability.

The major obstacle in making the navy effective in its primary military objective of deterrence is the lack of a well-demonstrated national resolve and an appropriate decision-making apparatus to use military force in a timely and even proactive manner, to safeguard national interests. This erodes the credibility of the navy's deterrent posture developed painstakingly over time, with alert and robust deployments and action. It is essential to integrate the military in higher security decision-making at the national level, as in most democratic nations. To be able to achieve this, first, the Ministry of Defence needs to be restructured so as to give due importance to the professional military expertise available at the Services Headquarters, while integrating this expertise holistically with the overall national defence framework. Second, an empowered Chief of Defence Staff must be appointed as a single point of military advice to the government. Without these measures and a demonstrated national resolve, which can be brought about only through a strong commitment of the political leadership, no amount of military capability enhancement will be able to deter another 26/11 incident which has been setting the nation back in its path of socio-economic development time and again.

Notes

1. The assessments take the form of annual reports by the Office of Naval Intelligence, the Department of Defence, several Congressional Research Service papers and reports/writings from professional military service institutions like the Navy/Army War Colleges, and perceive that the ongoing PLAN development could challenge the supremacy of the USN.

2. The four different types of SAM systems available give AAD cover from 20 to 80 miles.

3. The available SSM systems have ranges of 65 to 130 miles.

4. A total of five or six of the Jin-class SSBNs are scheduled to be commissioned.

5. The strategy relies on simultaneous application of electronic warfare and computer network operations (CNO) against an adversary's command, control, communications, computers, intelligence, surveillance, and reconnaissance (C4ISR) networks.

6. The first Joint Maritime Strategy document of the US Navy, Marine Corps, and Coast Guard promulgated in October 2007 clearly states this. See, U.S. Navy, Marine Corps, and Coast Guard, 'A Cooperative Strategy for 21st Century Seapower' (Washington, D.C.: Department of the Navy, October 2007).

7. US Navy, Marine Corps, and Coast Guard, 'A Cooperative Strategy for 21st Century Seapower' (Washington, D.C.: Department of the Navy, October 2007).

8. China has old disputes with Japan, the Philippines, Vietnam, Malaysia, and Brunei, and new ones with the two Koreas and Indonesia.

9. India has yet to establish a sea-based nuclear deterrence, and also because the scope of this chapter is generally limited to conventional forces/capabilities.

10. '1999 Kargil Conflict'. Available at www.globalsecurity.org/military/world/war/kargil-99.htm.

11. One incident of the Indian dhow MV Bhakti Sagar in 2006 and the other of MV Stolt Valour with Indian crew on board in September 2008.

12. Admiral Arun Prakash, 'India's Deterrent Capabilities', talk delivered at the Netaji Bose Memorial Lecture on 23 January 2010.

13. There was a vast shortfall of 19–58 per cent in the capital budget of the navy between 1995–6 and 1999–2000.

14. From personal experience of the author, who was part of the crew of a destroyer purchased from the USSR.

15. The first three indigenous destroyers of the Delhi-class and the first three indigenous frigates of the Brahmaputra-class took an average of nine years per ship, as against international standards of just three/four years.

16. As reported by *Defense News* and accessed on www.defensenews.com, the Chief of Naval Staff, at a media briefing on 2 December 2009 stated that the IN's major concern related to the delays in construction of ships.

17. The major weapon/sensor fit on the Talwar-class being built in Russia and the Shivalik-class frigates being built in India is common and includes the SS-N-27 Klub-N SSM, the SA-N-7 Kashmir SAM, and the indigenous HUMSA sonar.

18. Both these indigenous missiles are contemporary in their class, even by world standards, and have a range of 350 km (157 nautical miles).

19. However, there have been delays that will also affect the ordering of another six boats, to be selected from the Scorpene/German type 214/Russian Amur 1650 classes.

20. A total of 45 aircrafts have been ordered.

21. They have been upgraded from 2001 onwards, including fitment of air-to-ship missiles.

22. They are to be equipped for modern ASW, ASuW and intelligence, surveillance, and reconnaissance.

23. Some of these will be imported initially, before setting up facilities to manufacture them in India.

24. It is reported that the navy can ultimately acquire as many as twenty of these aircrafts. This is essential to move closer to the optimum 1:1 ratio between

major war vessels and LRMP aircraft, stated in *India's Maritime Military Strategy 2007*, pp. 112–13.

25. See Ganesh, 'Evolving Maritime Challenges', wherein he states that the navy cannot afford to reduce its capability or lose its effectiveness by restructuring to meet lesser threats.

26. See http://ajaishukla.blogspot.com/2009/08/coastal-security (accessed March 2010).

27. As stated by Prime Minister Dr Manmohan Singh at the Combined Commanders' conference of the Indian Armed Forces on 20 October 2005.

28. For details, please see http://ions.gov.in/?q=about_ions (accessed February 2010).

29. Admiral Nirmal Verma, during an interview with the Indian Defence Review, New Delhi, in February 2010, stated that in addition to the annual joint naval exercise Malabar, the two navies are progressing in explosive ordnance disposal, salvage operations, and expeditionary warfare exercises.

30. The Joint Action Plan concluded between the two Prime Ministers in 2009 has a strong focus on maritime-security.

31. Indian Minister of State for Defence Pallam Raju quoted as saying, 'India was happy to assist China to keep open vital sea lanes between Middle East and Asia in order to guard against piracy and conflict', as reported on www.defence.pk/forums/india-defence dated 22 February 2010.

32. The author makes a strong case that there is a growing realization in both countries that there is more to be gained through cooperation.

References

Agnihotri, K.K. 2010. 'Chinese Quest for a Naval Base in the Indian Ocean-Possible Options for China', 12 February, The National Maritime Foundation, New Delhi. Available at http://maritimeindia.org/sites/all/files/pdf/Chinese%20naval%20base%20KKA-12%20Feb.pdf (accessed March 2010).

Athwal, Amardeep. 2008. *China-India Relations: Contemporary Dynamics*. New York: Routledge.

Behera, Laxman K. 2009. 'India's Defence Budget 2009–10: An Assessment', IDSA, New Delhi. Available at www.idsa.in/idsastrategiccomments/IndiasDefenceBudget2009-10_LKBehera (accessed 18 February 2010).

———. 2012. 'Defence Spending in India and Its Neighbourhood, IDSA Asian Strategic Review 2012', pp. 20–1. New Delhi: Pentagon Press. Available at http://www.idsa.in/system/files/book_ASR2012.pdf.

Cordner, Lee. 2010. 'Rethinking Maritime Security in the Indian Ocean Region', *Journal of the Indian Ocean Region*, 6 (1): 67–85.

Das, P.S. 2010. 'China and India at Sea', *Business Standard*, 31 January.

De Silva-Ranasinghe, Sergei. 2011. 'Why the Indian Ocean Matters', *The Diplomat*, 2 March. Available at www.thediplomat.com/2011/03/02/why-the-indian-ocean-matters/?all=true (accessed July 2012).

Downs, Erica. 2006. *The Brookings Foreign Policy Studies Energy Security Series: China*. Washington, DC: The Brookings Institution Press. Available at http://www.brookings.edu/fp/research/energy/2006china.pdf.

Eaglen, Mackenzie and Jon Rodeback. 2010. 'Submarine Arms Race in the Pacific: The Chinese Challenge to U.S. Undersea Supremacy', Backgrounder #2367, The Heritage Foundation. Available at http://www.heritage.org/research/reports/2010/02/submarine-arms-race-in-the-pacific-the-chinese-challenge-to-us-undersea-supremacy (accessed February 2010).

Energy Information Administration (EIA). 2008. 'World Oil Transit Chokepoints', *Country Analysis Briefs*. Available at http://www.eia.gov/countries/analysisbriefs/World_Oil_Transit_Chokepoints/wotc.pdf (accessed February 2010).

Feuerberg, Gary. 2010. 'China Reverts to Aggressive Stance in the South China Sea', *The Epoch Times*, 22 February. Available at http://www.theepochtimes.com/n2/world/china-reverts-to-aggressive-stance-in-the-south-china-sea-30193.html (accessed March 2010).

Ganesh, R.N. 2009. 'Evolving Maritime Challenges', *Indian Defence Review*, 24 (3). Available at http://www.indiandefencereview.com/interviews/evolving-maritime-challenges/3/.

Global Security.org. '1999 Kargil Conflict'. Available at www.globalsecurity.org/military/world/war/kargil-99.htm (accessed 16 February 2010).

Gokhale, Nitin. 2011. 'India's Quiet Counter-China Strategy', *The Diplomat*, 16 March. Available at http://the-diplomat.com/2011/03/16/india%E2%80%99s-quiet-counter-china-strategy-2/ (accessed June 2012).

———. 2012. 'India's Quiet Counter-China Strategy', *The Diplomat*, 16 March.

Government of India, *Ministry of Defence Annual Reports* 2006–7, 2007–8, and 2008–9.

Government of India, *Ministry of Defence Annual Report 2008–09*, para 1.26. Available at http://mod.nic.in/reports/AR-eng-2009.pdf (accessed March 2010).

Hindustan Times, Washington DC, 20 December 2011. 'First US-Japan-India trilateral meeting'. Available at www.hindustantimes.com/world-news/Americas/First-US-Japan-India-trilateral/Article1-784695.aspx (accessed July 2012).

Hindustan Times. 2009. 17 December.

Holslag, Jonathan. 2009. 'The Persistent Military Security Dilemma between China and India', *Journal of Strategic Studies*, 32 (6): 811–40.

IANS. 2009. 'The IN had escorted 700 merchant ships, including about 600 foreign flagged vessels from 45 countries, through the Gulf of Aden since October 2008', 25 November. Available at http://blog.taragana.com/politics/2009/11/25/un-commends-indian-navy (accessed 16 February 2010).

———. 2012. 'India, China, Japan join hands for anti-piracy operations', 14 March. Available at http://maritimesecurity.asia/free-2/piracy-2/india-china-japan-join-hands-for-anti-piracy-operations/ (accessed June 2012).

Indian Defence Review, New Delhi, 20 February 2010. Available at www.indiandefencereview.com

Indian Ocean Naval Symposium. 2008. Knowledge World and National Maritime Foundation, New Delhi.

Information Office of the State Council, Beijing. 2009. 'China's National Defense in 2008'. Available at http://english.gov.cn/official/2009-01/20/content_1210227.htm (accessed February 2010).

Integrated Headquarters, Ministry of Defence [Navy], New Delhi. 2007. *Freedom to Use the Seas: India's Maritime Military Strategy.* •

Jane's Fighting Ships 2009–10. Available at www.englishnews@chosun.com (accessed 8 February 2010).

Japan Ministry of Defense, Defense of Japan 2009 (Annual White Paper). Available at http://www.mod.go.jp/e/publ/w_paper/2009.html (accessed March 2010).

Kaplan, Robert D. 2009. 'Center Stage for the 21st Century-Power Plays in the Indian Ocean', *Foreign Affairs*, 88 (2): 16–32.

Khurana, Gurpreet S. 2008. 'China's String of Pearls in the Indian Ocean and its Security Implications', *Strategic Analysis*, 32 (1): 1–39.

Kondapalli, Srikanth. 2001. *China's Naval Power*. New Delhi: Knowledge World.

Krekel, Bryan. 2009. 'Capability of the People's Republic of China to Conduct Cyber Warfare and Computer Network Exploitation'. Report prepared for the U.S.-China Economic and Security Review Commission, Northrop Grumman, October 2009, p. 6.

Krishnan, Ananth. 2012. 'Chinese Navy calls for trust building with India', *The Hindu*, Shanghai, 15 June 2012. Available at http://www.thehindu.com/news/international/article3529270.ece (accessed July 2012).

Majumder, Sanjoy. 2012. 'Russia-built Nuclear Submarine Joins Indian Navy', BBC News India, 4 April. Available at www.bbc.co.uk/news/world-asia-india-17606829 (accessed 13 June 2012).

Ministry of Defence [Navy]. 2007. *Freedom to Use the Seas: India's Maritime Military Strategy.* New Delhi: Integrated Headquarters, Ministry of Defence.

Moore, Malcolm and Praveen Swami. 2010. 'Vietnam Offers Navy Base to Foil China', *The Telegraph*, 8 November.

Mukherjee, Anit. 2012. 'Next Generation Defence Reforms: A Road Map', in B.D. Jayal, V.P. Malik, Anit Mukherjee, and Arun Prakash (eds), *A Call for Change: Higher Defence Management in India*, Monograph Series No. 6. New Delhi: Institute for Defence Studies and Analysis.

Mukherjee, Anit and Manohar Thyagraj. 2012. 'Competing Exceptionalisms: US-India Defence Relationship', *Journal of Defence Studies*, 6 (2): 12–28, April.

Office of the Assistant Secretary of Defense (Public Affairs), US Department of Defense. 2010. 'Remarks by Secretary Gates at ASEAN Defense Ministers Meeting Plus', 12 October. Available at http://www.defense.gov/transcripts/transcript.aspx?transcriptid=4700 (accessed 30 July 2012).

Office of Naval Intelligence. 2009. *The People's Liberation Army Navy, A Modern Navy with Chinese Characteristics*, Suitland (MD).

Office of the Secretary of Defense. 2009.'*Military Power of the People's Republic of China, 2009*', Annual Report to Congress, p. 40. Washington, DC: US Department of Defense.

O'Rourke, Ronald. 2009. *China Naval Modernization: Implications for U.S. Navy Capabilities—Background and Issues for Congress*, Congressional Research Service, 23 November, p. 10. Available at http://www.dtic.mil/cgi-bin/GetTRDoc?AD=ADA511396&Location=U2&doc=GetTRDoc.pdf (accessed March 2010).

Pant, Harsh V. 2009. 'India in the Indian Ocean: Growing Mismatch between Ambitions and Capabilities', *Pacific Affairs*, 82 (2): 279–97, 183–4.

Pardesi, Manjeet S. 2011.'India, US in East Asia: Emerging Strategic Partnership', *RSIS Commentary*, No. 54/2011, 8 April. Available at http://www.rsis.edu.sg/publications/Perspective/RSIS 0542011.pdf (accessed July 2012).

Pasricha, Anjana. 2010.'India, South Korea to Establish Strategic Partnership', *VOA News*. Available at http://www.voanews.com/tibetan-english/news/a-28-2010-01-26-voa3-90317852.html (accessed February 2010).

Prakash, Arun. 2009. 'The Menace of Piracy: India, the International Community and a UN Response', New Atlantic, Policy and Analysis Blog, 21 May. Available at www.acus.org/new_atlantic/menace-piracy-india-international-community-un-response (accessed 18 February 2010).

———. 2012. 'Defence Reforms: Contemporary Debates and Issues', in B.D. Jayal, V.P. Malik, Anit Mukherjee, and Arun Prakash (eds), A Call for Change: Higher Defence Management in India, Monograph Series No. 6. New Delhi: Institute for Defence Studies and Analysis.

Prasad, K.V. 2009. 'India-Japan Finalise Action Plan to Advance Security Cooperation', *The Hindu*, 30 December. Available at http://www.hindu.com/2009/12/30/stories/2009123054771000.htm (accessed 30 July 2012).

Press Information Bureau, Government of India. 2012. 'India, Oman extend MOU on cooperation for Maritime Security'. Available at http://www.safety4sea.com/page/8688/4/india,-oman-extend-mou-on-cooperation-for-maritime-security (accessed July 2012).

Rai, Ranjit B. 2011. 'Nerpa and Arihant will augment Indian Navy's declining submarine strength', *India Strategic*. Available at http://www.indiastrategic.in/topstories886.htm (accessed 9 February 2011).

Rai, Ranjit B. and Gulshan R. Luthra. 2009. 'Indian Navy Power Packed for A Strong Nation', *India Strategic*, 4 (12) December. Available at http://www.indiastrategic.in/topstories454.htm.

Roy Chaudhury, Dipanjan. 2009. 'Casting the Net Wide', *Mail Today*, November 25.

Roy-Chaudhury, Rahul. 2000. *India's Maritime Security*. New Delhi, Knowledge World.

Sakhuja, Vijay. 2006. 'Indian Navy: Keeping Pace with Emerging Challenges', in Laurence B. Prabhakar, Joshua Ho, Sam Bateman (eds), *The Evolving Maritime Balance of Power in the Asia-Pacific*. Singapore: Institute of Defence and Strategic Studies.

————. 2010. 'The Indian Navy's Agenda for Maritime Security in the Indian Ocean', *Terrorism Monitor*, 8 (8). Available at http://www.jamestown.org/single/?no_cache=1&tx_ttnews%5Bswords%5D=8fd5893941d69d0be3f378576261ae3e&tx_ttnews%5Bany_of_the_words%5D=PKK&tx_ttnews%5Bpointer%5D=2&tx_ttnews%5Btt_news%5D=36086&tx_ttnews%5BbackPid%5D=7&cHash=3bbf85ba5f#.UdTtyrS6bVI.

Sengupta, Prasun K. 2009. 'Full Steam Ahead', *Force*, November, 52–3.

Siagian, Sabam. 2011. 'India's Role in the Indian Ocean, E. Asian Regions', *The Jakarta Post*, 29 March.

Sikri, Rajiv. 2007. 'Why Russia and India Matter to Each Other?', Paper No. 2111, South Asia Analysis Group. Available at http://www.southasiaanalysis.org/%5Cpapers22%5Cpaper2111.html (accessed 20 February 2010).

Suryanarayana, P.S. 2009. 'India, China Discuss Anti-piracy Cooperation', *The Hindu*, 31 May.

Thayer, Carlyle A. 2010. 'Recent Developments in the South China Sea: Grounds for Cautious Optimism?' RSIS Working Paper, No. 220, p. 4. Available at http://www.rsis.edu.sg/publications/WorkingPapers/WP220.pdf (accessed July 2012).

The Economic Times, PTI, 29 June 2012. 'India, Republic of Korea, Japan hold trilateral meet; discuss South China Sea'. Available at http://economictimes.indiatimes.com/news/politics/nation/india-republic-of-korea-japan-hold-a-trilateral-meet-discuss-south-china-sea/articleshow/14504878.cms (accessed July 2012).

The Hindu. 'INS Vikramaditya Will Be Ready by 2012, Says ENC Chief'. Available at http://www.thehindu.com/news/cities/Visakhapatnam/ins-vikramaditya-will-be-ready-by-2012-says-enc-chief/article59982.ece.

Times of India. 2007. 'Amphibious Warship INS Jalashwa Inducted into Navy', September 14. Available at http://articles.timesofindia.indiatimes.com/keyword/ins-jalashwaa (accessed 26 August 2013).

U.S. *ONI Report*, 2009, 'The People's Liberation Army Navy, A Modern Navy with Chinese Characteristics', August, Suitland (MD), Office of Naval Intelligence.

Verma, Nirmal. 2012. 'Metamorphosis of Matters Maritime: An Indian Perspective', Key address delivered at the International Institute for Strategic Studies, London, on 25 June. Available at http://www.iiss.org/en/events/events/archive/2012-4a49/june-7879/metamorphosis-of-matters-maritime-an-indian-perspective-e8cf (accessed June 2012).

Yan, Zhang. Ambassador of China to India. 'Bonding at Copenhagen Cemented India-China Relations', OutlookIndia.com, 18 January 2010. Available at http://www.outlookindia.com/article.aspx?263645 (accessed June 2010).

2 The Indian Air Force of Tomorrow

Challenges

PRAMOD K. MEHRA

INDIAN AIR FORCE is the fourth largest Air Force in the world. This is a statement made very often in the professional literature as well as spoken during seminars but what it fails to quantify and qualify is its capability in terms of numbers,[1] fire power, level of technology, self-sufficiency in aviation related industry, doctrine and concept of operations, trained manpower, and the future plans to maintain/improve the status. All the qualifications stated above, which indicate force projection capability, are variable and need to be considered together to denote strength as an aerospace power. It also implies that Indian aerospace power must grow in all the above stated aspects to remain an effective force in the future. More often than not, the debate is limited to numbers albeit very important for a country of India's size, but the aerospace power of a potential great power has to have a credible deterrent capability in the entire range of military operations (Naik 2011: 11–14).

In India, air power and in fact, aerospace power holds the key to maintaining an edge over the likely adversaries, and it surely cannot happen with three to four decades old inventory of fighter aircraft, rapid build-up of air power by some of the neighbours, limited airlift capability, and lack of combat support equipment. Besides military hardware, there is a need to develop capabilities to hit the soft ribs of the adversaries and affect their ability to conduct war using cyber space. Additionally, space power is needed to give our war fighters the precise advantage in surveillance, persistence, assessment of results, and thereafter reengage with decisive and overwhelming force. The challenge is to go from where we are to where we should be in years to come. This chapter seeks to assess India's present air power capability and its future potential in the face of changing security challenges to its major power status. I argue that to face such challenges, India would require a greater role by its Air Force which is however limited in its capability and is at various stages of its transformation. This chapter proceeds with a section that briefly introduces the historical evolution of the Indian Air Force (IAF). The section that follows discusses the operational experiences of the Air Force in the past. The following section endeavours to demonstrate the key security challenges to India's emergence as a major regional power and the role of the IAF. The final section looks into the force projection capability of the IAF and various challenges at the force and policy levels.

Formative Years

The formative years have played a very important role in the philosophy for growth, leadership, ethos, war fighting, and developing a world view of other countries and their air forces. The hallmarks of the IAF growth have been initiative, innovative spirit, and charting of its growth independently.

Pre-Independence

Two centuries of British Raj had left India essentially de-industrialized, impoverished, and faced with an appalling state of human resources, yet civil aviation came to India within seven years of the first flight by the Wright Brothers. This was possible since the Maharajas and a few rich entrepreneurs had a very strong spirit of adventure, enterprise, and also the aircraft manufacturers in Europe saw opportunities to sell the aircraft in India. Aviation in India was not far behind that in Europe and according to the *The Hindu*, the first flight is credited to a Corsican, Mr Giacomo d' Angeli, in March 1910. He was a hotelier in Madras (now named Chennai) who flew in an aircraft made in Madras by the Simpson's (*The Hindu* 2003). The other notable pioneers were the Maharaja of Patiala, whose British-built Farman biplane and a two-seat Gnome-Bleriot monoplane flew at Allahabad on 10 December 1910 (Bhargava). The Indian Army was not far behind and the first aerial reconnaissance demonstration for the military was carried out at Aurangabad, Maharashtra, on 16 January 1911 with four cavalry brigades participating and 12 British Generals witnessing the display (Chaudhry 2010: 117–35). The world's first airmail was carried in India from Allahabad to Naini on 18 February 1911 and thereafter to Kolkata on 22 February 1911 (Chaudhry 2010: 117–35). Civil aviation continued to grow with Indian pilots participating in air races like the one between England and India and establishment of Tata Airlines in 1933 by Tata Sons Ltd. The growth of civil aviation was even more remarkable after the Second World War when a large number of war surplus Dakotas were left behind by the United States Army Air Force (USAAF) and were auctioned at throwaway prices and thereafter overhauled and refurbished by Hindustan Aircraft Limited (HAL) for the fledgling airlines. These Dakota aircraft were even requisitioned to move troops to Srinagar after the Maharaja of Kashmir signed the document of accession to India on 26 October 1947 (Singh 2007: 52).

Military aviation came to India in the form of the Royal Air Force (RAF) squadrons being deployed to secure the frontiers of India in the North Western Frontier Province (NWFP). However, before that, a number of Indians, such as Lt Indra Lal Roy DFC and Sardar Hardit Singh Malik, had served with great distinction with the British Royal Flying Corps during World War I (Bhargava). The IAF was established by a legislative act passed by the legislative assembly and the Indian Air Force Act (XIV of 1932) came into force on 8 October 1932. It was modelled around the establishment and principles of the RAF, but the role assigned to the IAF squadrons was a tactical role in support of the army, envisaging artillery support and armed reconnaissance. It took more than eight years and the pressure of the Second World War to build up the IAF to its full strength of 10 squadrons. The aircraft and the equipment with IAF were inferior to those of the RAF and other allied forces since the RAF and the United States Air Force (USAF) were tasked with bombing and other combat roles. During the war years, the bravery, innovative skills, and leadership of IAF pilots and airmen was recognized through awards of wartime gallantry medals and once by no less than the Supreme Allied Commander himself at an operational airfield (Singh 2009: 54–5).

Post-Independence Era (1947–90)

After independence, the IAF was left with six squadrons of fighter aircraft and half a squadron of transport aircraft. All the IAF squadrons had undergone reconversions since their raising and at the time of independence, they were equipped with Tempest, Spitfire, and Dakota aircraft. Even after the prolonged war of 1947–8, the Government of India authorized an IAF strength of 15 squadrons in 1953 followed by 23 squadrons (18 combat and five transport) in 1959 (Singh 2009: 106–7) when Pakistan was seen to be receiving supersonic F-104 and F-86 aircraft from the United States after joining the Central Treaty Organization (CENTO) and the South-East Asia Treaty Organization (SEATO). It was very evident that the Government of India was greatly influenced by the reports submitted by British advisors namely, Wansborough Jones and the physicist P.M.S. Blackett, who wanted the IAF to retain a tactical role and acquire surplus weapons from Britain (Singh 2007: 64–6). Meanwhile, the IAF with the help of HAL built a light bomber squadron of about 42 B-24 Liberator aircraft through repair and cannibalization from the 100-odd deliberately damaged maritime reconnaissance aircraft left behind at Kanpur (Bhargava).[2] By then, even though China had already annexed Tibet, the build-up of defence capability remained Pakistan-centric.

In January 1963, the Emergency Committee of the Cabinet accepted in principle the recommendation of the IAF to build up 64 squadrons, but the actual strength was limited to 45 squadrons (35 combat and 10 transport squadrons) (Singh 2007: 68–9). Strong links with Britain in the early years meant that the IAF entered the jet age with aircraft like Vampire and thereafter Hunter, Gnat, and Canberra aircraft from the UK, but in between the IAF diversified through the purchase of Ouragon and Mystère aircraft from France in the mid-50s after a perceived slow-down in the supply of spares by Britain during the period (1951) when there was a threat of war with Pakistan (Singh 2009: 73). These aircraft were purchased to build up strike capability, but the emphasis shifted to air defence aircraft as soon as Pakistan acquired F-86 and the supersonic F-104 aircraft. After a rebuff from the United States, India approached the Soviet Union in the early 60s to purchase MiG-21 and later on Su-7 aircraft, but these aircraft had been designed for a specific threat environment, had a short radius of action, limited throw weight, and were a part of the larger Soviet air defence weapon system against the North Atlantic Treaty Organization (NATO) (Singh 2007: 67). This build-up of the IAF inventory with Mig-21 variants, MiG-23BN/MF, MiG-25, MiG-27, MiG-29, and Su-7 marked an increase in dependence on the Soviet Union. Four variants of the MiG-21 were inducted into service in phases and at one time, in the late 70s, about 60 per cent of the fighter force comprised these variants (Singh 2007: 68). The Gnat also had a very short radius of action and required substantial development work to make it safe and operational. This was carried out by HAL in the 60s and 70s.[3] The short operating ranges of the MiG-21 and the Gnat necessitated construction of new airbases close to the borders and the attendant air defence requirements for both ground-based systems and airborne platforms. 30 Pechora SAM squadrons and a battery of various radars were inducted in the 70s to protect the forward bases, which had a big impact on manpower distribution but, more importantly, emphasized the defensive operational doctrine.

Some change in the mindset from defensive to offensive did take place with the induction of the Jaguar aircraft (often called 'Deep Penetration Strike Aircraft'), but without the long-range fighter escort aircraft, aerial refuelling, and Airborne Warning and Control Systems (AWACS), it did not have the necessary operational reach. Four additional squadrons (over and above the 35 combat squadrons) equipped with Mirage 2000 and MiG-29 aircraft were raised in 1985–9 as part of the next phase of capability development after Soviet intervention in Afghanistan and the supply of F-16 aircraft to Pakistan as a part of massive American aid.[4] The IAF's growth story indicates a reactive response to developments in the neighbourhood, but it still maintained a favourable equation with its neighbours with the induction of better technology platforms and their innovative usage.

In this entire series of air power build-up through imports, there was one silver lining of indigenous research and development effort. This saga of a state-of-the-art design and development and subsequent failure due to lack of a suitable engine is covered later.

Operational Experience

What did this young Air Force learn from the wars? The IAF cut its operational teeth as an army cooperation force in the NWFP during the Waziristan campaign from 1936–9. During the Burma campaign, the finest example of initiative, innovative skills, leadership, and morale was displayed in 1942 when No.1 Squadron under Sqn Ldr Jumbo Majumdar locally modified a Lysander aircraft to carry two bombs and bombed the operating airfields of the invading Japanese in Burma (Singh

2009: 34–6). Similar examples of the IAF squadrons engaged in airfield bombing, escort roles, and interdiction tasks, besides the close support role and reconnaissance were seen in 1944 during the Second Arakan campaign and advance to Rangoon. It was during these campaigns that the IAF was faced with an organized military and a hostile Air Force for the first time. After the war, the IAF again faced testing times when, during demobilization, British officers were withdrawn and this very young Air Force was faced with the challenge of running itself without any experience and time for consolidation.

The IAF was still going through the pangs of Partition and the division of assets when Pathan tribesmen, aided by Pakistani regulars, invaded Kashmir on 22 October 1947. Soon after the accession of Jammu & Kashmir (J&K) to India on 26 October, Dakotas from civil airlines were requisitioned to augment the very limited IAF transport assets to move an entire brigade to Srinagar in five days. Lord Mountbatten wrote that in his war experience, he had 'never come across an airlift of this order being successfully undertaken with such slender resources, and at such a short notice' (Kumar 2007: 48). Either the lack of political will or lack of control over the armed forces was in evidence when, even though independent India's leadership wanted much greater use of the combat aircraft for interdiction and for sanitising the western approach to the Srinagar valley, these were not carried out as all the three arms of the defence forces were headed by British officers who took decisions keeping in mind British interests in coordination with the British Government (Singh 2007: 52–4). So much so that the Tempest aircraft of the IAF were not fully mobilized to fight this very long war in J&K and half their strength was kept at places far away (Singh 2007: 54–5). The IAF crew displayed courage, bravery, and the finest examples of Army-Air Force cooperation when they undertook some very hazardous missions in J&K—landing the guns at Poonch at night without airstrip illumination and troops at Leh, the highest landing strip (10682ft AMSL), in an unpressurized Dakota. Apparently, these missions were carried out without obtaining clearance from headquarters and may have been in violation of the instructions laid down (Singh 2007: 57).

In 1962, the IAF was only used to provide logistical support to the Army and combat aircraft were not used. The probable explanation for this is the kind of advice received from non-professionals unaware of IAF capability and the wish to avoid the destruction of cities and the sufferings of the population during the Second World War. There was an exaggerated fear that China would bomb Indian cities in retaliation, but there is no evidence that any study was carried out on the Chinese combat aircraft, their air bases, and the ability of IAF fighters to defend the air space. In hindsight, it is very clear that IAF combat power could have achieved a strategic effect, reduced casualties, and probably averted a loss of face (Tiwary 2006).

Much has been written about the Indo-Pakistan war of 1965, but a thorough analysis of the air war has been lacking. A recent analysis by Air Cmde Jasjit Singh in *Defence from the Skies* has highlighted some aspects (Singh 2007). During the 1965 Indo-Pakistan war, IAF initially lost a number of aircraft on the ground because of lack of preparedness and the element of surprise, but it was subsequently able to dominate the Pakistan Air Force (PAF). This was possible since PAF had devoted a very large air effort towards airfield defence, which could not be sustained because of paucity of numbers (Tiwary 2007). The IAF suffered initial reverses since it was in the throes of expansion and had not developed a coherent doctrine for its role and tasks in the use of air power and the support to be provided to surface forces. It did manage to blunt the enemy armour attacks, but could not maintain control of the air because of lack of suitable aircraft both in numbers and technology. From the foregoing, a very important lesson was drawn that both numbers and level of technology matter and the concept of 'Defensive Air Defence' cannot win wars.

Unlike 1965, there was adequate coordination and better understanding of use of air power by all the forces during the 1971 war for the liberation of Bangladesh. After gaining air supremacy in the east in the first three days, the IAF mounted relentless attacks in support of the Army in the form of close air support, interdiction, and attacks on the airfields to keep them inoperative. Simultaneously, transport aircraft were used for para-drops and helicopters for transporting troops across the countless waterways. The strategic impact of the attack on the Governor's house at Dhaka is too well known to be recounted (Singh 2007: 144–5). In the western sector, the IAF played a crucial role in the famous 'Battle of Longewala' where a handful of Hunter aircraft blunted the Pakistan armour thrust. At the same time, there appeared to be a lack of coordination between the Pakistan Army and the PAF since no PAF aircraft came to intercept the Hunters (Singh 2007: 131).

The most recent experience of the IAF in combat was in Kargil in 1999 when it was required to support the Army on icy heights to evict Pakistani intruders. This war brought to the fore the need to maintain capability to fight in the high mountains. The vulnerability of slow-moving platforms like helicopters, the challenge of target acquisition of small targets in the mountains, weapon release from altitudes above 30,000 ft, weapon system limitations and delivery accuracy, use of precision guided munitions (PGMs), and the need for innovative tactics were highlighted (Singh 2007: 161). Air attacks on supply dumps and enemy placements had a strategic effect, forcing the enemy to rethink their plans and this did not lead to an escalation. Although the political direction to not to cross the Line of Control (LOC) for fear of escalation was not sound from the operational point of view, it helped in image building in the international arena.

Besides the above-mentioned operations, the IAF also learnt some valuable lessons from the year-long deployment during the stand-off against Pakistan in 2002 (code-named 'Operation Parakram'), employment of IAF helicopters to support the Indian Peace Keeping Force (IPKF) in Sri Lanka in 1987–90, and during Operation Cactus in November 1988 to quell an externally engineered rebellion in the Maldives.

The IAF has also taken part in peace-time operations under the UN mandate and has provided disaster relief in many areas across the world. The earliest operation was in Congo (1961–2) followed by Somalia (1993–4), Sierra Leone (2000), Congo (2003–11), and Sudan (2005–11). Noteworthy recent relief operations undertaken by IAF are the evacuation of Indians and citizens of neighbouring countries from Cyprus after the Lebanon war and from Iraq and Kuwait in 1990, the Bhuj earthquake in India's Gujarat state (2001), the Indian Ocean Tsunami (December 2004), a major snow storm in J&K (2005), the Pakistan earthquake (October 2005), relief material flown to the USA in the aftermath of Hurricane Katrina (August 2005), and flood rescue in Sri Lanka.

Challenges to India's Emergence as a Regional Power

The Indian subcontinent has seen four wars in the last 60 years or so because of the geo-politics of this region. Southern Asia itself has been on the boil for over 50 years, whether through regular or irregular warfare. Even though India has risen to help its neighbours in times of their need, it has not built up the political capital essential for a regional power. On the other hand, China has used defence diplomacy and economic clout to convert the recipient states into client states. Is there a lesson for India to change track and give a greater chance to its defence diplomacy in concert with the use of economic power? A 'Hands Off' policy does not make a great power and hence realization of India's greater legitimate role in the regional affairs extending from the Horn of Africa to beyond the Malacca straits and from Central Asia to the Indian Ocean is a must. India can play this role only by becoming strong both economically and militarily.

The causes of a conflict are numerous and too complex to be predicted, but it is always worthwhile to consider their presence so as to prepare in advance. Moreover, in a number of countries in the wider Middle East and Africa, the prevailing political system remains autocratic and faces instability due to internal turmoil, poor governance, and limited popular participation. The instability which had started from Tunisia, Libya, Yemen, and Egypt has somewhat abated but is still continuing in Syria. It is hoped that these movements lead to democracy, remain non-violent, and are not hijacked by extremist elements. International relations have undergone a sea change thanks to globalization, but it does not mean that wars will not take place. It is only the nature of wars which will change. The Asia-Pacific region has been a witness to muscle flexing between China and Japan in 2010, and the lesson to be drawn is that economic power and control over scarce resources is the source of strategic tension during this period of recession.

India's boundary dispute with China is unlikely to be resolved soon. China has now gone to the extent to call Arunachal Pradesh and J&K a disputed territory, but has recognized Pakistan Occupied Kashmir (POK) as part of Pakistan (George 2010; Ramachandran 2011). These pinpricks are constant reminders that, in spite of Confidence Building Measures (CBMs) being in place, India needs to develop both economically and militarily. Both China and Pakistan are nuclear powers and are cooperating extensively in developing their strategic strike capability. As long as India does not possess a credible deterrence and capability to thwart a ballistic missiles attack, this will be their principal weapon of choice. The IAF has to take note of the wide spectrum of conflict from the likely use of missiles with conventional warheads with increased accuracies in a limited war to fourth-generation warfare.

The PAF has received more F-16 from the USA in 2011 and the older ones are being upgraded (Avalon 2011: 28). In addition, China and Pakistan have a joint development programme to develop JF-17 combat aircraft and about a dozen have already been delivered and many more being assembled in Pakistan.[5] The PAF has become more effective with the induction of Beyond Visual Range systems (BVRs), PGMs, Harpoon missiles, tankers, and Advanced Early Warning (AEW) aircraft. The IAF does not retain the same superiority in numbers as in the past and it will have to strategize and work out the force employment of the technologically superior but numerically limited aircraft to achieve air dominance against an increasingly potent opponent.

China, on the other hand, has adopted a policy of winning the wars through 'command of the air' and has been relentlessly developing the latest generation aircraft. China is way ahead in building their infrastructure in Tibet and can mount operations from a number of airfields opposite the Indian border or further inland with the support of aerial refuellers and early warning aircraft. China has shown to the world their own fifth-generation aircraft indicating that they will be able to field a very sophisticated air force along with combat support elements by the next decade. The air-launched cruise missiles and other long range anti-access missiles developed by China along with ballistic missiles with ranges of more than 3,000 km. means that IAF has a long way to go to ensure air defence of its territory.[6] China's successful test of anti-satellite capability in January 2007 (Office of the Secretary of Defense: 36) and manoeuvring satellites in 2010 is a warning that it can knock out India's communication and imaging satellites, thus blinding both its defence forces and civil entities.

With both China and Pakistan modernizing their fleets, the IAF will have fewer aircraft to support the surface forces because of heavier commitments toward achieving air superiority and preventing the opponent's aircraft from interfering with its Army's ground operations. Although the possibility of a war with China in the near future is remote, if China does start a war, it is possible that Pakistan may join to take advantage of India's limited capability to fight on two fronts. The Indian military is rewriting its doctrine for a war on two fronts, developing its border infrastructure in the north, and acquiring suitable weapon systems to fight in the mountains (Blumenthal 2010). At present, the IAF may be able to defend against attacks by Su-27 aircraft of the People's Liberation Army Air Force (PLAAF) operating from the high altitude airfields of Tibet or from Chengdu region airfields, but it is woefully short in capability against the Second Artillery.

War between nuclear-armed and potent neighbours is expected to be a short-duration limited war in the subcontinent and the tempo of air operations is expected to be very high. Between two matching adversaries, total combat fire power will play a crucial role and its employment to gain asymmetry will be the key to success. Under a nuclear overhang, the land forces will have limited objectives and it will be only the IAF which can take punitive action. This punitive action has to be well calibrated to have the desired strategic effect and targets so selected that India retains control over escalation and avoids nuclear risk.

In the context of the above challenges, can there be more than one power centre in the region and can India rise to that status? The answer is 'Yes', but with the caveat that India has to display the necessary self-confidence. This confidence will depend upon the extent it develops its economic, diplomatic, and military clout. India does not covet the territory of other countries and its diplomatic and economic clout can become credible only if it can grow in a peaceful environment. The region can prosper only when disputes are resolved in an atmosphere of trust and long-term peace prevails in the region. Moreover, the region will expect India to resolve disputes with a benevolent approach. India can influence the countries in the region only when its intrinsic strength based on poverty alleviation; human resource development, education, health, good governance, and equality before law are addressed. The spirit of competition with China will prevail, but regional support is more likely for India if it is a benign power. Regional multilateral alliances in South-East Asia, East Asia, and West Asia are more likely to accept India as a member for both military and joint technology development programmes and that will ultimately help in its role as a regional power.

India is not a member of any military grouping but has developed bilateral strategic partnerships and defence cooperation agreements with a number of countries like the United States, the United Kingdom, France, Russia, Malaysia, and Singapore. The bilateral defence agreements have elevated the relationship with some countries to a higher plane through regular exercises instead of only a buyer-seller relationship. India took nearly four decades to graduate to cooperation and joint development with USSR/Russia; it is not known when, if ever, the new relationship with the United States will mature to this level.

India's growing economic and military might will require its armed forces to be increasingly prepared for all spectrums of conflict jointly. The limitation typically faced by the Indian Army due to the geographical spread is being overcome through a doctrinal shift to 'active defence,' which is primarily a pro-active deterrence strategy for joint operations to be effective. There is thus a need to institutionalize those unified operational structures based on joint operational doctrine.

Force Projection Capability

In order to discuss the capability of the IAF, it is important that its role and tasks are clearly defined, understood, and are in tune with the doctrine laid down. The role of the IAF to achieve national goals using the vertical dimension in conjunction with other Indian military forces is well accepted but the question is whether it has established the structures for joint planning, equipping, and operations. The IAF has the well-recognized task of achieving air dominance, which implies offensive air defence, unhindered army operations, ability to hit the enemy target system deep into enemy territory, and expansion of the battle space at will to facilitate Intelligence, Surveillance and Reconnaissance (ISR) and communications over the area of interest. The IAF also has the task to support surface forces in all their operations including counter-insurgency and counter-terrorism.

Essentially, the central logic of the IAF is not the use of air power against tactical or strategic targets, but to strike the adversary's vulnerabilities and cause functional paralysis. A networked environment further provides parallel application of air power, which weakens the adversary's capability and also his will to wage war. This means that the IAF has to develop agility and flexibility in all levels of operations including the expeditionary role while making optimum use of limited available resources. For the long term, the IAF has to build a favourable asymmetry both in numbers and technology levels over the adversary in order to achieve air dominance. Meanwhile, in case of negative asymmetry, innovative force employment and selection of targets will determine the outcome.

The IAF has continuously improved its capability through force build-up as discussed earlier, but it was only with the induction of Jaguar, Mirage 2000, and MiG-29 aircraft that it began to consider itself capable of carrying out all the classical tasks stated above. The subsequent acquisition of Su-30 MKI armed with PGMs and BVRs markedly enhanced IAF's ability to dominate the adversary. The IAF has already displayed its force projection capability, acquired through the induction of IL-78 aerial refuellers along with IL-76 heavy airlifters, through participation in exercises with friendly foreign countries in Europe and USA.

Transforming the Indian Air Force in the Near Term

The IAF commenced its drive to transform itself in the last decade and is well set on that trajectory through the induction of aircraft to achieve dominance, arresting the decline in numbers, revisiting its doctrine/ concepts, and bringing in some organizational changes. The question is whether it has addressed the challenges of building a balanced force through a planned induction of aircraft, systems, weapons, missiles, combat support systems, space-based systems, and indigenous programmes in the next decade or so? The IAF also needs to develop techniques and a Concept of Operations (CONOPS) to fight tomorrow's war with tomorrow's weapons, as with the fully integrated and systems intensive aircraft under development. Future aircraft will display a solution based on fused/integrated information from all on-board sensors and other combat elements and not what any single system would give.

A balanced force structure is essential for credible deterrence and achieving the national objective, that is, to win a war if deterrence fails but it is related to threat, enemy Order of Battle (Orbat), joint campaign requirements, concept of operations, state of the economy, self-sufficiency, international relations, geo-politics of the region, and so on. What constitutes a balanced force structure? The force structure of any air force would consist of aircraft, weapons, combat support systems, space-based systems, ground environment for surveillance and communication, manpower and so on. For the IAF, the force in being should have the capability to achieve air dominance while fighting a very capable adversary, deliver nuclear weapons when ordered, fight an intense limited war, especially under a nuclear overhang, and even accomplish the tasks in fourth-generation warfare. The IAF must have the means to deliver its firepower accurately in all kinds of weather during day and night, conduct surgical strikes, and also provide credible air defence against the matching capabilities of an adversary using aircraft and even ballistic missiles.

In the case of aircraft, the force structure mix would include air defence aircraft, strike aircraft, bombers, multi-role aircraft, transport aircraft, helicopters, unmanned aerial vehicles (UAVs), and so on. This aircraft and weapons force mix can be divided into categories of heavy, medium, and light aircraft. Further sub-divisions can be based on high, medium, and low technologies and levels of obsolescence. Similar categorization can also be worked out when discussing combat support systems.

The IAF has been facing these force structure issues since independence when its task was basically meant to provide army support. Subsequently, during the growth period, aircraft had to be procured from different countries, and these were designed to meet the producer country's requirements. These acquisitions perforce depended on availability and did not address categorization in terms of capability and technology levels. Broad distribution of numbers into fighter, transport, and helicopter squadrons should have been further divided into varying degrees of capability of platforms and weapon systems. The force structure is linked with the capability of the adversary and threat perception. The IAF has to maintain a credible force deployed on both the fronts and must maintain a very favourable asymmetry on the western border and capability to augment the force, if required, at the northern border.

A broad breakdown of the types, numbers, level of technology, and so on, of weapon systems can be suggested considering the present equation which exists with India's neighbours, but this must be reviewed periodically or whenever the equation is disturbed. The IAF needs to have a majority of medium multi-role aircraft with medium-to-high technology against the western neighbour so as to maintain control of the airspace and support ground operations. The IAF must maintain a favourable asymmetry both in numbers and technology for high-tempo operations and for escalation control. The requirement of weapon systems against the northern neighbour will be different. All three categories of aircraft will be required, with a greater number of heavy and high-technology aircraft as well as of air defence aircraft and weapon systems. The IAF has already proposed to increase its sanctioned strength to 45 Combat Squadrons to meet existing threats.[7]

Manned Aircraft

The IAF is presently suffering from delay in recapitalizing old aircraft inducted over 30 years ago. Delays in the indigenous development of Light Combat Aircraft (LCA) coupled with hold-ups in decision-making for new aircraft induction have allowed the force levels to deplete considerably. The induction of the hybridized version of the Russian

Su-30MKI has helped the IAF to retain its effectiveness but it is well known that 'quantity has its own quality' and, for a country of India's size, numbers matter. India is expected to sign the contract for 126 medium multi-role combat aircraft (MMRCA) in the near future and the numbers could easily stretch if there is further slippage in LCA induction or if the government accepts the necessity of building up capability to fight on two fronts.

Presently, USA, Russia, China, and India are the only countries developing more advanced aircraft which fall into the fifth-generation category in collaboration, except for China, which is on its own. China has the largest number of development programmes running to replace old aircraft and has also flown its fifth-generation aircraft. Other developments of note are the Indian LCA and its future versions and the joint venture between Russia and India to develop a fifth-generation aircraft. The LCA programme has been a successful technology demonstrator and plans to develop other operational versions and graduate to an indigenous Advanced Medium Combat Aircraft (AMCA) by developing fifth-generation technologies are afoot.[8] The IAF should propose a redesigned operational version of the LCA, which will be operationally relevant for the next thirty years to have a balanced air force, but time is of essence since indigenous development holds the key to arresting the decline. Another reason to stress on indigenous development is the issue of Intellectual Property Rights (IPR) in an unequal joint development partnership. Considering planned fighter inductions and the phase outs, the IAF will have only about 35 squadrons by the end of this decade. This fighter fleet is definitely inadequate for the future tasks discussed earlier.

The IAF has now focused on improving the transport aircraft fleet considering the future area of operations. Steps have also been taken to fill in the niche special operations requirements through the induction of the C-130J and purchase of C-17 aircraft to address the mobility requirement in the high mountains. The need to induct a 20-tonne payload class of transport aircraft has been recognized and there are plans to develop the same jointly with the Russians through a 50: 50 joint venture with HAL.[9] The An-32 aircraft have served IAF well for intra-theatre needs for over 20 years and are planned to be upgraded, but they will require replacement in the next 10 years or so with a 5-10-tonne class of aircraft.

New helicopters are being inducted in all the three forces and the fleets are being upgraded to maintain their effectiveness. The procurement processes for the heavy lift, Mi-17, utility helicopters, light armed helicopters, and VIP helicopters are going on. The need to recapitalize the attack helicopters is being taken up through both direct purchase and indigenous development by HAL. During counter-insurgency operations, the IAF will mostly be tasked for air mobility and hence the current induction plans of the Army, Navy, and the Air Force need to be addressed urgently and in an integrated manner.

Unmanned Aerial Systems

The IAF is in the midst of a build-up of manned aircraft inventory and appears to be devoting a little less attention to developing the unmanned combat air vehicles (UCAVs) and UAVs. All the three defence forces have been operating the Israeli Heron and Searcher UAVs for over a decade and the Indian Army has recently accepted the indigenous Nishant UAV. The DRDO is also developing the Rustom UCAV, but progress has been slow owing to technological hitches. Although the sensors on board the UAVs of the Army, Navy, and Air Force are identical, there is no interoperability of these UAVs owing to differences in their command and control systems. The role played by UCAVs in Afghanistan, Iraq, and Yemen is well known to the IAF and the development of a wide range of UAVs/UCAVs has been planned by the DRDO. Considering the limitations of India's indigenous capability, development of these platforms can be hastened only through a joint collaboration. Joint collaboration suffers from the restrictions imposed by the Missile Technology Control Regime (MTCR) and this limitation has to be overcome through diplomacy and politics. There is also an urgent need for research and development of sensors/sensor data fusion, satellite communication, engine technology, ground control stations, automatic take-off and landing, weapon integration, and so on, since these technologies will help in achieving self-sufficiency and will have spin-offs in weapon systems development.

Weapon Systems Development

The DRDO and ordnance factories have lagged behind in developing air-to-surface and air-to-air guided weapons. This is an indirect result of import and licensed manufacture of aircraft since the IAF has always purchased weapons for immediate operational capability and thereafter has not pushed for design and development of indigenous PGMs. The

DRDO has successfully tested a Laser Guided Bomb (LGB) kit and is also developing BVRs for the LCA and other aircraft, but these are yet to be operationalized. The IAF has planned to have a mix of precision and unguided weapons due to reasons of quantity and the cost. The vast improvements in the accuracy of the Nav-attack (that is, navigation and attack) systems have considerably reduced the Circular Error Probable (CEP) or accuracy of unguided bombs and have enhanced their utility against some target systems even when attacked from medium-to-high altitudes. Development of the air-launched version of the BrahMos cruise missile for Su-30 aircraft, long-range standoff guided missiles, and LGBs, though very expensive, will have to be part of the inventory for usage against strategic well-defended targets. Although the DRDO is focusing on smaller high-precision warheads and is developing the requisite technologies, its track record has not been encouraging. The IAF is the repository of knowledge on air-to-air and air-to-surface weapons and should become the stakeholder in weapons development.

Aerospace Power and Combat Support Elements

A study of recent inductions in the IAF indicates a shift in focus to combat support elements. Major organizational restructuring and doctrinal changes are taking place through the assimilation of these new elements into the IAF. AWACS and aerial refuelling aircraft, along with aerostat, ground-based radars, air defence systems, precision weapons, and electronic warfare systems are the key to achieving air dominance.

The number of AWACS, aerial refuellers, and aerostat radars is barely enough for tactical operations in a limited war at present. The IAF has to calculate the total requirements based on the likely operational tasks and acquire more aerial refuelling and AWACS aircraft (including aerostats) to enhance its strategic reach. The DRDO is already developing an Airborne Early Warning (AEW) aircraft based on an Embraer Legacy aircraft, but this platform is too small and hence will have a very limited capability. It is understood that DRDO has succeeded in developing Active Electronically Scanned Array (AESA) ground-based surveillance radar. This AESA radar, along with other types of radars, is required for a layered defence around a Vital Area/Vital Point (VA/VP) and gap-free coverage. The joint development of the Barak system by the DRDO and Israel Aircraft Industries (IAI) is progressing and, after successful sea and land trials, this system will be operationalized.[10] The IAF has already accepted the indigenous Akash system and more will be ordered after its usage in field conditions. Meanwhile, Quick Reaction Surface-to-Air Missiles (QRSAMs) are being acquired to arrest the declining numbers of Surface-to-Air Missiles (SAMs).

Hopefully, the IAF has learnt a lesson from the import of Electronic Warfare (EW), Electronic Counter Measures (ECM), and Signal Intelligence (SIGINT) systems in the past. The DRDO should be tasked to further develop its earlier versions of EW, Electronic Intelligence (ELINT), and Communication Intelligence (COMINT) ground and airborne hardware. It is hoped that they are in a better position to overcome the technological hurdles of the past. If successful, various versions, both externally and internally carried, will have to be developed for different aircraft. The IAF already has systems for Suppression of Enemy Air Defences (SEAD) and Destruction of Enemy Air Defences (DEAD).[11] but they need to be more versatile for usage against different targets in a layered defensive system.

From the foregoing, it is clear that radar and communication are the most important sensors and that is why maximum efforts are also being made to defeat them through Stealth and EW. Simultaneously, more research is being done to make the platforms stealthier and overcome the limitations of the past. A balanced inventory implies that there is a suitable mix of weapons and systems with different performance levels and should be hardened against electro-magnetic pulse.

The foregoing may sound like a platform-centric approach to developing a force structure, but it is not so. The IAF has gone ahead with plans to set up a force-wide communication network with adequate bandwidth and made considerable progress in developing an Integrated Air Command and Control System (IACCS). The IACCS is the first step to network all the sensors, but unless the Operational Data Link (ODL) is available on all platforms, both airborne and ground-based, and linked through a military communication satellite, the networking will be incomplete. The networking of these sensors will not be easy since the sensors belong to different vintages, countries of origin, and levels of accuracy, especially the radars. Doctrinally also, the IAF has to prepare the commanders for this information explosion and formulate control and decentralization guidelines. The issue of networking with other services, joint security, and a robust joint cyber warfare plan have assumed greater importance considering some of the events in the past.

Surface-to-Surface Missiles and Nuclear Weapons

Ballistic missiles are proving to be the greatest force levellers and a very potent deterrent since even smaller countries can threaten the major powers. Missiles have become such attention getters that whenever and wherever a missile is launched, it is taken note of by all countries irrespective of their threat perception. India launched its own indigenous missile development programme called the 'Integrated Guided Missile Development Programme' (IGMDP) in 1983 and a joint development programme with Russia for supersonic cruise missile BrahMos in 1998. The short-range Prithvi missile series and land and naval versions of BrahMos have been developed, and inducted into all three services, while the middle-range Agni-I and intermediate-range Agni-II have been inducted into the Indian Army. Two successful tests of 500km range *Agni V* have raised hopes of early operationalization. The integration of BrahMos with Su-30 MKI is expected during 2013–14. The DRDO is continuing to improve the performance and accuracy of all these missiles, but it is taking too long to operationalize these systems and hence cannot match the numbers available with the neighbours. More important than the numbers are the organizational and operationalization issues of the induction of ballistic missiles into the Indian military. There should be a clear policy on induction of different types of ballistic missiles into the three armed forces and the Strategic Forces Command (SFC) based on their role and responsibilities. Since air defence is the exclusive responsibility of the IAF, ballistic missile defence (BMD) should also be under the command and control of the IAF.

India carried out nuclear tests first in 1974 and thereafter in 1998 after a gap of 24 years. The decision to develop nuclear weapons and subsequently test it was taken in utter secrecy and the armed forces were not aware of it. Initially, IAF aircraft were the only platforms readily available for delivering a nuclear bomb in retaliation but it is possible that in these intervening years the nuclear warhead has been integrated with the missile. Nuclear weapons are under the control of the SFC, with actual decisions on launch under the Nuclear Command Authority. Since India has adopted the nuclear doctrine of no first use (NFU), the dilemma is to ensure survival of the nuclear arsenal and make it a credible deterrent. The Indian policy of NFU has not stopped Pakistan from indulging in low-intensity conflicts, but on the other hand, has forced India to consider Pakistan's nuclear threshold for fear of escalation in any limited or full scale war. As discussed earlier, it is clear that in any future war with Pakistan, the Indian Army will not be able to make any deep foray and only the IAF will be able to launch calibrated punitive strikes without breaching Pakistan red lines. Development of tactical missiles and cruise missiles by Pakistan has added another dimension to the difficulties in defending against them, hence ballistic missiles and cruise missiles are likely to be the principal weapon of choice and India should build up its arsenal to be credible.

Battle Space Information and Intelligence

Aerospace power and battlefield intelligence are inseparable. Success of an air campaign depends upon situational awareness, which in itself is dependent on availability of timely, accurate, and comprehensive information about the on-going battle and deployed military assets of the enemy. Wars in the last two decades have shown that the United States could direct a large number of sensors and communication systems, both airborne and space-based, for continuous surveillance at the place and time of its choosing. India has a long way to go in developing these sensors and will face an uphill task to integrate them since the systems are either being purchased or developed and need to be integrated with platforms sourced from different countries. Another limitation in the existing system is lack of capability for automated collation, fusion, analysis, and transfer of intelligence to the war fighter in time. Indian defence forces lack the capacity to handle even the existing amount of data and unless urgent steps are taken to train and equip them, the intelligence personnel will be flooded by the huge amount of data available through networking in future. Some steps have been taken after the Kargil war to ensure availability of intelligence from all sources, with the establishment of one agency for analysis by trained and dedicated analysts, but in practice there is very little to show in this regard and different agencies continue to work in silos.

Space-based Assets and Missile Defence

It is well known that Indian space research has largely been civilian-oriented, with the laudable aims of social and educational development and remote sensing for natural resources. The Indian Space Research Organisation (ISRO) has made considerable progress in providing satellite-based communication and even multi-spectral imagery through its CARTOSAT series and is well on the way to developing the GPS Aided GEO Augmented Navigation (GAGAN) system for satellite-based navigation (*The Economic Times* 2008). The Indian Ministry of Defence issued a document 'Defence Space Vision' (DSV) in 2005 (Ministry of Defence), which laid down the short, medium, and long term goals for acquiring space-based assets in the areas of communication, navigation, and ISR. But the issue of establishing an integrated command structure manned jointly by all the three services has not been resolved and therefore military space systems development has not taken concrete shape. The IAF has all along asked to be designated the lead agency for space since air and space are a continuum. Moreover, the IAF will be tasked to defend space assets and will also be the major user of space-based assets and BMD systems to defend against missiles. It is also worth noting that cyber space has aptly been linked with air and space in the USAF White Paper of 2008—'Since the air, space and cyber domains are increasingly interdependent, loss of dominance in any one could lead to loss of control in all' (Moseley 2007). In any future war, the warring sides will make extensive use of space-based assets; hence the IAF must take note of the adversary's capability to attack/interfere with the satellites. In this regard, China has already proven its capability in January 2007 and subsequently its satellite manoeuvre capability in 2010. The IAF also needs to have sensors in space for missile defence and also to develop matching indigenous capability to be able to disable the adversary's satellites.

The proliferation of missiles has pushed a number of countries to seek or develop BMD systems. India has launched the BMD development programme in the endo- and exo-atmospheric regions for missiles with a range of about 2,000 km. This capability is inadequate, especially considering the range of missile threats from the neighbours, which varies from tactical missiles to intermediate range ballistic missiles having a range of 5,000 km. A BMD system is required to protect both countervalue and counterforce targets. With India's stated policy of NFU, it is essential that the second-strike capability remain intact. Moreover, an effective BMD will once again make the Indian conventional superiority potent by negating the threat of a nuclear attack by Pakistan. The decision to initially deploy BMD selectively to protect Delhi and Mumbai is sound since the cost is prohibitive and experience gained through deployment will help in further improvements of the system.

Quest for Technology Development and Self-Reliance

Self-reliance has been the mantra ever since India's independence, but it initially posed its own challenges, like a very limited technology base, no industry to support defence, only 1.6 per cent of GDP committed to defence, priority commitment of resources for poverty alleviation, and industrialization in core sectors. The preference for self-reliance was further strengthened when the IAF could not obtain new Spitfire aircraft from the UK during the Indo-Pak conflict of 1947–8. Furthermore, in 1951, it came to light that the frontline fighter aircraft Vampire was deficient of a crucial component required for gun firing (Singh 2011: 160). Subsequently, as a matter of abundant caution, purchase of aircraft was diversified. This policy helped India to purchase and licence manufacture aircraft and equipment from different countries, but it led to a logistical nightmare due to diversified inventory and technical training of personnel on different aircraft. Meanwhile, the expectation that licensed manufacture would bring in self-reliance was belied—when the Soviet Union broke up, the IAF found itself unable to meet the spares and repair demand without supplies from the erstwhile states of the Soviet Union.

The story of combat aircraft development in India makes a very interesting study. IAF issued an Air Staff Requirement (ASR) for an advanced combat aircraft in 1955 based on which HAL invited Dr Kurt Tank and his team to design and develop a combat aircraft in India. This German-led Indian team commenced design work in 1957 and the first flight took place in June 1961. This design of the multi-role HF-24 aircraft at that time was at par with those being developed in the United States and had no match anywhere else in the world, but it suffered from the lack of a suitable engine (Singh 2011: 132). A number of factors, including the preference for indigenous efforts at development, were responsible for the inability to obtain an engine to make this excellent airframe achieve its designed performance. Although about 140 aircraft were produced and even successfully used in the 1971 war, the fact remains that the HF-24 was under-powered even with two Orpheus engines of the Gnat aircraft (Chatterjee). It was finally phased out in 1990 with some of the aircraft having barely flown a hundred hours. There was no serious effort to design and develop new fighter aircraft from the 60s to the late 80s, except for the design and development of Ajeet, a derivative of the Gnat (GlobalSecurity.org). This was partially because aircraft from the erstwhile

Soviet Union were available on easy terms and the Soviets carried out limited modifications as and when the requirements arose, but this had a very debilitating effect on the design and development capability of India's aircraft industry.

The Government of India had taken the initiative for research and manufacturing activities in the defence sector from the Second Five-year Plan onwards but the expenditure on R&D has always been less than 1 per cent of India's GDP. For over two decades, HAL did not carry out any Design and Development (D&D) activity due to depletion in its D&D resource and neither the Government nor the user (IAF) formally tasked HAL to even develop a replacement for the MiG-21 aircraft. Even when the LCA was mooted for development, the task was given to an independent agency, the Aeronautical Development Agency (ADA) under the DRDO that was connected with neither the HAL nor the user, the IAF (Singh 2011: 165–8). This vertical and horizontal disconnect among the ADA, HAL, and IAF has been the bane of our quest for self-reliance.

Nearly 50 research laboratories under the DRDO alone, Defence Public Sector Undertakings (DPSUs), and research laboratories under the Council of Scientific and Industrial Research (CSIR) have been set up, but the end result is continued dependence on foreign suppliers. Committees like the Kelkar Committee[12] and the Rama Rao Committee[13] have been set up in the past to identify the causes, but the results are yet to be seen. Technology development has been successful wherever there has been continuous user participation, like in the case of EW equipment and during the initial phases of LCA development, but without permanent cadres and involvement of the user, these successes have been very few.

India is at a stage where research in technology development should have an application by the user and hence must be tied up with an industry to ultimately manufacture an improved product. Simultaneously, fundamental research should also be undertaken to bridge the gap with the other technologically advanced countries. There is a need to sponsor research with academic institutions, private/public sector industry; research labs with both DRDO and CSIR, but the sponsor should drive the programme. There are enough examples worldwide where technologies are developed in a competitive environment so that the user has a choice. Ultimately, technologies should be developed to ensure that a budding major power does not have to ride on the shoulders of more advanced countries. Developing new technologies is a continuous process—once a technology is developed, research is targeted to either defeat that technology or develop a better one since by then it is also available with the opponent. A case in point is stealth technology.

Another key technology which must be mastered for self-reliance is the development of jet engines. India cannot become an aerospace power with dependence on imported aero engines. Aero engines are presently the preserve of a few countries and all other military powers without this capability cannot develop their own aviation industry. China is trying to develop their own jet engines to be in the same league as the US, UK, Russia, France, Germany, and so on, so as to power its combat aircraft and helicopters. India has already suffered the consequences of lack of capability and therefore has embarked upon the development of the Kaveri engine for the LCA. There has been very limited success and the only way is to persevere and perhaps even join hands with a recognized aero-engine design house in India or abroad. The scientific community should identify their weaknesses and study success stories to learn their lessons. They will find that wherever they had user participation or a joint development like BrahMos, they have achieved success. There is an urgent need to introduce a collaborative approach—between the user and Indian and even foreign manufacturing industry—to research undertaken in India.

Indian Aviation Industry

The foremost question that comes to the mind is—how come the fourth largest air force in the world is a net importer of aircraft and equipment? Is it due to the temptation of each military commander at the helm to ensure preparedness at all times through imports even at the expense of indigenous capability? Some answers have been found in pre- and post-independence history in earlier pages, but they still do not fully explain the lack of progress in developing defence industry, and aircraft industry in particular, in the last three decades or so. The aircraft factory set up by Seth Walchand Hirachand in December 1940 was nationalized within two years of its establishment[14] and, after independence, control was passed on to the Ministry of Industries, Government of India. In 1958, control of HAL was transferred to the Ministry of Defence Production and simultaneously, the Scientific Advisor (SA) to the Defence Minister was appointed with the Chief Controller of Research and Development (CCR&D) placed under him, thus transferring the executive role to the SA (Singh 2011: 104–7). The negative effect of both these developments is that the Ministry of Defence became the researcher, developer, manufacturer as well as the buyer all rolled in one.

During the war years, HAL had become a hub for repair and overhaul of combat aircraft and lost its earlier vision of design and development, but not for long. D&D work at HAL commenced with HT-2 piston trainer aircraft, which first flew in August 1951 and thereafter a number of basic trainer (HPT-32, Pushpak) and other utility aircraft for artillery observation (Krishak) and crop spraying (Basant) were designed and manufactured. HAL designed and developed the first jet trainer HJT-16 in the early 60s and the first flight took place on September 4, 1964. Variants of HJT-16 were developed in the following years and this design has proven to be the workhorse of all fighter pilots' training in the IAF and the Indian Navy. It is not known why HAL did not press hard to design and develop the Advanced Jet Trainer (AJT), although the requirement existed since 1982 (Singh 2011: 146) (with the recommendation made by the La Fontaine Committee). The contract for AJT was signed only in 2004. Meanwhile, HAL was tasked to develop an Intermediate Jet Trainer (IJT) in 1999 and the first flight of the prototype took place in March 2003. The IAF has already placed the order, but the date for initial operational clearance and the aircraft's entry into service cannot be known with any certainty because of problems being faced.[15] The IJT has benefited from the learning experience and infrastructure created for the LCA and has faced some hurdles directly connected with an IJT and also a decision on the engine, which had to be taken mid-way during the D&D.

Except for the sporadic efforts to develop more improved versions of the HF-24 with different engines, no serious D&D of a new aircraft was undertaken till the LCA, which commenced in 1987. Although the licensed manufacture was expected to build up the indigenous capability for D&D, the reverse was true since no indigenous D&D work was approved by the government and most of the experienced and trained manpower left HAL. The DRDO was hence tasked to develop and build 'technology demonstrators' and, since the reservoir of knowledge and experience in aeronautics was with HAL, most of the engineers from HAL were deputed to work in the ADA. ADA was set up as an ad hoc organization, which was neither integrated with HAL nor with the IAF and thus neither the downstream manufacturing agency nor the user were on board. This was just one more example of lack of integration between the DRDO laboratories and the manufacturing agencies leading to disjunction and consequently to performance shortfalls and cost/time overruns.

D&D of the LCA was started as a 'technology demonstration' programme in 1987 with the building of two aircraft and further decisions were to be taken based on the success of the programme. Except for the drawbacks mentioned earlier, setting up the ADA was a very good idea with a mandate to coordinate the development of technologies, integrate the efforts of various specialist institutions, develop a vendor base, and uplift the aeronautical technology base through creation of infrastructure. Even though the task was underestimated both in terms of cost and time frame, the ADA was able to establish world-class facilities for the technology leap. It was a roller-coaster ride for the ADA since there was a need to seek help from vendors abroad and the sanctions imposed after the nuclear test in 1998 caused a setback during the most critical phase of digital fly-by-wire development. These sanctions caused delays, but were also a boon since Indian scientists developed most of the technologies in-house, leading to greater self-sufficiency. As mentioned earlier, delays and shortfalls in LCA programme can also be attributed to converting a technology demonstrator platform into an operational aircraft without going through the intermediate step of redesigning an operational aircraft based on the developed technologies with the participation of the user and the manufacturer.

The latest collaborative efforts to develop the Fifth Generation Fighter Aircraft (FGFA) and also set up a joint equal partnership venture for developing multi-role medium transport aircraft are laudable, but has HAL done an audit of its capacity to simultaneously undertake all these massive projects? HAL is even now feeling the pinch of not recruiting manpower in the late 80s and 90s and hence faces a shortage of middle-level experienced technicians. The customer and the manufacturer being under the same ministry is not good for either, especially when the civilian bureaucracy in the ministry can show artificial progress through loading the DPSUs/ordnance factories with work and brushing under the rug problems of quality and cost escalation. The behaviour of the same ministry is very different and bureaucratic when dealing with the private sector industry. It will be more than welcome if the same yardstick is applied to DPSUs and ordnance factories as well.

Policy, Manpower, and Defence Budget

India has a unique higher defence organization where the service chiefs in uniform are not a part of the decision-making hierarchy on matters of security. Moreover, no 'White Paper' has ever been issued by the Government of India to articulate its security policy. The decision makers in the ministry are not the ones responsible for the outcome of their decisions and only wield the authority. Even the decision to go nuclear and the requirements of the nuclear force capabilities were never discussed with the heads of the services, who are meant to operationalize the systems developed by Indian scientists. The Kargil Report had identified this weakness and had even suggested a 'National Defence Headquarters' to integrate the three service headquarters with the Government,[16] but so far the change has been superficial. The procurement procedures are even more entangled since even the Ministry of Defence cannot take an independent decision for large procurement without consulting the Ministry of External Affairs and Ministry of Finance, thus creating a web, which can only choke the pipeline.

Time and again, a call for the establishment of a Chief of Defence Staff has been raised, but it has never been pursued because there is no clear understanding of the charter and, of course, grave apprehensions exist in the minds of the bureaucracy and the political leadership about concentrating power in the hands of a single military officer. What is essential as a first step is cross-posting of uniformed personnel in the Ministry of Defence to remove existing apprehensions, which will lead to greater civil-military cohesion and understanding. The apprehension that the person in uniform will provide only the tutored advice of his parent establishment and will interfere with the independent advice of the generalist bureaucrats in the Ministry of Defence only highlights the disconnect. *Basically, the political authority in the government should get independent views of the civil and military in equal measure and not comments of the civil bureaucracy on the proposals of the defence services. The Defence Minister/political authority should then decide on the proposal and issue his orders.* It is implied that the political authority must be well versed with the individual defence forces and matters 'military' wherein he should understand the dynamics of inter-service operations. Even amongst the services, joint-ness is understood by many as 'how the other service can be integrated in their war plan' and not as developing a joint plan keeping the strengths and weaknesses of each of the services in mind. Unless 'joint-ness' is accepted as 'interdependence', there will be costly redundancies and only a political authority will be able to intervene.

The IAF has a sanctioned strength of 131,174 airmen and 12,183 officers (Standing Committee on Defense). Its manpower is very technology savvy and has been able to handle the most advanced weapon systems with ease. But the distribution of technical trades amongst the airmen dates back to British times and is inefficient, especially since the concepts of maintenance have undergone a sea change in modern aircraft. Efforts have been made in the past to change the training pattern, but as long as the IAF has older generation aircraft, it has to continue to follow the older system. It is a dilemma for the IAF, but the present reduced strength and recapitalization of the fleet provides the opportunity to implement far-reaching changes in the airmen technical trades and training pattern.

There is no critical pilot shortage at present because the number of squadrons has reduced, but with the imminent induction of more twin-seat Su-30MKI aircraft and the development of a twin-cockpit fifth-generation aircraft, the requirement of numbers will increase considerably. Sortie generation in war is a very critical factor and that depends upon the number of aircraft, pilots, and maintenance crew. The number of pilots per aircraft also depends upon the type of aircraft and the task allotted, for example, the more the number of missions, the more the pilots required. A ratio of 1.5 pilots per cockpit is the minimum and will be greater for an intense campaign of the kind expected in the region. With the non-availability of a basic trainer and delays in induction of the IJT, the output of trained pilots cannot be stepped up. It takes at least six years to train an operational pilot and unless the capacity build-up is taken up earnestly, there may be a shortage of pilots when the decline in number of squadrons is reversed. There is also an urgent need to revisit the operational training of pilots since the CONOPS will undergo major changes with the induction of fifth-generation aircraft in the next decade. A lead in fighter aircraft may help in reducing the overall cost of operational training and producing a more professional pilot.

There is a dichotomy in the Indian defence budget allocation. On one hand, there is a demand for increasing the allocation to about 3 per cent of the GDP from the current rate of less than 2 per cent of GDP, and on the other there is shortfall in expenditure and funds are returned year after year. This shortfall in expenditure can only be corrected by improving our procurement procedures and also through increased indigenous R&D and manufacturing. Fortunately reforms are being introduced in both these directions, but they are inadequate. Issuance of new defence procurement manuals/procedures every alternate year does indicate that the reforms are under active consideration, but may indicate lack of deeper understanding of the acquisition process. The net effect will be visible when the capacity of the bureaucracy (both civil and military) to spend the allotted funds increases and the time taken between the acceptance of a proposal and the system becoming operational is cut down considerably. The 'offset policy' has also seen frequent changes and its likely contribution to self-reliance is suspect since India's defence industry is yet to build capacity to absorb these huge offset amounts. The expectation that the offset policy will help in indigenous development of cutting edge technology is misplaced since foreign vendors will only source the equipment to meet the offset commitments and will not invest in joint development of technology unless they are permitted to invest more than 49 per cent in a joint venture. There is also a lack of professionalism in negotiating and contracting since the persons dealing with the acquisitions have learnt on the job and have no formal qualifications.

The Air Force budget is around 25 per cent of the total defence budget for 2012–13, which is about 4 per cent less than the allotment for the preceding year, but the problem is not the amount but rather the pattern of spending. Acquisitions are increasingly being done through a transparent process and also using the Foreign Military Sales (FMS) route in the case of the United States. Approval of the 12th Defence Plan 2012–17 and the first ever 'Long-Term Integrated Perspective Plan 2012–27' by the Defence Ministry (Pubby)[17] is certainly very good news, but unless the system is geared up to meet the time frames and allocations are made as per the plan, these plans will remain only on paper.

The defence budget for 2012–13 is INR 193,407 crores (US$ 37.58 billion), which is an increase of 17.6 per cent over the budget allocation of 2011–12. The capital outlay of INR 79,578 crores has also seen a jump of 15.7 per cent over the last year. When compared with China's published defence budget, it is seen that China spends approximately three times the Indian defence budget and their spending on R&D is much larger than that in India.[18] The Indian Air Force has been allotted the largest share of capital outlay at INR 28,504 crores (US$ 5.54 billion), but the problem is not the amount; rather, it is the pattern of spending. In the recent past, the IAF has been able to spend the allocated budget for capital acquisition, but the moot point is whether the allocation had been made as per the approved long-term re-equipment plan or is just incremental to the last allocation.

***

The IAF was established on the same lines as the RAF and within three years of its formation was fighting a war in the NWFP. There are many firsts to its credit, thanks to the quality and spirit of its personnel. The trajectory of its growth has been based on its performance and the experience gained during the wars, notably in the high mountains of Kashmir—Siachen and Kargil—at heights where no air force in the world has operated. The IAF has become a full-spectrum force equipped with very capable platforms and trained manpower, but the numbers are inadequate for intense and lengthy operations. Any future campaign led by it must maintain an edge over the adversary through technology and force employment. The IAF, like other air forces, operates at the forefront of technology, but needs to push for self-sufficiency since the country has to develop its own technology and defence industrial base. Unfortunately, India's track record in research and development has been dismal and only far-reaching changes in defence manufacturing policies through the involvement of the private sector and the development of linkages with the user may help.

Notes

1. Flight International special report on 'World Air Forces 2011-12' on page 6 states that the Indian Air Force is fifth in total number of aircraft but is placed fourth in terms of combat aircraft.

2. These aircraft were on lend-lease from USA to RAF and could not be handed over to any other country so they were damaged to prevent their usage.

3. Available at www.vectorsite.net.

4. 'History of IAF'. Available at http://indianairforce.nic.in/show_page.php? pg_id=98 (accessed March 2011).

5. 'Pakistan & China's JF-17 Fighter Program', 23 May 2011. Available at http://www.defenseindustrydaily.com/stuck-in-sichuan-pakistani-jf17-program-grounded-02984/ (accessed June 2012).

6. Annual Report to Congress, Office of the Secretary of Defense. 2010. 'Military and Security Developments Involving the People's Republic of China 2010', pp. 29–33. Available at http://www.defense.gov/pubs/pdfs/2010_ CMPR_Final.pdf (accessed March 2011).

7. See www.defencenews.in.

8. Asia-Pacific staff, 'New Design for Advanced Medium Combat aircraft'. Available at http://www.aviationweek.com/Article.aspx?id=/article-xml/AW_ 03_04_2013_p72-548182.xml&p=1 fe (accessed June 2013).

9. 'MRTA: HAL and Irkut's Joint Tactical Transport Project', 12 September 2010. Available at http://www.defenseindustrydaily.com/hal-and-irkuts-joint-tactical-transport-project-02931/ (accessed March 2011).

10. Available at www.defenseindustrydaily.com 2011.

11. Available at www.defense-update.com 2006.

12. Committee was set up to enhance India's self-reliance in defense industry, nominating a few private sector industries for parity with Defense PSUs and setting up a technology development fund.

13. The report has not been declassified. The committee was to look into restructuring DRDO, HRD policies, and improving interaction with the user.

14. Available at www.hal-india.com.

15. Available at www.airforce-technology.com.

16. Available at www.fas.org.

17. Available at www.m.indianexpress.com.

18. Available at www.defencereviewasia.com.

References

'Ajeet', www.GlobalSecurity.org, n.d. Available at http://www.globalsecurity.org/military/world/india/ajeet.htm (accessed 9 July 2012).

Avalon, Leithen Francis. 2011. 'Pakistan in Negotiations with U.S. for more F-16s', *Aviation Week & Space Technology*, March 7: 28.

Bhargava, Kapil. 'Beginning of Aviation in India, a peep into its early history'. Available at http://www.bharat-rakshak.com/IAF/History/Aircraft/AviationIndia.pdf (accessed March 2011).

———. 'India's Reclaimed B-24 Bombers'. Available at http://www.bharat-rakshak.com/IAF/History/Aircraft/Liberator.html (accessed June 2012).

Blumenthal, Dan. 2010. 'India Prepares for a Two-Front War', *Wall Street Journal*. Available at http://online.wsj.com/article/SB10001424052748704240004575085023077072074.html (accessed March 2011).

Chatterjee, K. n.d. 'Hindustan Fighter HF-24 Marut: Part I – Building India's Jet Fighter'. Available at http://www.bharat-rakshak.com/IAF/History/Aircraft/Marut1.html (accsessed 9 July 2012).

Chaudhry, A.B.S. 2010. 'Combat Support Operations in the Indian Air Force: A Historical Appraisal', *Air Power Journal*, 1 (5): 117–35. Available at http://www.aerospaceindia.org/Air%20Power%20Journals/Spring%202010/Chapter%205.pdf

Defence Industry Daily. 2011. 'India & Israel's Barak SAM Development Project,' 3 June. Available at http://www.defenseindustrydaily.com/india-israel-introducing-mr-sam-03461/ (accessed June 2012).

Defense News Admin. 'IAF seeks to increase squadron strength to 45', 12 February 2011. Available at http://defencenews.in/defence-news-internal.asp?get=old&id=344 (accessed March 2011).

George, T.J.S. 2010. 'Options We Have; Have We the Will?', *Mainstream*, XLVIII (40). Available at http://www.mainstreamweekly.net/article2332.html (accessed March 2011).

'Harpy Air Defense Suppression System', *Defence Update*, 4 March 2006. Available at http://defense-update.com/directory/harpy.htm#cont (accessed June 2012).

Hindustan Aeronautics Limited. Available at http://www.hal-india.com/aboutus.asp (accessed March 2011).

'HJT-36 Sitara Intermediate Jet Trainer, India', Airforce Technology, n.d. Available at http://www.airforce-technology.com/projects/hjttrainer/ (accessed 7 July 2012).

'India's Defence Budget, 2012-13', *Defence Review Asia*, 3 June 2012. Available at http://www.defencereviewasia.com/articles/169/India-s-Defence-Budget-2012-13 (accessed June 2012).

'Kargil Committee Report–Executive Summary'. Available at www.fas.org/news/india/2000/25indi1.htm (accessed March 2011).

Kumar, Bharat. 2007. *An Incredible War: Indian Air Force in Kashmir War, 1947-48*. New Delhi: Centre for Air Power Studies.

Ministry of Defence, Government of India. Available at http://mod.nic.in/aboutus/welcome.html.

Moseley, T. Michael. 2007. 'The Nation's Guardians: America's 21st Century Air Force', CSAF White Paper, 29 December. Washington, DC: Department of the Air Force, Office of the Chief of Staff. Available at www.af.mil/shared/media/document/AFD-080207-048.pdf (accessed March 2011).

Naik, Air Chief Marshal Pradeep Vasant. 2011. Interview with T.R. Rama-chandran and Anil Tyagi, *Gfiles*, 4 (11): 11–14.

Pubby, Manu. 'Procurement Gets a Push after Anthony, General Meet', *Indian Express*, n.d. Available at http://m.indianexpress.com/news/procurement-gets-a-push-after-antony-general-meet/931676/ (accessed 9 July 2012).

Ramachandran, Sudha. 2011. 'China ramps up pressure over Kashmir', *Asia Times*, 4 January. Available at http://atimes.com/atimes/South_Asia/MA04Df01.html (accessed March 2011).

Singh, Jasjit. 2009. *The Icon: Marshal of the Indian Air Force Arjan Singh, DFC: An Authorised Biography*. New Delhi: KW Publishers in association with Centre for Air Power Studies.

———. 2011. *Indian Aircraft Industry*. New Delhi: KW Publishers and Centre for Air Power Studies 2011, pp. 104–7.

———. *Defence from the Skies: Indian Air Force through 75 Years*. New Delhi: Knowledge World.

Standing Committee on Defense, Ninth Report. Available at http://164.100.47.134/lsscommittee/Defence/FINAL%20-%209TH%20REPORT.pdf (accessed March 2011).

'The Folland Gnat / HAL Ajeet'. Available at http://www.airvectors.net/avgnat.html (accessed March 2011).

The Economic Times. 2008. 'India to Get Global Navigation System for ISRO, AAI', 3 August. Available at http://articles.economictimes.indiatimes.com/2008-08-03/news/27715692_1_navigation-system-gagan-system-aai (accessed March 2011).

The Hindu. 2003. 'The Flying Corsican', 16 July. Available at http://www.hindu.com/thehindu/mp/2003/07/16/stories/2003071600310300.htm (accessed March 2011).

Tiwary, A.K. 2006. 'No Use of Combat Air Power in 1962', Indian Defence Review, 21 (3). Available at http://www.indiandefencereview.com/military%20&%20aerospace/No-Use-of-Combat-Air-Power-in-1962.html (accessed March 2011).

———. 2007. 'IAF defeated PAF in 1965 War', Indian Defence Review, 22 (1). Available at http://www.indiandefencereview.com/2007/04/IAF-defeated-PAF-in-1965-War.html (accessed March 2011).

'World Air Forces 2011/2012', *Flightglobal Insight*, p. 6. Available at http://www.flightglobal.com/airspace/media/reports_pdf/world-air-forces-2011-2012-90190.aspx (accessed 11 June 2012).

3 India's Nuclear Forces

Doctrine and Operationalization

Gurmeet Kanwal

Since its independence in August 1947, India has faced many external threats and challenges and has for long had to endure the vicissitudes of a dangerous nuclear neighbourhood. China became a nuclear power in 1964, soon after the India-China border war of 1962. Pakistan is reported to have acquired nuclear weapons capability in 1986–87 with covert help from China. Though India had conducted a 'peaceful' nuclear explosion in May 1974 to showcase its technological capability, the government continued to resist nuclearization and strongly advocated total nuclear disarmament. However, India's deteriorating security environment and the likely entry into force of the discriminatory Comprehensive Test Ban Treaty (CTBT) forced the government to reconsider its nuclear option. After conducting five nuclear tests over two days at Pokhran in May 1998, India declared itself a state with nuclear weapons. India's nuclear doctrine is built around an NFU policy with 'credible minimum deterrence'. In the interest of strategic stability, India is willing to absorb a 'first strike' and has declared its intention of launching massive punitive retaliation to cause unacceptable damage to the adversary. Consequently, India follows a 'counter value' targeting strategy.

According to the Indian government's official declared policy, India's nuclear weapons are political weapons whose sole purpose is to deter the use and threat of use of nuclear weapons against India. Hence, nuclear weapons are not considered weapons of war-fighting and India has abjured the use of tactical/theatre nuclear weapons. India's nuclear force structure is based on a triad—nuclear-tipped SSMs (Prithvi, Agni-I, Agni-II, and

Agni-III) manned by the army, nuclear glide bombs under slung on Jaguar, Mirage 2000, and SU-30 fighter-bomber aircraft with the air force, and, in due course, submarine launched ballistic missiles (SLBMs) on SSBNs with the navy. India is generally estimated to have approximately 60 to 80 nuclear warheads and enough plutonium to manufacture another 50 to 60 warheads. During peace time, the atomic cores of nuclear warheads are in the custody of the Atomic Energy Commission (AEC) and the high explosive trigger assemblies are in the custody of the DRDO. India's nuclear warheads are not kept mated with the launchers, which are held by the armed forces. Nor are these launchers deployed. This reduces the risk of accidental and inadvertent launch and enhances peace time safety.

India's nuclear weapons development programme and its command and control systems are firmly under the control of its civilian political leadership. The National Command Authority (NCA) guides India's nuclear command and control system (see figure 3.1, figure 3.2, and figure 3.3). The Political Council of the NCA, which is charged with nuclear decision making at the apex level, is headed by the Prime Minister. The National Security Advisor heads the Executive Council of the NCA, which is responsible for threat assessment, planning, and preparation. Within the armed forces, the Commander-in-Chief Strategic Forces Command advises the Chairman, Chiefs of Staff Committee on all aspects of nuclear warfare and exercises operational and technical control over the nuclear forces. The delivery assets (SSM groups and nuclear-capable fighter squadrons) are raised, equipped, and maintained under the guidance of the respective Services HQ. A clear chain of succession has been established to overcome a decapitating first strike. During crisis situations, nuclear decision making will be undertaken from a National Command Post (NCP) outside New Delhi.

India has for long been a strong advocate of total universal nuclear disarmament. Despite not having signed the NPT and the CTBT, India has been in compliance with all the provisions of these key treaties. India has voluntarily renounced further nuclear testing and has an unblemished non-proliferation record among the nuclear weapon powers. India practices strategic restraint and believes in entering into nuclear confidence-building and risk-reduction measures. The country has for long been a committed votary of total nuclear disarmament.

This chapter analyses the efficacy of India's nuclear doctrine and concludes that an NFU doctrine with a 'credible minimum nuclear deterrent' posture are the right policies for India. It evaluates the current status of the operationalization of India's nuclear deterrence and notes that major progress has been made in this field since May 1998. It also examines whether India's nuclear deterrence is credible in the light of minimal warhead and missile testing and many negative controls over the arsenal.

India's Nuclear Doctrine

India's nuclear policy is underpinned by a categorical and unambiguous commitment to NFU of nuclear weapons against nuclear armed adversaries and the non-use of nuclear weapons against non-nuclear weapons states. This is rooted in a deeply ingrained cultural belief that the use of force to resolve inter-state disputes is a repugnant concept. Though India had the potential to develop nuclear weapons since the first so-called 'peaceful' nuclear explosion at Pokhran in May 1974, India steadfastly refrained from exercising its nuclear option and, despite a deteriorating security environment, chose instead to work for nuclear disarmament. For several decades, India opted to maintain a 'recessed deterrent'. When India finally decided to declare itself a state with nuclear weapons, it opted for only a 'credible minimum deterrent' due to the widespread recognition in the country that nuclear weapons are political weapons and not weapons of war-fighting and their sole purpose is to deter the use and threat of use of nuclear weapons. There is a broad national consensus on the development of a credible minimum nuclear deterrent capability and the doctrine of NFU. Minimum deterrence may be defined as 'a small force of survivable nuclear weapons (that) would deter an adversary from initiating military action that would threaten a nation's vital interests' (Gallucci 1991: 110–11). India is not looking at establishing any capability beyond this level of deterrence.

The concept of deterrence by punishment, rather than deterrence by denial, is central to Indian strategic thinking. However, by voluntarily renouncing its sovereign right of the first use of nuclear weapons to defeat nuclear threats and to prevent nuclear blackmail, India has made an immense strategic sacrifice and imposed a heavy burden upon itself. The government and key decision-makers recognize that should deterrence ever break down, India will have to pay an enormous price for a nuclear first strike by an adversary before retaliating in kind. Hundreds of thousands of Indian lives will be lost and more than one city may be turned into rubble. Hence, India's NFU doctrine demands a robust, infallible, and potentially insuperable nuclear deterrent capability to ensure that India never has to suffer a nuclear strike.

About one year after the Pokhran nuclear tests in May 1998, the National Security Advisory Board (NSAB) of the National Security Council (NSC) submitted a draft nuclear doctrine paper to the government that was released to the public for wider debate on August 17, 1999. The key features of the proposed nuclear doctrine are reproduced below (NSAB 1999)—

(1) India shall pursue a doctrine of credible minimum deterrence. In this policy of 'retaliation only', the survivability of our arsenal is critical. This is a dynamic concept related to our strategic environment, technological imperatives, and the needs of national security. The actual size, components, deployment, and employment of nuclear forces will be decided in the light of these factors. India's peacetime posture aims at convincing any potential aggressor that–

   (a) Any threat of use of nuclear weapons against India shall invoke measures to counter the threat; and

   (b) Any nuclear attack on India and its forces shall result in punitive retaliation with nuclear weapons to inflict damage unacceptable to the aggressor.

(2) The fundamental purpose of Indian nuclear weapons is to deter the use and threat of use of nuclear weapons by any state or entity against India and its forces. India will not be the first to initiate a nuclear strike but will respond with punitive retaliation should deterrence fail.

(3) India will not resort to the use or threat of use of nuclear weapons against states that do not possess nuclear weapons, or are not aligned with nuclear weapons powers. (Some analysts interpret this to mean that India might contemplate a retaliatory strike against such a power if struck first with nuclear weapons from its soil, which nuclear weapons belong to those of the nuclear power it is 'aligned with'. This is a contingency with a very low probability and the NCA will make an appropriate judgement if and when it arises.)

The draft nuclear doctrine, while generally following the policy guidelines enunciated by the Prime Minister in Parliament (www.fas.org), fleshed out his pronouncements and provided 'a broad framework for the development, deployment and employment of India's nuclear forces' (Zuberi 2000). The draft paper proposed that India should establish a credible, minimum nuclear deterrent capability comprising sufficient, survivable, and operationally ready nuclear forces based on the principle of no first use of nuclear weapons. It emphasized that the level of India's nuclear capability should be consistent with credibility, survivability, effectiveness, safety, and security. It provided for the establishment of effective intelligence and early warning systems. It recommended that India's nuclear forces be based on a triad of strategic bombers, land-based ballistic missiles, and SLBMs. Though a sea-based nuclear capability was expected to take many decades to develop, the requirement of SLBMs was considered inescapable due to their relatively lower vulnerability. Nuclear forces that need to survive a first strike have no option but to ensure that at least 50 to 60 per cent of the arsenal is made comparatively invulnerable by being maintained as SLBMs on SSBNs. The draft paper proposed that India's nuclear strike capability be configured to inflict punitive retaliation. It was envisaged that the consequences of assured retaliation would be unacceptable to a potential adversary who will therefore be deterred from doing the unthinkable. The doctrine highlighted the cardinal supremacy of civilian control over India's nuclear weapons and proposed that the final authority for the release of nuclear weapons must vest with the Prime Minister or his designated successor(s).

The proposed doctrine rejected the concept of nuclear war-fighting and did not, hence, consider it necessary for India to match its nuclear warheads and delivery systems with those of its potential nuclear adversaries in terms of numbers. A small number of survivable nuclear warheads and delivery systems capable of inflicting damage which would be unacceptable to the adversary were considered adequate for the purposes of deterrence. Although the doctrine paper left some ambiguity by not clearly rejecting the need for tactical or battlefield nuclear weapons in India's context, the tenor of the paper and its emphasis on a retaliatory policy appeared to rule out any thinking towards tactical nuclear weapons.

Consequent to strident criticism of the draft nuclear doctrine by Western analysts on the grounds that it advocated a posture that was far from 'minimal', it was hastily disowned by the Ministry of External Affairs and the debate about what India's nuclear doctrine should be continued. Consequently, several years later, on January 4, 2003, the government made a statement in Parliament that has come to be accepted as India's official nuclear doctrine. The statement retained all the essential features of the NSAB's draft doctrine and by and large followed the contours, the tone, and the tenor of the draft. If there are any major differences, these have only made the doctrine firmer and somewhat more strident in its tone. For example, the word 'massive' was introduced before 'punitive retaliation' and nuclear retaliation was threatened even against chemical and biological strikes. A decade's experience with India's nuclear doctrine has revealed that it has served its purpose well, even though there are some critics who question the government's wisdom in being ready to suffer substantive damage in a first strike. Also, some analysts argue that massive punitive retaliation may be a good declaratory strategy but it is not a practical one as it would be more prudent to adopt a strategy of flexible response so as to minimize the damage that might occur if deterrence failed. However, it is not well understood that flexible response would undermine deterrence by lowering the nuclear threshold.

Many analysts and even foreign governments have sought to raise doubts about India's draft nuclear doctrine. The US government was critical of the Indian desire to develop a nuclear arsenal. In many world capitals, the doctrine conjured up dark visions of a nuclear arms race in Southern Asia and spurred fears of a new arms race in the Middle East (Blanche 1998). However, not all Western powers denounced India's attempts to establish a credible weaponized nuclear deterrent. France welcomed the release of India's draft nuclear doctrine as a 'logical and indeed wanted step' (*Hindustan Times* 1999). The worst criticism of the nuclear doctrine has been that opting for a triad of nuclear forces is not indicative of a minimalist posture but of a maximalist one, particularly as sea-based nuclear weapons have been envisaged to form part of the nuclear force (*The Economic Times* 1999). This criticism fails to take into account the fact that the credibility of a nuclear deterrent that is limited to retaliatory strikes only hinges around the ability of the nuclear force to survive a first strike in sufficient numbers to inflict unacceptable punishment in retaliation. Since submarines offer the best survival potential, India has no option but to rely on a small number of SSBNs armed with SLBMs for credible deterrence. Some critics have averred that the nuclear threats that India faces have not been enunciated and that the doctrine does not define the nuclear force levels that India considers 'minimum' (*Hindustan Times* 1999). Others have protested that the costs of India's nuclear deterrent have not been spelt out. India's declaration of its NFU doctrine has focussed international debate on the efficacy of NFU policies, even though India has repeatedly reiterated that it is willing to negotiate NFU treaties bilaterally or multilaterally with all nuclear weapons states including China and Pakistan.

An NFU policy works best during conditions of mutual deterrence. An NFU commitment is not merely a verbal or even a negotiated assurance; it can and must be seen to be reflected in the nuclear force structure, the deployment patterns, the types of surveillance assets in place, and the state of readiness of a country's nuclear forces. China announced an NFU commitment immediately after its nuclear test in October 1964. In recent years, it has diluted this policy by emphasizing that such a declaration does not apply to territories that belong to China. While Taiwan falls in this category, so does Arunachal Pradesh in India which China still claims as its own territory. Hence, it can be plausibly stated that China could contemplate the use of nuclear weapons during a war over Taiwan or a border conflict with India in Arunachal Pradesh. The former Soviet Union had also subscribed to the NFU policy.

India's NFU doctrine was not hastily formulated to win brownie points from the international community. It is a carefully thought through policy that has taken decades to mature, even if it was not publicly well articulated. The External Affairs Minister Jaswant Singh wrote in *Foreign Affairs*—'No other country has deliberated so carefully and, at times, torturously over the dichotomy between its sovereign security needs and global disarmament instincts, between a moralistic approach and a realistic one, and between a covert nuclear policy and an overt one' (Jaswant Singh 1998: 43). K. Subrahmanyam had written in 1986:

> Today the international system is dominated by nuclear dacoits who are refusing to disarm and there is nothing unethical if India were to secure for itself necessary self-protection capabilities to ward off coercive use of nuclear diplomacy... If India is to make a serious intervention in the disarmament debate and contribute to nuclear disarmament, acquiring nuclear capability is a fee that has to be paid (Subrahmanyam 1986: 10).

Even during the mid-1980s, defence analysts like General K. Sundarji, Chief of Army Staff (COAS), and K. Subrahmanyam were advocating a minimum deterrent capability for India and had ruled out the need for tactical nuclear weapons as these were meant for nuclear war-fighting—a concept that India does not subscribe to (Subrahmanyam 1986: 275–9).

Efficacy of NFU

Ever since the May 1998 nuclear explosions and the Indian government's advocacy of the doctrine of NFU and a minimum credible deterrent, a major debate has been raging in the strategic community in India on the issue of no first use of nuclear weapons. Supporters of the credible minimum deterrence doctrine see inherent virtue in three crucial aspects—the NCA will 'control' all nuclear weapons and prevent them from falling into unauthorized hands or being handled in unsafe ways; the authorization for a nuclear strike is unambiguously vested solely in civilian, not military, authority; and, the doctrine retains a commitment to no first use, which is a sober posture that can inhibit a nuclear arms race. Many analysts have averred that India has gained nothing and has unnecessarily elected to bear the horrendous costs of a nuclear strike by choosing to adopt a purely retaliatory nuclear policy.[1] Praful Bidwai reported that the NFU policy, 'unpopular among many hawks, has now come under sharp attack from the National Security Advisory Board, no less. The Board, headed by C.V. Ranganathan, a former ambassador, recommended in a 160-page report submitted on December 20, 2002 that "India must consider withdrawing from this commitment as the other nuclear weapons-states have not accepted this policy"' (Bidwai 2003).

Rear Admiral Raja Menon asked in his *A Nuclear Strategy for India*—'Will India… be committed to absorbing a nuclear strike in case deterrence fails?' And answers—'Hardly, because in the event that an intelligence warning of a "definite" nuclear strike is received, the NCP (National Command Post) will have to consider, among other options, a first launch' (Menon 2000: 248). It is often argued that after all India's NFU doctrine is only a declaratory doctrine and if other nuclear powers are not willing to accept India's offer of a negotiated NFU treaty, why should India subject itself to the ravages of nuclear destruction? (Sethi 2009: 119–46). Though it is not very likely that eventually one or more Nuclear Weapon States (NWS) (including Pakistan) will come around to accepting India's offer of a negotiated bilateral or multilateral NFU treaty, it cannot be ruled out as realization is gradually dawning among civilian populations that everything possible needs to be done to prevent or at least substantially reduce the probability of a first strike. Given the groundswell of public opinion against the continuation of nuclear weapons almost all over the world, it may happen sooner rather than later. Meanwhile, some hard questions need to be asked. Is India likely to be faced by situations occasioned by operational realities when it might become necessary for the Indian political leadership to order the first use of nuclear weapons? When will the situation become operationally so critical that India might be forced to do the unthinkable? So, is India's NFU doctrine merely a rhetorical statement or is it based on sound operational reasoning? These issues pose a strategic dilemma and present a complex challenge that is not at all easy to rationalize.

NFU is Operationally Justified

It is now universally accepted that nuclear weapons are political weapons and not weapons of 'war-fighting'. However, the close link between nuclear weapons and a nation's conventional military capabilities is undeniable. If a nation's conventional capability is extremely low *vis-a-vis* a nuclear armed adversary, it may be necessary for that nation to adopt an *in extremis* 'first use' strategy to thwart a conventional military offensive that may threaten to undermine its territorial integrity and lead to its break up. This is the situation that Pakistan finds itself in at present. While India may have no intentions of launching a major conventional offensive into Pakistan, given India's conventional superiority (no matter how slender the edge may be), Pakistan has based its national security strategy on the first use of nuclear weapons to prevent its comprehensive military defeat like in 1971 and, consequently, its disintegration as a nation. The rational for Pakistan's nuclear weapons is to counter India's conventional force superiority. It is for this reason that Pakistan does not accept India's offer of a bilateral NFU treaty as a nuclear confidence-building and risk reduction measure.

Though overall China's conventional military forces far outnumber India's, due to China's problems in inducting, deploying, and logistically sustaining large forces in Tibet, India enjoys a reasonable defensive capability at present and, therefore, does not need a 'first use' nuclear strategy to deter a conventional Chinese offensive backed by nuclear-tipped ballistic missiles deployed in Tibet. However, India's existing defensive capability is being quickly eroded as China is modernizing its armed forces at a brisk pace, raising rapid deployment divisions, and improving the logistics infrastructure in Tibet while exhibiting extreme intransigence in resolving the outstanding territorial and boundary dispute with India. If India continues to neglect the upgradation of its conventional military capability and military modernization by investing the grossly inadequate sum of less than 2.0 per cent of its GDP for defence, as it is doing at present, the nation may again have to suffer the ignominy of large-scale military reverses, should China choose to fight even a limited border war after completing its military modernization by 2015–20.

While nuclear doctrine must undoubtedly be based on sound theoretical underpinings, it has to be ultimately tested in the crucible of operational reality. Inherent in an Indian nuclear first strike option, as advocated by the opponents of NFU, is the Pakistani nuclear retaliation that would inevitably follow on Indian cities and military targets. Cities like Jodhpur, Bikaner, Ahmedabad, Jalandhar, Jaisalmer, Ludhiana, and perhaps even New Delhi and Mumbai would be the likely targets of a retaliatory Pakistani nuclear strike. In all the above scenarios, given the limited gains that an Indian first strike may achieve and the real possibility of successful Pakistani nuclear retaliation, a first use nuclear option by India is not worth the risk of inevitable retaliation. An Indian nuclear first strike would not be justified as the costs of Pakistani retaliation would be prohibitive. Nor would it be operationally expedient.

Across the full spectrum of conventional conflict with either China or Pakistan, the first use of nuclear weapons by India does not make sound strategic sense as the gains will be marginal and the potential losses colossal. Besides, a first use doctrine would invite international opprobrium, seriously undermine India's efforts towards total nuclear disarmament, and be prohibitively costly to implement. It is not generally well appreciated that a first use doctrine requires a massive investment in surveillance and target acquisition infrastructure by way of satellite and aerial reconnaissance and human intelligence to execute 'launch on warning' and 'launch under attack' strategies, with the nuclear forces being maintained on permanent hair-trigger alerts. A first use doctrine also requires quick political decision making and decentralization of the control of nuclear weapons to theatre commanders in the armed forces during high level alerts. Hence, such a doctrine is inherently more risky and more likely to lead to the accidental, even unauthorized, use of nuclear weapons.

Need for Caveats to NFU

It would, of course, be far better to mutually negotiate an NFU treaty with adversarial nuclear armed states as that would be the best nuclear risk reduction measure. Russia and China have signed a mutual NFU treaty. In case India's nuclear-armed adversaries continue to be recalcitrant in signing a binding NFU pact, it would be worthwhile for India to consider some essential qualifications to its unilateral NFU doctrine. The first is to clearly spell out that a nuclear strike on Indian soldiers even within Pakistani territory would be deemed to be a nuclear strike on India and would invite massive punitive nuclear retaliation. The absence of this rider would negate India's conventional edge over Pakistan as the army would be forced to plan on launching only shallow-offensive operations to achieve limited objectives so as to avoid risking nuclear strikes on the mechanized spearheads leading India's advance. Only the capability of executing deep offensive strikes can ensure conventional deterrence and present viable policy options to prevent Pakistan's predilection for attempting salami slicing in J&K.

The second caveat should be that even a conventional bombing or missile attack on India's nuclear establishments and nuclear weapons storage sites during war, which results in casualties due to a nuclear explosion or even radiation leaks, would invite a nuclear response. Though India and Pakistan have signed an agreement to desist from targeting each other's nuclear facilities, such agreements have little value when war is declared. Also, state-sponsored acts of terrorism or sabotage of India's nuclear establishments and storage sites should also result in nuclear retribution against the sponsoring country. With better surveillance systems and improvements in the intelligence gathering apparatus, it should be possible to accurately determine the identity of the originator of such heinous crimes. Without these inescapable qualifications, with others to be added when necessary, it would be extremely difficult for India to implement a credible NFU doctrine. Adding these riders would substantially enhance the quality of India's deterrence.

Warheads and Delivery Systems for Credible Deterrence

The number of nuclear warheads that India needs for credible minimum deterrence has remained a contentious issue. In the absence of any statement from the government, the estimates put forward by Indian analysts range from one to two dozen 'survivable' warheads at the lower end of the spectrum to over 400 warheads at the upper end. However, these appear to be mainly based on intuitive judgments and not on dispassionate cold logic. When the doctrine being followed is not mutually assured destruction (MAD), nuclear warheads are not required in very large numbers in order for deterrence to function. The threat of effective punitive retaliation should be adequate to deter the adversary from resorting to the first use of nuclear weapons.

A nation's nuclear force structure depends on its nuclear doctrine and deterrence philosophy. These are essentially based on its civilizational values, its national security strategy, and its assessment of how much would be enough to deter its adversaries. The number of nuclear warheads that a nation must stockpile depends on the availability and quality of weapons-grade fissile material, its mastery of nuclear weapons design technology, the accuracy and reliability of its delivery systems, the fiscal constraints that govern its defence budget, the present and future air and missile defence capability of its adversaries, and their ability to absorb retaliatory nuclear strikes.

If deterrence fails, in keeping with its nuclear doctrine, India will have to absorb a nuclear strike before retaliating against the adversary's major cities and industrial centres. India's targeting philosophy is based on a 'counter value' (as against 'counter force') strategy of massive punitive retaliation to inflict unacceptable damage to the adversary's major population and industrial centres. Hence, India's nuclear forces have been so structured that the warheads and their delivery systems are able to survive a first strike in sufficient numbers to be able to inflict the required amount of punishment on selected targets in a retaliatory strike. The survivability of India's nuclear arsenal can be ensured by redundancy in numbers, through wide dispersion of nuclear warheads and delivery systems over Peninsular India, by having rail- and road-mobile missiles in addition to air-delivered warheads, and by investing in a limited number of difficult-to-detect SSBNs armed with SLBMs. Only SSBNs provide true assured retaliation capability.

How Many Warheads Does India Need?

Dr Ashley J. Tellis has written—'Since India's preferred outcome is defined solely in terms of deterrence, the possession of even a few survivable nuclear weapons capable of being delivered on target, together with an adequate command system is seen as sufficient to preserve the country's security' (Tellis 2001: 261). While that is true, in practical terms, the number of nuclear warheads required to be stockpiled for credible minimum deterrence is directly proportional to the number of targets to be destroyed. A retaliatory strike capability to destroy eight to 10 major population and industrial centres of the adversary would be adequate to meet the requirements of deterrence. However, this number must be based on intelligence assessments of the adversary's strategic culture, personality traits of his political leadership, dispersion of his economic and military power centres, and the resilience of his population. Together these factors determine the extent of damage that an adversary is prepared to absorb in retaliation for launching a first strike. The present yield of India's fission, boosted fission, and thermonuclear warheads ranges from 15 kiloton (kt) to 300 kt. The warheads are reported to be of the dial-a-yield (DAY) class, that is, in simple terms, the yield can be varied in the field by turning a dial on the warhead.

For 10 counter value targets to be destroyed in the adversary country, a total of 40 nuclear warheads, at the scale of four 15 to 50 kt warheads per target, would be adequate to cause unacceptable damage in a retaliatory nuclear strike if the CEP of the Agni IRBM delivery systems is taken to be less than 500 metres and a destruction assurance level of 0.7 (about 70 per cent) is considered acceptable. If the functional efficiency or overall reliability of India's nuclear delivery system is taken to be between 0.5 and 0.6 (50 to 60 per cent), a reasonable assumption for a modern nuclear force, then 75 to 80 warheads must actually be launched for about 40 to 45 warheads to explode successfully over their targets as some missiles may fail to take off, some may veer off course, some may be intercepted, and some warheads may either fail to explode or may explode in a sub-optimal manner. Hence, a minimum of 75 warheads and, of course, their delivery systems, must survive the enemy's first strike on Indian targets and be available for retaliation.

Despite the best possible concealment and dispersion measures, approximately 50 per cent of the nuclear warheads and delivery systems may be destroyed in a counter force first strike by the adversary. It would, therefore, be reasonable to plan a warhead stocking level of at least twice the number of warheads that are actually required to be launched, that is, 150 warheads. The last aspect to be catered for is a prudent level of reserves for larger than anticipated damage to own nuclear forces in a first strike and for unforeseen eventualities. Escalation control and war termination strategies would also be dependent on the ability to launch counter-recovery strikes and some fresh strikes. One-third the required number of warheads should be adequate as reserves. Hence, the total requirement works out to 200 nuclear warheads for credible minimum deterrence with an NFU strategy if 10 major population and industrial centres are to be attacked in a retaliatory strike to achieve a 70 to 80 per cent level of destruction assurance. In case the number of targets to be destroyed increases, the number of warheads required will increase proportionately.

Operationalization of India's Nuclear Deterrence

After an initial period of vacillation soon after the nuclear tests in May 1998, when nuclear deterrence was in hands primarily of the civilian scientists of the Department of Atomic Energy (DAE) and the DRDO and the armed forces had nothing to do with it, the Indian government has taken many cogent steps towards operationalizing India's nuclear deterrence. According to Brig. Arun Sahgal (Retd)—'...consequent to the formation of Strategic Forces Command (SFC), there has been substantive movement towards a coordinated effort between DRDO, DAE and SFC working in tandem to achieve the goals of providing a credible minimum deterrence capability to the country' [Sahgal (forthcoming)].

India has based its nuclear force structure on a triad—nuclear-tipped Short-range ballistic missiles (SRBMs) and Intermediate-range ballistic missiles (IRBMs) manned by the Regiment of Artillery of the Indian Army; nuclear glide bombs to be delivered aerially by fighter-bomber aircraft of the IAF; and, SLMBs to be launched from SSBNs of the Indian Navy, as and when these are introduced into service.[2] While India does not at present have nuclear-tipped cruise missiles in the arsenal, it is an option that can be exercised as the technological capability to launch cruise missiles is available. The surface component of India's triad comprises Prithvi SRBMs (150 km range) and Agni-I (800 to 900 km range) and Agni-II (2,500 km range) IRBMs. While these SSMs are already in service, the Agni-III IRBM (some analysts have wrongly called it an Inter-continental ballistic missile [ICBM]) with a range of 3,000 to 3,500 km approximately is still in development stage as only one successful test was carried out in 2007. The Prithvi, Agni-I, II, and III are all road- and rail-mobile missiles. The rate of production of Agni missiles is reported to be 12 to 18 per annum. The Prithvi SRBM is in service with the IAF and the Navy, with ranges up to 300 km. It can also be launched from surface warships with either a conventional or nuclear warhead.

With its demonstrated prowess in launching satellites indigenously, including the launch of 10 satellites on one launch vehicle in April 2008, India is well on its way to acquiring a capability for the employment of multiple, independently targeted re-entry vehicles (MIRV) technology. This should be possible in the next five to 10 years with the Agni-III IRBM as the platform of choice. However, various other factors will need to be considered before multiple warheads are placed on a single IRBM, and at present there does not appear to be any movement in this direction.

Credibility of India's Nuclear Deterrence

The designs of India's nuclear warheads are based on a very small number of nuclear tests. Though these are backed by computer modeling and simulation, the database is extremely small. The efficacy of some of the nuclear tests had been questioned by prominent atomic scientists soon after the 1998 Pokhran-II explosions. Most of the doubts, including those raised in the *Bulletin of Atomic Scientists* (Albright 1998: 22–3), had died out almost completely after the AEC released some test data selectively. However, in view of the statement made by former DRDO scientist K. Santhanam in August 2009, doubt has once again been cast on the efficacy of the thermonuclear device that had been tested in May 1998. (Mr Santhanam has called the thermonuclear test a fizzle (*Times of India* 2009), that is, it did not achieve the planned yield, but Dr P. Chidambaram, former Secretary, Department of Atomic Energy, and Dr A.P.J. Abdul Kalam, former SA to the Raksha Mantri, have denied that the test was a fizzle (*Times of India* 2009)). The number of nuclear warheads available to India—60 to 80 by most international and Indian estimates (*Times of India* 2011)[3]—does not fulfill even the low-end requirements of minimum deterrence and this number must be rapidly enhanced. The Agni series of missiles have also not been adequately tested to inspire confidence among the users that these missiles will function correctly. Also, India still lacks an IRBM that can reach value targets deep inside China.

The Advanced technology vehicle (ATV) project that was expected to provide the capability to design and manufacture nuclear-powered SSBNs has not become fully operational as yet, with the result that India has not yet operationalized the third and most important leg of the triad, that is, operational SSBNs armed with nuclear-tipped SLBMs. While

India's successful experience in space research, particularly the launch of multiple satellites on a single rocket, has endowed the scientists with the capability to master MIRV technology, there is no move at present to develop such a capability. In view of the R&D developments in China, it would be prudent to commence a research programme on MIRV technologies as a technology demonstrator.

Both the NDA and UPA governments have tended to play down discussion of nuclear issues in the public domain, other than the routine flaunting of models of Agni missiles at the Republic Day parade. No nuclear drills are known to have been held to ensure that the missile groups can deploy in a realistic time frame and that the warheads can be mated with the launchers in real time for early retaliation in the eventuality of a nuclear strike, even though some of these measures may have been practised in secret. Nuclear signaling is an extremely sophisticated art and India appears to have ignored this aspect completely.

In view of these major shortcomings, in purely theoretical terms, India's nuclear deterrence appears to lack credibility at present. However, nuclear deterrence is ultimately premised on the ability to successfully destroy value objectives in the adversary's territory and this crucial criterion can be met by India's nuclear forces. As long as three out of four nuclear warheads can be successfully detonated over the intended target every time, deterrence holds in practical terms even if one or more of those warheads do not provide the maximum intended yield. Notwithstanding this, India must demonstrate its resolve to use nuclear weapons, if it ever becomes necessary, through a carefully formulated process of signaling and must visibly upgrade the quality of its warhead and missile technology. The additional steps necessary to fully operationalize India's nuclear deterrence must not only be taken early, but must also be seen publicly to have been taken—within the bounds of security of information and materials.

Command and Control

Even though over 10 years have passed since India's nuclear tests in May 1998, there has been very little informed debate on the issue of Command and Control. If at all the subject of Command and Control of India's nuclear weapons comes up in the writings of defence analysts, it is mentioned *en passant* to highlight that contrary to the case in Pakistan,

India's nuclear weapons are firmly under civilian control. Western scholars, in particular, have noted disapprovingly that the Indian armed forces have been kept away from the nuclear planning process and nuclear decision-making. In fact, the armed forces were completely unaware of the work being undertaken by the DAE and the DRDO prior to the May 1998 nuclear tests (Joeck 1997: 53).

National Command Authority

India's duly elected PM heads the Cabinet Committee on Security (CCS) and exercises ultimate control over all nuclear decision-making. On January 4, 2003, the CCS adopted and made public the key elements of India's nuclear doctrine and Command and Control structure. The PM and the CCS now comprise India's NCA. In the NCA, the Political Council headed by the PM, is the 'sole' authority for ordering a nuclear strike. The Political Council is advised by an Executive Council that is headed by the NSA. The Executive Council provides inputs and advice to the Political Council and executes its decisions through the Chairman, Chiefs of Staff Committee (COSC), and the Commander-in-Chief (C-in-C) SFC.

Single Point Military Advice

It is important that in nuclear decision-making, the Cabinet must get 'single point military advice'. At present, all three Chiefs of Staff render military advice to the CCS through the Defence Minister. (While they may be invited to attend meetings of the CCS, they do not have institutionalized 'direct' access to the PM and the Cabinet, unlike in the erstwhile Defence Committee of the Cabinet (DCC) where the three Chiefs were permanent invitees as 'co-opted members'). The PM's decision-making dilemma can be imagined if two Chiefs of Staff were to advise the CCS to desist from using nuclear weapons to retaliate against an enemy nuclear strike during on-going conventional military operations and the third Chief, particularly the army Chief, was to insist that the retaliatory use of nuclear weapons was an inescapable operational requirement in the prevailing circumstances due to the situation on the various battle fronts. Due to the inter-dependence of the three Services on each other in modern warfare and because of the repercussions of the operational activities of one on the other, it is imperative that differing viewpoints among the Services are resolved by military professionals themselves and that the political masters get professional military advice from only one source. Such a source can only be the Chief of Defence Staff (CDS) or a permanent Chairman, Joint Chiefs of Staff, and not the Chairman, COSC, as it is presently constituted. Also, the CDS must be a permanent invitee to the meetings of the Political Council as a co-opted member. Till a CDS is appointed, all three Chiefs of Staff should be permanent invitees to meetings of the Political Council.

The tri-Service SFC exercises command and operational control over the nuclear weapons delivery systems and oversees the functioning of the surveillance, early warning, nuclear forces intelligence, attack, and damage assessment systems.[4] It is also responsible for all aspects of professional training pertaining to nuclear launch, safety and security and dispersal, camouflage, and concealment. The Services HQ are responsible for raising, equipping, initial training, and logistics support. Targeting, another major command function, is increasingly becoming more and more dynamic due to rapid industrialization and the creation of new strategic assets. Targeting is also a function of the SFC. It is based on inputs received directly from the national-level intelligence organizations as well as from the Defence Intelligence Agency (DIA) and the intelligence agencies of

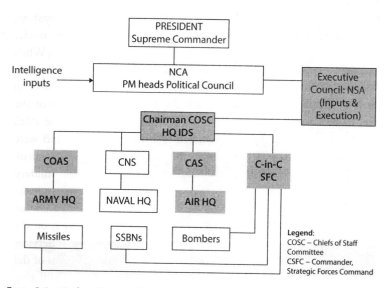

FIGURE 3.1 Nuclear Command and Control (overview)

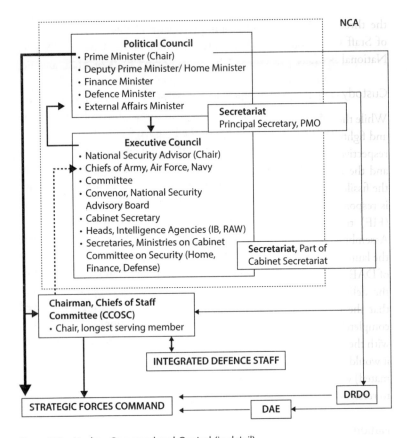

FIGURE 3.2 Nuclear Command and Control (in detail)

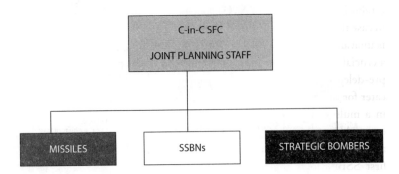

FIGURE 3.3 C-in-C SFC

the three Services. The C-in-C SFC reports to the Chairman, Chiefs of Staff Committee. In practice, however, he takes his orders from the National Security Advisor (NSA).[5]

Custody and Storage of Nuclear Warheads

While the delivery systems (missile launchers, nuclear-powered submarine, and fighter-bombers) are 'manned' by the army, the navy, and the air force, respectively, the custody of nuclear warheads is divided between the DAE and the DRDO. The DAE machines the atomic core of warheads from the fissile material produced in India's un-safeguarded nuclear reactors and is responsible for their custody. The DRDO produces the high explosive (HE) triggers for the warheads and is responsible for their custody. Assembling the warheads during the preparatory stage and mating them to the launchers (missiles and aircraft) is a joint responsibility of the scientists of DAE and DRDO and has not been delegated to the SFC units manning the delivery systems. This system of storage during peace time ensures that the probability of an accidental or unauthorized nuclear launch is completely eliminated.[6] However, over a decade after overt nuclearization, with the advent of sophisticated permissive action links (PALs) technology, it would be reasonable to assume that a finite number of assembled (but not mated) warheads are likely to be in storage, both to reduce reaction time and to retaliate in case necessary during the early stages of a conflict.

National Command Post, Chain of Succession, and Delegation

NCP is reported to be under construction outside New Delhi and, as an interim measure, an Interim National Command Post (INCP) has been established (IANS 2003). A clear line of succession has been established in case the political leadership is decapitated by a nuclear strike or the PM is unavailable for some reason, so that decision-making is not stymied at a crucial juncture in the nation's history. However, it is not clear whether pre-delegation of authority to the armed forces has also been approved to cater for the probability of the entire civilian leadership being eliminated in a multi-warhead first strike—an improbable but not an impossible event. Also, no information is available about the command and control arrangements intended to be introduced when the INS Arihant, India's first SSBN, joins the nuclear forces by 2012–13. Some delegation of authority is necessary when SSBNs are away on long patrols at sea.

Communications and Logistics

Dedicated communications have been provided between the NCP and HQ SF and between HQ SFC and all nuclear forces units, storage sites, and likely launch sites. Communications encompass several layers of redundancy and have been hardened to withstand Electro-magnetic Pulse (EMP) strikes [Sahgal (forthcoming)]. The logistics arrangements necessary to transport warheads from their storage sites to the delivery systems have been streamlined and are periodically rehearsed.

Peace-time Locations of Missile Groups

In the interest of strategic stability, India's nuclear-armed missile groups have been stationed at locations that are deep in the interior and are well away from their likely launch pads. However, plans have been made for their rapid move to and deployment in their launch pads and for 'marrying up' with the teams responsible for mating the warheads with the missiles. These plans are periodically rehearsed and updated.

Impact of Nuclear Deterrence on Military Modernization

There is some evidence to suggest that concerted efforts are being made to tailor operational plans for defensive and offensive operations to the prevailing nuclear environment. Various army and air force joint exercises held in recent years, including *Vijay Chakra* (February 2000), *Poorna Vijay* (May-June 2001), *Divya Astra* (May 2004), *Vajra Shakti* (May 2005), Desert Strike (November/December 2005), *Sanghe Shakti* (May 2006), and *Vijayee Bhava* (May 2011), were aimed at concentrating and coordinating firepower and fine-tuning Army-Air Force joint operations in a strategic setting that was premised on operations in a nuclear environment. The COAS had said during Exercise *Vajra Shakti* that it had been conducted with a nuclear backdrop, and that battle procedures had been refined and 'high synergy' had been achieved with the IAF (Kanwal 2006). According to Brigadier Arun Sahgal (Retd),[7] these exercises were carried out in an environment where nuclear, biological, and chemical weapons had been employed; giving the army much needed operational experience.

From the statements made during recent military exercises it can be deduced that operational plans are being made to ensure that all new weapons and equipment acquisitions upgrade the ability to operate in a nuclear environment. However, there is no evidence to suggest that the doctrines underpinning military modernization programmes have been revised and integrated to draw full benefit from the umbrella provided by credible nuclear deterrence.[8] Part of this is due to the fact that most military modernization programmes are aimed primarily at the replacement of obsolescent or even obsolete weapons and equipment with more modern ones, and do not contribute substantively towards upgrading the combat potential of the armed forces. As Stephen P. Cohen and Sunil Dasgupta have brought out in their recent book *Arming without Aiming* (Cohen and Dasgupta 2010), India's military modernization process lacks political support and guidance, is haphazard and bereft of strategic direction, and is not in consonance with evolving doctrinal and organizational changes. Cohen and Dasgupta have examined the contours of India's emergence as a 'reluctant' nuclear power and discussed the fragility and ambiguity of strategic stability in South Asia. They correctly point out that India's politico-military strategy has not evolved in concert with its nuclear power status. For example, the element of proactive planning is lacking in India's national security strategy.

Ballistic Missile Defence

Given India's NFU doctrine, BMD capability makes eminent sense for India as it will increase the uncertainty of the success of a first strike by the adversary and will, hence, reinforce deterrence. The only credible counter action against BMD is to substantially enhance the number of missiles to be fired against each target so as to saturate the BMD system and ensure that at least some of the missiles get through. BMD systems are a combination of national missile defence (NMD) for the defence of the whole nation and theatre missile defence (TMD) for a given war zone.

The DRDO's successful anti-missile defence test conducted in December 2007 was a significant step in the country's air defence system. The DRDO conducted the test with two missiles—a modified Prithvi missile fired from Chandipur-on-Sea to simulate an incoming enemy missile and an Advanced Air Defence interceptor missile fired from Wheeler Island in the Bay of Bengal to defend against and destroy the hostile missile. Conducted at an altitude of 15 km., this test was endo-atmospheric. In 2006, a missile was successfully intercepted in an exo-atmospheric test at an altitude of 60 km. The two tests are part of an effort to provide a two-layered anti-missile air defence capability to the armed forces.

Another Indian anti-missile system under trial is a version of the indigenously designed and developed Akash medium range SAM. The anti-missile technology was based on the foundation technologies, manpower, expertise, experience, and infrastructure developed for the Akash SAM that formed part of the Integrated Guided Missile Development Program started in the early 1980s. The anti-missile defence system involves integration of long-range tracking radars, fire control radar, mobile communications terminal, and mobile launcher-fired interceptor missiles, which make it technologically complex. Interception of an incoming missile demands high levels of precision and accuracy in terms of identification, tracking, and point kill capabilities, and several tests will be required to refine the system. To that extent, this test was a successful demonstration of technology. However, the test assumes strategic significance because it signals to China and Pakistan the sophistication of Indian techno-military capabilities and thereby strengthens India's nuclear deterrence.

The development of a BMD system is in India's national interest as it will make India's deterrence more credible and provide a limited shield to high value targets. It would also be in India's national interest to collaborate with Israel, Russia, and the US, and other strategic partners to gain technical know-how for the development of a BMD system. Since these countries are likely to be unwilling to accept one-way transfer of such cutting edge technology, India should consider entering into the joint development of BMD systems with one or more of them. India cannot afford to be left behind in this technological race as success will enhance the quality of India's nuclear deterrence.

The proliferation of SRBMs and IRBMs in India's neighbourhood has spurred a new sense of urgency regarding air defence and anti-ballistic missile (ABM) defences. India's retaliatory strike nuclear force must survive a disarming first strike in sufficient numbers to be able to deliver punitive counter value retaliation to an adversary who chooses to cross the *Lakshman Rekha* [9] and does the unthinkable. Besides the nuclear force units and storage sites, India's leadership that comprises the NCA must also survive a decapitating first strike to be able to assess the situation and make the necessary decision to retaliate. Hence, not only must New Delhi, the capital city, be defended against nuclear attack, but also the NCP and other command and control centres. The enhanced role of air defences and ABM defences in a nuclear environment emerges quite clearly.

The debate between increasing the effectiveness of air defences and instituting viable ABM defences, on the one hand, and enhancing the effectiveness of the nuclear deterrent, on the other, is a perennial one. An ABM system for the defence of Delhi has been estimated to cost approximately between US $1 billion (Bedi 1998) (Rs 4,600 crores) and 2 billion (Raghuvanshi 1998). Though it has been reported that a sum of Rs 2,000 crores has been allotted to the DRDO to develop an indigenous ABM system (Singh 1998), the only low-to-high altitude air defence-cum-ABM system that may be readily available to India is the Russian S-300V. Because of the high cost of ABM systems, some defence analysts and editorial writers argue that it would be better to increase the size of India's nuclear forces in terms of additional nuclear warheads and better, more modern ballistic missiles with longer ranges rather than expend limited funds on dubious air defences.

It is well known that an ABM system can be saturated with simultaneous attacks from a large number of ballistic missiles, some of which may even carry conventional warheads while some others may be decoys. Lt Gen. Harwant Singh (Retd) has written—'An adversary's missile launch pads can be fairly close to Delhi (in missile distance terms) and given the advancements in multi-targeting, multi-warhead, jamming technology and techniques and low level flight profile, interception will be almost impossible' (Harwant Singh 1998). Others have been equally skeptical and have suggested alternative measures—

> An ABM system to protect Delhi will cost one billion dollars plus... there will (then) be a clamour to protect Bombay (Mumbai)... which has two reactors and then other places... (an ABM system) can never provide assured defences... For less than one quarter of the price, we can develop Prithvi and Agni versions which will provide absolute deterrence against the USA, China and Pakistan...
>
> (*Chanakya Aerospace Defence and Maritime Review* 1998).

Whether or not to opt for ABM defences is indeed a dilemma. However, it would be prudent to purchase equipment for at least one or two batteries off the shelf and then commence indigenous development efforts by reverse engineering or undertake licensed production.

Impact of Indo-US Nuclear Deal on India's Strategic Weapons Programme

Within India, the nuclear deal with the US initially met with stiff resistance among detractors in the right wing as well as the left wing political parties, a handful of analysts and journalists, and from some members of the community of nuclear scientists (A. Gopalakrishnan, A.N. Prasad, Bharat Karnad, and P.K. Iyengar 2010; *The Hindu* 2007). Opponents of the deal aver that it will cap India's nuclear weapons programme, that India will be forced to refrain from nuclear tests in future, that the separation plan is flawed (Karnad 2006: 49),[10] there is no assurance on continued fuel supplies, it will result in US inspectors storming Indian nuclear establishments if the International Atomic Energy Agency (IAEA) fails to ensure that safeguards are observed, and that Indian foreign policy will become subservient to that of the US, for example on the Iranian nuclear imbroglio (Chellaney 2007).[11] Perhaps the most misunderstood aspect about the deal is about its possible impact on the nuclear weapons programme, despite several reassuring endorsements to the contrary by respectable members of the strategic community (Ghose 2007).[12]

The opposition was also exercised about the provisions relating to enrichment and re-processing technologies even though the leaders are well aware that the US has a well-established policy of not exporting these technologies even to its allies, and India has independently gained sufficient expertise in them. India's vote against Iran at the IAEA was also seen as a compromise with national interests in order to placate the US (Rasgotra 2005).[13] However, the government's efforts to explain the key advantages of the nuclear deal have paid dividends and most opposition has withered away. One of the major factors was the emergence of the fact that India already has an adequate stockpile of fissile material to meet the needs of minimum deterrence.

***

The current international trend is towards more modern, high quality nuclear forces, even though the present efforts of the US and Russia to reduce the number of warheads and missiles will continue. Both China and Pakistan are engaged in the upgradation of their nuclear warhead and delivery systems capabilities. With nations like Iran and various terrorist groups expressing their nuclear ambitions openly and the probability of a political-military meltdown in Pakistan, the proliferation of nuclear weapons around India remains a cause for concern. Hence, it can be deduced that credible nuclear deterrence will continue to play a crucial role in India's national security calculus over the next few decades. In line with the emerging trends, India too must endeavour to modernize its nuclear warheads and delivery systems and keep its option to test open— if it ever becomes necessary in future. In particular, India must close the missile technology gap with both China and Pakistan as early as possible, or else the credibility of India's nuclear deterrence will remain suspect.

India's desire to develop a credible minimum nuclear deterrent against nuclear blackmail and the threat of use of nuclear weapons is an eminently justifiable national security imperative. India's NFU, retaliation-only nuclear doctrine is not only morally befitting and worthy of India's civilizational heritage, it is also operationally sound strategy. However, deterrence hinges on credibility and India is still far from demonstrating strong political resolve to execute a massive retaliatory nuclear strike. India's adversaries will be deterred only when they are convinced that India has both the political and military will and the hardware necessary to respond to a nuclear strike with punitive retaliation that will inflict unacceptable loss of human life and unprecedented material damage. Only then will the nuclear monster remain tightly leashed in and around India's neighbourhood. The adoption of graduated or flexible response strategies will weaken the quality of India's deterrence and may tempt its adversaries to test India's resolve and capabilities.

Notes

1. While the probability of a city busting first strike is low if deterrence fails, it can never be completely ruled out. Even a strike on a small urban centre with a single nuclear warhead with a yield of 10 to 20 kt would cause hundreds of thousands of civilian casualties as Indian towns are extremely densely populated. The consequences of a multi-warhead nuclear strike on a city like Delhi or Mumbai are indeed unthinkable.

2. INS Arihant, India's first SSBN, is undergoing sea trials and is expected to join the nuclear forces by 2012–13. India would need at least four SSBNs, each armed with 10 to 12 SLBMs with a range up to 5,000 km.

3. The report was attributed to David Albright of ISIS and was published in almost all Indian newspapers.

4. It needs to be debated whether the communications channel for the execution of a nuclear strike should be a single channel from the C-in-C SFC to the concerned unit(s) or if it should be duplicated by execution orders being also sent on the channels of the operations directorate of the Service concerned.

5. 'Even the Assistant Chief of Integrated Defence Staff (Strategy) in the Operations branch of HQ IDS has been taken out of the loop which is now the sole prerogative of SFC, taking directions not so much from Chairman COSC but the NSA and his staff', Arun Sahgal.

6. According to Ashley Tellis, 'Indian pre-war storage facilities in India, both civilian and military, are relatively secure, since they enjoy high levels of physical protection against penetration and unauthorized access. Moreover, the sheer size, numbers, and locations of these facilities render them ideal sanctuaries for storage of critical strategic components', p. 419.

7. Interview with the author.

8. The *Indian Army Doctrine 2004* does not at any place emphasize that future operations will be conducted in a nuclear environment.

9. A mythological barrier.

10. '... the nuclear "separation plan"... is tantamount to a noose the government has put round the country's neck. Unless the Manmohan Singh regime wakes up and restricts the damage by agreeing on only a minimal separation (leaving a number of civilian power plants and all weapons production support and ancillaries out of the safeguards trap), the country may find Washington, prompted by the American non-proliferation lobby, pulling on the rope'. Karnad 2006, p. 49.

11. 'That the deal has brought India within the US strategic sphere is evident from a number of instances: the two Indian votes against Iran in Vienna; Indian acquiescence to an overt US role in countries in India's strategic backyard, such as Nepal, Sri Lanka and Bangladesh; and the increasing alignment of Indian policy with US policy on Pakistan'. Brahma Chellaney.

12. Among others, see Arundhati Ghose, 2007. Ms Ghose is a former Indian ambassador to the UN at Geneva.

13. Not all Indian analysts and opinion makers agree with this approach. Convener of the NSAB and former Foreign Secretary M.K. Rasgotra opposed such thinking in an interview with the author. He has written—'India's IAEA vote on Iran's uranium processing problems is not a vote for the US or against Iran. It is a vote for India's own national security interests'.

References

Albright, David. 1998. 'Shots Heard Round the World', Bulletin of Atomic Scientists, pp. 20–4. Available at http://books.google.ca/books?id=vAsAA

AAAMBAJ&pg=PA20&dq=shots+heard+'round+world&hl=en&sa=X &ei=qbXXUYrdOsbprAeDw4H4BA&ved=0CD0Q6AEwAg#v=onepag e&q=shots%20heard%20'round%20world&f=false (accessed 11 February 2011).

Bedi, Rahul. 1998.'India and Russia to Sign Pact', *Jane's Defense Weekly*.

Bidwai, Praful. 2003. 'Nuclear South Asia: Still on the Edge', *Frontline*, 20 (2). Available at http://www.tni.org/archives/bidwai/edge.htm (accessed 11 February 2011).

Blanche, Ed. 1998.'Nuclear Reactions', *Jane's Defense Weekly*.

Chanakya Aerospace Defence and Maritime Review. 1998. 'Minimal Nuclear Deterrence and the Systems it Renders Obsolete', editorial.

Chellaney, Brahma. 2007.'Taken for a Ride', *Hindustan Times*, 3 April.

Cohen, Stephen P. and Sunil Dasgupta. 2010. *Arming without Aiming: India's Military Modernisation*. Washington D.C.: Brookings Institution Press.

Gallucci, Robert L. 1991. 'Limiting US Policy Options to Prevent Nuclear Weapons Proliferation: The Relevance of Minimum Deterrence', in James C. Gaston (ed.), *Grand Strategy and the Decision-making Process*, pp. 110–11. Washington D.C.: National Defence University Press.

Ghose, Arundhati Ghose. 2007. 'The 123 Agreement: No Threat to India's Strategic Programme', *The Tribune*, 12 November.

Gopalakrishnan, A., A.N. Prasad, Bharat Karnad, and P.K. Iyengar. 2010. *Strategic Sell-Out: Indo-US Nuclear Deal*. New Delhi: Pentagon Press.

Hindustan Times. 1999.'France Welcomes India's N-doctrine', 27 August.

Hindustan Times. 1999.'India Spells out Draft N-doctrine', 18 August.

IANS. 2003. 'India Building Nuclear-proof Bunkers for top Leaders', 2 September. Available at http://www.siliconindia.com/shownews/India_ building_nuclearproof_bunkers_for_top_leaders___-nid-20887.html (accessed 11 February 2011).

Joeck, Neil. 1997.'Maintaining Nuclear Stability in South Asia', *Adelphi Paper 312*, 1997 (312): 53.

Kanwal, Gurmeet. 2006.'Strike Fast and Hard', *The Tribune*, 23 June. Available at http://www.tribuneindia.com/2006/20060623/edit.htm (accessed 11 February 2011).

Karnad, Bharat. 2006. 'Strategic Implications of Nuclear Cooperation', *The Debate on Indo-US Nuclear Cooperation*, Delhi Policy Group, Nuclear Policy Stewardship Project.

Menon, Raja. 2000. *A Nuclear Strategy for India*. New Delhi: Sage Publications.

NSAB. 1999. See paragraphs 2.3, 2.4, and 2.5 of 'Indian Nuclear Doctrine', a Draft Paper. Publicly released by the New Delhi: Ministry of External Affairs in New Delhi on 17 August 1999.

Raghuvanshi, Vivek. 1998. 'Russia Will Continue Defence Ties With India', *Defense News*, 14–20 September.

Rasgotra, M.K. 2005. *The Economic Times*, 4 October.

Sahgal, Arun. (forthcoming). 'Operationalisation of India's Nuclear Doctrine', Issue Brief. Centre for Land Warfare Studies (CLAWS).

Sethi, Manpreet. 2009. *Nuclear Strategy: India's March Towards Credible Deterrence*. New Delhi: Knowledge World.

Singh, Harwant. 1998.'Costly Missile Shield for Delhi!', *The Tribune*, 11 November.

Singh, Jaswant. 1998.'Against Nuclear Apartheid', *Foreign Affairs*, 77 (5).

Subrahmanyam, K. 1986. 'Introduction', in K. Subrahmanyam (ed.), *India and the Nuclear Challenge*, p. 10. New Delhi: Lancer International.

Suo Motu Statement by Prime Minister Atal Behari Vajpayee in Parliament on 27 May 1998. Available at http://www.fas.org/news/india/1998/05/980527-india-pm.htm (accessed 11 February 2011).

Tellis, Ashley J. 2001. *India's Emerging Nuclear Posture*. Santa Monica: RAND.

'The Cabinet Committee on Security Reviews Operationalisation of India's Nuclear Doctrine', 4 January 2003. Available at http://pib.nic.in/archieve/lreleng/lyr2003/rjan2003/04012003/r040120033.html (accessed 6 July 2013).

The Economic Times. 1999. 'N-doctrine Speaks of Credible Deterrence, Strike Capability', 18 August.

The Hindu. 2007. 'P. K. Iyengar Cautions Against Nuclear Deal', 28 January. Available at http://www.hinduonnet.com/2007/01/28/stories/2007012804520600.htm (accessed 11 February 2011).

The Times of India. 2009a.'Pokhran-II not fully Successful: Scientist', 27 August. Available at http://articles.timesofindia.indiatimes.com/2009-08-27/india/28210828_1_thermonuclear-device-pokhran-ii-ctbt (accessed 11 February 2011).

———. 2009b. 'Kalam Certifies Pokhran-II, Santhanam Stands his Ground', 28 August. Available at http://articles.timesofindia.indiatimes.com/2009-08-28/india/28199613_1_santhanam-thermonuclear-device-pokhran (accessed 11 February 2011).

———. 2011.'Pakistan has 110 N-warheads, Edges Ahead of India: US Report', 31 January. Available at http://articles.timesofindia.indiatimes.com/2011-01-31/us/28377446_1_weapons-fissile-material-nuclear-arms.

Vishwakarma, Arun. Available at http://www.bharat-rakshak.com/MISSILES/Agni.html (accessed 11 February 2011).

Zuberi, Matin. 2000.'The Proposed Nuclear Doctrine', *World Focus*, 244 (April): 5.

4 The Indian Defence Industry

Struggling with Change

Richard A. Bitzinger*

GREAT NATIONS, IT CAN BE SAID, have great arms industries. To put it another way, it is nearly impossible for a country to be a great power if it must rely on foreign suppliers to outfit its military. Not only would that country be susceptible to arms embargoes and other sanctions that could constrain or constrict its military power, but it would leave itself vulnerable to outside forces who could use those dependencies to intimidate and coerce that country into engaging in actions or pursuing policies—political, economic, or otherwise—that might go against its wishes. Consequently, many countries automatically equate great power status with autarky, or self-sufficiency, when it comes to armaments production.

India is an aspiring great power that has long harboured the goal of possessing a technologically advanced self-sufficient arms industry (Cohen and Dasgupta 2010; Bedi 2005; Mohanty 2009, 2004; Pardesi and Matthews 2007; Singh 2000). These ambitions go back to more than 50 years, when the country attempted to design and build its own fighter aircraft, the HF-24 *Marut*. Although a technological failure, it did not dampen India's determination to one day becoming a major arms-producing nation, capable of meeting most, if not all its requirements for self-defence—and therefore great-power status—through indigenous means. This quest for autarky *and* stature, for example, drove the country's

---

* The author would like to thank Deba R. Mohanty for his comments and suggestions on an earlier draft of this paper.

nuclear weapons programme. As India's economic power has expanded, and as its technological prowess in certain areas (such as information technologies) has grown, it has become more determined than ever to create a world-class, globally competitive defence industry.

India already possesses one of the oldest, largest, and most diversified defence industries in the world. It produces fighter aircraft, surface combatants, submarines, tanks, armoured vehicles, helicopters, artillery systems, and small arms. The country also has a huge defence R&D establishment with considerable experience in indigenous weapons design and development going back more than 50 years. That said, India has long been confronted with serious impediments to its efforts to build a state-of-the-art arms industry. While the rest of India appears to be racing into the 21st century, powered by a dynamic, free market-oriented economy, the defence sector seems mired in the country's Nehruvian socialist and protectionist past. Consequently, the nation is still predominantly saddled with a bloated, non-competitive, non-responsive military-industrial complex—capable, it seems, of only producing technologically inferior military equipment, and even then, never on time and nearly always way over their original cost estimates. Given such longstanding deficiencies in its defence industrial base, it is little wonder why India's drive for great power status has been so fitful.

This may be changing. The economic liberalization that began in India 20 years ago may finally be pervading the local arms industry. For more than a decade, the Indian government has been engaged in a number of initiatives designed to open up the defence sector to competition; more recently, too, it has expanded efforts to bring in foreign technologies to improve the capabilities of home-grown armaments and establish the foundation for a more high-tech defense R&D base. At the same time, however, many of these reforms face strong resistance, and for the present it is still uncertain what impact, if any, these efforts may eventually have on invigorating the Indian military-industrial complex.

India's Traditional Policy of Self-Reliance in Arms Production

Self-reliance has long been a fundamental goal of indigenous armaments production in India. Such an objective had military, political, and economic salience. As Ajay Singh put it—'After independence, and the adoption of a policy of non-alignment, it was…obvious that foreign policy would need to be reinforced by a policy of self-reliance in defense...Prime Minister Jawaharlal Nehru believed that no country was truly independent, unless it was independent in matters of armaments' (Singh 2000: 126–7).

Early on, a distinction was made between 'self-sufficiency' and 'self-reliance'. Singh defined the former as requiring that 'all stages in defense production (starting from design to manufacture, including raw materials)...be carried out within the country'. He added that, 'to be self-sufficient, a country must not only have the material resources required for defense production, but also the technical expertise to undertake design and development without external assistance'. Self-reliance, on the other hand, was much more modest, as while it entailed the indigenous production of armaments, it allowed for the importation of foreign designs, technologies, systems, and manufacturing know-how (Singh 2000: 127).

While self-sufficiency was the preferable approach, self-reliance has long been the practice when it comes to Indian armaments production. As such, New Delhi has long conceded the need to import considerable amounts of foreign military technology—mostly from the Soviet Union/ Russia but also from France and the United Kingdom—in order to establish and expand its indigenous military-industrial complex. Thus, from the 1960s to the 1980s, India undertook the licensed-production of several foreign weapons systems, including MiG-21 and MiG-27 fighter jets, Jaguar strike aircraft, Alouette III helicopters, T-55 and T-72 tanks, Milan antitank weapons, and *Tarantul* corvettes (Baskaran 2004: 211–13, 221–6).

At the same time, however, it was always New Delhi's intention to gradually and incrementally replace licensed production with indigenously developed and designed weaponry. Hence, starting as far back as the 1950s, the manufacture of foreign-sourced military systems was complemented with local products (Pardesi and Matthews 2007: 421–9).[1] India, for example, began development of its first indigenous fighter jet, the HF-24 *Marut*, in 1956, with the first flight occurring in 1961. Truly indigenous armaments development and production, however, did not really take off until the 1980s, with the inauguration of several new home-grown projects, such as the LCA, renamed the *Tejas* in 2005, the Advanced Light Helicopter (ALH), the *Arjun* tank, and, especially, the IGMDP, which involved the development of a number of tactical missile systems. While many of these 'indigenous' programmes still incorporated considerable amounts of foreign technology or subsystems, the objective has always been to reduce this dependency along the lines of the evolutionary 'ladder-of-production' model, and eventually achieve true 'self-sufficiency' (Bitzinger 2003: 16–18). This intent was underscored, for example, in 1995 when New Delhi announced that within 10 years it would increase its 'local content' of weapons systems in the Indian armed forces from 30 per cent to 70 per cent (Singh 2000: 151).

India's Military-Industrial Complex: An Overview

Until quite recently, Indian armaments production was entirely embedded within a huge government-run military-industrial complex. Even after some modest reforms (discussed later below), the vast bulk of defence manufacturing remains in the hands of the state. The Indian defence industrial base consists of eight government-owned DPSUs, 39 Ordnance Factories (OFs), and, at the top, the powerful DRDO (Behera 2010: 34). The Indian state-run defence sector employs more than 1.4 million workers (of which about 105,000 work in the OFs), including some 30,000 scientists and engineers within the DRDO, and in 2010 it enjoyed revenues of approximately US$7.8 billion (Defense News 2011; Behera 2010: 31–4).

The DPSUs and OFs carry out the bulk of Indian arms manufacturing, often operating mainly as monopoly suppliers. HAL, for example, is the sole DPSU engaged in aircraft production, including combat aircraft, helicopters, trainers, and transport planes, as well as avionics and engines (Behera 2009: 4). HAL was established in 1964 with the merger of Hindustan Aircraft Ltd. and Aeronautics India Ltd.; it is headquartered in Bangalore and operates four main manufacturing and design complex. HAL both license-produces foreign-designed aircraft—including the MiG-21, MiG-27, MiG-29, Jaguar, and (currently) Su-30 fighter jets— and manufactures indigenously developed combat planes, such as the HF-24 *Marut* and, currently, the *Tejas* LCA. Other military aircraft programmes include the ALH, the LCH, and the IJT.

Bharat Dynamics Ltd (BDL) builds tactical and strategic missiles for the Indian military. Most important, BDL is the production base for India's IGMDP, which was launched in the early 1980s. The IGMDP entailed the development and production of several types of missile systems, initially two surface-to-surface ballistic missiles (the short-range *Prithvi* and the medium-range *Agni*), the *Akash* and *Trishul* SAMs, and the *Nag* antitank guided missile (ATGM). Additionally, Bharat Dynamics builds the *BrahMos* antiship cruise missile, the *Sagarika* (a submarine-launched version of the *Prithvi* missile), and the *Astra* air-to-air missile.

Bharat Electronics Ltd (BEL) is India's DPSU responsible for the production of electronic systems for the Indian armed forces. Established in 1954, BEL is based in Bangalore and operates nine factories producing radios and other communication gear, radars, sonars, electronic warfare systems, opto-electronics, and electronic components for tanks and other weapons systems (Behera 2009: 4). BEL is also designing and developing the Indian Army's Tactical Communications System, as well as the Battle Management System, an army-wide network-centric 'situational awareness' solution, linking and integrating data from a wide range of sensors and transmitting this information in near real-time to forces on the battlefield (Raghuvanshi 2010a).

The various OFs are responsible for the manufacture of ground forces and miscellaneous military equipment, such as tanks and armoured vehicles, artillery systems, small arms and ammunition, uniforms, tents, and so on. The 39 OFs are split into five operating divisions—Ammunition and Explosives (10 factories); Weapons, Vehicles, and Equipment (10 factories); Materials and Components (nine factories); Armoured Vehicles (five factories); and the 'Ordnance Equipment Group of Factories' (five factories). Two more OFs are in the offing (Behera 2010: 34).

Intra-sectoral competition appears to exist only in the shipbuilding industry. The three chief DPSUs in charge of naval construction are Mazagon Dock Ltd (MDL), Garden Reach Shipbuilders and Engineers Ltd, and Goa Shipyard Ltd. Mazagon Dock, located in Mumbai, is the country's oldest shipyard, founded in 1934 and nationalized in 1960. MDL is India's main naval shipbuilder; in the past, it has produced the *Delhi*-class destroyers, the *Godavari*-class frigate, and the *Khukri*-class corvette, as well as German Type-209 submarines assembled under license. Currently, it is building the *Kolkata*-class destroyer, the *Shivailk*-class frigate, and the Franco-Spanish *Scorpène*-class submarine (six of which are currently being constructed under license). Garden Reach Shipbuilders and Engineers Ltd. is based in Kolkata and was founded in 1960. It is currently building the *Kamorta*-class corvette, along with various fast-attack craft and patrol vessels. Goa Shipyard Ltd, founded in 1967 and based in Vasco Da Gama (Goa), produces offshore patrol vessels, missile corvettes, and fast patrol vessels.

Interestingly, India's indigenous aircraft carrier, the INS *Vikrant*, which is currently under construction, is *not* being built at a naval DPSU, but rather the Cochin Shipyard, in Kochi. Cochin was traditionally a commercial shipbuilder (but still a state-owned firm, or PSU), manufacturing bulk carriers, tankers, and platform supply vessels. Given the likely construction of two or more indigenous carriers, however, Cochin could come to compete heavily with other shipbuilding DPSUs for naval contracts.

At the very top of India's military-industrial complex stands the DRDO. The DRDO has primary responsibility for the design, manufacture, and management of indigenous weapons programmes and weapons systems for the Indian armed forces. The DRDO comprises more than 50 state-owned laboratories engaged in the R&D of defence technologies; it employs over 30,000 workers, including 5,000 scientists and about 25,000 other scientific, technical, and supporting personnel. The DRDO's budget in 2010 was approximately US$1.88 billion, or 6 per cent of overall Indian military expenditures (Cloughly 2010).

The DRDO is presently engaged in over 400 research projects, such as the development of missile systems, combat and trainer aircraft, radars, EW systems, and other types of armaments. Key R&D programmes include the *Tejas* LCA, the next-generation Medium Combat Aircraft (MCA), an advanced unmanned aerial vehicle, an airborne warning and control system for the IAF, and a 'mini nuclear submarine' for the Indian Navy (Raghuvanshi 2010d). In addition, the organization has primary responsibility for all indigenous missile development programmes, particularly the *BrahMos* antiship cruise missile, the *Shaurya* and *Sagarika* sea-based missiles, and the entire IGMDP. The DRDO also manages the ADA, a consortium of over 100 defence labs and academic and industrial institutions established in the mid-1980s to specifically oversee R&D of all aspects of the *Tejas* LCA, including airframe, propulsion, radar, and flight control systems (www.ada.gov.in).[2]

The DRDO has traditionally had very close ties with the DPSUs and OFs. In particular, the DRDO has acted as the Defence Ministry's principle investigator and evaluator of defence procurement programmes. Consequently, the organization frequently serves as the mediator between the military services and the local defence industry, particularly when it comes to determining requirements and coordinating weapons R&D and production.

To pay for all this, India has greatly increased military expenditures in recent years. Indian defence spending grew by two-thirds between 1998 and 2008, according to data provided by the Stockholm International Peace Research Institute (SIPRI) (SIPRI 2011). In 2011, the Indian defence budget stood at US$36.5 billion, a rise of 11.6 per cent over the previous year; this was equal to 1.83 per cent of the country's GDP. Procurement alone grew by 14 per cent in 2011 to US$15.4 billion; of this amount, US$6.6 billion went to the IAF, US$4.2 billion to the army, and US$2.9 billion to the navy. Approximately, US$1 billion was allocated for defence R&D (Raghuvanshi 2011).

Enduring and Endemic Problems in India's Defence Industry

Despite more than 50 years of effort, the history of India's defence industry is a nearly unbroken story of spectacular failures. For several decades, the Indian armaments production process has been a vicious cycle of ambitious programme overreach, followed by technological setbacks and lengthy delays, too often resulting in equipment that has typically been of substandard quality and suboptimal performance. In 2006, for example, a government audit of the OFs revealed that about 40 per cent of OF products had 'not achieved the desired level of quality despite the fact that most items were in production for decades'. This included T-72 tanks built under license, the INSAS assault rifle, and various ammunition (Raghuvanshi 2006). Overall, the technology gap between Indian and foreign weapons systems has widen over the past two decades as the country has tried, unsuccessfully in most cases, to move from self-reliance to self-sufficiency (Author interviews 2011; Baskaran 2004: 213, 216–18; Mohanty 2004: 28, 36–7; Pardesi and Matthews 2007: 432–4). At the same time, costs have skyrocketed; according to one source, the country's five most important weapons programmes—including the *Tejas* fighter, the *Arjun* tank, and the *Kaveri* engine—are at least two and a half times over their original budgets (Cloughly 2010).

For example, India's supposedly state-of-the art *Tejas* fighter jet is more than 12 years behind schedule, while R&D costs have nearly doubled. The *Tejas* LCA was intended to propel India's aerospace industry into the 21st century, advancing this sector in several key areas, including composites (carbon-fiber composites account for 45 per cent of the aircraft, by weight), a modern 'glass cockpit', a fly-by-wire (FBW) flight-control system, a multimode pulse-doppler radar, and an afterburning turbofan engine. Unfortunately, India has run into several development problems regarding the *Tejas*, including delays in finalizing the aircraft's FBW software, and, more significantly, failures to deliver both an effective indigenous radar *and* jet engine; in both cases, a foreign substitute had to be found (Aroor and Ranjan 2006a). In particular, the indigenous *Kaveri* engine has suffered so many setbacks (in particular, it has been deemed overweight and underpowered) that it was 'de-linked' from the *Tejas* programme in 2008, and for the foreseeable future, all *Tejas* aircraft will be outfitted with the US General Electric F404 turbofan.

Originally, the *Tejas* was to be initially deployed with the IAF around 2002, but the first 'proof-of-concept' model did not fly until 2001, and a production-model LCA did not achieve first flight until 2007; the aircraft finally achieved initial operating capability with the IAF in 2011. Up to 260 LCAs could be built, in both IAF and naval versions (for India's future aircraft carriers), but so far only 40 aircraft have been ordered. The *Tejas* went into production in 2010 and will be manufactured as a very low rate of around 10–12 aircraft a year for the next 20 years; at that rate, the aircraft could be obsolete before the last one is delivered.

For its part, the *Arjun* main battle tank only just entered service with the Indian Army (IA) in 2011, more than 30 years after the programme was initiated. The *Arjun* has had a history of technical problems, resulting in horrendous delays and cost overruns—according to one source, the tank is more than 16 years behind schedule and 20 times over its original cost estimates (Aroor and Ranjan 2006b; Behera 2010: 20–2). Its engine had a tendency to overheat, while its excessive weight and width made it too big for the IA's current tank transporters. The interior would become so hot that the tank's fire control system, thermal imager, and laser range-finder would be rendered useless; its rifled gun barrel prevents it from firing anti-tank rockets. In addition, government reports have pointed to problems with the tank's powerpacks, 'low accuracy and consistency', 'failure of hydropneumatic suspension', and 'chipping of gun barrels' (Government of India 2008). So far, the army has committed to buying only 248 *Arjuns*.

Even the country's much-vaunted IGMDP, initiated in 1983 as a comprehensive, intensive effort to make India self-sufficient in tactical missile systems, has so far produced few successes. Only two IGDMP projects—the *Prithvi* and *Agni* surface-to-surface ballistic missiles—have so far been deployed to the Indian armed forces. Even then, the *Prithvi* is a relatively short-range, liquid-fueled missile (maximum range–350 km.) of limited tactical use, while the *Agni* 'does not appear to have been produced in large enough numbers for induction into the services' (Cohen and Dasgupta 2010: 33). Moreover, some missiles under the IGDMP, including the *Trishul* SAM system and the *Astra* air-to-air missile, are still in development decades later and will likely never be anything more than 'technology demonstrators' (Joshi 2006; Aroor and Ranjan 2006c). For its part, the *Nag* ATGM is still undergoing test and validation trials after more than 20 years of development, and it was only accepted into the Indian Army (on a trial basis, with just 443 missiles being ordered) in 2011 (Shukla 2010a; Gordon 2009: 13–14). So far, only the *Akash* surface-to-air missile has gone into serial production and deployment.

The Indian defence industry even apparently has problems with programmes as simple and technologically straightforward as small arms. The INSAS, the Indian Army's standard assault rifle, costs nearly $400 apiece, or three times that of an imported AK-47 (Bedi 2005). Even so, the INSAS was found to have a number of defects, including poor performance in extremely cold and high-altitude situations; for these reasons it was removed from use in the Siachen glacier area. The Nepalese Army, which bought 100,000 INSAS rifles, claimed that the gun could only operate for about an hour or two before malfunctioning, resulting in heavy casualties in firefights with Maoist guerrillas (Raghuvanshi 2006).

Overall, endemic delays and setbacks in domestic weapons programmes have forced the Indian military to continually scrounge for foreign stopgaps to compensate for these shortfalls and to sustain force recapitalization. For example, due to ongoing delays in the *Tejas* programme, the IAF in the mid-2000s instituted the Medium Multi-Role Combat Aircraft (MMRCA) competition to buy 126 foreign fighter jets (with an option for up to 74 additional aircraft), at a cost of up to US$10 billion; in early 2012, New Delhi, after several years of deliberations, finally chose the French *Rafale* as its MMRCA finalist.[3] In addition, the IAF is currently acquiring up to 240 Russian Su-30MKIs, which are being licensed-produced by HAL. For its part, because of interruptions in the indigenous *Arjun* programme, the IA is buying several hundred Russian T-90 tanks, again locally built at Indian ordnance factories; the IA could acquire up to 1,400 T-90s, which would severely cut into purchases of the *Arjun* (Arthur 2009: 13–14). The IA is also buying 15,000 Russian-made *Konkurs*-M and 4,100 French *Milan*-2T antitank missiles, due to setbacks in the *Nag* programme; both will be licensed-assembled by Bharat Dynamics (Arthur 2009: 14). Finally, the IN has had to acquire Russian and Israeli SAMs for its ships because local missile systems are still unavailable.

If anything, Indian efforts to move from self-reliance to self-sufficiency in armaments production has taken a huge step backwards over the past 15 years. The Indian military is as dependent as ever on foreign systems and technologies. Around 60 per cent of the components for the *Arjun* tank are imported, for example, while the *Tejas* fighter utilizes US jet engine and either European or Israeli radar (Aroor and Ranjan 2006; Pubby 2010). Even India's highly touted *BrahMos* supersonic cruise missile (available in both antiship and land-attack variants) is heavily based on the Russian-designed P-800 *Yakhont* missile; India's particular contribution to this programme, other than money, is hard to identify (Author interview 2011; www.Globalsecurity.org).[4] Indeed, the most advanced armaments coming out of Indian factories are still predominantly licensed-produced versions of foreign weapons systems—Su-30MKI combat aircraft, T-90 tanks, the *Konkurs* and *Milan* ATGMs, *Scorpène* submarines, and so on. Additionally, most of the *Rafale* fighters acquired under the MMRCA programme will be locally built under license.[5]

Consequently, the Indian arms industry still functions mainly as an assembler, rather than an across-the-board innovator (Author interviews 2011). In 1995, New Delhi announced that within 10 years it would increase its 'local content' of weapons in the Indian armed forces from 30 per cent to 70 per cent. By 2005, however, foreign weapons systems (that is, both imports and licensed production) still comprised around 70 per cent of the Indian military's acquisitions (Singh 2000: 151; Bedi 2005). In 2010, the percentage of imported systems hovered around 70 per cent (Cloughly 2010; Anderson 2010: 68).

At the same time, India has become the second largest arms buyer in the world; according to the US Congressional Research Service, during the period 2002–9 New Delhi placed orders for US$32.4 billion worth of arms, just behind Saudi Arabia (US$39.9 billion) (Grimmett 2010: 46). In addition to the aforementioned systems that will be licensed-built in India, the country has made such off-the-shelf purchases as Phalcon airborne early-warning aircraft, Barak SAMs, and UAVs from Israel; C-130J and C-17 transport aircraft, P-8 maritime patrol aircraft, and artillery-locating radar from the United States; and lightweight howitzers from the United Kingdom (Bedi 2011).[6]

The problems with India's defence industry are structural, financial, and, most of all, cultural. A cabal of monopolistic state-owned enterprises has traditionally dominated the arms-production process. In turn, these DPSUs and OFs are larded with bloated workforces and excess productive capacity; estimates are that much of the defence industry operates at barely 50 per cent of capacity (Bedi 2005: 25–6; Singh 2000: 155). At the same time, the defence industry has been starved of capital for modernization, for keeping pace with the global state-of-the-art in arms production. India's defence budget constituted less than 2 per cent of the country's GDP in 2011 (Bedi 2011). Funding for defense R&D amounted to barely US$1 billion in 2011—barely three per cent of total military expenditures; in contrast, the United States spent US$78 billion on defense R&D in FY2010, while's China's military R&D budget is estimated to be around US$5 billion to US$6 billion. One result has been that the Indian defence sector has been unable to train enough highly qualified technicians, engineers, and scientists (Pardesi and Matthews 2007: 424). Finally, there has also traditionally been a lack of coordination between the defence sector and the armed forces when it comes to requirements, planning, and production (Pardesi and Matthews 2007: 432–4; Singh 2000: 148–9).

Despite these obvious deficiencies, there was for a long time little incentive from within the arms industry to reform and restructure itself. A 'statist' mindset generally permeated the Indian military-industrial complex, and the government, DPSUs, and OFs operated in a cozy, sealed environment. Under the guise of 'self-reliance', state-run defence firms were pretty much guaranteed production work; little stress was put on meeting project milestones or ensuring quality or operational effectiveness. Moreover, the private sector was not permitted to bid on major weapons contracts. For their part, the Indian armed forces were essentially forced to accept indigenous military equipment, whatever their preferences (Author interviews 2011). Consequently, as recently as 2005, one Indian defence ministry official was quoted as stating—'the DPSUs have no need to be competitive as they face no competition and have a captive market in the military' (Bedi 2005: 28).

At the same time, defence industry employees were organized within a powerful union, and altogether these workers constituted an influential 'vote bank'. This, in turn, made it difficult to shed excess labour or engage in other kinds of structural reforms, such as privatization or plant closures. Even where some downsizing was achieved—the OFs, for example, cut their workforce from 150,000 in 1989 to 105,000 in 2010—this was accomplished mainly by instituting a hiring freeze, resulting in the loss of new talent; moreover, according to Rahul Bedi, personnel reductions in many OFs were 'lopsided', resulting in labour surpluses in those factories 'where production lines face closure or are winding down' (Bedi 2005: 26).

Much of the blame for the failure of the Indian military-industrial complex to perform adequately has been laid directly upon the DRDO. The DRDO has frequently been criticized for its poor performance in overseeing the country's overall weapons development process (Bedi 2005: 27, 2007, 2010; Joshi 2006). In particular, the institution has been accused of arrogance, self-promotion, and weak leadership, and with a stronger emphasis on the *acquisition* of technology and know-how than on its actual *application*. Cohen and Dasgupta, in their 2010 book on Indian military modernization, put it bluntly—

> The reasons for DRDO's failures are multifaceted. One review concluded that poor planning, over-optimistic timelines, and a lack of coordination with the armed forces led to cost and time overruns of major defense projects. However, the most important reason is the agency's lack of political leadership. DRDO officials engaged in exaggerated and wildly over-optimistic statements of their own capabilities, and civilian politicians with little knowledge about strategic or military affairs, alone the intricacies of military technology and hardware, allowed DRDO a free hand for decades (Cohen and Dasgupta 2010: 33).

Insisting that maintaining an indigenous defense R&D and industrial base is a strategic technological and economic imperative, the DRDO historically took a reflexive approach that overwhelmingly and relentlessly favoured indigenous solutions over foreign options. Particularly during the 1980s and 1990s, when India began its attempts to move from licensed production-based 'self-reliance' to more autarkic 'self-sufficiency', the DRDO

> 'made it a practice to claim that it could provide services in, and make any product related to, aeronautics, armaments, electronics, combat vehicles, engineering systems, instrumentation, missiles, advanced computing and simulation, special materials, naval systems, life sciences, training and information systems...' (Joshi 2006).

Consequently, the organization has had the persistent tendency to overestimate the technological abilities of the local defence sector while also low-balling weapons costs and development timelines—

'The organization has adopted a classic foot-in-the-door strategy: winning initial support by promising products on the cheap but later citing sunk costs to demand more money' (Cohen and Dasgupta 2010: 33).

At the same time, the DRDO has long had 'the power to kill any procurement proposal from the armed forces', and could furthermore 'set the hardware-modernization agenda through its power to veto or delay acquisition from overseas in favour of indigenous research and development' (Cohen and Dasgupta 2010: 33).

The challenges to the Indian defence industry will likely only increase over the next several years, especially as the country embarks on a massive recapitalization of its armed forces. Estimates are that the military will, over the next two decades, need to buy up to 450 combat aircraft, 100 transport aircraft, 200 helicopters, 1,500 tanks, 500 combat vehicles, 1,500 artillery pieces, and 140 naval ships, including up to 20 submarines and two to three aircraft carriers (Raghuvanshi 2007; Bedi 2005: 28; Author interviews 2011). It is arguable whether the Indian military-industrial complex is up to the task of supplying state-of-the-art systems to the nation's armed forces within this timeframe.

Reforming the Indian Defence Industry, 2001–11

To be fair, the Indian government has long been aware of the deficiencies affecting the country's defence industrial base, and for roughly a decade it has pursued a number of initiatives intended to reform and revitalize the defence sector. These reforms generally fall under one of several categories—(1) opening up defence contracting to private sector; (2) permitting foreign firms to invest in India's defence industry; (3) encouraging more joint R&D and co-production arrangements with foreign firms; (4) formalizing offsets and leveraging them for technology acquisition; and (5) encouraging arms exports.

In order to shake the state-owned defence sector out of its complacency, the Indian government has increasingly invited the commercial sector to compete in defence bidding and production. In 2001, New Delhi allowed private sector participation in defence contracting up to 100 per cent of the value of the programme (Bedi 2007). As a result, local commercial firms have begun to win military contracts. Two local firms, Larsen and Toubro (L&T) and Tata, were recently awarded a joint contract to develop components for a new multiple rocket launcher. L&T was also selected to build hulls for India's new nuclear-powered *Arihant*-class submarine (formerly the Advanced Technology Vessel, or ATV), while Tata will produce control system for this submarine (Joseph 2008). In addition, L&T is investing heavily in modernizing its shipyards in Hazira, on India's east coast, in an effort to win away from Mazagon Dock a potentially lucrative follow-on contract to build up to six *Scorpène*-class submarines for the IN (Grevatt 2011).

For its part, Tata is seeking a tie-up with AgustaWestland of Italy to produce helicopters. Private companies may also bid to build a new armoured fighting vehicle for the Indian Army (Raghuvanshi 2010c). Altogether, the country's private sector did about US$800 million worth of defence work in 2010, compared to US$4.5 billion earned by the DPSUs and OFs (Raghuvanshi 2011).

In addition, the Indian military hopes to leverage the capabilities of local industry when it comes to commercial off-the-shelf (COTS) solutions, especially when it comes to information technologies (IT). The expectation is that COTS-based solutions would be quicker, more cost-effective, and more easily upgradeable, particularly in such areas as communications, command and control system, situational awareness, and network management (Author interviews 2011).

In order to promote increased commercial participation in defence bidding, the government proposed an initiative in 2007 to designate several private sector companies as 'Champions of Industry' (RURs) entitled to the same benefits as DPSUs. RURs would be able to design, develop, and manufacture military equipment, as well as produce defence systems developed by the DRDO. Additionally, they would be eligible for duty-free import of defence research-related equipment, to enter into technology-transfer and licensed-production arrangements with foreign firms, and receive government military R&D funding. Roughly a dozen local firms applied for RUR status (Anderson 2010: 69; Bedi 2007). To further encourage private-sector participation in armaments production, the Indian defence ministry, around this same time, proposed setting aside one billion rupees (US$2.2 million) to fund military R&D projects by commercial firms (Bedi 2007).

At the same time that the Indian commercial sector was permitted to compete for military contracts, the government also allowed foreign firms to invest in local defence enterprises, up to 26 per cent of value. The United Kingdom's BAE Systems, for example, has linked up with Mahindra & Mahindra Ltd, a private Indian conglomerate (one of its divisions builds automobiles and utility off-road vehicles), to develop land-defence systems in India. The European Aeronautic Defence and Space Company (EADS) has proposed a defence joint venture with L&T, while Elta of Israel has invested 2.5 billion rupees (US$56 million) in L&T and in Astra Microwave, to develop and build radar and other defence electronics systems (Anderson 2010: 69–70).

Joint ventures between foreign firms and the state-run defence industrial sector have also greatly expanded in recent years. The *BrahMos* cruise missile, for example, is the product of a joint venture between the DRDO and the Russian Federation's NPO Mashinostroyenia. In addition, in 2006, Russia's Irkut Corporation entered into a U$700 million joint venture with HAL to design and build a 60-ton multirole transport aircraft (MRTA) (Bedi 2007). Most important of all, perhaps, Moscow and New Delhi recently agreed to codevelop an FGFA based on the Russian PAK FA programme, which in turn is based on the Sukhoi T-50 prototype. Under the terms of this joint venture, HAL will work with Sukhoi to develop a two-seater version of the T-50, in exchange for a 25 per cent work share in the aircraft's design and development, including the mission computer, navigation systems, cockpit displays, and countermeasure systems. The project will also entail considerable Russian technology transfers to India. Altogether, New Delhi could invest up to around US$30 billion to US$35 billion into the FGFA, including R&D and the procurement of 250 aircraft. Russia and India would also set up a joint marketing company to export this fighter (Author interviews 2011; Shukla 2010b and 2010c).

Other countries besides Russia are entering into joint ventures with Indian arms producers. Israel Aerospace Industries (IAI) is cooperating with the DRDO to develop a longer-range version of the Israeli *Barak* air-defence missile. Boeing and Tata have set up a joint venture to manufacture defence systems. The French jet engine manufacturer SNECMA is collaborating with HAL on improving the *Kaveri* turbofan engine, and the European missile consortium MBDA is working with the DRDO and BDL to develop a new short-range SAM (Author interviews

2011; Tran 2009). The United Kingdom's Cobham plc is cooperating with HAL on air-to-air refueling probes for the IAF's Su-30MKI fighters. Finally, France, as the winner of the MMRCA contest, will have to provide considerable technology transfers to enable India to produce the *Rafale* in-country.

In an effort to formalize technology transfer obligations, the Indian government has over the past decade inaugurated and refined an official defence offsets policy.[7] In the 2000s, the New Delhi's Defence Procurement Procedures (DPP) guidelines outlined three broad acquisition strategies for the Indian armed forces—'Buy', 'Buy and Make', and 'Make'. 'Make' refers to military products that would be more or less wholly designed, developed, and manufactured within India; its basic objective is to ensure the maintenance and expansion of indigenous R&D, design, and production capabilities on the part of the local defence sector, both state-owned and private (Behera 2010: 36). The 'Buy' category entails products that are intended to be imported; under the terms of the 2006 DPP, any such arms import greater than 3 billion rupees (approximately US$67 million) required a minimum 30 per cent direct offset, either in the form of counter-purchases of Indian defence equipment or foreign direct investment (FDI) in the Indian defence industry (such as codevelopment or co-production arrangements, or joint international marketing efforts). The 'Buy and Make' category applies mainly to major military programmes, such as the MMRCA's *Rafale*, that entail licensed production inside India and which, therefore, demand considerable technology transfers and industrial participation. In such cases, a 50 per cent offset is usually mandated. To put it another way, the MMRCA programme, which could be worth as much as US$10 billion, could generate up to US$5 billion in offsets.

India's offset policy reportedly generated around Rupees 75 billion (US$1.68 billion) worth of offset work for the period 2006–09 (Anderson 2010: 69). Ultimately, the Indian government expects to sign US$10 billion worth of offset agreements over the course of the 11th Defence Plan (2007–12) (Behera 2010: 36).

Finally, India has a nascent effort underway to break into the global arms export business. Indian defence industries are increasingly present at major trade shows (such as Farnborough or the Singapore Air Show), in an effort to sell their wares overseas. In particular, India has pitched the *BrahMos* missile, which is marketed by a Russo-Indian joint venture. So far, however, Indian arms exports have been minimal, around US$100 million annually (Anderson 2010: 68).

In general, therefore, the Indian government is seeking to use private firms to put pressure on the state-owned defence sector to reform itself. By permitting commercial businesses to bid on defence contracts and to create joint ventures with foreign defence companies, it is hoped that the competition will force the DPSUs and OFs to become more market-oriented and cost-effective, and also more responsive to customer requirements (that is, the Indian military). In addition, a formalized offsets strategy is intended to inject critical technologies into the Indian military-industrial complex where they are most needed, and in a timely fashion (Author interviews 2011).

Perhaps it is too soon to tell if these initiatives will have their desired impact, but so far, however, these efforts have shown few tangible results. First of all, it has been difficult, for example, to encourage India's private sector to invest in a line of work that requires large, risky investments in R&D and infrastructure, in exchange for low returns. This effort is made all the more harder by the persistence of a 'statist mindset' on the part of the Indian Ministry of Defence—and especially the DRDO—that still tends to default to giving large military contracts (and defence offsets) to the DPSUs and OFs. This was most recently reflected in the defence ministry's 2010 awarding of a noncompetitive contract worth US$1 billion to BEL for the Indian Army's battle management systems (BMS) (Raghuvanshi 2010). Moreover, the RUR initiative was eventually abandoned, in part due to stiff resistance from trade unions representing workers in the DPSUs and OFs (Anderson 2010: 69; Grevatt 2007).

Additionally, while the government has permitted foreign firms to invest in Indian defence companies (up to 26 per cent of shares), so far there have been few takers. Overseas investors have no independent means by which to valuate these companies' stock, and they are not permitted much say in how these companies should be run. Additionally, the Indian government has frequently rejected foreign shareholding or joint venture efforts, and consequently only four such foreign-Indian defence joint ventures have been set up since 2001 (Author interviews 2011). According to one source, in 2009, such FDI amounted to less than US$142,000 (Anderson 2010: 69). At the same time, any privatization of the country's state-owned defence sector, that is, the DPSUs or OFs, is so unlikely as to be almost inconceivable.

Second, it is still uncertain how much of an impact these new offsets and technology transfers policies may have when it comes to injecting much-needed cutting-edge technologies into the Indian military-industrial complex. For example, even if India *does* succeed in accruing US$10 billion worth of new offsets, it may turn out to be more work than the local industry can handle, at least in the short run (Author interviews 2011; Raghuvanshi 2010b). At the same time, India's arms producers could be hard-pressed to exploit the foreign technologies they are acquiring, if they are unable to also upgrade their capacities for technology absorption, innovation, and production. This could, in particular, undercut their efforts to make substantive contributions to joint venture programmes, such as the FGFA (Bedi 2010).

Finally, rapidly increasing military expenditures have actually been counter-productive to reforming the state-run defence sector. India's defence budget has grown 60 per cent in just the past decade, and analysts expect New Delhi to spend at least US$200 billion on new weaponry over the next 15 years. This is enough to buy nearly every item on the military's 'wish-list', as well as providing a huge windfall of orders that should keep the DPSUs and OFs operating at full capacity for several decades. In light of such an expectation of 'fat years' out to the horizon, it will be doubly difficult to encourage state-owned industries to think about being more efficient and market-oriented, or to get the Indian military to exert such pressure on the defence sector (Author interviews 2011).

***

It is, of course, easy to be dismissive of Indian's defence industry—both of its current capacities for advanced armaments production, and of its likelihood of engaging in real, effective reform. In general, India's track record in both of these areas has not been encouraging, and overall the history of India's military-industrial complex has been particularly disheartening. After China, India possesses the largest and most ambitious defence industrial base in the Asia-Pacific, if not the entire developing world, and yet the performance of its defence industry over the past 50 years has been disappointing in the very least. Billions of dollars have been spent on domestic weapons programmes that have never performed up to their requirements or met their objectives when it came to costs and milestones. And while the rest of the world has marveled at India's globally competitive information technologies sector, the country's defence industry has remained, for the most part, an overwhelmingly statist enterprise undauntedly committed to autarkic armaments production. The Indian military-industrial complex was a huge white elephant of highly protected, monopolistic state-owned corporations, headed up by a bloated DRDO, which pressed for indigenous solutions with little heed paid to capabilities or timeliness. It is little wonder, therefore, that Cohen and Dasgupta would flatly state that the Indian military-industrial complex 'has not delivered a single major weapon system to the armed forces in five decades of existence' (Cohen and Dasgupta 2010: 32). And while such an assertion may strike one as unfair and exaggerated, the sad fact is that this claim was right more times than it was wrong.

All that said, change may be in the offing. Undoubtedly, restructuring and reforming the Indian defence industry will be slow and incremental. At the same time, recent reform efforts have already produced some tangible results. India's private sector has broken finally into the once-restricted arms-producing business, and by 2010, local commercial firms were earning about US$800 million annually from defence contracting (Raghuvanshi 2011). What's more, private-sector bidding for local defence contracts is likely only to grow, as these companies increase their investments in capabilities and facilities for armaments production, such as shipbuilding, military vehicles, and defence-related electronics. In addition, opening up the military contracting process to foreign firms, through joint ventures and offset arrangements, is also fundamentally altering the defence-industrial landscape of India.

Defence industrial reforms also have some powerful allies in the government and the military. In particular, both are keen to use the local private sector and foreign firm involvement to pressure the DRDO, DPSUs, and OFs to change their business-as-usual practices. In this regard, they are strongly supported by such powerful allies as the Confederation of Indian Industries (CII), which has long pressed for the liberalization and opening up of the country's defence business.

Nevertheless, reforming India's military-industrial complex remains an uphill battle. The state-owned defence sector is still very powerful, and the DPSUs and OFs will likely continue to strongly oppose any initiatives to remove or reduce their role as the primary producers of the nation's armaments, particularly when it comes to such big-ticket items as combat aircraft, warships, missile systems, and tanks and other armoured vehicles.

Moreover, the DRDO still wields considerable influence within the national armaments planning process, and is thus a strong advocate for the *status quo*. In particular, it still prefers, when it can, to pursue indigenous development programmes over licensed production or foreign joint ventures.

Ultimately, it is too soon to tell if these recent reform efforts will take root and flower. One thing is for certain, however—so long as India continues to shield and coddle its traditional military-industrial complex in the name of self-sufficiency and strategic imperative, it will never be able to remake the local defence industry into something capable of supplying the Indian armed forces with the equipment it requires. That, in turn, will mean that Indian ambitions of becoming a great power will always be circumscribed.

Notes

1. See also Chapter 5, 'India's Defence Acquisition and Offset Strategy', by Ron Matthews and Alma Lozano in this volume.

2. Available at http://www.tejas.gov.in/technology.html (accessed 12 August 2013).

3. Six aircraft originally competed for the MMRCA—the US F-16 and F/A-18, the Russian MiG-35, the Swedish *Gripen*, the French *Rafale*, and the Eurofighter *Typhoon*. In May 2011, the IAF shortlisted the *Rafale* and *Typhoon*; in late 2012, the *Rafale* was chosen to be the MMRCA finalist.

4. See www.Globalsecurity.org, 'PJ- 10 BrahMos'. Available at http://www.globalsecurity.org/military/world/india/brahmos.htm (accessed 12 August 2013).

5. The IAF will acquire the first 18 MMRCA aircraft directly from the foreign manufacturer; all subsequent aircraft will be licensed-produced in India.

6. Stockholm International Peace Research Institute (SIPRI), SIPRI Arms Transfers Database, available at http://www.sipri.org/databases/armstransfers/armstransfers (accessed 12 August 2013).

7. See the chapter in this same volume by Matthews and Lozano, 'India's Defence Acquisition and Offsets Policy', for a fuller explanation of India's new defence offsets policies.

References

Anderson, Guy. 2010. 'India's Defense Industry', *RUSI Defense Systems*, p. 68.

Aroor, Shiv and Amitav Ranjan. 2006a. '23 Yrs and First Fighter Aircraft Hasn't Taken Off', *Indian Express*, 14 November.

Aroor, Shiv and Amitav Ranjan. 2006b. 'Arjun, Main Battle Tanked', *Indian Express*, 14 November.

―――. 2006c.'Armed Forces Wait as Showpiece Missiles are Unguided, Way off Mark', *Indian Express*, 13 November.

Arthur, Gordon. 2009.'Indian Armed Force Programs: Large Budget Increases', *Defense Review Asia*, 3(2): 13–14.

Baskaran, Angathevar. (2004). 'The Role of Offsets in Indian Defense Procurement Policy', in J. Brauer and J.P. Dunne (eds), *Arms Trade and Economic Development: Theory, Policy, and Cases in Arms Trade Offsets*, pp. 211–13, 221–6. London: Routledge.

Bedi, Rahul. 2005.'Two-Way Stretch', *Jane's Defense Weekly*, 42 (5): 25–9.

―――. 2007a. 'India Launches "Thorough" Audit of DRDO's Effectiveness', *Jane's Defense Weekly*.

―――. 2007b.'India Plans Private Sector Defense R&D Project Funding', *Jane's Defense Weekly*.

―――. 2007c.'Eyeing the Prize', *Jane's Defense Weekly*.

―――. 2010.'Making Decisions', *Jane's Defense Weekly*.

―――. 2011. 'India Announces 12% Defense Budget Increase', *Jane's Defense Weekly*.

Behera, Laxman Kumar. 2009.'Background Paper on India's Defense Industry: An Overview', prepared for the National Seminar on the Defence Industry, New Delhi, 23–24 January, p. 4.

―――. 2010a.'The Saga of MBT-Arjun', *Defense Review Asia*, 4(4): 20–2.

―――. 2010b. 'India's Growing Defense Industry Base', Defense Review Asia, 4(7): 34.

Bitzinger, Richard A. 2003. *Towards a Brave New Arms Industry?* Adelphi Paper No. 356, International Institute for Strategic Studies. Oxford: Oxford University Press.

Cloughly, Brian. 2010.'Analysis: DRDO Fails to Fix India's Procurement Woes', *Jane's Defense Weekly*.

Cohen, Stephen P. and Sunil Dasgupta. 2010. *Arming without Aiming: India's Military Modernization*. Washington, DC: Brookings Institution.

Defense News. 2011.'Interview with M. Mangapati Pallam Raju, Minister of State for Defence, India'.

Government of India. 2008.'Arjun Battle Tank', press release, 5 May. Available at http://pib.nic.in/newsite/erelease.aspx?relid=38445 (12 August 2013).

Grevatt, Jon. 2007. 'India Delays Defense Reforms Again in Face of Multiple Pressures', *Jane's Defense Weekly*, 21 December.

―――. 2011. 'L&T Chief Attacks Indian Government Support for "Sick" Public-Sector Companies', *Jane's Defense Industry*, March 9.

Grimmett, Richard F. 2010. *Conventional Arms Transfers to Developing Nations, 2002–2009.* Washington, DC: Congressional Research Service.

Joseph, Josy. 2008. 'Private Sector Played a Major Role in Arihant', *Daily News & Analysis*, 27 July. Available at http://www.dnaindia.com/india/report_private-sector-played-a-major-role-in-arihant_1277435 (accessed 12 August 2013).

Joshi, Manoj. 2006. 'If Wishes Were Horses', *Hindustan Times*, 18 October.

Mohanty, Deba R. 2004. *Changing Times? India's Defense Industry in the 21st Century.* Bonn: Bonn International Center for Conversion.

———. 2009. *Arming the Indian Arsenal.* New Delhi: Rupa Publications.

Pardesi, Manjeet S. and Ron Matthews. 2007. 'India's Tortuous Road to Defense-Industrial Self-Reliance', *Defense & Security Analysis*, 23 (4): 419–38.

Pubby, Manu. 2010. 'Israel, EU in Contention to Co-develop Radars for *Tejas*', *Indian Express*, 14 July.

Raghuvanshi, Vivek. 2006. 'Report: Indian Products Defective', *Defense News*.

———. 2007. 'India May Increase Defense Spending as Percent of GDP', *Defense News*.

———. 2010a. 'Exec: Award Shows India Still Favors State Firms', *Defense News*.

———. 2010b. 'India Aircraft Tech Proposal May Be Hard to Enforce, Ministry Says', *Defense News*.

———. 2010c. 'Private Firms to Bid for Indian Vehicle Project', *Defense News*.

———. 2010d. 'Indian Research Agency Agrees to Tech Transfers', *Defense News*.

———. 2011a. 'Budget Hike in India', *Defense News*.

———. 2011b. 'Tata Seeks "Level Playing Field" in India', *Defense News*.

Shukla, Ajai. 2010a. 'Army Opts for Nag Missile as it Enters Final Trials', *Business Standard*, 8 March.

———. 2010b. 'India, Russia close to PACT on next generation fighter', *Business Standard*, 5 January; Available at http://www.business-standard.com/india/news/india-russia-close-to-pactnext-generation-fighter/381718 (accessed 12 August 2013).

———. 2010c. 'India to develop 25% of fifth generation fighter', *Business Standard*, 6 January; Available at http://www.business-standard.com/india/news/india-to-develop-25fifth-generation-fighter/381786 (accessed 12 August 2013).

Singh, Ajay. 2000. 'Quest for Self-Reliance', in Jasit Singh (ed.), *India's Defense Spending*, 125–56. New Delhi: Knowledge World.

Stockholm International Peace Research Institute. 2011. *SIPRI Military Expenditure Database.* Available at http://milexdata.sipri.org (accessed 12 August 2013).

Stockholm International Peace Research Institute (SIPRI). *SIPRI Arms Transfers Database*. Available at http://www.sipri.org/databases/armstransfers/armstransfers (accessed 12 August 2013).

Tran, Pierre. 2009. 'MBDA Looks to India for New Air Defense Missile', *Defense News*.

www.Globalsecurity.org, 'PJ-10 BrahMos'. Available at http://www.globalsecurity.org/military/world/india/brahmos.htm (accessed 12 August 2013).

5 India's Defence Acquisition and Offset Strategy

RON MATTHEWS AND ALMA LOZANO

T HE PURPOSE OF THIS CHAPTER is to explore the relevance and reality of defence offset in India's expanding defence industrial environment. Offset is a widely employed mechanism whereby the purchaser of military equipment requires foreign suppliers to engage in commercial and industrial transactions in the importing economy as a condition to grant a contract. These transactions are aimed at developing and enhancing the economic, technological, and industrial capabilities of the recipient country. Offset is an atypical market condition, as it places leverage in the hands of purchasing countries by going beyond conventional economic analysis of 'supply and demand', with the objective of creating opportunities to extract 'offsetting' concessionary benefits, normally technology transfer. This phenomenon derives from a market 'imperfection' known as a buyers' market that has characterized the global defence economy since the end of the Cold War. The emergence of a market where a limited number of major arms buyers hold dominance was caused by both a collapse in arms demand and an expansion in the global supply base; the latter due to increasing numbers of developing countries promoting local defence industrial capacity. India, in particular, has made huge efforts to build-up its defence industry, often via *ad hoc*, informal, case-by-case license production arrangements with overseas defence contractors. For two reasons, such deals will intensify—first, because offset is now mandatory, following India's implementation of the 2005 offset policy, and, second, because the number of offset agreements will rise, driven by the dramatic increase in India's defence acquisition budget.

New Delhi's appetite for offset is tied to rising defence expenditure, and especially India's overseas acquisition budget. Defence spending is rising not so much because of increased regional tensions but simply because abundant financial resources have become available from the country's impressively high rates of economic growth. India's capacity and preparedness to fund unprecedented levels of defence spending has thus positioned the subcontinent as Asia's most arms-attractive market, catapulting it into the vortex of the offset phenomenon.

India's 2010–11 defence budget was US$32 billion, of which US$13 billion was earmarked for weapons acquisition and related services. This acquisition budget was Asia's third biggest, behind China and Japan (Deloitte and Confederation of Indian Industry 2010: 5). Moreover, it is estimated that across the present five-year plan (2007–12) India will spend US$100 billion on defence acquisition and a further US$120 billion in the next period (2012–17) (Deloitte and Confederation of Indian Industry 2010: 5). The scale of aerospace acquisition is mesmerizing. For instance, India plans to procure around 250 FGFA through collaboration between Russia's Sukhoi Corporation and HAL at a cost of US$30 billion (*Outlook India* 2010).[1] This is additional to the 280 Sukhoi 30-MKI fighters that India has already committed to purchase (*Deccan Chronicle* 2011). Under a separate deal, India is preparing to spend at least US$10 billion acquiring 126 MMRCA. The French company, Dassault, has been down-selected as the winning bidder, and the attractiveness of its offset (technology transfer) arrangements almost certainly represented a critical discerning factor working in its favour.[2] Reportedly, the order is expected to increase to 260 aircraft, bringing the cost of the purchase to US$25 billion (*Deccan Chronicle* 2011). In parallel, India is buying 120 of the locally developed *Tejas* (LCA) and undisclosed numbers of another locally developed FGFA called AMCA. Both these aircraft are labelled as 'indigenous', but in reality they will likely require acquisition of major subsystems from foreign OEMs (Original Equipment Manufacturers). Given that India's offset policy mandates substantial offset-related investment and technology transfer, the coming years will see tens of billions of USD offset-induced investment flowing into India's economy. Clearly, then, offset is important to India, not least because policymakers view technology transfer as a primary vehicle for enhancing local defence industrial capability. Yet, the question is whether offset will in reality act as the catalyst for sustainable indigenous defence industrialization.

This is not an easy question to answer, but the fact is that India, as a major defence economy, became intoxicated with the offset phenomenon during the early 2000s, with large segments of the defence community persuaded by the apparent ease of policy success. The 2005 launch of India's first official offset policy and the subsequent changes implemented in the 2006 Defence Procurement Procedures (DPP) were the easy part, but the difficult challenges still remain to be tackled, especially the task of promoting defence indigenization through offsetting investment.[3] Although the challenges are obvious, they have not been totally recognized. New Delhi bureaucrats have been blinded by the lure of offset and its putative ability to leverage technology transfer. Policymaker denial has meant that the ambivalence of defence contractors to release technology has not been factored into the offset development calculus. The result has been uncritical adherence to the offset marketing mantra that extolls the virtues of 'win-win' vendor-recipient relations, without paying heed to the challenges of securing long-term sustainable 'next-generation' production.

Thus, the working hypothesis underpinning this chapter's analysis is that India's offset policy will likely fail to realize the long-term benefits anticipated from its offset policy. This will be the case unless the conditions for ensuring viable and sustainable development are secured, particularly given the relative technological immaturity of India's defence economy. The hypothesis is examined by exploring the evolving offset phenomenon set against India's unique defence industrial conditions. The chapter seeks to evaluate offset performance during the early decades of India's post-independence defence industrial development. This was a period characterized by both the lack of a formal offset policy and the government's failure to secure indigenous defence industrial capability. As India's offset policy is intended to address this defence industrial malaise, it is essential that its major features are highlighted to establish the relevance and workability of the policy. Based on a review of contemporary comparative 'best' (offset) practices, several weaknesses of India's offset policy are identified. These are weighed against the huge market leverage that India's burgeoning defence market can bring to ensure progress towards defence industrial self-reliance. The final concluding section draws together the interconnected discussion threads, offering policy-oriented conclusions on the Indian offset experience. This will then, hopefully, form the basis for further debate, particularly from Indian policymakers and analysts wishing to make their own contribution to this important debate.

Understanding the Offset Phenomenon

Judging by over 50 major countries having published official offset policies, it has become nigh impossible for global defence contractors to export weapon systems without being hit by offset obligations. The ubiquitous nature of offset suggests that academics, analysts, consultants, journalists, and, most importantly, policymakers are aware of the complexities of the subject, but this is often not the case. The sometimes unpalatable truth is that offset is akin to a 'black art', with most stakeholders blissfully unaware of the deeper nuances of the subject-area. Thus, a jaundiced stereotype of offset has developed, whereby it is viewed as the 'holy grail' for achieving dramatic growth in indigenous defence industrialization. In practice, this translates into an aim for a more robust indigenous technological capability, encompassing—higher utilization of existing defence-industrial capacity as well as the creation of new capacity; higher employment, particularly in higher skill fields; acceleration of local indigenous capability through growth of domestic R&D expertise; the expansion of a high value subcontracting base; and the enhancement of defence export potential.

Of course, this begs the question as to why offset and opacity go hand-in-hand. A major reason is that offset is a phenomenon that originally emerged and developed in the defence rather than the commercial environment, and the former always brings with it a degree of sensitivity due to its impact on national security. Moreover, historically, a majority of offset programmes are based around reciprocal defence-related investments, and, therefore, there is a sense amongst both governments and corporations that production relocation and/or technology transfer from an offshore vendor to the purchasing country is also secret. This view is reinforced by the fact that generally no statistics, national or international, exist on the value and volume of offset trade, save for the annual US Department of Commerce report submitted to the Congress. The absence of detailed empirical data on offset performance is also because offset is integral to the marketing strategies of major defence contractors. Their reticence to release data on offset strategy and performance is a natural corporate response to safeguarding a principal source of competitive advantage in creating defence sales opportunities. In this sense, offset is a significant non-price variable, with the quality of the offset package sometimes being more important than that of the primary defence contract.

A final consideration accounting for the mystique of offset is that it forms part of a broader counter-trade typology, thus further distancing defence trade from the classical liberal trade theories of Smith and Ricardo. Counter-trade expands the notion of reciprocal trading mechanisms to include counter-purchase and barter, reflecting other market transactions based on a mutual exchange of wants. The barter system, in particular, operates where cash is not the medium of exchange, and, instead, oil, diamonds, or 'rare earth' minerals are used as the means of payment for armaments. This was the practice employed by Hitler, in the 1930s, exchanging German manufactured goods for raw materials from the Balkans; by the Japanese, also in the 1930s, trading industrial products for oil from states belonging to Japan's Greater East Asian co-prosperity sphere; and by Saddam Hussein, in the 1980s, exchanging Iraqi oil for Soviet weaponry (Griffin and Rouse 1986: 181). This form of 'guns for butter' trade is explained by the fact that any form of counter-trade, including offset, is predicated on a 'buyers' market structure, skewed in favour of the purchasing country.

Searching for Rainbow's End: A 'Second-Best' Offset Policy?

Under strict classical economic reasoning, offset represents a marketing imperfection. This is because it undermines efficient resource allocation, acting to distort trade flows. Yet, as offset has become the norm in the international arms market; it makes sense for the pragmatist to replace the purist. This 'second-best' approach accepts that offset is a fact of economic life, and thus works to devise an optimal best-practice model that maximizes resource efficiency to create dynamic comparative advantages in high technology (defence) industrial development.[4] The goal of offset, then, is clear—to build competitive and hence sustainable economic, industrial, and technological capacity/capability in the recipient country. However, whilst the goal is clear, the means for achieving it are not. At the broadest level, the question arises as to whether the purchasing government should work in 'partnership' with the offshore vendors in the achievement of jointly agreed targets or should relations, instead, be based on clearly defined contractual boundaries? The distinction matters, because partnership connotes flexibility by the recipient authority to accept delays in the implementation of offset programmes, when warranted. For instance, Saudi Arabia responded supportively when BAE Systems in the 1990s faced difficulties in reaching the agreed GBP 1 billion Al Yamamah offset target.[5] However, such flexibility is not the norm, with national offset authorities seeking to impose penalties on unfulfilled obligations or underperformance. Here, offset agreements are legally binding contracts, and the foreign prime contractor will be obliged to comply with bureaucratic and prescriptive policies. Should the contractor fail to religiously comply with the agreed contractual requirements, then it must face the consequences, ranging from fines to blacklisting against future contracts.

Policymakers must also make judgments as to whether a country's offset strategy should be direct or indirect; that is, whether the policy goal is aimed at compensating the domestic defence industrial base for the acquisition of foreign defence equipment or whether defence offset is considered a vehicle for broader commercial development. The latter objective appears to be tailor-made for countries possessing 'small' defence economies. Direct offsets in such cases are likely to be inappropriate, but there is only limited empirical evidence available providing guidance to decision-makers on the viability of local defence production. Small acquisition volumes mean that offset-induced local production will suffer high unit costs, but determining what constitutes a short production run is, of course, a matter of judgment.

The lack of scale for a particular defence acquisition programme may not preclude defence offset being funneled into other areas of the local defence economy; that is, indirect offset into projects unrelated to the primary defence contract. An interesting case, here, is Singapore. The island-state is a small country with limited arms volume requirements. It possesses, however, a 'deep' defence economic base, crystallized in the high technology divisions of the ST Engineering group. Singapore often eschews local production of completed weapon systems, but not always. The country will procure submarines and AH-64D helicopters off-the-shelf, and offset programmes will be requested on a case-by-case basis to maximize industrial and technological benefits, as appropriate. Singapore's approach to offset is thus novel, seeking to identify licensing and technical transfer opportunities in a flexible way. The Singapore 'model' is held to be effective, because Singapore is firstly one of the few countries in the world that operates without any formal offset policy, and, second, it has developed a high degree of absorptive technological capacity, ensuring that offset is infused, adding to the accretion of high technology defence industrial capability. The Singapore case is instructive, because it suggests that offset policies must be thought through, reflecting not only the conditions and needs of the recipient country, but also the vendor's operating constraints.

For most states, the policy objectives will reveal first-order strategic goals, such as the attainment of defence industrial sovereignty and economic diversification. However, it is the second-order imperatives, such as job creation, skills enhancement, supply-chain development and export penetration that provide the metrics to evaluate the performance of offset programmes. Whilst such metrics are legion amongst country offset policies, there is little empirical evidence on the effectiveness of particular policies in the attainment of these objectives.[6] What evidence exists, however, suggests that offset-derived investments have maintained skilled jobs, albeit, not created them.

Additionally, there is no evidence that local subcontractors have come into existence because of offset. Yet, local companies may have benefitted from offset creating new capacity in specific manufacturing domains through subcontractor opportunities in the global supply chain of major OEMs. It is fair to state, though, that examples of such offset-induced production opportunities are sparse. Finally, offset has rarely led to the creation of export opportunities beyond 'piggy-backing' on OEM global supply chains. A major reason for this is presumably the reluctance of offshore vendors to release technologies for export to third countries. This makes it difficult for offset recipient countries to penetrate overseas markets in the absence of IPR ownership. For instance, both Malaysia and South Korea have suffered US prohibitions on export of 'indigenous' military production, due to the extent of US technologies integrated into locally developed platforms.

The problems highlighted in the preceding discussion signal that the moulding of an optimal national offset policy is challenging. Moreover, this merely concerns the measurement of performance by reference to outcomes, and does not account for the fact that offset, particularly licensed production, may incur considerable additional financial cost when compared to off-the-shelf acquisition. The question, given such costs, is why countries continue to seek offset, and this remains a subject of ardent debate. Recently, however, there are international efforts to eradicate offset. For example, the European Commission and the European Defence Agency are actively seeking to marginalize, if not ultimately remove, offset from the intra-European defence market. Additionally, the US is advocating global consortia, such as the F-35 combat aircraft programme, as the way forward, to move beyond offset; and Australia has taken the extreme step of abandoning offset, concluding that in spite of two decades of implementation, offset had failed to deliver what was expected. As an alternative to offset, the Australian acquisition authorities now seek to encourage offshore vendors to partner with local defence companies for long-term mutual economic benefit, based on the proven competences of local defence companies.

Similarly, the UK Industrial Participation (IP) approach has evolved from a voluntary offset policy aimed at simply providing OEMs with awareness of what are deemed competitive UK defence subcontractors— albeit with demanding requirements including a 100 per cent offset target to be met exclusively through direct compensations, to voluntary partnership, where there is no offset target and no coercion is exercised.[7] The objective of this flexible approach is to encourage offshore vendors to collaborate with local suppliers in order to generate mutual economic benefit in an environment of partnership and trust, having the operational advantage of knowing that foreign OEMs will only engage with UK defence companies, provided that the latter are globally competitive. Technology transfer may play a part in the arrangements, but equally, it may not. In the long-term, all stakeholders, local and foreign, recognize that it is in their interests to ensure that both product and process technologies are at the competitive frontier.

This brief review of different offset policy approaches leads to the judgment that there are neither ideal offset policies nor generally applicable recommendations to make the strategy work. Rather, the suitability of an offset policy has to be assessed on a case-by-case basis, taking into account the economic, technological, industrial, and even political factors in the recipient country. This is required in order to adequately align existing industrial needs, objectives, and capabilities with the offset implementation mechanisms and management processes. Such an assessment may determine that defence offset is not a suitable industrialization strategy for a particular country, and, if that is the case, national industry and the economy as a whole will benefit from the removal of the opportunity costs imposed by offset.

The scene is thus set to establish, first, the role that offset has played in India's pattern of defence industrialization, examining especially the difficulties and challenges the country has faced in this process; second, the extent to which offset has been effective in contributing to India's defence industrial development; and, third, the likely outcomes that the presently crafted policy might yield in the future.

Defence Acquisition and the Curse of Foreign Dependency

Upon independence, India regarded domestic defence industrial capacity as a strategic imperative. The rationale was simple—immersed in a hostile geopolitical environment, the country could not afford to be highly dependent on external defence manufacturers, as the implementation of an independent foreign policy requires supply sovereignty. Furthermore, as a by-product, the development of a domestic defence industry would also contribute to the achievement of economic growth, thereby propelling the country to a higher international status. Political and economic incentives led to the establishment of a defence acquisition self-sufficiency policy, and, accordingly, substantial resources were channelled into indigenous defence development and production. These activities were undertaken exclusively under government control. As such, the 1948 Industrial Policy Resolution restricted entry of the private sector into defence production, putting in place an enormous bureaucratic system to work towards the achievement of defence self-reliance. The 1956 Industrial Policy further entrenched the position of the public sector in defence production. State ownership was strengthened in several fields, including electronics and composites, through the creation of new companies, such as BEL. Since then, in spite of multiple attempts at defence modernization, through strategies ranging from licensed production to joint ventures, the outcome has been an unbalanced mix of success and failure, resulting in India continuing to rely on foreign sources to meet 70 per cent of its military equipment requirements (The International Institute for Strategic Studies 2010: 477).

Examination of acquisition programmes, and accompanying indigenization efforts, reveals that the main cause of failure to indigenize is to be found in the government's excessive intervention in the defence industrialization process, as well as in its incapacity to plan, design, implement, and manage a suitable long-term strategy. Indeed, far from facilitating indigenization through a coherent strategy suitable for the country's industrial needs and production capacities, the government has implemented a series of inefficient policies that have, to a large extent, prevented domestic industry from maximizing the industrial benefits to be gained from defence acquisition. Furthermore, over-ambitious objectives, unmatched by the country's level of industrial and economic development, have been pursued with little regard for the high costs incurred. These factors have resulted in India's defence industry following a pattern of dependency on foreign technologies.

Notwithstanding national security concerns, the Indian government has recognized that re-inventing the wheel is not a cost-effective approach to industrial development. Hence, from 1947 to the early 1960s, India's defence industrialization strategy was characterized by a strong belief in the country's capacity to achieve self-sufficiency. The chosen route was through foreign purchases accompanied by technological and industrial assistance, enabling a quick-start to the industrialization process. Thus, in the early 1950s, the vast majority of India's weapon systems were procured off-the-shelf from Western European countries. Offset was not a major feature of these early acquisitions, but this changed in the late 1950s when, in an attempt to obtain production technology, India requested German, Japanese, and British contractors to assemble purchased land-based systems in India, making use of domestic resources.

As a result, in 1956, the state-owned HAL undertook the licensed production of the HF-24 *Marut* fighter. To the dismay of the Ministry of Defence (MoD), the final outcome was an under-performing aircraft whose cost would have been lower had it been purchased off-the-shelf, and, worse still, due to long delays, it was technologically obsolete by the time it was ready for deployment (Gupta 1990: 850). Failures during this early industrialization period can be attributed to insufficient R&D investment, lack of qualified human resources, excessive reliance on foreign suppliers for the provision of critical components, general organizational inefficiencies in the operations of both the government-run DRDO and the DPSUs and poor coordination between the Ministry of Finance in charge of managing offset agreements and the MoD responsible for implementing the defence industrialization policy.

Whilst licensed production has undoubtedly contributed to the enhancement of HAL's industrial capabilities, by the late 1960s the Indian government had realized that the absence of an adequate industrial infrastructure meant that pursuit of total self-sufficiency was futile. Therefore, a policy of self-reliance was implemented. This policy recognized the need for foreign acquisition, but regarded it as a stepping-stone to indigenization. Defence acquisition would only be used as an instrument to acquire and develop local production capabilities. This gave birth to a new era in which offset through Soviet co-production and joint ventures would prevail. Indeed, during this period the main source of military supplies was the Soviet Union. There are two main factors explaining the Indo-Soviet partnership—(1) the political relationship with Western countries had deteriorated as a result of conflicting geopolitical interests, leading to US reluctance to supply defence equipment to India, or even upgrade the existing inventory, and (2) the Soviet Union's willingness to supply not only advanced equipment, but also offset in the form of technology transfer and collaborative production agreements.[8]

Nevertheless, India tried to diversify its supplier base so as not to be totally dependent on Soviet military equipment provision. In consequence, agreements were reached with the UK and France to license produce Leander-class frigates, Alouette-3 helicopters, and Jaguar strike aircraft. In spite of these diversification efforts, by the early 1970s the Indian military, particularly the Air Force and Army, were overwhelmingly reliant on Soviet equipment—HAL licensed-produced Soviet MiG-21s, MiG-23s, and MiG-27s, but was incapable of designing and engineering its own products. In addition, the absence of a local subcontracting base meant that components and subsystems had to be imported. In the late 1970s, the failure of the Vijayanta and HS-748 programmes further evidenced the fact that the self-reliance policy was not working. In effect, the inability of local manufacturers to absorb licensed technologies to enhance their industrial assets, combined with several other features, such as the refusal of the Soviets to transfer technology beyond basic manufacturing processes, the insufficiency of government R&D investment, and the absence of local backward linkages, resulted in an uncompetitive domestic industry where time delays and cost overruns were the norm and the production level was largely limited to low- and mid-tech items (Mohanty 2004: 13). Inevitably, this unsatisfactory state of affairs led to a widening of the technological gap between India and Western countries and an increased reliance on foreign suppliers.

In general, the 1980s saw more of the same, with both the domestically designed Arjun main battle tank (MBT) and Tejas LCA repeatedly delayed and over-budget. To compound the problems, the LCA was heavily reliant on foreign technology inputs, with up to 70 per cent of electronics and avionics imported (Bristow 1995: 42). This, once more, proved that the self-reliance policy was not delivering the desired results. To make matters worse, the failure of the Arjun to meet the Indian Army's performance requirements prompted the MoD to order T-90 tanks from Russia as substitute platforms, raising serious doubts as to the practicality of manufacturing equipment that was easily available in international markets and whose off-the-shelf acquisition would be more cost-efficient. Importantly, during this period, due to strategic pressures, there was a shift in priorities and the government started to focus on guided missile development, instead of combat aircraft. The success of the IGMP, first launched in 1983, is largely attributable to the domestic industrial base possessing the necessary R&D infrastructure and technological assets to undertake production of this middle-technology project without foreign assistance. There were two additional and equally influential factors—(1) the DRDO coordinated the collaboration between the public and private sectors, thereby forming a 'public-private partnership' that worked for mutual benefit, and (2) unlike all other domestic production projects, the officers in charge of managing the programme were qualified scientists and engineers rather than senior civil servants.

In the 1990s, rapid development of the IT sector enabled India to go from licensed production to co-production and joint industrial partnerships. Thus, acquisition of MiG-29 aircraft, Hawk advanced jet trainers, and the Phalcon early warning defence system, from Russia, the UK, and Israel, respectively, were accompanied by joint development agreements. Moreover, India and Russia agreed on a partnership involving the joint R&D, design, and production of Sukhoi aircraft. Undoubtedly, the most remarkable indigenous programme undertaken in this period was *BrahMos*, a supersonic cruise missile, jointly developed by India and Russia. Its production required the implementation of an unprecedented collaborative and organizational structure. In fact, after decades of operating under a licensor-licensee scheme, the BrahMos programme gave rise to the establishment of an 'equal' relationship between the two parties. In this regard, although the BrahMos programme is a government-owned enterprise, it operates as a self-governing entity under corporate principles. More importantly, its production incorporates a wide range of components manufactured by local Indian subcontractors, therefore having the potential to generate industrial multipliers.

In 2002 the Russian Inter-Governmental Commission (IRGC) for Military-Technical Cooperation was established for the development of FGFA and the joint development and production of the *BrahMos* anti-ship cruise missile. As part of this industrial collaboration, India obtained a full license to manufacture the SU-30MKI fighter and its accompanying AL-31FP engine. Crucially, the agreement included the build-up of production facilities in India for subsystems manufacturing. These developments suggest that the self-reliant policy is working, but fails to acknowledge that India continues to import most of its equipment in order to keep the Armed Forces operational and the national industry afloat. Indeed, an industry that has been unable to undertake production of major systems without importing crucial technologies or subsystems, given the absence of a consolidated domestic network of subcontractors, cannot claim to be self-reliant. Consequently, although relative success has been achieved in low-end domestic defence production, such as the Indian Small Arms System (INSAS), the Nishant UAV, and the Lakshya pilotless target aircraft (PTA), the fact remains that the largest, most strategically, and economically relevant projects have delivered unsatisfactory results (Pardesi and Matthews 2007: 427–8).

In effect, the multiple mechanisms put in place to facilitate the indigenization process have failed to meet their objective. Evidence suggests that after 66 years, as an independent nation and engaged in an unrelenting search for self-reliance, India has not developed the indigenous production capabilities it requires to be able to claim a strategic position in the international system to match its increasing economic prowess. Granted, offset has been successful, but they are situated at the lowest end of the production spectrum and, therefore, does not make a significant contribution to technological and industrial development. Thus, in general terms, local industry has been incapable of manufacturing equipment to meet the demand of the Armed Forces. The DRDO has accused the military/MoD of contributing to programme failure by constantly changing requirements and making unrealistic demands (Jane's Information Group 1999: 2). Yet, failure cannot simply be attributed to demanding clients. Rather, it is explained by the existence of complex obstacles preventing efficiency and innovative operations in both government and industry.

First, due to India's threatening geopolitical environment, its military perceives the need to constantly modernize equipment. Hence, the Armed Forces cannot afford to wait until local industry negotiates its slow passage towards indigenization before it secures the right 'fit' between the equipment and military specification. This, in turn, has led to Indian industry not having a strong enough incentive to meet deadlines and quality standards, since its only client has been supplied with foreign equipment on a regular basis. Second, emphasis has been on licensed production rather than on design and R&D. As a result, local added-value has been limited and there has been insufficient technology learning and absorption, both of which are prerequisites for achieving long-term sustainability. Third, the opportunity-cost of domestic manufacturing has been too high due to the absence of a strong local subcontracting base. In a circuitous way, this has prevented the establishment of backward linkages and, in consequence, crucial components and subsystems have had to be imported, leading to unanticipated cost overruns. Lastly, the bloated bureaucratic system responsible for managing defence industrialization strategy is a classic example of government inefficiency in economic affairs. Indeed, not only has the government proven to be incapable of performing basic management tasks, but has also failed to correct implementation mistakes once programmes have started, as evidenced by a reluctance to cancel projects in spite of multiple time delays spanning across decades and budget overruns amounting to billions of USD.

In 2001, for the first time since 1948, Indian private companies were allowed to manufacture defence products under MoD license. Furthermore, in 2005, the first official offset policy was implemented in an attempt to accelerate the defence industrialization process. Given India's disappointing track record, the question that remains is whether the deep structural problems and challenges that the country has faced in its defence industrialization journey can be overcome by formalizing offset as a major instrument in the development process. International experience demonstrates that the results obtained from offset-driven industrialization strategies vary considerably.[9] Is India right, therefore, to pursue the offset path? More important, is the current Indian offset policy fit for purpose?

India's Offset Strategy: An Appropriate Path for Indigenous Defence Industrialization?

India's informal *ad hoc* approach towards offset-linked arms acquisition has proved a failure. The stated goal of reversing the 70 per cent dependence on foreign arms acquisition and 30 per cent indigenous production has not occurred. Accordingly, since the early 2000s, New Delhi has progressively moved towards engaging with the private sector to inject commercial and innovation dynamism into the public sector-dominated defence industrial base. To formalize this commercialization process, DPP was introduced in 2002. Different acquisition categories were delineated and typologies such as 'Buy' and 'Buy and Make' began to evolve over the decade. The expansion of categories occurred regularly between 2002 and 2011. DPP bi-annual amendments have been published with the purposes of broadening industrial participation in defence acquisition and improving the process of transparency via regular transmission of policy directives. Arguably, the most significant DPP was the 2006 offset policy. The purpose of launching this policy was to accelerate progress towards indigenous defence industrialization through the generation of world class capabilities, the improvement of technical know-how for sustainable developmer and production, and the creation of skilled employment across India's defence economy, broadly defined. For this purpose, New Delhi determined that the threshold to initiate offset requirements be set at a relatively high INR 3 billion (US$75 million).

Offset obligations range between 30 and 50 per cent, decided on a case-by-case basis. Thus, in the offset arrangement for the prospective acquisition of India's multirole combat aircraft, worth US$10–25 billion, a 50 per cent obligation has been imposed (Deloitte and Confederation of Indian Industry 2010: 13). The policy thrust is on defence (including both direct and indirect offset), with the DPP 2008 specifying 13 defence product categories qualifying for offset. However, the defence focus is increasingly being relaxed. For instance, dual-use technologies have been accepted, and the 2011 DPP indicates that qualifying products would henceforth be expanded to include civil aerospace, internal security, and training (Laxman 2011: 1).

The offset policy also led to the creation of the Defence Offset Facilitation Agency (DOFA) to administer and monitor the performance of offset programmes. Essentially, offshore vendors will seek approval from DOFA that their offset proposals conform to one or more of the three established 'gateways' for discharging offset obligations, namely— (1) direct purchase or execution of export orders, (2) FDI in Indian defence industry, and (3) FDI in Indian defence R&D organizations. Additionally, the banking of offset credits is allowed, but as the regulations stand, credits are maintained only for a maximum of two and a half years.

Offset will be applied to all acquisition categories created under the DPP regulations. Figure 5.1 presents the differing offset requirements

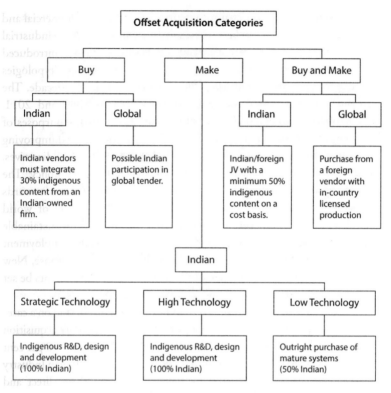

FIGURE 5.1 Typology of India's Offset Acquisition Categories

Source: Compiled from *Prospects for Global Defence Export Industry in the Indian Defence Market*, Deloitte/Confederation of Indian Industry (2010), pp. 50–5, and *Enhancing the Role of SMEs in Indian Defence Industry*, Ernst & Young/Confederation of Indian Industry (2009), pp. 27–30.

according to the respective offset acquisition category. As illustrated, there is a spectrum of offset permutations, including zero offset requirements, 30 per cent indigenous content, 50 per cent indigenous content, and 30 per cent of the foreign exchange cost of the investment.

India's offset policy has a number of other standard and novel features. For instance, multipliers have not been specified and this makes achievement of offset credit targets far more challenging, as only 1:1 investment to offset credits will be awarded by DOFA. In addition, the offset obligation must be completed within the delivery period of the primary defence contract, otherwise penalties will be imposed on the unfulfilled value of the commitment. This penalty, moreover, has the potential to become crippling. Specifically, an obligor that fails to fulfil its obligations in the specified timeframe must pay a penalty equivalent to 5 per cent of the under-performance incurred, and if the under-performance continues over subsequent years, then the penalty will be compounded, resulting in the extreme, in a cumulative compound penalty (5 per cent penalty on a 30 per cent offset value) over a 10-year period of 27.5 per cent, given no offset fulfilment whatsoever (CTO Data Services Company 2010: 102–16).

A final unique provision in India's offset policy is the so-called anti-corruption clause. This bans defence contractors from using commissioning agents, with punitive penalties applied in the event that the provision is circumvented. In recent years, agents have been involved in a number of high profile corruption cases involving major Indian defence acquisition programmes (Vogel 2006), and the anti-corruption provision is an attempt by the authorities to implement high ethical and governance standards in Indian defence acquisition.

From this broad sweep of India's offset policy, there is a clear sense that the multiplicity of provisions amounts to a profoundly complex and prescriptive approach towards encouraging offset investment into the country's defence economy. Evaluation of the policy should be undertaken from two perspectives—(1) the broad strategic level (addressed in this section), and (2) the micro level by reference to the individual policy attributes (evaluated under section 'Defence Acquisition and the Curse of Foreign Dependency').

At the strategic offset policy level, there is a spectrum of possible approaches ranging from complete policy abandonment (open defence trade, as in the case of Australia) to minimal foreign acquisition, and, thus, zero offset requirements (defence industrial self-sufficiency, as in the case of Russia). India's offset policy falls somewhere between these two extremes. There is no question that in the case of India a degree of regulation is required. This is because the country's defence industrial base is technologically insufficient to satisfy substantive offset requirements and, therefore, government direction is necessary to ensure that foreign commitment enhances the capabilities of relatively underdeveloped local defence companies. However, coercion rather than encouragement may prove counterproductive, in that it is likely to deter long-term mutually beneficial offset partnerships. In fact, there has already been one case where an overseas defence contractor withdrew from an Indian defence acquisition competition because of the risk and uncertainty associated with the offset obligations (Jane's Information Group 1999).

By contrast, the UK and Australian models are liberal in application, not least because both these countries already possess an advanced and diversified defence industry, and thus the role of offset is primarily to access existing defence companies rather than create new ones. Such policies are held to work efficiently because they are flexible and non-prescriptive, allowing offshore vendors to invest in the local defence industry without the threat of penalty—the goal of both the UK and Australia is to promote partnerships with foreign defence contractors through local systems development and integration into the prime contractor's global supply networks.

Arguably, Japan and Singapore are the two countries that have enjoyed the greatest success in offset implementation. Yet, in both cases a formal offset policy had not been formulated. Instead, each offset programme was agreed on a case-by-case basis, with arrangements regarding technology packages and targets based on what is feasible under the circumstances of the particular acquisition programme. Also significant is that both Japan and Singapore have employed government interventionist policies to promote civil-military strategic industries in the development of dual-use technologies; the aim being to develop synergies from defence-driven technology spin-offs to the civil sector and, simultaneously, commercial-driven technology spin-ons to the defence sector.[10] India has attempted to emulate this model through the 2006 guidelines for the selection of *Raksha Udyog Ratnas* (RURs). Here, high technology systems developers, producers, and integrators would be accorded preferential status, enjoying tax and investment concessions. However, the RUR policy has faltered, due to political wrangling from stakeholders with vested interests.

What lessons do these comparative offset models provide for India's policymakers? The most important lesson is that flexibility is the key to offset success.[11] Hence, a case could be made that flexibility should be introduced into certain features of India's offset policy. In this regard, there are several major areas requiring attention—

(1) First, FDI needs to be liberalized. Presently, there is pressure on the offshore contractor to engage with local defence companies through co-development, co-production, joint ventures, maintenance, and upgrades, but full mergers and acquisitions are not allowed. Indeed, FDI into an Indian defence company is capped at a 26 per cent

equity stake. Inevitably, this has acted as a disincentive to foreign defence contractors, because they carry a substantial financial risk, as investment comes without management control. Increasing the foreign equity share to 49 per cent or even 51 per cent is perhaps long overdue (Grevatt 2011).

(2) Second, policy emphasis on using offset to raise India's penetration in the international arms market is misplaced. There are two reasons for this misjudgement. The principal reason is that no causal link exists between offset performance and export promotion. Japan, for instance, has used offset to good effect, particularly focused on arms capacity-widening and technological deepening. However, the country prohibits the export of weapons systems, so it is impossible to establish the link between offset and export penetration.[12] Singapore has also been successful in using offset as a catalyst for enhancing defence industrial transformation, but the city-state's arms exports have been modest.[13] Equally, Malaysia's offset policy has sought to raise the competitiveness of its defence industry, but its defence exports are so low that they fail to even appear on the databases of both *The Military Balance* and *SIPRI*. It is possible that selected 'advanced' countries have fared better, and thus in these cases, there may be a positive relationship between offset performance and export promotion, but at the present time no empirical research has been undertaken to prove this hypothesis. In any case, advanced countries will enjoy higher levels of technological absorptive capacity compared to developing countries and so a direct read-across to evidence the potential for Indian defence exports would be inappropriate.

(3) The third concern lies with the ability of India's defence offset policy to successfully effect inward technology transfer. As mentioned earlier, New Delhi seeks technology transfer through licensed production, including design, manufacturing know-how, and blueprints. The aim is for the local Indian partner to acquire the capability to progress from assembly to indigenous development, production, and Maintenance, Repair and Overhaul (MRO). There is, therefore, an expectation that the foreign vendor will commit to 'complete' technology transfer of phased manufacture to the Indian partner of the system's subsystems, modules, assemblies, and specific parts/components. Moreover, support must be provided for a minimum period of 20 years after the last unit of local production is completed

(CTO Data Services Company 2010: 102–16). These OEM commitments are far more challenging than most other countries' national technology transfer-related offset policies. And this is not all; there are two further technology transfer policy requirements— first, the 'availability' of technology is a pre-condition for winning the contract; second, technology transfer falls outside the offset arrangement, and, thus, does not qualify for offset credits. As such, it remains to be seen whether India's robust technology transfer provision is 'successful'. The country's future defence market leverage will undoubtedly act as a powerful tool to obtain technology from offshore contractors. Yet, evidence from offset programmes across the globe suggests, powerfully, that foreign contractors are exceedingly reluctant to release technology, not least because huge expenses have been incurred in cumulative R&D, in the propagation of brands, and in the protection of proprietary knowledge.

(4) A final concern linking India's defence offset policy to export promotion is that expectations are overly ambitious. Industrial exports are a measure of competitiveness with respect to price, quality, and product 'surround'. Depending on the type of product, the key attribute for success will be customer-supplier trust. This normally evolves over decades and is symbolized via an internationally recognized 'brand'. Market reputation is built on quality and reliability, engendering brand loyalty. This is important in any commercial high technology market, but is even more important in high technology defence markets. The problem for India, however, is that it suffers from low international brand recognition, compounding the difficulties of inadequate defence capacity and capability. Therefore, the possibility of building on India's existing low US$114 million defence export figure looks bleak (Deloitte and Confederation of Indian Industry 2010: 47). Moreover, given that potentially the export-route for satisfying Indian offset credits is up to US$1 billion annually, it suggests that 10 times the present defence export level requires to be achieved (Deloitte and Confederation of Indian Industry 2010: 48). Thus, whilst India's huge future defence acquisition values will no doubt generate high levels of offset credits, there is little likelihood that the defence export gap will be closed in the short-run. In the longer-term, improved export performance may arise through piggy-backing on offshore vendor brands and markets, principally via

subcontracting work in their global supply chains. However, this in no way represents indigenous technological development. Greater export opportunities may be feasible if offset can contribute to local technological development, but this will depend on whether substantive technology transfer is achieved.

India's Offset Performance: A New Dawn Beckons?

It is clear that India's offset programmes, undertaken in the absence of a formal policy, did not produce the expected results. The objective of this section, therefore, is to determine whether policy formalization will make any difference. At present there is not enough evidence to assess the extent to which the policy has been effective, as after only seven years of implementation, insufficient time has elapsed to produce tangible effects. However, by examining the policy's main features, it is possible to identify the weaknesses that may well undermine its workability. Understanding the reasons why the policy may not work and suggesting appropriate alternatives is of vital importance. This is because according to the current trends, in the next four years, India's acquisition budget will increase by 15 per cent to reach US$19.20 billion in 2015 (Deloitte and Confederation of Indian Industry 2010: 64). Most of the contracts will be awarded to offshore vendors that will return at least 30 per cent offset investment to India (KPMG and Confederation of Indian Industry 2010: 22–3). In 2011, out of the US$13.4 billion budget allocated to acquisition, US$11.1 billion were spent on imports (Jane's Information Group 1999: 2) and it is estimated that by the year 2030 the total value of received offset could amount to US$50 billion (PricewaterhouseCoopers and Confederation of Indian Industry 2009: 31). The stakes are therefore high. Should India fail to manage these imminent offset deals in an appropriate manner, not only will it be missing the opportunity to overcome its dependency, but it will also be condemning the domestic defence industrial base to more years of backwardness, and the military to increasing strategic pressures and operational difficulties.

Offset has the potential to contribute towards the achievement of India's long-awaited defence industrial self-reliance, principally because of the impending mega defence acquisition deals over the next 15 years. For instance, in 2010, the Navy released a tender for six diesel submarines, having an estimated cost of US$3.4 billion each (Deloitte and Confederation of Indian Industry 2010: 29). Additionally, several warships including destroyers and frigates with a total cost of US$11.33 billion are on the list of future acquisitions (Deloitte and Confederation of Indian Industry 2010: 29). Between 2010 and 2015, the Navy will procure 29 MiG-29Ks from Russia's Mikoyan and 20 long range maritime patrol aircraft from Boeing (Deloitte and Confederation of Indian Industry 2010: 29). With respect to land-based systems, the Army plans to purchase missiles, tanks, vehicles, and artillery, though most of these contracts are likely to be awarded to domestic manufacturers. In contrast, however, due to the limited indigenous capacity of the aerospace sector, the Air Force is upgrading existing equipment with foreign assistance and procuring major systems from offshore vendors. As mentioned in the introduction, the largest contracts include the purchase of 272 Su-30 MKIs and 126 MMRCA, valued at between US$10 and 12 billion, reportedly one of the world's biggest defence imports (Waldron 2011). In addition, the Air Force plans to order 134 more aircraft, increasing the value of the contract to US$25 billion (Waldron 2011). These acquisitions will be accompanied by their respective offset packages.

Since the implementation of the official policy, leading OEMs such as Northop Grumman, Boeing, Lockheed Martin, EADS, Saab, Thales, and Sikorsky, have agreed to undertake the joint-development and production of both civil and defence applications with public and private Indian manufacturers. However, not all the agreements between a foreign defence contractor and Indian companies are established under an offset framework. For instance, in 2008, HAL won a five-year contract on a competitive basis to supply doors to EADS for the A318, A319, A320, and A321 civil aircraft (Deloitte and Confederation of Indian Industry 2010: 57). In contrast, in the same year, Thales signed an agreement with Tata's Strategic Electronic Division to transfer technology specifically to meet its offset obligations. This demonstrates that whilst foreign companies will try to align sourcing needs with the fulfilment of offset commitments, they are also willing to grant contracts, establish partnerships, and integrate local firms into global supply chains provided that they offer a competitive advantage in terms of value for cost.

Since 2007 several offset contracts have been signed between OEMs and Indian local industry. Russia's Rosoboronexport is offsetting 30 per cent of the US$700 million that the Indian MoD is paying for the upgrade of its Sukhoi 30-MKI fighter jets (Deloitte and Confederation of Indian Industry 2010: 63). Other currently on-going offset projects include Lockheed Martin's obligation from the US$1 billion sale of six C-130J-30 aircraft (Deloitte and Confederation of Indian Industry 2010: 63). IAI has also agreed to offset 30 per cent of the US$1.4 billion contract for the supply of 2,000 Barak SAMs for the Indian Navy (Deloitte and Confederation of Indian Industry 2010: 63). Foreign defence contractors have also set up joint ventures with both DPSUs and India's private defence industry. For example, in 2008, Boeing and the Tata Group established a joint venture for the manufacture of civil and defence subsystems to be integrated into various Boeing programmes (Boeing Media 2008). Similarly, in 2009, Tata and IAI formed a US$200 million joint venture for the production of missiles and electronic warfare systems (Joseph 2009). EADS has also invested in a joint venture with the private company L&T to design, develop, and manufacture electronic warfare items and defence avionics (*The Hindu* 2009).[14] Rolls Royce and BAE Systems forged joint ventures with HAL and Mahindra & Mahindra, respectively (PTI 2010; www.mahindra.com). In all instances, foreign ownership is restricted to 26 per cent of total equity. As discussed earlier, this cap hinders the potential for international collaboration and offset because without a large stake in the enterprise, foreign partners are unlikely to release know-how and crucial technologies.

A further perceived weakness of India's offset policy is the wide scope of its objectives. Traditionally, geopolitical imperatives have led New Delhi to establish over-ambitious targets for the industry as well as involvement in high-tech undertakings without prior assessment of existing assets and absorptive capacities, a crucial factor for successful offset programmes. Such arbitrary planning combined with attempts to indigenize across all military production sectors, instead of focusing on the development of competitive advantages in niche sectors, is unlikely to produce satisfactory results.

Yet another aspect that requires prompt attention is the different treatment that local public and private firms receive. Not only do the DPSUs enjoy excessive government protection, they are also sheltered from real competition, putting the private sector at a clear disadvantage when it comes to the granting of MoD contracts. The reason this is an important issue is because the industry as a whole needs competition to encourage innovation and efficiency. Without this, there is no incentive for companies to perform to optimal standards, and, under such conditions, national defence industrial development is hard to achieve. This implies that for the offset policy to be effective, the Indian government needs to let go of nationalistic sentiments and liberalize the defence sector, or, at the very least, give government-owned companies the necessary autonomy to operate under a corporate rationale. Subsequently, the full integration of the private sector into the defence industrial base and global supply networks of foreign prime contractors can take place, in turn, facilitating the development of offset programmes.

To additionally strengthen India's offset policy, industrial diversification is of vital importance. However, the Indian government has continuously concentrated on indigenizing defence technologies, underestimating the potential of dual-use innovations. As a result, fields such as IT, nanotechnology, and biotechnology are mostly the domain of the private sector. This explains the backwardness of government-owned companies and further justifies the need to consolidate both sectors. Given India's relatively strong IT and electronics industries and their high potential for spin-ons, restricting OEMs to fulfil their obligations in the form of defence-related direct offsets represents a serious mismanagement of resources.

The 2011 DPP provision allowing offshore vendors to discharge offset in the commercial aerospace and homeland security sectors is an important advancement, but more needs to be done in order to fully harness the positive synergies resulting from the application of dual-use aerospace technologies. Indeed, given the expansion of civil aviation, the present goal of developing commercial and defence aerospace simultaneously has to be the way forward. Not doing so when the same product and process technologies suffice to undertake both endeavours is as uneconomical as it is irrational. There is no major aerospace company in the world that caters exclusively for the defence sector. India's aerospace and defence industry has the potential to build up a competitive commercial sector through spin-ons. For this purpose the implementation of a civil offset bias has become an imperative. Such an approach would subsequently contribute to the development of the defence sector by creating a self-reinforcing cycle of spin-ons and spin-offs that ultimately lead towards higher levels of indigenization and industrial development in both the civil and defence sectors.

***

India has implemented its offset policy with the objective of achieving self-reliance in the production and maintenance of military equipment. From the Indian perspective what is at stake goes far beyond economic gains, involving national security and the capacity to be an independent player in the international community. This explains the government's decision to exercise strict control over the defence industry, implementing rigid policies designed to safeguard its development. Yet, industrial development is not determined by strategic needs or political will. Rather, it is essentially an economic phenomenon and, as such, is influenced by market forces. Under these conditions, India needs to take some drastic steps at the level of both defence industrial strategy and the offset policy itself, in order to derive maximum benefit from increasing offset investment.

Restructuring the national defence economy is crucial for avoiding the earlier failures of defence indigenization and industrialization strategies. To a large extent, those roadblocks are still in place in the form of undiversified government-owned companies, restrictions to FDI, and a peripheral private sector. International offset experience demonstrates that such conditions are not precursors for successful implementation and sustainability of offset programmes. On the contrary, they are likely to hinder industrial progress and undermine indigenization efforts. Addressing these deficiencies and ensuring that a proper environment exists is, therefore, a prerequisite for success in developing defence industrial capacity.

The fundamental weakness of India's offset policy is that it is based on an inflexible doctrine of indigenization. This, in turn, is the result of a defence industrialization strategy that has put in place government controls characteristic of centrally planned economies while attempting to get industrial benefits from global defence corporations operating under economic rationality conventions and responding to market incentives. India's approach may be politically appealing, but it shows poor understanding of defence industry dynamics and is certainly not economically feasible. Thus, it is imperative that the government overcomes political opposition to industry reform for the defence industrialization strategy to secure sustainable outcomes. To achieve this goal, India's offset policy must be made compatible with the economic dynamism of global defence industry, so that it makes commercial sense for OEMs to want to generate value from partnering with Indian defence companies. Indeed, several major deficiencies in India's offset policy have to be addressed, namely, the policy's obligatory nature, the broadening of objectives, and, most importantly, the reduction of complexity.

India is a relatively new entrant in the international offset field and, accordingly, its policy is undergoing a process of evolution and refinement based on trial and error. The recent decision to accept offset in the commercial aerospace sector suggests that the government is beginning to acknowledge that enhancement of domestic industry through offset cannot afford to have a policy ruled exclusively by strategic objectives. This is because, above all, a sound offset policy has to make economic sense. Nevertheless, the future looks promising—India's defence market is buoyant and there exists strong offset leverage. It is now incumbent on the government to implement the necessary changes to ensure that the offset policy works.

Notes

1. Early Russian development of this fighter has led to two single-seater prototypes—the T-50 and the PAK-FA. India's version is a two-seater officially called the FGFA.

2. To fulfil offset requirements, Dassault will grant contracts to Indian aerospace and defence companies for a total value of US$8 billion. Recipients include India's leading manufacturers and approximately 400 SMEs operating in both the civil and military sectors. For a partial list of beneficiary companies see, *The SupportBiz Bureau.*

3. India's 2005 offset policy was non-obligatory, but failure to obtain significant benefits led to the implementation of a mandatory policy and the establishment of the DOFA in 2006. For a review of the evolution of India's offset policy see, Matthew 2009.

4. For the theory of the second-best see, Lipsey and Lancaster 1965.

5. See Matthews 1996. Note that Saudi Arabia's Offset Committee has pursued both indirect (UK – Al Yamamah) and direct (US – Peace Shield) offset programmes, whereas India's policy approach focuses solely on direct offsets.

6. However, see Balakrishnan and Matthews 2009.

7. The European Union Defence and Security Procurement Directive 2009/81/EC, which came into force in August 2011, imposed open cross-border competition on all European defence acquisitions, thereby limiting the use of offset to the protection of national security interests. This in turn led to the UK's elimination of its official Industrial Participation policy. See, *Official Journal of the European Union* 2009. See also, *Offsets: A Portal of European Defence Agency*, 16 June 2012.

8. In addition, the Soviets agreed to favourable terms of payment such as countertrade, barter, and credit with low interest rates.

9. For country case studies on offset policy and programme performance see, Martin 1996 and Brauer and Dunne 2004. For in-depth case analyses of unsatisfactory offset performance, see Matthews 1996 and Balakrisnan and Matthews 2009. For a review of successful offset country cases see Mitra 2009.

10. For further discussion on technology spin on/off in relation to Japan and Singapore see, Matthews and Chinworth 1996, and Matthews 1999.

11. This is evidenced by the relatively successful outcomes obtained by countries that have implemented case-by-case and best-endeavours policies and by the stark contrast between results obtained by countries with flexible policies and those that adopted an inflexible approach. See, for example, Bitzinger 2004.

12. Since December 2011, Japan's export ban has been eased to allow Japanese defence manufactures to participate in international development and production programmes with major players in the US and Europe. The move is intended to enhance the capabilities of the local defence industry, reduce defence expenditure, and promote the export of weapon systems to peaceful states. See Agence France-Presse 2011.

13. Whilst Singapore's arms exports remain modest, its arms industry made an important export breakthrough in December 2009, with its first major export deal to a first-tier power (the UK). See Matthews and Maharani 2008.

14. In 2011, another joint venture was formed between EADS Cassidian and L&T. See ET Bureau 2011.

References

Agence France-Presse. 2011. 'Japan Eases Long-Standing Arms Export Ban', *Defense News*, 27 December.

Balakrishnan, Kogila and Ron Matthews. 2009. 'The Role of Offsets in Malaysian Defence Industrialisation', *Defence and Peace Economics*, 20 (4): (341–58).

Bitzinger, Richard A. (2004). 'Offsets and Defense Industrialization in Indonesia and Singapore', in Jurgen Brauer and Paul Dunne (eds), *Arms Trade and Economic Development: Theory, Policy, and Cases in Arms Trade Offsets*. London and New York: Routledge, 249–63.

Boeing Media. 2008. 'Boeing and Tata Industries Announce India Joint Venture', News Release, 14 February. Available at http://www.boeing.com/news/releases/2008/q1/080214a_nr.html (accessed 15 July 2013).

Brauer, Jurgen and Paul Dunne (eds). 2004. *Arms Trade and Economic Development: Theory, Policy, and Cases in Arms Trade Offsets*. London: Routledge.

Bristow, Damon. 1995. 'India's New Armament Strategy', *Whitehall Paper Series*, London: RUSI.

CTO Data Services Company. 2010. 'India's Offset Policy', *The Offset Guidelines Quarterly Bulletin*, 2010(October): 102–16. Available at http://www.cto-offset.com/qb-issue/4/2010-10-01.

Deccan Chronicle. 2011.'Fighters deal bigger: 126 will rise to 260', 13 February.

Deloitte and Confederation of Indian Industry. 2010. 'Prospects for Global Defence Export Industry in Indian Defence Market'. Available at http://www.deloitte.com.br/publicacoes/2007/Prospects_for_global_defence_export_industry_indian_defence_market.pdf (accessed 15 July 2013).

ET Bureau. 2011.'L&T in pact with EADS arm', *The Economic Times*, 11 February.

Grevatt, Jon. 2011. 'India mulls FDI limit increase in bid to boost technology transfer', *Jane's Defence Industry*.

Griffin, John and William Rouse. 1986.'Counter-Trade as a Third World Strategy of Development', *Third World Quarterly*, 8(1): 181.

Gupta, Amit. 1990. 'The Indian Arms Industry: A Lumbering Giant?', *Asian Survey*, 30 (9): 850.

Jane's Information Group. 1999. 'Features, Mixed Fortunes for India's Defence Industrial Revolution', *Jane's International Defence Review*, 32 (5): 2.

Joseph, Josy. 2009. 'Tata, Israel Aero in $200m Joint Venture', *Daily News & Analysis*, 12 February.

KPMG and Confederation of Indian Industry. 2010.'Opportunities in the Indian Defence Sector: An Overview', 22–3. Available at http://www.kpmg.com/ca/en/industry/industrialmarkets/documents/opportunities%20in%20the%20indian%20defence%20sector.pdf (accessed 15 July 2013).

Laxman, Kumar B. 2011. 'A Critical Review of India's Defence Procurement Procedure 2011', *IDSA Issue Brief*. Available at http://www.idsa.in/issuebrief/ACriticalReviewofDefenceProcurementProcedure2011 (accessed 15 July 2013).

Lipsey, R.G. and Kelvin Lancaster. 1965. 'The General Theory of Second Best', *The Review of Economic Studies*, 24 (1): 11–32.

'Mahindra and BAE Systems sign Joint Venture agreement', Press Release. Available at http://www.mahindra.com/News/Press-Releases/1293536379 (accessed 15 July 2013).

Martin, S. (ed.). 1996. *The Economics of Offsets: Defence Procurement and Countertrade*. Amsterdam: Hardwood.

Matthew, Thomas. 2009.'Essential Elements of India's Defence Offset Policy – A Critique', *Journal of Defence Studies*, 3 (1): 19–42.

Matthews, Ron. 1996. 'Saudi Arabia's Defence Offset Programmes: Progress Policy and Performance', *Journal of Defence and Peace Economics*, 7: 233–51.

———. 1999.'Singapore Buys Longbows and Grows Its Defence Industry', *Asia-Pacific Defence Reporter*, 25(7): 20–1.

Matthews, Ron and Curie Maharani. 2008.'Beyond the RMA: Survival Strategies for Small Defence Economies', *Connections*, NATO Journal, 7 (2): 67–80.

Matthews, Ron and Michael Chinworth. 1996. 'Defence Industrialisation through Offsets: The Case of Japan', in Stephen Martin (ed.), *The Economics of Offsets: Defence Procurement and Countertrade*, 177–218. Netherlands: Harwood Academic Publishers.

Mitra, Anuradha. 2009.'A Survey of Successful Offset Experiences Worldwide', *Journal of Defence Studies*, 3 (1): 43–62.

Mohanty, Deba R. 2004. 'Changing Times? India's Defence Industry in the 21st Century', Bonn International Center for Conversion, Paper 36, p. 13.

Official Journal of the European Union. 2009. 'Directive 2009/81/EC of the European Parliament and of the Council of 13 July 2009', 20 August.

Offsets: A Portal of European Defence Agency. 2012.'United Kingdom', 16 June.

Outlook India. 2010.'India, Russia Sign FGFA Joint Development Deal'. Available at http://news.outlookindia.com/items.aspx?artid=705905 (accessed 15 July 2013).

Pardesi, Manjeet S. and Ron Matthews. 2007.'India's Tortuous Road to Defence-Industrial Self-Reliance', *Defense & Security Analysis*, 23 (4): 427–8.

PricewaterhouseCoopers and Confederation of Indian Industry. 2009.'Changing Dynamics: India's Aerospace Industry'. Available at http://www.pwc.com/gx/en/aerospace-defence/pdf/india-aerospace.pdf (accessed 15 July 2013).

PTI. 2010. 'HAL and Rolls-Royce Announce Manufacturing Joint Venture in India', *Daily News & Analysis*, 30 March.

The Hindu. 2009.'L&T, EADS form joint venture', 6 May.

The International Institute for Strategic Studies. (2010). 'Reforming India's Defence Industries', *The Military Balance*, 110 (1): 477.

The SupportBiz Bureau. 2012. 'Indian SMEs to Benefit from Dassault Rafale Offset Deals', 17 February.

Vogel, Ben. 2006.'India Strives for Balance in Defence Industrial Policy', Industry Briefing, *Jane's Defence Industry*, 1 October.

Waldron, Greg. 2011. 'Battle Royale for India's MMRCA Crown', *Flight International*. Available at http://www.flightglobal.com/news/articles/battle-royale-for-indias-mmrca-crown-352411/ (accessed 15 July 2013).

6 Internal Security Challenges and Role of the Central Armed Police Forces

BIBHU PRASAD ROUTRAY

INDIA, THE LAND OF A MILLION MUTINIES, has witnessed since its independence a number of armed insurrections with demands ranging from secession and autonomy to greater constitutional rights for the tribal population. Since the transfer of power from the British in 1947, the north-eastern region of the country, consisting of seven states, has remained a land of turmoil, marked by an unceasing growth of insurgencies, many of whom have found bases in neighbouring countries. The late 1960s saw the rise of a left-wing extremist movement in the eastern state of West Bengal that gradually spread to Andhra Pradesh in the south. The western state of Punjab witnessed an extremely violent militancy supported by Pakistan across the border in the 1980s and early 1990s. The early years of the 21st century witnessed a fresh consolidation of the dormant left-wing extremists. The last years of the 1980s witnessed an externally sponsored-cum-indigenous militancy in the state of Jammu & Kashmir, which continues till date.

Achievements at meeting the challenges posed by these armed extremist movements have been a mixture of stupendous successes and disastrous failures. The first phase of the left-wing Naxalite movement was crushed in 1971. The armed Sikh militancy in Punjab was quelled by the early 1990s. In the north-east, insurgency has been defeated in Mizoram and Tripura. Militancy related fatalities have reduced significantly in J&K. However, these success stories notwithstanding, several challenges remain. Peace in J&K remains fragile and reversible, linked to the tenuous nature of India-Pakistan relations. Several north-eastern states are still affected by the remnants of the old insurgency movements and also by the emergence of new outfits attempting to fill the vacuum. And, most importantly, the Left-Wing Extremist (LWE) or Maoist movement since 2005 has emerged as the most formidable internal security challenge for the country, in spite of the near decimation it suffered in the southern state of Andhra Pradesh.

The Central Armed Police Forces (CAPFs) (Ministry of Home Affairs 2011)[1] have remained pivotal to India's predominantly force-centric approach to deal with the armed uprisings. Supplementing the efforts of the state police forces and the Army, the CAPFs have played a critical role in each of the aforementioned conflict theatres. On the other hand, each of these conflicts has shaped and nurtured the outlook, the ideology, and the growth pattern of these forces. The CAPFs, thus, can be projected to remain a critical component of the continuing and future counter-insurgency (COIN) efforts of the state.

This chapter argues that in spite of the prolonged history and vast experience at responding to the country's security needs in various conflict zones, the CAPFs have failed to break the threshold of mediocrity to emerge as effective security providers. In spite of their centrality to the national security architecture, their performance has been limited both externally as well as internally. While the external requirement of being part of a COIN strategy inked by the state police forces limits their functional autonomy, in the internal sphere, lack of leadership and ability to adapt to new operating environments has made their performance severely error prone. As a result, they have remained a part of the stopgap arrangements that the country uses to deal with armed insurrections. In addition, being products of a lackadaisical modernization project, the CAPFs on occasion have resembled a huge ham-fisted force, whose impressive numerical strength gives them significant capacities to withstand losses, but as far as responding effectively to India's growing security needs is concerned, they suffer from significant limitations.

The chapter focuses on the role of the CAPFs in three conflict theatres—the LWE affected states, the North-east, and J&K. While analysing their role in terms of contribution to conflict resolution and conflict management, the chapter also explores their relationship with the politico-strategic environment consisting of the armed forces, state police forces, intelligence agencies, and the political elites, and seeks to assess the impact of these relationships on their performance. While the chapter does refer to the history of the CAPF engagement in the three conflict theatres, it limits itself largely to analysing contemporary trends.

The first section provides a brief backgrounder to the origin and growth of different CAPF organizations. The second section assesses the performance of the CAPFs in the three aforementioned conflict theatres. The third section is an evaluation of the relationship of the CAPFs with the politico-strategic environment they operate in, and the latter's impact on the performance of the forces. The fourth and last section consists of recommendations for effecting improvements in the CAPFs' COIN capability.

The CAPFs

The CAPFs are not clubbed under a single monolithic organization, but are divided into seven different units with diverse roles. India's international borders are guarded by the Border Security Force (BSF), Indo-Tibetan Border Police (ITBP), Sashastra Seema Bal (SSB), and Assam Rifles (AR) in different theatres. The Central Reserve Police Force (CRPF) looks after internal security while the Central Industrial Security Force (CISF) is entrusted with the security of industrial installations and airports. The National Security Guards (NSG) is an elite anti-terror commando outfit. In 2011, the combined strength of the CAPFs reached 777,788 divided into 516 operational battalions; an increase of 36 operational battalions since 2008 (Chidambaram 2011).

Three distinct trends are perceptible from the available numbers—(1) the strength and resources allocated to each of the CAPF organizations have risen at a steady rate over the past decades and the pace is likely to be sustained with successive regimes in New Delhi reiterating their intent to raise more battalions over the next two decades. Tables 6.1 and 6.2 indicate the significant growth in CAPF numbers and consequent rising expenditures respectively; (2) the original mandate with which each of the CAPF organizations was raised has since been expanded enormously and almost all the CAPF units today have designated roles in COIN operations; and (3) the expansion in mandate and consequent overlapping of responsibilities has led to a significant erosion in the functional distinctiveness among the CAPFs. Consequently, each of these CAPF organizations has raised its profile and developed strategies to adhere to COIN requirements.

TABLE 6.1 Manpower Status in the CAPFs (2000–7)

Year	AR	BSF	CISF	CRPF	ITBP	NSG	SSB	Total
2000	51056	181839	95992	181136	30356	7357	32141	579877
2001	59899	185590	95366	184538	32992	7357	31750	597492
2002	62399	204885	94534	204531	34657	7357	31625	639988
2003	63649	208103	91347	229699	34788	7357	31554	669497
2004	61395	208422	93935	248790	36324	7357	31554	687777
2005	65185	208937	93521	248689	34636	7354	47147	705469
2006	63142	209361	100764	248712	34798	7334	55351	719462
2007	65290	210261	103860	260873	50326	7334	48934	746878

Source: Compiled from Annual Reports (various years), Ministry of Home Affairs, Government of India.

TABLE 6.2 Actual Expenditure on the CAPFs: 2000–1 to 2009–10 (in crores of Rupees)

Year	AR	BSF	CISF	CRPF	ITBP	NSG	SSB	Total
2000–01	655.32	2157.78	802.30	1653.25	416.06	90.34	322.28	6077.33
2001–02	776.25	2399.02	860.55	1894.42	417.08	82.79	327.03	6757.14
2002–03	711.20	2668.41	936.55	961.13	470.25	95.90	325.77	6169.31
2003–04	929.15	2970.24	982.19	2087.78	468.32	113.81	315.92	7867.41
2004–05	1005.64	2635.76	1061.24	2516.96	552.72	128.00	381.84	8282.16
2005–06	1314.17	3560.45	1131.07	3228.05	576.25	140.28	581.97	10535.22
2006–07	1478.29	3398.85	1225.59	3642.40	707.99	151.19	779.92	11384.23
2007–08	1541.81	3879.00	1376.23	3911.69	1000.73	163.90	943.70	12817.06
2008–09	2016.27	5398.50	2169.28	5557.82	1433.24	210.52	1241.63	18027.26
2009–10	1599.02	4472.66	1978.88	5262.33	1134.05	231.70	801.31	15479.95
2010–11	2814.79	7366.87	2780.44	8128.10	1862.35	491.77	1630.36	25074.68

Source: Compiled from Annual Reports (various years), Ministry of Home Affairs, Government of India.

Performance Assessment

Since all categories of armed insurrections pertain to the 'law and order' category, which is a 'state'[3] subject according to the Indian Constitution, the primary responsibility of dealing with the extremist movements has with the state governments. Only on the request of the state government can the Centre send the CAPFs to assist the efforts of the state police forces and the CAPFs, under all circumstances, work under the direction of the state police authorities. Thus, the performance of the CAPFs in domestic conflict theatres is largely limited to being a supporter or enhancer of the activities of the state police forces and an executor of the broad security strategy of the state government. They are required by law to play only a subsidiary role to the state police forces. As a result, the available literature on conflict situations tends to provide only a cursory analysis of the CAPFs performance.

Operationally, however, this strategic constraint is subject to on-field alteration, inherently linked to the existing capacities of the state police forces to deal with the emerging threats. More often than not, given the inadequacies of the state police forces, the CAPFs have assumed a lead role in COIN scenarios. From the point of view of the chapter, this enormously widens the scope of the CAPFs' performance assessments, both in theatres where conclusive victories against extremism have been secured and in ongoing conflicts. The CAPFs' role has varied in different cases.

For example, in Punjab, where the COIN campaign under the leadership of the state police scripted a significant success against Sikh militancy in 1992, CAPF organizations—the CRPF and the BSF—played a crucial role in augmenting the capacities of the state police forces. The COIN campaign led by Director General of Police (DGP) K.P.S. Gill integrated the CAPFs into a neatly crafted strategy that went on to work outstandingly well against the Pakistan-sponsored militants. The 'Gill Doctrine' (Mahadevan 2008) with some modifications has been adopted in almost all the conflict theatres subsequently. On the contrary, in the north-eastern state of Mizoram, where a brutal campaign by the Indian Army, marked by large scale human rights abuses, quelled a violent secessionist movement by the Mizo National Front (MNF) cadres in the mid-1980s, neither the state police nor the CAPFs had any significant role to play. Some of these aspects will be elaborated on in subsequent sections of the chapter.

This section broadly assesses the role of the CAPFs in three conflict theatres—the LWE affected states, the North-east, and the state of J&K—both in terms of their successes and failures. It attempts to highlight the strength that the CAPFs added to the COIN campaigns and also the shortcomings that affected the outcomes.

The LWE Theatre

The LWE movement, also known as Naxalism, which had been comprehensively crushed in 1971, again emerged to become the 'biggest internal security challenge' for India by 2005. The movement seeking to overthrow the prevailing system of governance through a violent 'people's war' enlisted the support of 20,000 armed cadres. It also had the sympathies of thousands of the tribal population, whose rights of land, forest produce, and livelihood were being curtailed by the intrusion of multi-national companies, public sector undertakings, and other state agencies. As Table 6.3 shows, there was a tide of fatalities arising from LWE-related violence between 2006 and 2010. Extremists, estimated to be operating in one third of the country's geographical territory, not only carried out attacks on every symbol of the state's presence, but also launched repeated swarming militia attacks on police stations and armouries, killing personnel and looting arms and ammunition.

In spite of the fact that the southern state of Andhra Pradesh had been able to script a success story against the extremists by 2005, other states—Chhattisgarh, Jharkhand, Bihar, Odisha, West Bengal, and Maharashtra—failed to respond effectively to the LWE surge.

Table 6.3 LWE-related Fatalities (2006–11)

Incidents/Deaths	2006	2007	2008	2009	2010	2011
Incidents	1509	1565	1591	2258	2213	1755
Civilians	521	460	490	591	720	464
Security Forces	157	236	231	317	285	142
Extremists	274	141	199	219	172	99
Total Fatalities	952	837	920	1127	1177	705

Source: Compiled from Annual Reports (various years), Ministry of Home Affairs, Government of India.

Maoists, in each of these states, managed to carve out liberated zones and implemented a system of parallel administration called *Janathana Sarkar* (people's government), mostly implementing instant justice on anybody with official contacts. Central to the collapse of the state administration in the areas under Maoist influence was the enduring weakness among the state police forces, who were no match against the marginally skilled, yet highly motivated extremists. State police departments, in many of these states, took conscious decisions to disarm their own personnel located in remote police stations to guard against extremist attacks and looting of the weapons available with the police personnel.[4]

In this backdrop of a comprehensive retreat of governance from vast stretches of the country's geographical expanse, it became expedient for the fire power of the state police forces to be supplemented by that of the CAPFs. Since the over-stretched Indian Army refused to be drawn into a non-secessionist rebellion that involved the country's own population bereft of any external assistance, the CAPFs became the backbone of the force-centric approach of the government against the extremists.

Till 2009, 30-odd CAPF battalions were deployed in the LWE affected states carrying out operations in tandem with the state police forces. By late 2009, when the annual LWE related fatalities reached 1127, an increase of 22 per cent over 2008, the total deployment was enlarged to 70 battalions—comprising not just the CRPF, which had been projected to become the country's lead COIN force, but also the BSF, CISF, ITBP, and the SSB. The last three had no previous COIN experience and had been deployed purely to make up for the acute shortages in security forces in the LWE belt. In addition, the CRPF also deployed its newly raised Combat Battalion for Resolute Action (COBRA), a 10-battalion strong anti-Maoist commando unit, for exclusive 'seek and engage' operations in the LWE areas.

Induction of a large number of well-armed CAPF personnel into the LWE strongholds was no doubt a much needed move aimed at correcting the skewed security force vs. extremist ratio. It also formed a critical component of Operation Green Hunt, the multi-theatre synchronized operation against the extremists. However, apart from merely adding a large number of uniformed men into the war zone, the stratagem clearly failed to overcome the flaws that the CAPF engagement in the LWE theatre had previously been marked by. Within six months of its early 2010 launch, the operation had to be called off. What went wrong?

First, the CAPFs were constrained by the ineffectual strategies of the state police establishments reflected in their indiscreet deployment, on which the state police establishment is the final arbiter. Instead of using the CAPFs in focused area operations supporting the state police, these forces were either left idle owing to lack of operational planning or were used for solo operations without the intelligence support of the state police. On most occasions, the overall CAPF deployment hardly matched their operational or developmental requirements, necessitating intervention by the Ministry of Home Affairs (MHA).[5]

Second, in addition to being constrained by a directionless strategy, the CAPF operations suffered from a lack of leadership. Inquiry reports on some of the attacks that resulted in serious losses for the CRPF substantiate this. On 6 April 2010, extremists organized the biggest attack known till date on a CRPF company in Chhattisgarh's Dantewada district. The ambush, in which about 1,000 extremists participated, resulted in the loss of an entire company of the CAPF organization consisting of 75 fighting men. Inquiry into the attack underlined serious 'command and control' failure and violation of Standard Operating Procedures (SOPs) by the CRPF personnel led by a Deputy Commandant (Gupta 2010). The investigation revealed that a Walkie-Talkie set belonging to the CRPF Deputy Commandant had fallen into the hands of the extremists, allowing them to monitor the movement of the forces and set up the ambush (Routray 2011).

Narratives from the LWE theatre routinely point at similar SOP violations by the CAPFs. These include personnel operating with drained Walkie-Talkie sets, travelling on top of open tractors, not using seat-belts and helmets while travelling in landmine-proof vehicles, not walking in single-file formation, using motorcycles during long range patrolling on non-tarred roads which are most likely to be mined, frequently using the same route for operations thereby making themselves vulnerable for ambush, and so on—all pointing to the lack of able leadership.

Inherently, the lack of leadership is linked to a rushed recruitment procedure. The CRPF, for example, nearly doubled its size in a span of eight years—from 120 battalions in 2003 to 220 battalions in 2011. Experts argue that this rapid expansion has resulted in a crippling shortage of officers within the CRPF ranks, as the training procedure for the officers to command the newly raised units are much longer than those for training the soldiers. While nine months are required to train a constable, officers need two years of instruction (Swami 2009). In a scenario when the demand for CAPF deployment has reached a feverish pitch in all the conflict theatres, many frontline units are not equipped with adequately trained leadership.

Third, in the LWE theatres, much more than in other areas of conflict, it was crucial that the CAPFs bring in drastic transformation into their rules of engagement, shifting from a traditional and rather strait-jacketed 'we versus them' confrontational approach to a more nuanced one. The forces are mandated to neutralize foreign-backed militants by maximum use of force, for example, in J&K. In contrast, the LWE-ridden theatres required that the CAPFs, mostly consisting of personnel alien to local conditions, cultivate the host population among whom the insurgents and extremists take refuge into their operations. It was important that the forces adopt a typical counter-insurgency doctrine of 'isolating the fish from the sea' into their operations and win the trust of the civilian population by taking adequate precautions to minimize collateral damage. However, the history of COIN operations in such areas indicates that the CAPFs were either not briefed to bring about such changes in their approach, or simply did not feel the necessity to transform themselves. Moreover, the operations suffered due to the lack of ground level intelligence and resulted in an unacceptable level of human rights violations.

Fourth, CAPF operations suffered from lack of adequate cooperation from the civil administration. The official strategy of 'clear, hold, and develop' in the LWE areas was hinged on the support of the civil administration being provided to the security forces. It was necessary that the civil administration start operating on an urgent basis in areas cleared of extremist presence, under protection provided by the security forces. However, on most occasions, the administration chose either to remain conspicuous by its absence or was an unenthusiastic implementer of the development schemes. An example can be cited in the context of the Saranda Development Plan which was initiated in October 2011 after a month-long security force operation freed the Saranda forests, a bastion of the LWE leadership stretched over an 820 sq. km. area in the state of Jharkhand, from extremist presence. However, the efficiency of utilization of resources to the tune of Rupees 2.64 billion allocated by New Delhi to be spent on building roads and houses for the tribal population continued to lag way behind schedule. The administration either complained of procedural hurdles for not utilizing the money or simply procrastinated on the implementation of the schemes (Mukherjee 2012). The spectre of an extremist return to such areas could not be ruled out once the security forces withdrew.

The North-east

Since India's independence, its north-eastern region comprising of seven states has remained the theatre of a multiplicity of tribal insurgencies. Insurgency in the state of Nagaland is considered to be the 'mother of all insurgencies' in the region, for having risen first in the mid-1950s (Sinha 2011) and inspired the formation and growth of others. With demands ranging from outright independence to autonomy within the Indian union, these movements have attempted to espouse the cause of both the tribal and non-tribal population. Popular support, hostile topography, contiguity with countries like Bangladesh, Bhutan, and Myanmar, each separated by a porous international border from India, external support, and weak police establishments in each of these states have ensured longevity for most of these insurgencies. Barring the state of Mizoram, where armed insurgency ended as a result of excessive army action and subsequent political cooption, insurgencies have thrived in the region.

In recent years, however, the region has witnessed a significant transformation. Owing to a combination of factors such as police action, peace negotiations with insurgent outfits, and diplomatic successes in persuading neighbouring countries to take action against the insurgents, there has been a dramatic decline in the level of violence (see Table 6.4).

TABLE **6.4** Insurgency-related Fatalities in the North-east (2006–11)

Incidents/Deaths	2006	2007	2008	2009	2010	2011
Incidents	1366	1489	1561	1297	773	627
Civilians Killed	309	498	466	264	94	70
Security Forces Killed	76	79	46	42	20	32
Extremists (Killed, Arrested, and Surrendered)*	3231	2875	4318	3842	3306	3377

* The MHA does not provide disaggregated figures reflecting fatalities among the extremists.

Source: Compiled from Annual Reports (various years), Ministry of Home Affairs, Government of India.

While Tripura has been able to score a comprehensive victory over insurgency, the majority of the armed movements in other states such as Assam, Manipur, Nagaland, and Meghalaya have suffered a series of setbacks, affecting their capacities to indulge in subversive activities.

The decision to induct the CAPFs into the North-east, beginning with Nagaland in the 1950s, was primarily to make up for the weak police forces, which were found incapable of dealing with the armed insurgents. A policy of neglect pursued by New Delhi towards the north-eastern region, connected by the narrow 21 km.-wide Siliguri corridor, had not only resulted in an impoverished region, but also a thoroughly marginalized police force. The frailty of police capacities vis-a-vis the insurgents was acknowledged in the MHA's Annual Report for the year 2001–02, which noted that the insurgents are far better armed than the state police forces.[6] It was unimaginable that the state police would have been able to contain the situation without external assistance.

Compared to the LWE affected states, where CAPFs are the only central forces assisting the state police, the Indian Army too had been inducted into the north-eastern region, considering both the region's contiguity with foreign countries and also the active support insurgents generated within countries like Bangladesh, Bhutan, Myanmar, and China from both state and non-state actors. The presence of the Army provided operational support for CAPFs, although it did give rise to additional requirements of coordination between three distinct forces, compared to only two in the LWE theatres.

Unfamiliarity with local conditions, the central weakness of CAPFs, has been addressed to a large extent by the deployment of AR in some of the conflict ridden states such as Nagaland and Manipur. Raised in the year 1835 'to guard the alluvial plains of Assam from the wild and unruly tribes' (Website of the Assam Rifles), AR is the oldest CAPF organization in the country, and is officered by the Indian Army. Consisting of a sizeable number of soldiers from the north-eastern region, the AR resembles a local force and has a competitive advantage over both the other CAPF organizations and the Army. Adoption of slogans such as 'The Sentinels of the North-East' and 'Friends of the Hill People' has further helped the force augment its acceptability among the local population.

However, even with these advantages, CAPF operations against the insurgents suffered from a range of deficiencies, both external as well as internal. Externally, for decades, the campaign against the insurgents was limited by India's diplomatic failure in persuading ruling regimes in Bhutan, Bangladesh, and Myanmar to act against the insurgents who had found refuge in those countries. In the absence of such cooperation, insurgents simply crossed over the porous international borders to avoid security force operations launched inside the region. 'Hit and run' attacks carried out from those countries wreaked havoc in states like Manipur, Tripura, and Assam. Until 2003, when Bhutan launched a military operation displacing insurgents operating in Assam from its soil, insurgency in the north-east appeared to be without solution. Dhaka started cooperating in 2009 after the Awami League-led government pursued a policy of arresting and handing over insurgent leaders to India. Lack of adequate cooperation from Myanmar, however, keeps insurgency alive in Manipur.

Second, weak and inefficient policing in most of the states remained the bane of CAPF operations. Lack of adequate progress in police modernization programmes in almost all the states of the region was a handicap for the central forces both in terms of intelligence as well as the operational support that the latter received from the state police forces. The fact that a section within the police force in states like Assam, Manipur, and Nagaland had been compromised and for a number of years maintained a nexus with the insurgents, regularly providing them with counter-intelligence regarding planned offensives, greatly neutralized the projected gains of CAPF operations.[7]

Third, in the internal sphere, CAPF operations have been affected by a deficit of officers in their ranks. The previous section dealt with the reason for such a phenomenon in the LWE theatres. The north-east faced an additional problem in the form of a rivalry between the MHA, which controlled the AR, and the Ministry of Defence (MoD), which supplied the AR with officers. It ensured a perennial short supply of officers for the AR, affecting the organization's performance and to a large extent, the level of discipline.

Repeated failure to adhere to strict norms of engagement tarnished the image of the CAPFs, including the AR. The central forces were accused of frequent human rights violations—allegations of rape, custodial torture, and fake encounters—in almost all the north-eastern states they operated in (Human Rights Watch 2008). Among such incidents was the infamous case of Manorama Devi, a former insurgent in Manipur. On 11 July 2004, she was picked up from her residence by the AR personnel and her dead body with signs of torture was recovered the next day. The refusal of the AR authorities to initiate legal proceedings against the guilty personnel was the starting point of a popular agitation for withdrawal of the central forces from the state. Such popular disenchantment was exploited by the insurgent organizations and violence spiked in the subsequent years. From 205 recorded fatalities in 2003, deaths among civilians, security forces, and insurgents reached 258 in 2004 and 410 in 2005.[8]

Fourth, CAPF performance in the north-east suffered from inadequate force presence. Terrorism in J&K dominated New Delhi's attention and as a result, the north-eastern states received far less deployment of central forces than demanded. The AR, with a strength of 46 battalions, performed the dual function of a counter-insurgent force with 31 battalions as well as a border guarding force along the 1,643 km long Indo-Myanmar border with 15 battalions. The severe deficit in numerical strength resulted in the curious phenomenon of AR deployments 40 km off from the international border, thereby allowing the insurgents an unhindered ability to ingress and egress. Repeated proposals by the MHA for replacing the AR with the BSF along the Indo-Myanmar border and assigning the AR an exclusive COIN responsibility have met with opposition from the MoD. The latter argues that dismantling or replacement of the AR would rob the government of domain knowledge of the area that could be useful to hold off a probable Chinese military offensive.[9]

Jammu & Kashmir

Since 1989, militancy in J&K has been the most important issue in India's internal security scenario. The state has been disputed by India and Pakistan since 1947. Pakistan made two unsuccessful attempts to seize the territory in 1947 and 1965. In the subsequent years, it largely refrained from making any direct attempt at gaining control in the area of J&K still in India's possession. Rather, its efforts shifted to aiding Pakistan-based militant groups waging a proxy war against Indian security forces in the state. According to an estimate, the 'proxy war has claimed 26,226 lives between 1988 and 2000 in an estimated 43,956 incidents of terrorist violence. Of these casualties 10,310 (40 per cent) were civilians, 3,520 (13 per cent) were security forces personnel, and 12,396 (47 per cent) terrorists'.[10]

Since 2001, during which 4,507 lives were lost in militancy in the state, violence has been on a consistent decline. In 2011, only 164 fatalities were recorded, the lowest since 1990 (see Table 6.5). Three factors are identified

TABLE **6.5** Militancy-related Fatalities in Jammu & Kashmir (2006–11)

Incidents/Deaths	2006	2007	2008	2009	2010	2011
Incidents	1667	1092	708	499	488	340
Civilians	389	158	91	71	47	31
Security Forces	151	110	75	79	69	33
Militants	591	472	339	239	232	100
Total Fatalities	1131	740	505	389	348	164

Source: Compiled from Annual Reports (various years), Ministry of Home Affairs, Government of India.

as the reasons behind such decline in militancy—the preoccupation of the Pakistani facilitators with cross-border militancy along the Pakistan-Afghanistan border; the strengthening of the counter-insurgency grid in J&K which has neutralized much of the local militancy; and the unveiling of a range of confidence building measures between India and Pakistan (Routray 2012). However, Indian authorities maintain that the terrorist training camps are still active across the border and the gains made in the state are fragile.

The CAPF operations in J&K can be divided into two distinct phases—one led by the BSF from 1990 to 2005 and the subsequent one led by the CRPF since 2005, following a Group of Ministers (GoM) recommendation to replace the BSF. The latter, the border guarding force along the India-Pakistan border, was the natural choice for the government to contain the spike in militant violence in J&K in 1990,[11] in spite of the fact that the force had no prior COIN experience. Six battalions of the BSF filled up the vacuum of a counter-insurgent force as the Indian Army, to begin with, expressed its reluctance to commit its soldiers for COIN duties. The BSF's strength rose to 34 battalions by 1993 (Hussain 2005). However, its relative inexperience was demonstrated in its rather brutal, yet unsuccessful anti-militancy campaign which was marked by large scale allegations of human rights violations.

Since 2005, the CRPF has played a critical role in the CI grid in J&K. With a 69 battalion strength in the state, the image of the CRPF, unlike the other theatres such as the LWE affected states and the North-east, has remained that of a comparatively more acceptable force, occasional outbursts by locals against it notwithstanding. Experts attribute this to a soft approach or restraint in using force against the civilian population during COIN activities pursued by the CRPF. In addition, unlike the BSF, the CRPF is 'considered to be less corrupt' (Hussain 2005) by the people, thereby providing it with some measure of acceptability and approachability.

The operational potency of the CRPF is also linked to its sheer size, even subsequent to its reduction in battalion strength, following the improvement in the ground level situation and implementation of New Delhi's confidence building measures in the state. The force is, however, present in most of the militancy marred zone. Such uninterrupted deployment has ensured continuity in policy decisions and implementation. Further, experts attribute CRPF's COIN success to the force's socio-economic composition. 'The jawans of the CRPF are closer to the areas they serve, in terms of class background. This in turn, helps them carry a better image and get better intelligence' (Hussain 2005).[12]

On the negative side, CRPF personnel continue to suffer from a serious deficiency of logistics, training, and leadership, which is a legacy of its rushed induction into J&K in 2005 without the assets required to make it an effective force. These include a theatre-specific training school, an intelligence service, and communications-interception capabilities (Swami 2009). 'Even today, you could see jawans serving with torn socks and *banyans*, and with bad shoes and insufficient ration (especially kerosene)'.[13] Quite evidently, the pace of modernization that aims at capacity building and improving logistics for the forces has remained tardy.

Experts further opine that the CRPF could be buckling under the wide array of responsibilities it handles in the state—COIN duties, VIP protection, providing security to religious pilgrimages, and the frontline charge of fighting the Islamist-led street protests that gathered momentum in J&K in 2008. As organized mobs pelted stones on the security forces presenting a whole new law enforcement challenge, the state police assigned the CRPF the responsibility of dealing with the protesters. The result was catastrophic. Between January 2009 and June 2010, 682 CRPF personnel were severely injured in stone-pelting incidents. The retaliation by the forces was equally brutal. A media report referring to rioting in the town of Baramulla in July 2009 noted—'Eight of fourteen people injured in CRPF fire were hit above the waist—a sign that the bullets were intended to kill, not injure' (Swami 2009). Information made available by the state police following petitions filed under the Right to Information Act has revealed that since 2009, 'hundreds of CRPF men and people from other law enforcing agencies' (www.siasat.com) have been indicted in stone pelting and other related offences. The fatigue factor among personnel has had other manifestations too—growing number of desertions, firing on superiors on being denied leave, and human rights abuses.

Engagement with Politico-Strategic Environment

The COIN success in Punjab in the early 1990s demonstrated the criticality of unfettered engagement of the security forces with the existing politico-strategic environment. Not only did the police establishment enjoy the support of the political class, it managed to carefully define a role for each of the agencies involved in the anti-militancy campaign— the army, the CAPFs, the intelligence agencies—and assimilated them to achieve the end objective. Each agency was made aware of its role in the campaign, was provided with a sense of participation and ownership, thereby minimizing the scope for friction.

Part of a series of unique experiments demonstrating a synergy of operations between the security forces, in 1991, the CRPF and the BSF functioned under the 'cooperative command' structure along with the Punjab Police and the Indian Army, enhancing coordination, joint actions, and unity of effort by the forces. CAPF officers were made part of joint interrogation teams to handle prisoners. The command structure ensured sharing of intelligence between all the organizations. The radio network of the state police was interlinked with those of the CAPFs (Mahadevan 2008). A unique practice, which has since been repeated across conflict theatres, was initiated allowing the Inspector General of Police (Operations) to dual-hat for the CRPF and the Punjab Police (Mathur 2011). This minimized turnaround time on intelligence inputs and enhanced their actionability. Prolonged interaction between local and central forces dissipated the initial suspicions that each held of the other (Mahadevan 2008). As an expert points out, all the forces acted in 'complete concert, with a clearly defined institutional structure of cooperation and consultation'.[14]

This section critically examines the dynamics of engagement between the CAPFs and the politico-strategic environment prevailing in each of the three conflict zones in order to assess the impact of the relationship on the overall performance of the forces.

The LWE Theatre

The lack of operational success against the extremists in the LWE theatres, barring the state of Andhra Pradesh, points to a poor synergy between the CAPFs and the prevailing politico-strategic environment. It is attributable to the divergent end-state vision between the political class and the security forces in some states. In others, it is due to the persisting difficulty of operating together between the state police and the CAPFs. The lack of intelligence support for the operations merely accentuates the problem.

First, India does not have a consensus on dealing with the LWE problem. In this context, the states affected by the problem can be divided into three categories—first, those which support a force-centric approach; second, those which support a peace dialogue and developmental approach; and third, states which want the central forces to manage the bulk of the counter-extremist operations (Routray 2012). This poses enormous operational difficulty for the CAPFs, who perennially swing between a state of operations and a state of disengagement.

Second, in spite of the extended deployment of the CAPFs in the LWE affected states, the relations between the state police departments and the CAPFs have been marred by frictions on two counts—(1) the patterns of deployment, and (2) the absence of operational 'jointness', indicating lack of synergy and cooperation during joint operations. As pointed out earlier, the states pay scant attention to the patterns of CAPF deployment which on most occasions do not conform to the requirements on the ground. Further, the operational differences often result in public sparring, with negative effects on the morale of the forces.

For example, the relations between the two forces reached their nadir in Chhattisgarh in 2010. Following repeated extremist ambushes claiming the lives of CRPF personnel, the state DGP remarked, 'We cannot teach the paramilitary personnel how to walk' (*Hindustan Times* 2010). The subsequent war of words between the CRPF authorities and the state police establishment led to the relocation of the CRPF's regional headquarters from Chhattisgarh to West Bengal. An attempt was made to address such regular frictions and establish a coordination mechanism by the creation of unified commands in four states—Chhattisgarh, Odisha, Jharkhand, and West Bengal. However, differences have persisted as these new commands have failed to meet regularly.

Third, the lack of ground level intelligence rather than the absence of coordination with the intelligence agencies, has seriously affected the operational abilities of the CAPFs (Singh 2011; CNN-IBN 2012). A campaign of annihilation targeting the 'police informers' pursued by the extremists has considerably weakened the intelligence infrastructure of both the state and central intelligence agencies in the LWE affected theatres, resulting in a highly vulnerable environment for the forces. On account of this, the CRPF set up its own intelligence wing solely for the LWE belt in 2011, although the effectiveness of this endeavour remains to be tested.

The North-east

A common factor between both the LWE affected states and the North-east is the frantic demand for the deployment of central forces by the state governments. A senior police official in Assam revealed a novel tactic to ensure the presence of a 'close to sufficient' number of CAPF battalions, during an interview. 'States normally demand at least double the number of battalions than actually required and settle for a reduced number allotted by the MHA', he said.[15] Purely on the basis of such dire need, the engagement of the CAPFs with their politico-strategic environment should have been smooth and trouble free. However, the experience has varied from state to state.

COIN operations in Tripura, which defeated a tribal insurgency primarily through police action, fulfilled three of the critical criteria—political support, a synergy between the state police department and the CAPF establishment, and leadership. The Left Front government provided a free hand to the police to deal with the insurgents. As the police took the lead, the CRPF and BSF personnel performed able supporting roles, both in COIN operations and also along the Indo-Bangladesh border, controlling the movements of the insurgents who had found safe haven in that country. Meticulously planned joint operations, sharing of intelligence, and regular coordination meetings between the police and CRPF authorities removed the possibility of friction. The COIN operations in the state resembled the operations in Punjab and replicated the success story. It was no coincidence that Tripura DGP GM Srivastav, who oversaw the anti-insurgent operations, had served under Punjab DGP K.P.S. Gill as a junior officer and had followed the Punjab experiment in great detail.[16]

In Assam, the state government attempted to coordinate the activities of the Army, the CAPFs, and the state police by establishing a unified command structure in 1997. Primarily aimed at the 'pursuit of the terrorists in a coordinated offensive to weaken their resolve and to undermine their cohesiveness' (Hussain 2008), the setup aimed at addressing a practical problem of division among the forces. Infiltration of the police department by the insurgents had made the state police an unreliable partner for both the Army and CAPFs. Several tactical joint force operations failed to achieve desirable results as insurgents deserted their hideouts after being tipped off. Similarly, state police nurtured a grievance against the CAPFs for indulging in human rights violations.

However, instead of providing a single chain of command and establishing a modicum of cohesiveness among the forces, the unified command structure degenerated into a 'competitive command' (Hussain 2008), thereby grossly limiting the achievements of the forces. The fact that the Army was allowed to head the command structure, instead of a civilian authority, thereby attaching a stamp of superiority on one of the three constituents of the security establishment, led the other two to go on an overdrive to claim credit for the success of specific COIN operations. An unhealthy competition became the hallmark of inter-force relations.

Similarly, allegations of human rights violations by the AR personnel in Manipur created a division between the political administration and the state police on the one hand and the CAPFs on the other, with a negative impact on the success of the COIN operations. Following the 2004 Manorama Devi killing episode, the state government, in response to the growing popular demand for the withdrawal of the controversial Armed Forces (Special Powers) Act [AFSPA], withdrew the Act from certain areas of the state, much to the angst of the AR establishment. The latter, claiming that the Act is an enabling piece of legislation, providing its personnel the right to raid, arrest, and even kill suspected insurgents, refused to operate in those areas (Talukdar 2004). The continuous bickering between the CAPFs and the state police department has been one of the key reasons for the failure of COIN operations in Manipur. The establishment of a unified command structure in the state in 2004 has not been able to address the problem of inter-force coordination.

Jammu & Kashmir

As mentioned before, continued deployment of the CRPF in certain areas of J&K has ensured a continuity in COIN practices. The state set up a Unified Command Structure (UCS) to coordinate the activities of the Army, the CAPFs, and the police in 1993, becoming the first Indian state to do so. Under the UCS, CRPF authorities claim a measure of operational autonomy in carrying out anti-militancy operations, thus indicating a high degree of functional synergy between the forces. For instance, elaborating on the joint operations carried out by the forces, in a May 2012 media interview, a senior CRPF official claimed—'Operations are conducted based on intelligence. And once intelligence is received, it is the question of response time. Depending upon who can respond in what time frame, each force is given a role to play' (Interview with B.N. Ramesh 2012).

Experts, however, differ in their opinion on the level of inter-force coordination. According to K.P.S. Gill, former DGP Punjab, in J&K—

> the command and control system has been the weakest element of strategy, pitting force against force in an abrasive and antagonistic context that emphasises the paramountcy of one force over others, and dissipates energies in an unhealthy competition at the operational level. Narrow fiefdoms have been created, and individual commanders feel threatened by the operations and presence of other forces, and consequently adopt an attitude of hostility and contempt towards these (Hussain 2008).

Gill goes on to say that—'an efficient system of command, control and co-ordination between diverse forces has been one of the greatest lacunae in every theatre of internal strife in India' (Hussain 2008). While instances of such lack of coordination are difficult to cite, the stone pelting incidents that began in 2008 and continued till the summer of 2011 brought out the operational schism between the state police and the CRPF personnel.

A commissioned study conducted by the Institute of Defence Studies & Analyses (IDSA) on the role of the CRPF in J&K revealed that the state police could be using the central forces as a shield and passing on the blame to them while committing human rights violation themselves. 'In several instances, while the firing was done by the local police, the blame was passed on to the CRPF. In some cases, when the CRPF wanted to lodge First Information Reports (FIRs), they were not lodged while people's FIRs against the CRPF were quite easily lodged', the study said (Kumar 2012). Experts, pointing at an erratic deployment pattern, suggest that the police and not the CAPFs, should be dealing with the stone pelting crowd.[17]

The political elites' opinion on the presence of the CAPFs in the state swings perilously between their ambition to decrease the footprint of the central forces in accordance with the improving security situation and retaining the CAPFs, citing lack of confidence in the capacity of the state police to deal with the remnants of militancy. Following a series of civilian deaths in CRPF firing during the stone pelting incidents in 2010, Chief Minister Omar Abdullah termed the force as one which has 'gone out of control'[18] and declared his intention to get rid of the central forces from the state. That stance, however, was soon reversed. The Chief Minister clarified that unless the state has adequate numbers of police personnel, it cannot replace the CRPF.

Recommendations

In sum, the CAPFs' performance has suffered internally due to a crisis of leadership, the inability of the forces to adapt to the demands of the conflict zones, and a modernization process which has failed to take care of the basic needs of the forces. Externally, the CAPF ability to deliver has been constrained by the legal requirements of making them a supporting force and also by the dynamics of inter-force coordination. As a result, the potential of this mammoth force remains underutilized. While some of these operational constraints are unavoidable and are common to many countries, problems in the logistical sphere can certainly be addressed and improved. It is essential that policy to deal with the problem consider the following short-term and long-term measures.

First, a revision of the mandate of the CAPFs needs immediate consideration. Limiting their role only to support the state police and making them a part of the state's strategy, which on many occasions has been found to be inadequate, wastes the energy and resources of the CAPFs. An element of functional autonomy needs to be built into the CAPFs' mandate. Since this has implications for India's federal polity, a national consensus on this needs to be evolved.

Second, in the long term, India's national security requirements would be better served by way of merging the different CAPF organizations into a single unit. In view of the near liquidation of the operational and functional differences between these seven CAPF organizations, the proposed unification would effectively address the problem of modernization by bringing the entire force under a single plan; would facilitate unimpeded switch between peace time and COIN duties, thereby addressing the problem of stress and consequent indiscipline; and would result in better management of the force.

Third, on an immediate basis and thereafter, the expansion programme of the CAPFs needs to factor in the necessity of acquiring both officers and soldiers. As explained earlier, the deficit in the number of entry and mid-level officers is the source of a serious command and control problem in the CAPFs. The criticality of discipline and balance cannot be overlooked while implementing a rushed recruitment programme.

Fourth, in the long term, an arrangement for transfer of personnel between the Army, CAPFs, and the police can address the problem of inter-force coordination. 'Class division' is one of the serious problems that impedes bonhomie and unity of purpose among the forces, with implications for their effectiveness.

Fifth, in the long term, modernization of the state police forces could hold the key to halt the perennial need for expanding the CAPFs. The operational weakness among the state police forces creates a condition of dependency of the states on CAPFs. Moreover, this dependency accentuates the problem by allowing the state governments to pay scant attention to modernizing their police forces. The MHA could consider evolving an incentive system for providing additional funds to states performing well on police modernization projects.

Sixth, developing close contact between the civilian population and the CAPFs is a critical necessity in the conflict zones. The civic action programmes of the CAPFs in their present forms are stand-alone initiatives and hence are ad hoc-ish in nature. An expansion of and institutionalization of the programme to be implemented in coordination with the civil administration could be considered. The overall objective of such programmes should be to extend the reach of the state administration in conflict zones and not merely to cultivate a friendly population to elicit intelligence.

Lastly, in the long term, a process of infusion of external wisdom relevant to the functioning and modernization of the CAPFs needs to be institutionalized. Setting up of a think tank to serve the needs of the CAPFs would possibly go a long way in addressing the deficit of ideas that has been the bane of CAPF operations in many of India's conflict theatres.

Notes

1. The CAPFs were previously known as the Central Para Military Forces (CPMFs). On 18 May 2011, a government notification effected a change in the nomenclature. See, Office Memorandum, Ministry of Home Affairs, Government of India.

2. Disaggregated data regarding detailed manpower in individual CAPF organizations is not available for years beyond 2007.

3. Article 246 of the Indian Constitution divides legislative powers into three lists—Union, State, and Concurrent. While 97 subjects under the Central category are the responsibility of the Central Government in New Delhi, 66 'state' subjects are the exclusive jurisdiction of the State governments. Residuary legislative powers rest with the Centre. Moreover, the Centre can enact laws on items in the 'state' list in case of declaration of a state of emergency. Law and Order is a 'state' subject.

4. Author's interview with R.K. Shukla, former Special Director General of Police, Sashastra Seema Bal, New Delhi, 12 January 2011.

5. Following an ambush that claimed the lives of 27 CRPF personnel in Chhattisgarh's Narayanpur district in June 2010, Home Minister P. Chidambaarm asked the state police department to revisit the CAPF deployment to reflect their operational or developmental requirements. The Home Minister said that the deployment reflects a strategy that had been decided a year earlier and not the current requirement. See Kumar 2010.

6. It noted, 'the condition of police forces in the North Eastern States is quite poor. Many of the militant groups have far more modern arms and equipment than the State Police'. Quoted in Routray 2002.

7. Author's interview with G.M. Srivastava, former Director General of Police, Tripura, at Guwahati (Assam), 14 February 2011.

8. See 'Insurgency Related Fatalities in Manipur: 2002–2010'. Available at http://www.satp.org/satporgtp/countries/india/states/manipur/data_sheets/annualreport.htm (accessed 24 June 2012).

9. A note circulated by the MHA in the Cabinet Committee on Security (CCS) in 2011 observed—'Assam Rifles has traditionally been a counter-insurgency (CI) force. The Assam Rifles is located not exactly at the border, but very much inside in the interiors to be also able to conduct CI operations. The attention of an essentially CI force to both guarding border and carrying out CI results in neither of the objectives being addressed effectively'. See Makkar 2011.

10. See 'Jammu and Kashmir Backgrounder'. Available at http://www.satp.org/satporgtp/countries/india/states/jandk/backgrounder/index.html (accessed 12 June 2012).

11. The year 1990 recorded a surge in militant activities over the previous year with 1,177 deaths in 3,905 incidents. In comparison, 1989 had recorded only

92 fatalities. See South Asia Terrorism Portal, 'Fatalities in Terrorist Violence 1988–2012'. Available at http://www.satp.org/satporgtp/countries/india/states/jandk/data_sheets/annual_casualties.htm (accessed 12 June 2012).

12. The foot soldier in the Indian armed forces is known as a 'jawan'.

13. Telephonic interview with Dr Suba Chandran, Director, Institute of Peace and Conflict Studies, New Delhi, on 21 June 2012.

14. See 'Backgrounder-Punjab'. Available at http://www.satp.org/satporgtp/countries/india/states/punjab/backgrounder/index.html (accessed 15 June 2012).

15. Author's interview with Bhaskar Jyoti Mahanta, Inspector General of Police, Assam, at Guwahati (Assam), 14 February 2011.

16. Interview with G.M. Srivastav, Guwahati (Assam), 14 February 2011.

17. Interview with E.N. Rammohan, former DGP, BSF. See G. Sampath 2010.

18. Interview with E.N. Rammohan, former DGP, BSF. See G. Sampath 2010.

References

Anonymous. 'J&K police indicts its own men, CRPF in stone pelting, other offences', 8 June 2012. Available at http://www.siasat.com/english/news/jk-police-indicts-its-own-men-crpf-stone-pelting-other-offences (accessed 12 June 2012).

Chidambaram, P. 2011. Ministry of Home Affairs, Government of India. Press Conference, 1 June. Available at http://mha.nic.in/pdfs/HM-OpenStat-010611.pdf (accessed 14 June 2012).

CNN-IBN. 2012. 'Anti-Naxal ops: Over 460 Posts for CRPF Intel Wing Announced', 31 January. Available at http://www.moneycontrol.com/news/wire-news/anti-naxal-ops-over-460-posts-for-crpf-intel-wing-announced_660163.html (accessed 24 January 2012).

Gupta, Shishir. 2010. 'Dantewada Massacre: Probe Finds Command Failure', *Indian Express*, 23 April.

Hindustan Times. 2010. 'We Can't Teach CRPF How to Walk: Chhattisgarh DGP', 2 July.

Human Rights Watch. 2008. 'These Fellows Must Be Eliminated', 15 September. Available at http://www.hrw.org/reports/2008/09/15/these-fellows-must-be-eliminated (accessed 20 June 2012).

Hussain, Aijaz. 2005. 'CRPF Replaces BSF in Kashmir', *Rediff*, 13 September. Available at http://www.rediff.com/news/2005/sep/13bsf.htm (accessed 13 June 2012).

Hussain, Wasbir. 2008. 'Multi-force Operations in Counter Terrorism: A View from the Assam Theatre', *Faultlines: Writings on Conflict & Resolution*, 9. Available at http://www.satp.org/satporgtp/publication/faultlines/volume9/Article2.htm (accessed 22 June 2012).

Interview with B.N. Ramesh, Inspector General (Operations- Kashmir), Central Reserve Police Force, *Force India*, May 2012. Available at http://www.forceindia.net/Interviewmay4.aspx (accessed 15 June 2012).

Kumar, Rakesh. 2012.'India's biggest police force are an unhappy lot in the Valley', *Daily Mail*, 27 May. Available at http://www.dailymail.co.uk/indiahome/indianews/article-2150541/Indias-biggest-police-force-unhappy-lot-Valley.html (accessed 20 May 2012).

Kumar, Vinay. 2010.'Revisit CRPF deployment in Chhattisgarh', *The Hindu*, 1 July.

Mahadevan, Prem. 2008.'The Gill Doctrine: A Model for 21st Century Counter-terrorism?' *Faultlines: Writings on Conflict & Resolution*, 19. Available at http://www.satp.org/satporgtp/publication/faultlines/volume19/Article1.htm (accessed 15 June 2012).

Makkar, Sahi. 2011. 'Defence, Home Ministries in Turf War Over Myanmar Border Security', *Live Mint*, 30 May. Available at http://www.livemint.com/2011/05/29222216/Defence-home-ministries-in-tu.html?atype=tp (accessed 12 June 2012).

Mathur, Anant. 2011. 'Secrets of COIN Success Lessons from the Punjab Campaign', *Faultlines: Writings on Conflict & Resolution*, 20. Available at http://www.satp.org/satporgtp/publication/faultlines/volume20/Article2.htm (accessed 15 June 2012).

Mukherjee, Soumik. 2012. 'Half-Baked Ideas and Empty Promises', *Tehelka*, 9 (25). Available at http://tehelka.com/story_main53.asp?filename=Ne230612half.asp (accessed 19 June 2012).

Office Memorandum, Ministry of Home Affairs, Government of India. 2011. 'Adoption of new nomenclature of Central Armed Police Forces', 18 March. Available at http://aicpmfewa.org/welfare/146-adoption-of-new-nomenclature-of-central-armed-police-forces (accessed 6 June 2011).

Routray, Bibhu Prasad. 2002.'Running Guns in India's Northeast', South Asia Intelligence Review, 1 (17). Available at http://www.satp.org/satporgtp/sair/Archives/1_17.htm (accessed 23 June 2012).

———. 2011.'Do our forces know their briefs in the Naxal heartland', Article No. 1935, Centre for Land Warfare Studies (CLAWS), 28 August. Available at http://www.claws.in/index.php?action=details&m_id=936&u_id=155 (accessed 16 June 2012).

———. 2012. 'India's Internal Security Outlook: Progress but Still Areas of Concern', Commentary No. 2/2012, Rajaratnam School of International Studies (RSIS), 3 January. Available at http://www.rsis.edu.sg/publications/Perspective/RSIS0022012.pdf (accessed 12 June 2012).

Routray, Bibhu Prasad. 2012. 'India's Response to Maoist Extremism: Force, Development or Both?', Policy Paper, S. Rajaratnam School of International Studies, May. Available at http://www.rsis.edu.sg/publications/policy_papers/Indias%20Response%20to%20Maoist%20Extremism.pdf (accessed 22 June 2012).

Sampath, G. 2010. 'Kashmir Police, Not CRPF, Should Confront Stone-pelting Mobs', *Daily News & Analysis*, 4 July. Available at http://www.dnaindia.com/opinion/interview_kashmir-police-not-crpf-should-confront-stone-pelting-mobs_1404969 (accessed 20 May 2012).

Singh, Rakesh K. 2011. 'Green Signal: CRPF's Own Intelligence Network for Maoist Heartland', *Pioneer*, 17 January. Available at http://crpf.nic.in/CRPF_NEWS/321.pdf (accessed 24 June 2012).

Sinha, S.P. 2011. 'Nagaland: The Beginning of Insurgency–I', *Indian Defence Review*. Available at http://www.indiandefencereview.com/news/nagaland-the-beginning-of-insurgency-i/2/ (accessed July 2012).

Swami, Praveen. 2009. 'Combat-fatigued CRPF needs intensive care', *The Hindu Blogs*, 17 July. Available at http://blogs.thehindu.com/delhi/?p=26136 (accessed 16 June 2012).

Talukdar, Susanta. 2004. 'Manipur on Fire', *Frontline*, 21 (18). Available at http://www.flonnet.com/fl2118/stories/20040910007400400.htm (accessed 24 February 2012).

Website of the Assam Rifles. 'The Assam Rifles: 177 Years of Glory and Sacrifice'. Available at http://assamrifles.gov.in/history.aspx (accessed 20 June 2012).

7   Civil-Military Relations and Military Effectiveness in India

Anit Mukherjee

In many ways, the state of civil-military relations, especially the tradition of civilian control over the military, along with free and fair elections, lies at the heart of the democratic ideal. In turn, civil-military relations can be defined as a continuous contest between politicians, civilian bureaucrats, and senior military commanders over policy matters. This contest is influenced by many factors including the strength of the political order, personality of political and military commanders, domestic political conditions, and the perceived threat environment. Huntington, in his seminal work *The Soldier and the State*, identified this contest as the main issue and argued that the problem in modern states is 'not armed revolt but the relation of the expert to the politician' (Huntington 1957: 20). Half a century after Huntington's observation, this debate continues to resonate and attracts attention in both academic and journalistic circles.[1] This chapter studies civil-military relations in contemporary India and argues that it has had an adverse impact on Indian military effectiveness.

The success of India's democracy, despite its formidable challenges in the decades following independence, has attracted much scholarly attention.[2] However, the Indian military— around a million strong and involved in numerous external wars and internal insurgencies—have rarely been scrutinized by scholars.[3] Even when studied, most scholars have focused on the reasons for the lack of military intervention in politics.[4] This should not be surprising as controlling the military has been one of the biggest challenges for most post-colonial democracies. Moreover, India's 'other' Pakistan, provided a suitable case study for scholars to use the comparative method.[5] While the question of lack of military intervention in domestic politics might have been an interesting post-independence concern, when India faced considerable nation-building challenges, it is perhaps less relevant today with strong democratic institutions and a professional military that has internalized the tradition of firm civilian control. As such, India can be considered a mature democracy, defined by Richard Kohn, as a democracy 'where civilian control has historically been strong and military establishments have focused on external defense' (Kohn 1997: 141). Perhaps the more interesting, and policy relevant question, is what are the causes and consequences of the form of civilian control in contemporary India? In response to internal and external challenges, how have civil-military relations evolved and what have been the major areas of contestation? Finally, why has the government undertaken episodic reforms aimed at streamlining the military and to what extent were these reforms successful?

The first section of this chapter briefly examines the theory of civil-military relations and situates the Indian experience of civilian control within. It argues that while Huntington's 'objective control' best describes civil-military relations in India, at the same time as it does not, contrary to Huntington's claim, maximize its military effectiveness. Thus it calls into question the Huntingtonian paradigm. Next it describes the three unique characteristics of civil-military relations in India which shape the defence policy process. The next section briefly describes the study of military effectiveness and the problems associated with defining it. It analyses Indian military effectiveness by examining its four crucial determinants—weapons procurement, defence planning, integration, and human resource development. While doing so, it focuses on how each of these processes are shaped by the unique characteristics of civil-military relations. The main argument is that the current structure of civil-military relations, more accurately described as an 'absent dialogue', has an adverse impact on its military effectiveness. This is followed by some suggested explanations. Finally it argues that the Indian state has acknowledged some of these problems and has made some attempts at defence reforms; though more forceful political intervention is required. However, the prospect of such political intervention, in the absence of a crisis, is uncertain.

The Theory of Civil-Military Relations and India

The Indian model of civil-military relations, on the surface, follows what Eliot Cohen has called, 'the normal theory of civil-military relations'.[6] The normal theory refers to Huntington's notion of 'objective control' in his classic *The Soldier and the State* (1957). 'Objective control' focuses on maximizing military effectiveness while ensuring civilian authority and requires 'the recognition (from civilian authorities) of autonomous military professionalism' (Huntington 1957: 83). In other words, an acknowledgement, by civilian authorities, that the military has an expertise that should not be interfered with. The politician sets the goal and the soldier is free to do what he wants to achieve it, relying on his 'professionalism'. Allowing military professionals autonomy within their own realm, according to Huntington, minimizes the danger of military intervention in politics by 'rendering them politically sterile and neutral' (Huntington 1957: 84) while, at the same time, ensuring that a professional officer corps carries out 'the wishes of any civilian group which secures legitimate authority within the state' (Huntington 1957: 84). The opposite of objective control, according to Huntington, is 'subjective control' which aims at maximizing civilian power by 'civilianizing the military, making them the mirror of the state' (Huntington 1956: 678). Crucially, subjective control denies 'the existence of an independent sphere of purely military imperatives', and 'presupposes military participation in politics' (Huntington 1956: 380–1). In other words, political regimes and, by extension, societies mould the military in its own image either by transplanting civilian elites into the military or by promoting senior military officers on the basis of their political beliefs. According to this definition, subjective control is practiced in the militaries of most communist and authoritarian states.

However, as this chapter argues, the Indian model of civil-military relations which closely adheres to Huntington's 'objective control' does not maximize its military effectiveness. As military effectiveness is one of the fundamental goals of objective control, the Indian case study calls for a revision to the Huntingtonian paradigm. Indeed, the theory of 'objective control' has been criticized, for a variety of reasons, by a new generation of scholars, most notably Peter Feaver and Eliot Cohen (Feaver 2003: 1–54; Cohen 2002: 225–48). Feaver's main criticism is that 'Huntington's theory does not adequately capture American civil-military relations'

(Feaver 2003: 38). Cohen argues that military professionalism is variable and a clear division between political ends and military means is not certain. Moreover, advocating the concept of the 'unequal dialogue', he cites instances where successful wartime commanders interfered in 'purely military' plans and challenged the assumption of military commanders.

Why Objective Control Best Describes Indian Civil-Military Relations

Indian civil-military relations represent the form of 'objective control' prescribed by Huntington. That is, the politician broadly sets the goals and the military enjoys considerable autonomy to achieve them. While this arrangement was largely followed post-independence, however, according to one narrative, this was upended by the wrongful 'political interference' by then Defence Minister Krishna Menon. This narrative blames India's forward policy and subsequent defeat in the 1962 China war to this interference. As a result, the 1962 war has had a major impact on the narrative of civil-military relations.[7] The Henderson-Brooks report, initiated by the army, and the sacking of Krishna Menon as Defence Minister, helped to perpetuate the 'story' that the defeat was caused due to political interference with promotions and because of 'the higher direction of war', or lack thereof.[8] Thereafter, the pattern of civil-military relations in India, closely follows 'objective control'—with limited political 'interference' and semi-autonomous military organizations. This pattern was cemented after the victorious 1971 Bangladesh war during which the then Chief of Army Staff, General Sam Manekshaw, 'asserted himself' and successfully postponed the invasion of East Pakistan against the wishes of the civilian principals including Prime Minister Indira Gandhi.[9] However, this arrangement came up short during the Indian Army's deployment in Sri Lanka in 1987. In an episode that has come to be known as 'India's Vietnam', the Indian Peacekeeping Force (IPKF) was ordered to militarily defeat the Liberation Tigers of Tamil Eelam (LTTE), and was consequently embroiled in an insurgency without any clear political guidelines. This operation, during which India attempted to flex its regional muscle, is still a subject of fierce controversy with the military blaming the civilians and vice versa.[10] The military's charge is that, despite warning from field commanders, the government embarked on an ill-advised and ill-planned mission to defeat the LTTE.[11] Moreover, they contend that the military action was ordered without a clear political mission, other than a nebulous objective of disarming the LTTE. This was bound to fail without a political endgame that responded to legitimate Tamil demands for autonomy. Civilian officials, however, argue that the then Army Chief, Gen. K. Sundarji, was well within the decision-making process and failed to communicate and prepare his troops for the 'inevitable' war. Despite the IPKF fiasco, and due to a changing political and international climate—including the assassination of former Prime Minister Rajiv Gandhi and end of the Cold War—structural reforms in the pattern of civil-military relations were not executed. Hence, as early as 1990, the then Prime Minister V.P. Singh, responding to criticism about inadequate civil-military integration, announced the formation of a National Security Council (NSC). However, for a number of reasons including bureaucratic opposition, this proved to be a stillborn measure. Although this organization was eventually created after the Kargil war in 1999, its current functioning has been deemed to be 'virtually dysfunctional'.[12]

Indian civil-military relations then, on the main indicators that differentiate objective from subjective control, appear to fulfill conditions in support of the former (see Table 7.1). However, even in recent times, Indian military officers frequently and incorrectly allege that they are under 'subjective control'.[13]

Characteristics of Civil-Military Relations in India

The strength of Indian democracy, legitimatized by regular elections, peaceful transfer of power, political parties and participation, free press, independent judiciary, and strong civilian institutions, is responsible for civilian control of the military. Civilian control, in turn, has been enhanced and implemented by bureaucratic institutions, which have evolved in composition, responsibilities, and organizational structure. Over time the Indian military has, in turn, internalized the idea of civilian control and its professional ethos prides itself of being 'apolitical'. However, while civilian supremacy has never been seriously questioned in India there is an underlying fear of unrestricted military power and of the Man on the Horseback, reinforced by the experiences of neighbouring countries.[14] To prevent such an occurrence, the military has been subjected to strong bureaucratic control. This ordinarily should not have been problematic or unique, for instance, the US military is controlled by a massive civilian

Table 7.1 Civilian Control in India

Civilian control and	Objective Control aimed at	Subjective Control aimed at	Civilian control in India
Society	Military to be a tool of society, career military isolated socially and physically from elements in the social structure.	Military to be a mirror of society, reflecting and embodying the dominant social forces and political ideologies of that society.	Objective- *Considerable physical and societal isolation of the Indian military from society. Moreover, social and political ideologies, like caste based reservation, not imposed on the military.*
Spheres of influence	Sharp delimitation between civilian and military interests, emphasis on militarizing the military.	Blending of civilian and military interests, emphasis on civilianizing the military.	Objective- *The Indian military enjoys considerable autonomy over its own sphere of activities and is mainly focused on war fighting.*
Politics	Military abstention from politics.	Military's participation in politics.	Objective- *The Indian military is removed from any political activity.*
Military expertise	Recognition that the military has an independent sphere of expertise and a clear distinction in role and function between military and civilian leaders.	Denying the existence of an independent sphere of purely military imperatives.	Objective- *Strong acknowledgement of military expertise.*
Power of the military	Minimizing military's power by confining it to a restricted sphere and rendering it politically sterile and neutral on all issues outside that sphere.	Minimizing military's power by rendering it indistinguishable from civilian power.	Objective- *Military's power is restricted only to its own sphere of activities. Minimal influence on political, diplomatic, or social issues.*
Difference between civilians and the military	Presupposing disagreement between military and civilian leaders but depends on obedience of the former.	Presupposes agreement between military and civilian leaders.	Objective/Mixed- *Despite some disagreements the principle of civilian supremacy is always maintained.*

Source: This distinction and differences between subjective and objective control relies on Samuel Huntington 1956: 380–5.

bureaucracy, except for the three unique characteristics of civil-military relations in India.

First is the lack of civilian expertise in military affairs—a characteristic applicable to both political and bureaucratic elements. In the first place, there are very few politicians who have an interest in the military. Curiously, a military veteran turned politician, Jaswant Singh, was responsible for pushing through major reforms in the military as a Defence Minister in 2001. Exceptions apart, the political class has to rely on the bureaucracy for advice on defence affairs. However, the bureaucracy itself lacks expertise in military affairs. In some ways, this is a problem inherited from the colonial era, with its emphasis on the generalist cadre instead of the specialist one, and it has had an impact on the functioning of most public institutions in India.[15] As an acknowledgement of this problem and in an effort to obviate it, the government has tried to post civilian bureaucrats in the Ministry of Defence (MoD) for longer tenures than usual. However, in the absence of in-depth knowledge and hindered by information asymmetries, inherent in civil-military relations, most bureaucrats focus on the process of decision-making instead of the outcome. Further, they lack the expertise to challenge the military on its logic and find it difficult to arbitrate between competing sectional interests. For instance, the Indian Air Force (IAF) opposed the creation of the Army Aviation wing, and still opposes the induction of attack helicopters in that wing, allegedly on 'turf' considerations—an issue that the Defence Ministry has not satisfactorily resolved even after decades.[16] Other than the problems that arise from the generalist system of administration in the civil services, there is a deeper, fundamental problem. The field of academic study on defence issues in India is largely underdeveloped, suffers from financial and institutional apathy, and offers few career opportunities for its graduates. Further as the state does not follow a declassification procedure there are few resources available to academics.[17] As a result, the discourse on defence affairs is dominated by retired military officials. Moreover, due to the underdevelopment of the field of defence studies, few incoming civil servants get an exposure to defence affairs during their graduate education.

The second characteristic of civil-military relations is strong but competing bureaucratic controls over the military. At the time of independence and in later years, the fear of a military coup preyed on both Jawaharlal Nehru and Indira Gandhi (Kundu 1998: 109–18, 163; Pant 2007: 242–3). While it is still a matter of controversy whether such a threat existed, but according to one narrative common within the military, this was used as a pretext by civilian bureaucrats to strengthen their power vis-à-vis the military. Hence, all actions which had financial consequences—a strong measure of control—had to be cleared by civilian bureaucrats. Over time, this led to two narratives within the military. First, that they were not under 'political control but were under bureaucratic control'.[18] Admittedly, this narrative is an oversimplification as politicians themselves, lacking in-depth knowledge of the military and deeply involved in political activities, prefer the bureaucracy to provide an alternative advice to proposals emanating from service headquarters. The second narrative within the military is that they are excluded from crucial decision-making forums, thus denying it a role in the policy-making process.[19] There is some truth to this. While the armed forces are consulted before decisions are made on the use of force, on crucial interagency deliberations the services are not adequately represented. The institution that was supposed to allow the military to have a role in decision-making was the Defense Ministers Committee (DMC). But, indicative of the lack of civil-military interaction, since independence the DMC has either functioned erratically or not at all.[20] Writing about the policy process in the 1980s, P.R. Chari identified the Policy Planning and Review Committee (PPRC) in the Ministry of External Affairs (MEA) and the Joint Intelligence Committee (JIC), under the Cabinet Secretariat, as the nodal agencies in charge of threat assessment and strategic planning. Although the PPRC has offered a permanent invitation to the Defence Secretary to participate in its meetings, there was no representation from the armed forces. Similarly, the development of nuclear weapons programme and its delivery mechanisms has been characterized by a strict separation between the civilians and the military.[21] To be sure there have been positive changes in the working relationship between the civilians and the military after the Kargil war, however, some recent episodes indicate that this is still a problem. For instance, the military was excluded from the deliberations of the recent pay commission leading to a mini-crisis in civil-military relations.[22] Tellingly, even when discussing issues like the use of the army in Kashmir, the Cabinet Committee on Security (CCS) met without any service representative.[23] In sum, one of the problems with civil-military relations in India is that, 'the military in this country does not participate in policy making, with inescapably deleterious consequences' (Malhotra 2005: xiv). To overcome this exclusion, military officers have tried, with varying degrees of success, to forge informal and interpersonal ties with political or bureaucratic figures. The results of these efforts, however, have been erratic and personality driven. Unsurprisingly, military officers, usually after retirement, have complained against this form of bureaucratic control.

Finally, to facilitate the acceptability to the military of the previous factors, considerable autonomy has been granted to the military on its own affairs. While the concept of strong bureaucratic control with military autonomy may appear paradoxical, the entire process plays out as a complicated game of negotiations, bargaining, threats, and contestation. However, by and large, the political class rarely interferes in what is considered purely military affairs. For instance, issues pertaining to doctrine, training, force structures, integration, and military education have very little, if any, civilian guidance. In practice, the military is allowed to do most of what it wants in its own sphere of activities— training and education, threat assessments, force structure, doctrine, innovations, appointments (up to a certain rank), and miscellaneous welfare activities.

These unique characteristics of civil-military relations in India can be characterized more appropriately as that of an 'absent dialogue' indicating the lack of communication and understanding between politicians, bureaucrats, and military officers.[24] According to K. Subrahmanyam, this directly translates into a system where 'politicians enjoy power without any responsibility, bureaucrats wield power without any accountability and the military assumes responsibility without any direction'.[25]

Military Effectiveness and Civil-Military Relations

There are issues with defining military effectiveness which have admittedly been problematic for its study.[26] To skirt around this problem, most scholars have eschewed a formal definition of the term altogether.[27] Complicating the issue is relating military effectiveness to political objectives. If 'war is a continuation of politics by other means', then evaluating war-fighting without referring it to political objectives is paradoxical. Lawrence Korb rightly argues that effective militaries are those that achieve the objectives assigned to them or are victorious in war (Korb 1984: 42).

If we were to apply that measure—militaries that fulfill political objectives—then the Indian military has acquitted itself well. Barring the 1962 China war and, to some extent, the IPKF expedition, the Indian military has succeeded on most, if not all, counts. During the 1965 war, it was able to prevent both Operations Gibraltar and Grand Slam, aimed at capturing Kashmir, from succeeding and when ceasefire was declared India was in a comparatively better negotiating position than Pakistan. During the 1971 Bangladesh and the 1999 Kargil war India was able to achieve all its political objectives and attained significant diplomatic victories. Even during the ill-fated IPKF expedition in Sri Lanka, the military was able to achieve the stated objective of conducting provincial elections in Jaffna and failed only in the highly improbable task of disarming the LTTE. Finally, the Indian Army has been extensively engaged in numerous internal insurgencies and has never been defeated in any of them as India has never seceded territory to insurgent groups. On the contrary, it has assisted in incorporating 'states' within the Indian union—Junagarh, Kashmir, Hyderabad, Goa, and Sikkim. Why, then, must we question and study the effectiveness of the Indian military?

A closer study of all of India's wars, except the 1962 China war, reveal that the Indian military enjoyed considerable superiority both in terms of men and material over the enemy. Despite that advantage the Indian military faced significant problems due to the absence of institutional integration. This, in turn, is partly the result of problematic civil-military relations. For instance, in the 1965 India-Pakistan war and the IPKF operations in Sri Lanka, there were major problems with inter-services integration.[28] Even in the victorious 1971 Bangladesh war, the Indian Army required considerable time to prepare itself for the campaign in the East.[29] Moreover, as Allan Millett, Williamson Murray, and Kenneth Watman point out, 'victory is not a characteristic of an organization but rather a result of organizational activity. Judgments of effectiveness should thus retain some sense of proportional cost and organizational process'.[30] This measure allows us to examine the effectiveness of the Indian military beyond a simplistic victory or defeat measure of effectiveness. Thus, despite the fact that India has not lost any territory in an insurgent campaign since independence, one can still examine the effectiveness of India's counterinsurgency capabilities. As argued elsewhere, India's counterinsurgency capability is significantly hampered by civil-military relations.[31] Indeed Indian officials seem to be aware about this and there is much debate in the parliament on 'defence preparedness'.[32] Finally, regardless of the performance of the Indian military, studying its effectiveness is a subject worthy in itself. As Peter Feaver warns, 'an inadequate military institution may be worse than none at all... it could lull leaders into a false confidence, leading them to rash behavior and then failing in the ultimate military contest' (Feaver 1999: 214).

For the purpose of this study, the concept of military effectiveness is borrowed from previous work on this subject by Risa Brooks. According to her, military effectiveness is defined as 'the capacity to create military power from a state's basic resources in wealth, technology, population size and human capital' (Brooks and Stanley 2007: 9). Risa Brooks further lists four *attributes* of military effectiveness as integration, responsiveness, skill, and quality, and stresses the importance of possessing all of them. Integration is defined as 'the degree to which different military activities are internally consistent and mutually reinforcing', responsiveness as the 'ability to tailor military activity to a state's own capabilities, its adversaries capabilities and external constraints', skill measures military personnel's 'ability to achieve particular tasks', and quality is the ability obtain 'highly capable weapons and equipment' (Brooks and Stanley 2007: 10–13). This chapter extrapolates on these four attributes to derive its main dependent variables. Hence it examines four processes within the Indian military— weapons procurement, defence planning, inter-services integration, and human resources development. These, in turn, correlate broadly with quality, responsiveness, integration, and skill, respectively. The attributes of military effectiveness, its definition, and the corresponding variables studied in this chapter are described in Table 7.2.

There are other competing explanations to military effectiveness— mainly culture, social structures, and threat environment (Brooks and Stanley 2007: 15–18). It is impossible to isolate a single factor explanation to military effectiveness as all these factors play an important role. Despite these problems, one of the approaches to the study of military effectiveness is to break it down to its components— weapons, officer skill levels, interagency, and integration. In other words, understand how each of these processes *work*. That institutional approach has been adopted in this study of military effectiveness.

The Attributes of Military Effectiveness

The structure and the three unique characteristics of Indian civil-military relations have had an adverse impact on its military effectiveness. In order to make this argument, this chapter analyses how the characteristics of civil-military relations have shaped the following processes—(1) weapons

TABLE 7.2 Attributes of Military Effectiveness

Attributes of Military Effectiveness	Defined As	Dependent Variables
Quality	'The ability to obtain highly capable weapons and equipment'.	Weapons and equipment.
Responsiveness	'The ability to tailor military activity to a state's own capabilities, its adversaries capabilities and external constraints'.	Defence planning.
Skill	'The ability [of military personnel] to achieve particular tasks'.	Human Resource Development (mainly Professional Military Education and Promotion).
Integration	'The degree to which different military activities are internally consistent and mutually reinforcing'.	Inter-services coordination.

Source: Brooks and Stanley 2007: 9–15.

procurement (2) defence planning (3) inter-services integration, and (4) human resources development. These factors, broadly, correspond with the manner in which the field is currently studied (Brooks and Stanley 2007: 9–13). The 'structure' of civil-military relations is unique for different states and is shaped by factors like culture, historical tradition and experience, external and internal threat environment, societal norms, and political institutions. Risa Brooks argues that these factors 'constitute the environment in which a state's military activities take place: for example, they influence how patterns and routines emerge and evolve for strategic and operational planning, selection of leaders, procurement of weapons, training of soldiers and creation of doctrine' (Brooks and Stanley 2007: 1). The structure of civil military relations, for the purposes of this chapter, is defined as the institutions, bureaucratic and procedural rules that capture the interaction between politicians, bureaucrats, and military commanders. It includes both formal and informal institutions that serve as decision-making, consultative or advisory forums.

Weapons Procurement

The weapons procurement process in India has been characterized as ad hoc and an instance of a country that 'arms without aiming'.[33] With regard to weapons procurement there are significant inter-agency and inter-ministerial issues that are exacerbated by a lack of planning and coordination between civilians and military officers.[34] India's domestic defence industry has been criticized for its inefficiency, lack of delivery, and exaggerated claims. This was even pointed out by the officials of the Soviet Union at a time when India was procuring most of its military hardware from them.[35] Service officers have made numerous complaints about the state of military hardware and have urged for structural and procedural reforms.[36] The characteristics of civil-military have shaped the weapons procurement process in a unique manner. First, a lack of civilian expertise has meant that civilians—both bureaucrats and politicians, have to rely on the military for technical recommendations. At the same time they possess strong bureaucratic controls, the second characteristic of civil-military relations, and are under pressure from the Defence Public Sector Units (DPSU), Department of Defence Production, and Defence Research and Development Organization (DRDO)—all within the MoD, to ensure that they get projects and funds. This is touted under the ideal of self-reliance and developing indigenous capability. However, for a number of reasons, most indigenous weapons development programmes have either suffered from long delays and/or have been costly and unsuccessful.[37] Tables 7.3 and 7.4 depict DRDO projects completed between 1996 and 2006 and those that are ongoing, respectively. All the projects have had massive cost and time overruns. To some extent this is inevitable as most initial estimates of projects are not only under priced but also optimistic on delivery schedules. These unrealistic claims relating to time and cost made it easier for DRDO to obtain project approval. This has been a perennial problem, as the former head of DRDO, V.S. Arunachalam, admitted—'in our eagerness to get major projects, we gave unrealistic timeframes and very low budgets' (Hoyt 2006: 64). Ultimately it is the military that suffers from non-delivery of weapons and delays. This has a direct impact on its effectiveness. In one of the more well known episodes, then DRDO head Dr Abdul Kalam's exaggerated claim of producing a weapon locating radar for the army and his subsequent inability to do so led General V.P. Malik to argue that 'if the DRDO had not come in the

TABLE 7.3 Major Projects (with time and cost overruns) Completed (1996–2006)

No.	Project	Date of Sanction	Projected Date of Completion (Original)	Projected Date of Completion (Revised)	Cost original in Crores	Cost revised in Crores	Date of Closure	Time overrun (in years)	Cost overrun in Crores and Percentage
1.	Light Combat Aircraft (LCA) Ph-I	August 1983	August 1993	March 2004	560	2,188	July 2005	12	1628 (390 per cent)
2.	Lakshya (Target Drone)	September 1980	September 1987	July 1994	17	30	July 1998	11	13 (176 per cent)
3.	Nishant UAV (Unmanned Aerial Vehicle)	October 1991	April 1995	March 2003	34	60.83	October 2005	10	26 (178 per cent)
4.	Pinaka (MBRL)	December 1986	December 1992	December 2000	26.47	55.33	February 2005	13	29 (212 per cent)
5.	Main Battle Tank (MBT) Arjun	May 1974	May 1984	May 1995	15.50	305.6	September 2000	16	290 (1971 per cent)
6.	Panchendriya (Naval Electronic Warfare)	November 1987	November 1993	December 1998	31.22	31.23	February 2000	7	0
7.	Sagardhwani (Naval sensors)	October 1987	June 1991	March 1999	44.90	80.01	December 2000	9	35 (178 per cent)
8.	AET	September 1987	August 1992	October 1999	12.51	24.43	May 2002	10	12 (195 per cent)
9.	Sarvatra (Bridging)	December 1992	December 1999	December 2000	17.58	22.80	December 2001	2	5 (130 per cent)

Note: Where MBRL stands for Multibarrel Rocket Launcher; AET for Advanced Experimental Torpedo

Source: Standing Committee on Defence, 14th Report: Defence Research and Development Organization.

TABLE 7.4 Ongoing Major Projects (with time and cost overruns)

No.	Project	Date of Sanction	Projected Date of Completion (Original)	Projected Date of Completion (Revised)	Cost (original) in Crores	Cost (revised) in Crores	Time overrun, continuing (in years)	Cost overrun (between revised and original) in Crores
1.	LCA (Ph-II)	November 2001	December 2008	No data	3301.78	No data	2+	
2.	Samvahak (Command and control systems)	May 1999	November 2003	September 2006	108.90	No data	7+	
3.	Samyukta (EW equipment)	May 1994	November 1999	November 2007	1200.22	1336.00	11+	116
4.	Sangraha	June 1995	June 2002	December 2006	491.97	No data	8+	
5.	IGMDP (Missiles)	July 1983	July 1995	December 2006	388.83	1771.43	15+	1381
6.	Kaveri (aircraft engine)	March 1989	December 1996	December 2009	383.00	2839.00	14+	2456

Source: Standing Committee on Defence, 14ᵗʰ Report: Defence Research and Development Organization.

way we would have got them [weapon locating radar] before the Kargil war and that would have definitely reduced our casualties'.[38]

The third characteristic of civil-military relations—of the military having considerable autonomy over its own processes—also creates problems. The most consequential aspect of it is in the drafting of General Staff Qualitative Requirements (GSQR's, often called QR's) for weapons and equipment.[39] GSQR are technical specifications of weapons and equipment on the basis of which they are evaluated and eventually inducted into service. These are drafted by the services and within the army by either the line or the Weapons and Equipment (WE) directorates. As such they are considered one of the most important documents as it specifies the parameters of the desired weapon systems. However, GSQR formulation has attracted much criticism on two issues—their manner of drafting and the frequent changes made in them.[40] Among the complaints made both by domestic and foreign defence companies operating in India, are that the services frame GSQR's by choosing 'BBC—best of brochure claims' and end up asking for products that do not exist. In other words, as the GSQR's are drafted by generalist officers possessing little specialized knowledge of weapons and equipment, they perforce rely on brochures and thereby pick and choose characteristics that they would like in their equipment. As a result, the GSQR's end up as an amalgamation of particular characteristics from different equipments, that none of the original equipment can match up to. Identifying this as one of the problems in indigenous weapons development, defence ministry sources noted that—'often Air Staff Requirements (ASR)/GSQR's are supersets of various latest technologies available in different foreign products combined together and, there, unrealistic for providing a complete or ultimate solution through development' (Standing Committee on Defence (2007: 40).

To be sure, since 2001, there have been a number of changes in India's approach to weapons procurement. Numerous versions of the Defence Procurement Procedure (DPP) have been released in an effort to bring transparency in the process. However, without structural changes in the pattern of civil-military relations, problems continue to plague the weapons procurement process. Admitting as such numerous committees, like the Kelkar, P. Rama Rao, and Defence Expenditure Review Committee, have been established in recent years to recommend changes. However, their implementation is still a matter of some debate.

Defence Planning

Long-term defence planning in India has been criticized for its manner of formulation, lack of assured budgetary support, and bureaucratic tussles.[41] While examining this process in 1996, the standing committee on defence scathingly observed that 'ad hocism in systemic planning in Defence Sectors is amply evident from the fact that in the period of 20 years, 6 Defence Five-Year Plans were prepared but none could be completed for one reason or the other and had either been deferred or reframed midway' (Standing Committee on Defence 1996: 21). Not much has changed in the plans made since then. The assumptions for the Ninth Plan (1997–2002) were upended by the nuclear tests in 1998 and Kargil war a year after. The Tenth Plan (2002–07) was 'tentatively approved at the end of its specified period'.[42] The Eleventh Plan (2007–12), currently in its fourth year, has still not been approved by the Cabinet.[43]

In turn, each of the characteristics of civil-military relations contributes to the continuing problems in defence planning. The first, a lack of civilian expertise, translates directly into an inability on the part of the civilians to play any useful role in the formulation of defence plans. As a result of this military planners have little strategic guidance from their political masters.[44] According to Admiral Arun Prakash— 'the defence planner does, therefore, start with a handicap and tends to grope a bit for direction'.[45] The absence of directives to guide defence planners is partly due to the lack of expertise and capability in the civilian realm to write these directives. The framing of the Defence Minister's Directives (known as the Raksha Mantri's Directives), which is meant to guide defence plans, is indicative of this problem. The first known RM's Directive was framed in 1983 but as it was believed to be generic in nature and a number of, ultimately unsuccessful, attempts were made to update it.[46] It was only in 2008 that this document was amended and adopted by the MoD.[47] However, reflecting the lack of capability on the civilian side, this document was largely prepared in the respective service headquarters and after being collated by the Integrated Defence Staff (IDS) was sent for approval to the ministry.[48] In other words, the services prepared their own planning guidelines. However, the reluctance of the politicians and civilians to assume a more pro-active role in defence policy making is not just due to a lack of expertise but also because of the traditional pattern of civil-military relations which resists such intervention.

The second characteristic of civil-military relations—strong bureaucratic control—which at times is in competition, has also shaped the defence planning process. Bureaucratic control by the defence ministry is evident from the manner in which the system is structured wherein the services get plan clearance and sanction from civilian counterparts. While the formulation of plans is an entirely service headquarters driven effort, they are frustrated with the delay and inability to obtain concurrence of civilian bureaucratic and political leaders. This is also hindered due to competing interests between the defence ministry and the office of Defence Finance and Finance Ministry. As the focus of latter two offices is primarily on cost-cutting measures and avoiding unnecessary expenditure, loosely defined, this leads to frequent correspondence between the concerned agencies. Admittedly, this is not entirely a function of civil-military relations and is indicative of inter-ministerial problems resulting in an inability to settle their differences. These differences, in turn, result in delay and non-approval of defence plans creating problems for the military. The system, according to Raju Thomas, is such that it 'allows the Finance Ministry to control the Defence Ministry and the Defence Ministry to control the armed service headquarters' (Thomas 1984: 251). In principle while this may not be a bad idea, however, in practice this frustrates the professional military as it leads to frequent delays and correspondence between them and a largely uninformed civilian staff. Some service officers argue that the inability to approve a plan is indicative of the divide between the service headquarters and civilian bureaucrats—whether in the defence or finance ministry.[49] Hence, they blame the inability of the service headquarters to make long term plans on the civil-military divide. The involvement of a number of different agencies in the defence planning process, including the department of defence production and department of defence research and development, with differing organizational interests and information asymmetries, also creates problems in interagency coordination.

The final characteristic—autonomy to the services—also influences the defence planning process. First, in the absence of overall strategic guidelines the services create their own service-specific plans. This understandably is done in a manner to increase own share of the defence budgets.[50] As a result, inter-services prioritization is one of the biggest problems in formulating defence plans. Ironically this function is carried out by civilian bureaucrats despite the fact that a lack of expertise meant that they were 'not equipped to handle the decision-making on inter-services prioritization'.[51] The second problem arising from considerable autonomy to the military is the strong powers vested in the service chiefs and his principal staff officers that make the process vulnerable to idiosyncrasies and personality-oriented plans. Hence, at times, defence plans are known to change in priority, equipment emphasis, and direction with a change in senior leadership. This can result in sectional interests trumping all-round organizational development. According to Air Commodore Jasjit Singh— 'the present process also permits frequent changes in force development plans due to changes in personalities in the service headquarters, reducing the sanctity of the plans' (Singh 2000: 76).

To be sure, problems in defence planning are not solely due to civil-military relations and some of it can be blamed on inter-ministerial and inter-agency disputes. However, the unique character of civil-military relations has exacerbated the defence planning process. While it is difficult to directly connect defence plans with military effectiveness, however, it stands to logic that non-approval of plans would have an influence on India's war-fighting capability.[52]

Jointness

Jointness or integration between the three services has always been a point of dispute and debate in almost all countries. Two decades after the Goldwater-Nichols Act in the US, there are still calls for re-examining this process. India follows the 'coordination' model to jointness whereby they have agreed to coordinate their operations when needed. This has historically been a source of problems.[53] The model of civil-military relations has only added to this problem.

First, a lack of expertise translates directly into an inability on the part of the civilians to force the services to integrate. They are also hindered by information asymmetries inherent in civil-military relations. At the same time, they are expected to arbitrate in inter-services disputes. For instance, both the functions of maritime and army aviation were finally ceded by the air force after intervention from civilians.[54] Due to this lack of expertise and a tradition of non-interference in military affairs, civilians have played a minimal role in fostering jointness within the services. The second characteristic—strong and competing bureaucratic control— does not really apply in this case. The final characteristic, autonomy to the military, adds considerably to the problem of integration. Due to this autonomy there is a single-service mindset and approach that is ingrained in officers of the three services. This adds to other problems with jointness, for instance, in turf wars and lack of interoperability in joint training and operations. The absence of political or bureaucratic pressure on the services to work together results in their operating in service-specific silos. This intellectual divergence adds to the organization and geographical separation between the services.[55] Indeed, the overall trends in jointmanship have been described by two air force officers in these terms—

> The force structure of the national Armed Forces has been created by the *institutionally independent* Services, acting in accordance with their own priorities and perceptions under debatable centralized control and direction. This un-integrated force structure and operational environment does not promote nor emphasize jointmanship. Insufficient attention has been paid to develop a joint military education system and the current Services career development practices do little to encourage specialists in joint military planning and operations. In addition, the Services have been reluctant to co-operate on joint requirements for equipment overlooking the advantage of commonality, compatibility and interoperability. This approach results in an un-integrated force structure.[56]

Jointness has historically been a problem in all of India's post-independence wars.[57]

Most recently, the Kargil war in 1999 led to an acrimonious exchange between the air force and the army.[58] Some of this is perhaps unavoidable but it is also indicates deep-rooted problems that obviously have an impact on the overall effectiveness of the Indian armed forces.

Human Resource Development

Human resources development or the skill set and the manner of promotion of senior officers plays an important role in the effectiveness of military organizations. On the whole, the Indian experience in this regard has been positive in some respect and negative in others. On the positive side, barring a few exceptions, politicians have not interfered with promotions and have prevented a politicization of the armed forces.[59] Moreover, among the Union Public Service Commissioned officers, the military devotes maximum resources to training and leadership development. At the same time there are some problems that arise from the form of civilian control.

First, other than specialization in the technical branches the Indian military is, by and large, a generalist cadre. The personnel policy of the military does not favour or place incentives on specialization. On the contrary, this may harm career prospects. As a result, there is little functional or regional specialization within the military. Second, excluding the teaching of technical subjects, there are no civilian instructors at institutions that impart military education.[60] As a result, organizational narratives, often self-serving, are perpetuated. Thus, the perceptions of the officer cadre are shaped with little civilian influence. Third, promotion and study leave policies do not encourage officers to pursue higher studies, thus curtailing their intellectual growth. Finally, the absence of declassification directly results in a lack of military historiography among the officer class. As a result, this leads to a loss of institutional memory and an inadequate understanding of the past.

This attribute of military effectiveness is also shaped by the unique structure of civil-military relations. The first characteristic—a lack of civilian expertise—translates directly into their inability to positively influence professional military education. The second characteristic—strong bureaucratic control—is exercised by the MoD which clears all files pertaining to creation of new educational courses, infrastructure, and even the deputation of officers for study abroad. Some argue that MoD policies discourage officers from gaining a broader education—at home or abroad.[61] Finally, considerable autonomy to the military in formulating its own education and promotion criteria means that these are open to ad-hoc and personality driven changes and there is little that civilians can do to influence this process. While civilian control and military autonomy might appear paradoxical, civilians exercise negative control instead of positive control. In other words, they exercise their power of turning down the requests from the services more than use their influence to shape professional military education.

The link between human resources development and military effectiveness in the Indian case is harder to make in the absence of overt politicization of the armed forces.[62] However, a lack of military historiography for obvious reasons would lead to a constant re-learning of lessons.[63] It can also be argued that with a broader education there will be also increased chances for military innovation and, in turn, effectiveness. To be sure, there are other problems with human resources—the shortage of officers, for instance, but it is difficult to link them with civil-military relations and hence they lie outside the purview of this study.

Defence Preparedness and Reforms

It is not as if these weaknesses are not recognized by many in India. The term 'defence preparedness', arguably a corollary of military effectiveness, has been used extensively without explicit definition in numerous reports by the Indian parliament's Standing Committee on Defence and by the Indian press.[64] One explanation for this form of civilian control has been offered by Ashley Tellis when he argues that—'the weaknesses of this [civilian] control system are widely recognized in India, but being content with the protection afforded by the country's great size and inherent strength relative to its adversaries, Indian security managers-historically-have consciously refrained from altering the structure of strict civilian control no matter what benefits in increased military efficiency might accrue as a result' (Tellis 2001: 285). Indeed this chapter argues that an absent dialogue best describes civil-military relations in India.[65] Hence, the three unique characteristics of civil-military relations present significant challenges in realizing the capabilities of the Indian military. This is further hindered by bureaucratic interests—both civilian and military—which perpetuate the status-quo and create little incentive for change.[66] The three services oppose radical changes as it can potentially threaten their autonomy. Moreover, they are opposed to the idea of civilians actively and constantly arbitrating inter-services disputes. The civilian bureaucrats, in turn, oppose some of the reforms as they fear a possible loss of power and influence. Confirming the problems with the Indian structure was this assessment made by the Kargil Review Committee—

> An objective assessment of the last 52 years will show that the country is lucky to have scraped through national security threats without too much damage, except in 1962. The country can no longer afford such *ad hoc* functioning. The committee, therefore, recommends that the entire gamut of national security management and apex decision-making and the structure and interface between the Ministry of Defence and the Armed Forces Headquarters be comprehensively studied and reorganized.[67]

Democracy's Self-correcting Characteristic

Despite the weaknesses in the Indian structure of civil-military relations, there have been at least two positive trends. First, as argued by Devesh Kapur and Bhanu Pratap Mehta while discussing Indian bureaucracy, the system while not allowing 'for easy change, but it also prevents sudden reversals…and gives opportunities for self correction' (Kapur and Mehta (eds) 2005: 12). In other words, a powerful bureaucracy and complicated rules and procedures have imbued a 'systemic stability'. For example, it is difficult for politicians or other vested interests to impose agendas within the military. This renders the armed forces relatively immune to politicization, and the potential dangers that come from that like caste based reservations, insertion of political ideologies, nepotism, political patronage, and corruption.

The second positive trend in civil-military relations can also be attributed to the democracy's self-correcting mechanism—the process of change and reforms attempted by the state. As a result of the Kargil Review Committee and the 2002 Group of Ministers report, new institutions have been established and considerable efforts have been made to implement both their recommendations. There is an effort to increase the accountability of different bureaucracies and to increase transparency in the decision-making process. For instance, the procurement process has been streamlined with the release of the Defence Procurement manuals. Similarly, attempts have been made at improving the long term planning and budgetary processes. The era of reforms is also being closely monitored by the Indian Parliament's Standing Committee on Defence, which is monitoring the implementation of the recommendations made by the two committees.[68]

But Old Problems Remain

Despite these attempts, however, structural problems remain. First, the political leadership has failed to build up a political consensus for the central recommendation of both the committees—the establishment of the Chief of Defence Staff (CDS) position. According to the MoD, the implementation of this recommendation is held up by the government's decision to seek the views of the main political parties. In turn, despite reminders, most of the parties have not presented their views and can, justifiably, be accused of political apathy.[69] Meanwhile, the problems that the CDS post was meant to obviate still remain.[70] Second, the armed forces headquarters are still not integrated with the MoD, a recommendation that was made by the Kargil Review Committee.[71] Instead, in what can be considered an act of bureaucratic sophistry, the nomenclature has been changed without much change in the functioning. Pointing it out the chairman of the Kargil Review Committee K. Subrahmanyam argued that—'so long as the armed forces are kept out of the government, there is a deep malaise (in the system)'.[72] Third, despite the limited attempts made at integrating the three services, operational integration has not been achieved. While some amount of inter-services rivalry is to be expected, and is inevitable, the failure to agree upon war fighting doctrines is a serious lapse. Hence, for instance, the IAF does not support and is not willing to commit resources to the Army's 'cold start doctrine'. In turn, the army is lobbying to acquire dedicated air assets for close air support. In sum, continued inter-services hostility and a failure of civilians—both bureaucrats and politicians to adjudicate these issues—has had an impact on the operational performance of the Indian armed forces.

In other mature democracies issues like integration are usually forced upon the reluctant services by a powerful political, or even bureaucratic, elite.[73] Usually this follows after setbacks suffered in a crisis.[74] While the results may not be perfect, improving the effectiveness of the military is a constant process. In India, however, as argued elsewhere, the defence reforms that were attempted after the Kargil war have largely failed to deliver.[75] Perhaps, responding to the public criticism, the Government appointed the Naresh Chandra Committee in June 2011 with a specific mandate to revisit the defence reforms process.[76] The report of this committee was submitted to the government in May 2012, and a public version of this report and its implementation is still awaited. While it would be unfair to prejudge this report and its implementation, however, many are already critiquing it.[77] One of the major criticisms is the lack of political interest and involvement in national security reforms.[78] Indeed it appears likely that in the absence of political will the weaknesses in India's approach to national security will remain. These institutional deficiencies in turn can be attributed to path dependency.[79] As bureaucratic institutions have a history of their own they limit the policy options that can facilitate a structural change. In many ways then, a mature and respectful civil-military relationship holds the key to facilitating the next generation of reforms. For that to happen, however, we need leadership from all constituencies. At this moment, however, the emergence of such leadership is still in question.

Notes

1. Some prominent academic works include Desch 1999, Cohen 2002, and Feaver 2003. Journalistic attention to civil-military relations has stemmed from

incidents like the dismissal of India's Admiral Vishnu Bhagwat in 1999 and General Stanley McChrystal in 2010 in the United States.

2. For some good works on India's democracy see Kohli 2001, Guha 2007, and Khilnani 1999.

3. Some notable exceptions are Cohen 1990 and Rosen 1996.

4. See Kundu 1998.

5. See Kukreja 1991, Bhimaya 1997, and Staniland 2008.

6. For a discussion on this theory of civilian control see Cohen 2002: 225–48.

7. For more on this see Raghavan 2009.

8. For more details about this charge made in the Henderson-Brooks report refer to the following: Hoffman 1990: 222, Mankekar 1968: 80–4, and Maxwell 1972: 438.

9. See Jacob 1997: 181–3.

10. For more on this issue see A.G. Noorani 2007.

11. See Singh 1992: 86–7.

12. For a critical view of India's NSC, see Babu 2003: 215–30.

13. For a typical view see Nayar 2008.

14. For a perspective on this, see Sinha 2011. More recently, there was a major controversy after a prominent newspaper made allegations of unauthorized military movement. See Gupta, Sarin, and Samanta 2012.

15. See Kapur and Mehta 2005: 1–24, and Singh 2007.

16. See Oberoi 2007. More recently there has been inter-services competition over the roles and ownership of assets in space.

17. For a good overview of this issue see Gautam 2011; also see Mukherjee 2012, 2010, and 2007.

18. The narrative of bureaucratic instead of political control has largely been internalized within the Indian military. For some typical perspectives, see Prakash 2007: 10, Kak 1998: 504, and Anand 2001: 86.

19. See Cohen 1990: 173–4 and Anand 2001.

20. For instance, the DMC atrophied in the years following independence and was only resurrected after the Indian army was defeated in the 1962 India-China war. Even then it existed in the form of the unstructured 'morning meetings'. Since then it has performed erratically dependent upon the operating style of the defence minister. See Sinha 1991: 26–8.

21. See Pant 2007: 254. For a fictional but influential account describing problems arising from a lack of coordination between civilians and the military, with respect to the nuclear weapons programme, see Sundarji 1993.

22. See Mukherjee 2011b.

23. See Ashiq 2010.

24. See Mukherjee 2009a.

25. Interview with K. Subrahmanyam, chairman of the Kargil Review Committee, New Delhi, 30 March 2008.

26. For some of the challenges associated with defining and studying military effectiveness, see 'Introduction' in Brooks and Stanley 2007: 1–26.

27. For instance, see Rosen 1995: 5–31, Pollack 2002, Reiter and Stam III 1998: 259–77, and Biddle and Long 2004: 525–46.

28. See Chakravorty 1992: 272, 329–30, Lal 1986: 162, Singh 1992: 164, and Kalyanraman 2012.

29. See Jacob 1997.

30. See Millett, Murray, and Watman 1987: 3.

31. See Mukherjee 2009b.

32. See Standing Committee on Defence 2005. There have been numerous debates on this issue in the Indian Parliament post-independence. For instance, see Unstarred Question No. 3317, 'Procedural Delays in Building Military Preparedness', in XIII Lok Sabha, answered on 16 March 2000. Also see Paranjpe 1998: 139–65.

33. See Smith 1994 and Cohen and Dasgupta 2010.

34. For some of these problems, see Singh (ed.) 1998: 48–87.

35. The Soviets were urging Indian DPSUs, Ordnance Factories, and even the private sector to step in and produce spares and tools but the capacity did not exist. See D.R. Kohli.

36. See Tripathi 2007.

37. For a critical audit of the DRDO's performance see the eight-part exposé by Aroor and Ranjan 2006, and a six-part special series by Iype 2000. For a contrarian view, see a three-part series by Kapisthalam 2005.

38. See Indian Express 06 September 2009.

39. There are other problems with the services procedure with respect to the procurement process, however, that is beyond the purview of this study. For problems with trials and evaluation, see Suman 2009.

40. See Behera 2007 and Suman 2006.

41. For some of the problems with defence planning, see Ghosh 2006.

42. See Standing Committee on Defence 2007c: 18.

43. See Standing Committee on Defence 2010: 25–7.

44. See Rahul Roy–Chaudhury 1993: 825–6.

45. Prakash 2007: 28. The author was a former Chief of Naval Staff and Chairman of the Chiefs of Staff Committee.

46. See Anand 2008: 20–4.

47. See Unnithan 2010.

48. Interview with an officer who served at that time in the Military Operations Directorate, New Delhi, 2 April 2010. Also see Kapur 2006: 114–15.

49. Interview with former Chief of the Defence Planning Staff, New Delhi, 28 January 2011.

50. For a good description of organizational interests in the preparation of service specific perspective plans and the limited role of civilians, see Ghosh 2006: 257–99.

51. Interview with P.R. Chari, former official in the Ministry of Defence, New Delhi, 15 September 2009.

52. For a reference to non-approval of plans and its impact on India's defence preparedness, see Standing Committee on Defence 2007b: 65.

53. The Group of Ministers report made public in 2001 commented upon the lack of jointness and synergy between the three services. See *Reforming the National Security System: Report of the Group of Ministers on National Security* 2001: 97–104.

54. For a description of the bureaucratic battle over maritime aviation, see Hiranandani 2000: 271–6, and for the fight for army aviation see Oberoi 2007.

55. The Indian armed forces have a total of 17 Commands, and with the exception of the joint Strategic Forces Command and the Andaman and Nicobar Command, none of the service commands are in the same location. See Prakash (2007) 'Keynote Address': 9.

56. See Tiwary and Gill 2006: 39, emphasis added.

57. For problems during the 1965 and the 1971 war, see Lal 1986: 162 and Chakravorty 1992: 329–30. For lack of jointness during IPKF operations see Singh (1992): 164.

58. Army and Air Force officers at that time have been involved in a war of words. See *Rediff News* 2004.

59. While there was some controversy during defence minister Krishna Menon's tenure in recent times, the only instances of such interference was the non-promotion of Lt Gen. S.K. Sinha as Army Chief in 1983 and the controversies during the tenure of defence minister Mulayam Singh. See Joshi 1998.

60. While prominent civilians are invited for guest lectures at schools of education, however, no classes are taught by them.

61. See Shukla 2010.

62. Unlike, for instance, cases wherein officer promotion policies are based on discrimination and ethnicity. For more on this, see Hoyt 2007: 55–79.

63. See Mukherjee 2009b.

64. See for instance, Standing Committee on Defence 2004: 20, Standing Committee on Defence 2005: 191, and Press Information Bureau 2013.

65. See Mukherjee 2009a.

66. For a description of bureaucratic politics, see Wilson 1989. Also see Allison and Zelikow 1999.

67. See *From Surprise to Reckoning: The Kargil Review Committee Report* 2000: 259.

68. See Standing Committee on Defence 2007d and Standing Committee on Defence 2008.

69. See Standing Committee on Defence 2007d: 12–15.

70. See Shukla 2006.

71. See *Kargil Review Committee Report*, para 14.19. Similar instructions were issued earlier under defence minister George Fernandes in 1999. See Diwanji 1999.

72. Interview with K. Subrahmanayam, New Delhi, 30 March 2008.

73. For instance, in the US, it was done through the enactment of the Goldwater-Nichols Act in 1986 (Available at http://www.ndu.edu/library/goldnich/goldnich.html) and in Australia it was done by implementing the Tange Report. See Edwards 2006.

74. See Mukherjee 2011c.

75. See Mukherjee 2011b, IDSA Occasional Paper18.

76. See Dixit 2011. For a perspective on what sort of reforms should have been considered by this committee, see Mukherjee 2011a: 30–7.

77. See Chandra 2011.

78. See Jayal, Malik, Prakash, and Mukherjee (forthcoming).

79. For more on this, see Pierson 2000.

References

Allison, Graham, and Phillip Zelikow. 1999. *Essence of Decision*. New York: Addison-Wesley Longman.

Anand, Vinod. 2008.'Integrating the Indian Military: Retrospect and Prospect', *Journal of Defence Studies*, 2 (2): 20–4.

———. 2001a. *Delhi Papers 16: Joint Vision for the Indian Armed Forces*. New Delhi: IDSA.

———. 2001b. 'Management of Defence: Towards an Integrated and Joint Vision', *Strategic Analysis*, 24 (11). Available at http://www.idsa-india.org/an-feb-2-01.html (accessed 1 August 2013).

Aroor, Shiv and Amitav Ranjan. 2006.'Delayed Research: Delayed Organisation'. *Indian Express*, 11–19 November.

Ashiq, Peerzada. 2010. 'Cabinet for use of army as deterrent in Kashmir', *Hindustan Times*, 07 July.

Babu, Shyam. 2003. 'India's National Security Council: Struck in the Cradle?' *Security Dialogue*, 34 (2): 215–30.

Behera, Laxman. 2007.'Indian Defence Acquisition: Time for a Change', *IDSA Comment*, 3 August.

Bhimaya, Kotera. 1997. *Civil Military Relations: A Comparative Study of India and Pakistan*. Santa Monica: Rand.

Biddle, Stephen and Stephen Long. 2004. 'Democracy and Military Effectiveness: A Deeper Look', *Journal of Conflict Resolution*, 48 (4): 525–46.

Brooks, Risa A. and Elizabeth A. Stanley (eds) 2007. *Creating Military Power: Sources of Military Effectiveness*. Stanford: Stanford University Press.

Chakravorty, B.C. (1992). *The History of the Indo-Pak War, 1965*. New Delhi: History Division, Ministry of Defence.

Chandra, Satish. 2011. 'Futile Review of National Security', *The Pioneer*, 4 August.

Cohen, Eliot. 2002. *Supreme Command: Soldiers, Statesmen, and Leadership in Wartime*. New York: Free Press.

Cohen, Stephen P. 1990. *The Indian Army: Its Contribution to the Development of a Nation*. New Delhi: Oxford University Press.

Cohen, Stephen and Sunil Dasgupta. 2010. *Arming without Aiming: India's Military Modernization*. Washington DC: Brookings Press.

Desch, Michael. 1999. *Civilian Control of the Military: The Changing Security Environment*. Baltimore: Johns Hopkins University Press.

Diwanji, Amberish. 1999. 'Service HQ to be integrated into defence ministry', *Rediff News*, 15 January. Available at http://in.rediff.com/news/1999/jan/05def.htm (accessed 1 August 2013).

Dixit, Sandeep. 2011. 'High level task force to review defence preparedness', *The Hindu*, 22 June.

Edwards, Peter. 2006. *Arthur Tange: Last of the Mandarins*. Sydney: Allen & Unwin.

Feaver, Peter. 2003. *Armed Servants: Agency, Oversight and Civil-military relations*. Cambridge, MA: Harvard University Press.

———. 1999. 'Civil-Military Relations', *Annual Review of Political Science*, 2: 214.

From Surprise to Reckoning: The Kargil Review Committee Report. 2000. New Delhi: Sage Publications.

Gautam, P.K. 2011. 'The need for Renaissance of Military History and Modern War Studies in India', IDSA Occasional Paper No. 21.

Ghosh, A.K. 2006. *Defence Budgeting and Planning in India: The Way Forward*. New Delhi: Knowledge World.

Guha, Ramachandra. 2007. *India after Gandhi: The History of the World's largest Democracy*. New York: Ecco Press.

Gupta, Shekhar, Ritu Sarin, and Pranab Dhal Samanta. 2012. 'The January night Raisina Hill was spooked: Two key Army units moved towards Delhi without notifying the Government', *Indian Express*, 04 April.

Hiranandani, G.M. 2000. *Transition to Triumph: History of the Indian Navy, 1965–75*. New Delhi: Lancer Publications.

Hoffman, Steven A. 1990. *India and the China crisis*. Berkeley: University of California Press.

Hoyt, Timothy. 2007. 'Social Structure, Ethnicity, and Military Effectiveness: Iraq, 1980–2004', in Risa Brooks and Elizabeth Stanley (eds), *Creating Military Power*. Stanford, California: Stanford University Press.

———. 2006. *Military Industry and Regional Defense Policy: India, Iraq and Israel*. London: Routledge.

Huntington, Samuel. 1957. *The Soldier and the State: The Theory and Politics of Civil-Military Relations*. Harvard University Press.

———. 1956. 'Civilian Control and the Constitution', *The American Political Science Review*, 50 (3): 678.

———. 1956. 'Civilian Control of the Military: A Theoretical Statement', in Heinz Eulau, Samuel J. Eldersveld, and Morris Janowitz (eds), *Political Behavior: A Reader in Theory and Method*. Glencoe: Free Press.

Indian Express. 2009. 'DRDO Came in the Way of Acquiring Key Radars Before Kargil: Malik', 6 September.

Iype, George. 2000. 'Chinks in the armour', *Rediff.com*, March.

Jacob, J.F.R. 1997. *Surrender at Dacca: Birth of a Nation*. New Delhi: Manohar Publications.

Jayal, B.D., V.P. Malik, Arun Prakash, and Anit Mukherjee. (forthcoming) 'A Call for Change: Defence Management in India', *IDSA Monograph Series*.

Joshi, Manoj. 1998. 'Playing with Fire', *India Today*, 16 February. Available at http://www.india-today.com/itoday/16021998/defence.html (accessed 1 August 2013).

Kak, Kapil. 1998. 'Direction of Higher Defense II', *Strategic Analysis*, 22 (4): 504.

Kalyanraman. 2012. 'Major Lessons from Operation Pawan for Future Regional Stability Operations', *Journal of Defence Studies*, 6 (3): 29–52.

Kapisthalam, Kaushik. 2005. 'DRDO: A Stellar success', *Rediff.com*, January.

Kapur, B.M. 2006. 'Integrated Tri Services Perspective Planning', in V.P. Malik and Vinod Anand (eds), *Defence Planning: Problems and Prospects*. New Delhi: Manas Publications.

Kapur, Devesh and Pratap Bhanu Mehta (eds). 2005. 'Introduction', in *Public Institutions in India: Performance and Design*. New Delhi: Oxford University Press.

Khilnani, Sunil. 1999. *The Idea of India*. New York: Fararr, Straus and Giroux.

Kohli, Atul. 2001. *The Success of India's Democracy*. New York: Cambridge University Press.

Kohli, D.R.. *Report on the Visit of Defense Secretary's Delegation to USSR (May 1976)*, Vol. 1, Top Secret, pp. 56–7, Subject File No. 300, III Installment. PN Haksar Files, Nehru Memorial Museum and Library.

Kohn, Richard. 1997. 'How Democracies Control the Military', *Journal of Democracy*, 8 (4): 141.

Korb, Lawrence J. 1984. 'How Well Can We Fight? For How Long?', in Stephen J. Cimbala (ed.), *National Security Strategy: Choices and Limits*, p. 42. New York: Praeger.

Kukreja, Veena. 1991. *Civil Military Relations in South Asia: Pakistan, Bangladesh and India*. New Delhi: Sage Publications.

Kundu, Apurba. 1998. *Militarism in India: The Army and Civil Society in Consensus*. New York: St Martin's Press.

Lal, P.C. 1986. *My Years with the IAF*. New Delhi: Lancer Publications.

Malhotra, Inder. 2005. 'Introduction', in K. Subramanyam and Arthur Monteiro, *Shedding Shibboleths: India's Evolving Strategic Outlook*. New Delhi: Wordsmiths.

Mankekar, D.R. 1968. *The Guilty Men of 1962*. Mumbai: Tulsi Shah Enterprises.

Maxwell, Neville. 1972. *India's China war*. New York: Doubleday.

Millett, Allan, Williamson Murray, and Kenneth Watman (1987). 'The Effectiveness of Military Organizations', in Allan Millett and Williamson Murray (eds), *Military Effectiveness, Volume I*. Boston: Allen and Unwin.

Mukherjee, Anit. 2007. 'Let Generals have their stories', Indian Express, 7 June.

———. 2009a. 'Absent Dialogue', Seminar, June.

———. 2009b. 'India's Experience with Insurgency and Counterinsurgency', in Sumit Ganguly, Andrew Scobell, and Joseph Liow (eds), *Handbook of Asian Security Studies*. London: Routledge.

———. 2010. 'Tell It Like It Is', *The Times of India*, 9 June.

———. 2011a. 'Facing Future Challenges: Defence Reforms in India', *RUSI Journal*, 156 (5): 30–7.

———. 2011b. 'Failing to Deliver: The Post Crises Defence Reforms in India, 1998-2010', IDSA Occasional Paper18, New Delhi: IDSA.

———. 2011c. 'Defence reforms shouldn't wait for another "Kargil"', *The Times of India*, 27 March.

———. 2012. 'Republic of Opinions', *The Times of India*, 18 January.

Nayar, V.K. 2008. 'Civil-Military Relations', *Journal of the United Service Institution of India*, CXXXVIII (574). Available at http://www.usiofindia.org/Article/?pub=Journal&pubno=574&ano=321 (accessed 1 August 2013).

Noorani, A.G. 2007. 'Shocking Disclosures', *Frontline*, 24 (18). Available at http://www.hindu.com/fline/fl2418/stories/20070921505807900.htm (accessed 1 August 2013).

Oberoi, Vijay (ed.). 2007. *Indian Army Aviation 2025*. New Delhi: Knowledge World Publishers.

Pant, Harsh. 2007. 'India's Nuclear Doctrine and Command Structure: Implications for Civil-military relations in India', *Armed Forces and Society*, 33 (2): 242–3.

Paranjpe, Shrikant. 1998.'India's Security Policy: An Evaluation after Fifty Years', *International Studies*, 35 (2): 139–65.

Pierson, Paul. 2000. 'Increasing Returns, Path Dependence, and the Study of Politics', *The American Political Science Review*, 94 (2): 251–67.

Pollack, Kenneth M. 2002. *Arabs at War: Military Effectiveness, 1948-1991*. Lincoln: University of Nebraska Press.

Prakash, Arun. 2007.'Keynote Address', *Proceedings of USI Seminar on Higher Defence Organization*, New Delhi: United Service Institution of India.

———. 2007.'Challenges of Defence Planning', *From the Crow's Nest*, 28.

Press Information Bureau. 2013. 'PM's speech at the Foundation Stone Laying Ceremony for the Indian National Defence University at Gurgaon'. Available at http://pib.nic.in/newsite/erelease.aspx?relid=96146 (accessed 1 August 2013).

Raghavan, Srinath. 2009.'Civil-Military Relations in India: The China Crisis and After', *Journal of Strategic Studies*, 32 (1): 172–4.

Rediff News. 2004.'Ex-Air Marshal returns army fire', 08 June. Available at http://www.rediff.com/news/2004/jun/08spec1.htm.

Reforming the National Security System: Report of the Group of Ministers on National Security. 2001. New Delhi: Government of India.

Reiter, Dan and Allan C. Stam III. 1998. 'Democracy and Battlefield Military Effectiveness', *Journal of Conflict Resolution*, 42 (3): 259–77

Rosen, Stephen Peter. 1995. 'Military Effectiveness: Why Society Matters', *International Security*, 19 (4): 5–31.

———. 1996. Societies and Military Power: India and its Armies. Ithaca: Cornell University Press.

Roy-Chaudhury, Rahul. 1993.'Higher Defence Planning in India: Critical need for Reassessment', *Strategic Analysis*, 16 (7): 825–6.

Shukla, Ajai. 2006.'The Problem with Indian Forces', Rediff News, 10 October. Available at http://in.rediff.com/money/2006/oct/10force.htm (accessed on 1 August 2013).

———. 2010. 'McChrystal Gazing', *Business Standard*. Available at http://www.business-standard.com/article/opinion/ajai-shukla-mcchrystal-gazing-110062900008_1.html (accessed on 1 August 2013).

Singh, Depinder. 1992. *IPKF in Sri Lanka*. New Delhi: Trishul Publications.

Singh, Har Swarup. 2007. *Indian Bureaucracy: Maladies and Remedies*. New Delhi: Shipra Publishers.

Singh, Jasjit. 2000. *India's Defence Spending: Assessing Future Needs*. New Delhi: Knowledge World.

Singh, Ravinder Pal (ed.). 1998. *Arms Procurement Decision Making, Volume I: China, India, Israel, Japan, South Korea and Thailand*. SIPRI: Oxford University Press.

Sinha, S.K. 1991. 'Higher Defence Organisation in India', USI National Security Lecture, No. 10, New Delhi: United Service Institution of India.

———. 2011. 'The Man on Horseback', Asian Age, 13 April.

Smith, Chris. 1994. *India's Ad Hoc Arsenal: Direction or Drift in Defense Policy*. New York: Oxford University Press.

Standing Committee on Defence. 1996. Sixth Report: Defence Policy, Planning and Management 1995–6. New Delhi: Lok Sabha Secretariat.

———. 2004. Demand for Grants, 2004–2005: First Report. New Delhi: Lok Sabha Secretariat.

———. 2005. Demand for Grants, 2005–2006: Second Report. New Delhi: Lok Sabha Secretariat.

———. 2005. Second Report: Demand for Grants, 2004–2005. New Delhi: Lok Sabha Secretariat.

———. 2007a. Fourteenth Report: Defence Research and Development Organization. New Delhi: Lok Sabha Secretariat, p. 40.

———. 2007b. Fifteenth Report: Action Taken on Recommendations of Eleventh Report. New Delhi: Lok Sabha Secretariat.

———. 2007c. Sixteenth Report: Demand for Grants, 2007–2008. New Delhi: Lok Sabha Secretariat.

———. 2007d. Report No. 22: Review of Implementation Status on Group of Ministers Report. New Delhi: Lok Sabha Secretariat.

———. 2008. 'Chapter I: Implementation of the Committee's Recommendations', Twenty-Ninth Report: Demand for Grants, 2008–2009. New Delhi: Lok Sabha Secretariat.

———. 2010. *Sixth Report: Demand for Grants*. New Delhi: Lok Sabha Secretariat.

Staniland, Paul. 2008. 'Explaining Civil Military Relations in Complex Political Environments: India and Pakistan in Comparative Perspective', *Security Studies*, 17 (2): 322–62.

Suman, Mrinal. 2006. 'Weapons Procurement: Qualitative Requirements and Transparency in Evaluation', Strategic Analysis, 30 (4). Available at http://www.idsa.in/strategicanalysis/WeaponsProcurementQualitative RequirementsandTransparencyinEvaluation_msuman_1006 (accessed on 1 August 2013).

———. 2009. 'Formulating rational field trials and evaluation plan', Indian Defense Review, 24 (3). Available at http://defenceforumindia.com/forum/

defence-strategic-issues/6367-formulating-rational-field-trials-evaluation-plan.html (accessed 1 August 2013).

Sundarji, K. 1993. *Blind Men of Hindoostan: India-Pak Nuclear War*. New Delhi: UBS Publishers.

Tellis, Ashley. 2001. *India's Emerging Nuclear Posture: Between Recessed Deterrent and Ready Arsenal*. Santa Monica: RAND.

Thomas, Raju. 1984. 'Defence Planning in India', in Stephanie Neuman (ed.), *Defense Planning in Less-Industrialized States: The Middle East and South Asia*, p. 251. Massachusetts: Lexington Books.

Tiwary, A.K. and A.S. Gill. 2006. 'Jointmanship–An Air Warriors Overview', *Purple Pages*, 1 (1): 39.

Tripathi, S.P.M. 2007. 'The truth about military hardware in our armed forces', *USI Journal*, CXXXVII (570). Available at http://www.usiofindia.org/Article/?pub=Journal&pubno=570&ano=363 (accessed 1 August 2013).

Unnithan, Sandeep. 2010. 'The Chipak threat', *India Today*, 23 October. Available at http://indiatoday.intoday.in/story/the-chipak-threat/1/117399.html (accessed 1 August 2013).

Wilson, James Q. 1989. *Bureaucracy: What Government Agencies Do and Why They Do It*. New York: Basic Books.

8 The Indo-US Defence Relationship

Prospects and Limitations

MANJEET S. PARDESI

INDIA HAS EMERGED AS THE second-fastest growing major economy in the world (behind China) in recent years.[1] As a consequence of its rapid economic transformation, long-time observers of India have begun to describe the country as an emerging great power with system-shaping capabilities (Nayar and Paul 2003; Cohen 2001). The management of the rise of a new great power is one of the primary concerns of international politics (Kennedy 1989; Gilpin 1981). However, the incumbent dominant great power, the United States, is viewing India's rise as a benign and positive development in the international system. Indeed, India itself views close relations with the United States as essential to its emergence as a major power in Asia and beyond. The consequent partnership that has emerged between India and the United States since the end of the Cold War is the result of 'a convergence of structural, domestic, and individual leadership factors' (Kapur and Ganguly 2007: 643).

In many ways, cooperation in the field of defence is spearheading the transformed Indo-US relationship. According to Meera Shankar, India's Ambassador to the United States, Indo-US 'defence cooperation has grown significantly and reflects deeper mutual *trust*' between the two countries (Embassy of India 2010). '[D]efense cooperation between us [the United States and India] is expanding in ways that were hard to imagine a decade ago'—in the words of William Burns, the US Under Secretary of State for Political Affairs (The White House 2010). In fact, in 2005, a US Department of State official even announced that America's 'goal' was 'to help India become a major world power in the 21st century', and further added that 'we [the United States] understand fully the implications, including military implications of that statement' (US Department of State 2005).

In light of these views, this chapter will analyse the Indo-US defence relationship as it has developed since the end of the Cold War, and especially after India's May 1998 nuclear tests. In particular, Indo-US defence relations will be analysed along three dimensions—the strategic logic guiding this relationship, military-to-military cooperation, and their bilateral defence trade (including trade in dual-use high-technology items). It will be argued that that the Indo-US defence relationship is likely to grow steadily in the years ahead as the two countries have overlapping grand strategic objectives—ensuring that China rises peacefully, confronting religious fundamentalism and terrorism, and managing the global commons in the maritime domain (primarily the Indian Ocean Region). However, there continue to remain perceptual and institutional impediments which are limiting this relationship from attaining its full potential. Consequently, even as the two countries have overlapping grand strategic objectives, they continue to have different policy preferences to achieve them. In spite of these differences, the Indo-US defence relationship will continue to grow in the years ahead, and their militaries will cooperate to hedge against unforeseen contingencies because there are no sources of fundamental bilateral tensions in the Indo-US relationship.

The next section of this chapter will provide a brief overview of Indo-US defence relations since India's independence until the end of the Cold War. The subsequent section will explain the dramatic transformation in Indo-US defence relations after the end of the Cold War, and especially in the aftermath of India's May 1998 nuclear tests. This will be followed by an analysis of their defence cooperation along three dimensions—the strategic logic guiding their relationship, military-to-military cooperation, and their defence trade (including trade in high technology dual-use items). It will be shown that both India and the United States have much to gain by fostering a close defence partnership even as some perceptual and institutional impediments remain.

Overview of Indo-US Defence Relations

The Cold War

The desire to pursue an independent foreign policy has been at the core of Indian strategic thinking since independence. India entered the Cold

War dominated international system in 1947 as an economically and militarily weak power. As a consequence of its lack of material power, India adopted the policy of nonalignment to safeguard its strategic autonomy in international affairs. Jawaharlal Nehru, the first Prime Minister of India, and the architect of its foreign policy, firmly believed that 'in no event should India be made to join any war without the consent of her own people being obtained' (Nehru 2004: 461). This quest for an independent foreign policy and opposition to global military blocs was a direct outcome of India's nationalist movement.[2]

Consequently, the United States became uninterested and dismissive of India.[3] In the then extant Cold War international system, the American Secretary of State, John Foster Dulles, showed his disdain for India's non-aligned status by calling it 'immoral' (*The New York Times* 1956). India's quest for an independent foreign policy clashed with the United States' Cold War priorities and the two democracies became 'estranged'.[4] This happened in spite of the fact that President Franklin D. Roosevelt had shown interest in India's independence during World War II.[5] Furthermore, even though Dr B.R. Ambedkar, the America-educated architect of independent India's constitution had drawn inspiration from the constitution of the United States, India did not pursue a strategic relationship with the United States.

The United States' alliance with Pakistan, a product of the Cold War geopolitical environment that began with the 1954 mutual defence agreement and continued with Pakistan's membership in the Southeast Asia Treaty Organization (SEATO) and the Central Treaty Organization (CENTO) further soured Indo-US ties.[6] Pakistan's alliance with the United States helped Islamabad counter India's relatively superior military and economic capabilities. 'The military importance of weapons transfers from the USA was historically crucial. Pakistan would not have become a serious military power without U.S. equipment' (Cohen 1980: 104). As such, the US-Pakistan alliance undermined India's conception of regional order predicated on Indian predominance in South Asia, and made India's strategic elite suspicious of America's intentions in the region.[7]

However, the war with China in 1962 proved that India itself needed military help from external powers to meet the Chinese challenge. India sought and received (limited) military assistance from the United States (and the United Kingdom).[8] India and the US also engaged in limited cooperation with regard to the Chinese occupation of Tibet after the

1962 Sino-Indian War (Kohli and Conboy 2002). This was the first time that the United States and India consciously aligned against another power (China).[9] However, Indo-US military co-operation proved to be of limited nature and short-lived.

Pakistan, a staunch military ally of the United States by this time, had profound misgivings about the US-India military relationship. In turn, India itself was uncertain about close military cooperation with the United States. The United States also demanded that India must commit to opposing communism globally prior to the establishment of a substantive military cooperation between the two countries (Barnds 1972: 195). Moreover, India was unable to obtain a nuclear umbrella from the United States (and other great powers) after China's first nuclear test in 1964 (Noorani 1967: 490–502). Finally, the outbreak of India's second war with Pakistan over Kashmir in 1965 led to an arms embargo by the United States against the subcontinent that ended the nascent US-India military cooperation. Consequently, India came to view the United States as an unreliable military-strategic partner—a sentiment that persisted for the rest of the Cold War in New Delhi.[10]

It was under these circumstances that India forged a strategic partnership with the former Soviet Union. So deep was the impact of India's military humiliation against China in 1962 that it had completely changed New Delhi's 'conceptual approach to international affairs' (Nayar and Paul 2003: 50). India forged a strategic relationship with the former Soviet Union to balance China as well as to procure advanced military hardware.[11] The Sino-Soviet split that had become apparent by this time paved the way for New Delhi's partnership with Moscow. This culminated in the 1971 Treaty of Peace, Friendship, and Cooperation between India and the former Soviet Union that was signed on the eve of the 1971 Bangladesh War. The treaty specifically forbade either side 'from giving any assistance to any third party taking part in an armed conflict with the other side' and called for 'mutual consultations' to 'eliminate' the threat when either side was attacked or threatened with an attack.[12] However, in order to maintain its strategic independence, New Delhi refused to partake in the Soviet Union's master plan for an Asian collective security system (Mastny 2010: 66, 71).

In the meanwhile, taking advantage of the Sino-Soviet split, the then US Secretary of State Henry Kissinger made a secret trip to China in 1971 after using Pakistan as a conduit to (tacitly) ally with Beijing in an attempt to shift the balance of power in the world.[13] During the 1971 Bangladesh War, the United States also gave China its consent to attack India, especially if India escalated the war in West Pakistan (Garver 2001: 322). The United States further dispatched a US Navy battle group, the USS Enterprise (believed to be nuclear-armed by strategists in New Delhi) to the Bay of Bengal, to warn India against escalating the war in the west. At the same time, it was also meant as a signal to the Soviet Union to desist from taking any military action against China in the event of a Chinese attack on India (Garver 2001: 322).

This pattern of American alignment with China and Pakistan against an Indian alignment with the Soviet Union continued through the 1970s and the early 1980s. Faced with a US-China-Pakistan entente, the Chinese nuclear threat, and now a presumed American nuclear threat from the Indian Ocean Region, New Delhi conducted its first nuclear test (dubbed as a 'peaceful explosion') in 1974 and immediately came under a host of international technology sanctions led by the United States.[14] The expansion of the American military base in Diego Garcia (leased from the British) in the Indian Ocean in the 1970s also strained Indo-US relations.[15] Indo-US relations further deteriorated after India's muted response to the Soviet invasion of Afghanistan in 1979 even as India was highly critical of the United States during the Vietnam War (Thakur 1979: 957–76. The United States also provided massive economic and military aid to Pakistan to check Soviet expansionism and cultivated Pakistan as a channel to aid Afghan freedom fighters. Finally, the United States turned a blind eye to Pakistan's clandestine nuclear activities until the withdrawal of Soviet troops from Afghanistan at the end of the Cold War in 1989 (Kux 2001: 227–321). All of these developments precluded any meaningful cooperation between India and the United States until the end of the Cold War.

The End of the Cold War and After

A number of developments in the 1980s had begun to soften these antagonistic alignments and paved the way for closer Indo-US relations when the Cold War ended. These included the Sino-Soviet rapprochement under the Soviet leader Mikhail Gorbachev as well as India's initial attempts to mend ties with the United States under Prime Minister Indira Gandhi.[16] India also began mending ties with China. Rajiv Gandhi made a landmark trip to China in December 1988, the first such visit by an Indian Prime Minister since 1954, to break the impasse between these Asian giants. Meanwhile, the 1989 Tiananmen Square protests and the Chinese government crackdown that followed it seriously damaged US–China relations (Foot 2008). The end of the Cold War between 1989–91 removed the rationale for strategic cooperation between the United States and China.

As a consequence of these developments, the rationale for any US-China alignment against Indian (and Soviet) interests came to naught. The implosion of India's superpower patron, the former Soviet Union, meant that an Indian foreign policy based on nonalignment was no longer viable.[17] After the 1991 balance-of-payments crisis, India also shed its socialist shibboleths and gradually began to embrace the market for its economic development. The path to a closer relationship with the United States was now open on both strategic and economic fronts. Under these structural and domestic conditions, Indian and American leaders have been gradually forging a close strategic partnership (Mohan 2006; Schaffer 2009).

Under Prime Minister V.P. Singh's National Front government (1989–90), India allowed US aircraft on supply runs from the Philippines to the Persian Gulf to refuel at airbases in India. His successor, Prime Minister Chandra Shekhar (1990–91) agreed to continue US refueling even after the US-led military action against Saddam Hussein's Iraq began during the 1991 Persian Gulf War (Kux 1993: 440–1).[18] In 1992, America's General Claude Kicklighter gave the Indian Army chief a document dubbed the 'Kicklighter Proposals' that identified several areas of mutual security cooperation (Datta-Ray 1992a; 1992b). Three years later, India and the United States signed a 10-year defence agreement under the governments of Prime Minister P.V. Narasimha Rao and President Bill Clinton that provided for joint exercises and defence trade (Burns 1995).

In the meanwhile, US-China relations continued to deteriorate after China conducted a series of missile tests in the Taiwan Straits in 1995–96 (Ross 2000: 87–123). It was in the context of this rapidly downward trend in US-China relations that India conducted a series of five nuclear tests in May 1998 (Ganguly 1999: 148–77). A few days before the May 1998 nuclear tests, the Indian Defence Minister George Fernandes declared China as India's 'potential threat number one' (*The Indian Express* 1998). After the tests, the Indian Prime Minister Atal Bihari Vajpayee sent a letter to the US President Bill Clinton in which he indirectly cited the threat from China and its proliferation of strategic technologies to Pakistan as the reasons for India's nuclear tests (*The New York Times* 1998).[19] However, in an ironic twist of events, India's nuclear tests provided the United States and China with an avenue for cooperation to salvage their deteriorating ties.

In the pursuit of its non-proliferation goals, the United States joined hands with China which was pursuing its own strategic rationale that included preempting an Indo-US alliance directed against it as well as the prevention of another (legitimate) nuclear weapons state in Asia. This resulted in a joint US-China statement on Indian (and Pakistani) nuclear tests in June 1998. According to Garver, the joint statement was tantamount to the United States endorsement of China's position that 'India should renounce nuclear weapons independent of China's nuclear arsenal' and that South Asia should become a 'nuclear weapon free zone' (Garver 2002: 26). India also came under a host of US-led multilateral sanctions on dual-use nuclear and high-technology commerce. Finally, the United States ended the nascent cooperation on defence issues with India that had begun as a consequence of the 1995 defence agreement between the two countries.[20]

While India was clearly upset with this US-China alignment against one of its core security issues, New Delhi sought to engage Washington in talks to make the United States understand the Indian point of view. This led to a sustained dialogue between India's External Affairs Minister Jaswant Singh and the US Deputy Secretary of State Strobe Talbott, which paved the way for the two countries to understand the strategic perceptions of the other.[21] Indo-US relations received a significant boost when the United States supported India's position in the 1999 Kargil War and blamed Pakistan for the crisis.[22]

That there was a dramatic reassessment in America of India's role in the emerging Asian security architecture became apparent when Condoleezza Rice—the US National Security Advisor and later the Secretary of State under President George W. Bush—wrote just before the beginning of Bush's first term that the United States must should pay close attention to India's role in the regional balance in Asia. 'There is a strong tendency conceptually to connect India with Pakistan and to think only of Kashmir or the nuclear competition between the two states. But India is an element in China's calculation, and it should be in America's, too. India is not a great power yet, but it has the potential to emerge as one' (Rice 2000: 56). Coming soon after the accidental American (NATO) bombing of the Chinese Embassy in Belgrade during the Yugoslav crisis in 1999 (BBC News 1999), and just before the emergency landing in China of the American surveillance plane EP-3 Aries after colliding with a Chinese fighter jet (that resulted in the Chinese pilot's death) in 2001 (CNN 2001)—events that severely strained US-China relations—the emergent bonhomie between the United States and India took added significance. Later in 2001, India was one of the few countries to cautiously support the Bush administration's missile defence plans—a development that further promoted their budding strategic partnership (Tellis 2006: 113–51).

Since the aftermath of the 9/11 terrorist attacks in New York and Washington, there has emerged a greater understanding between the United States and India on issues related to terrorism. In a dramatic display of its strategic intentions, India offered 'unlimited support' to Washington, including the use of specific air bases, three days after the 9/11 attacks (Fair 2004: 76–7). In return for Indian support on the US-led 'war on terrorism', the United States lifted most of the sanctions on dual-use high-technology items on India which were imposed after the latter's May 1998 nuclear tests (Kux 2002: 93–106). Defence cooperation between the two countries which was suspended after 1998 was also revived in the aftermath of 9/11 with an emphasis on counterterrorism initiatives (Raman 2006: 163–4). In April 2002, during Operation Enduring Freedom, Indian naval ships INS Sharda and INS Sukanya escorted high-value American ships passing through the Strait of Malacca (US Embassy). Later that year, the two countries formally launched the Joint Initiative on Cyber-Terrorism. When launched, the US did not have such a relationship with any other country. The US-India Cyber Security Forum was also launched in 2002 to promote bilateral cooperation in the information age (Fair 2004: 79).

The 2002 National Security Strategy of the United States listed India alongside China and Russia as one of the 'potential great powers … in the midst of internal transition' (The White House 2002: 26). The document further added that the United States wanted to move beyond issues related to nuclear and missile proliferation with India, as the United States saw India as 'a growing world power' with which it shared 'common strategic interests' (The White House 2002: 27).

In 2005, Indo-US relations witnessed a major transformation with the completion of the Next Steps in Strategic Partnership initiative that laid the foundations for close cooperation in civilian nuclear activities, civilian space programmes, dual-use high technology trade, and missile defence (US Department of State 2005). In June 2005, the two countries signed a new defence agreement that included provisions for collaborations in multinational operations, missile defence, and increased defence trade (Embassy of India 2005: 28 June). India and the United States also launched the US-India Global Democracy Initiative to assist other societies in transition that seek such assistance (Embassy of India 2005: 18 July). Later, the 2006 National Security Strategy added that 'India now is poised to shoulder global obligations in cooperation with the United States in a way befitting a major power' (The White House 2006: 39).

Most significantly, the United States changed its domestic law and played a leading role in changing several international agreements between 2006 and 2008 to bring India into the global nuclear regimes even as India is not a signatory to the Nuclear Non-Proliferation Treaty (NPT) and has an active nuclear weapons programme (Ganguly and Mistry 2006: 11–19). The US-India civil nuclear deal not only ended India's status as a nuclear pariah, but it also implicitly recognized India as a de facto nuclear weapons state while making provisions for civil nuclear (and dual-use high-technology) commerce with India. This deal has also served as a 'catalyst for New Delhi's increased trust toward Washington' (The National Bureau of Asian Research 2010: 5),[23] and paves the way for closer 'counterterrorism, defence, and intelligence cooperation' (Feigenbaum 2010).

There were some concerns regarding the tempo and direction of the Indo-US relationship after President Barack Obama assumed office in Washington in 2009. However, significant developments such as the signing of the Indo-US end-use monitoring agreement, the removal of several Indian organizations (such as the Indian Space Research Organization and the Defence Research and Development Organization) from the banned entity list that paves the way for dual-use high-technology exports from the United States, and Washington's strong push to enter the growing Indian defence market demonstrate that the relationship is back on track (The Indian Express 2009; Raj 2011; Najib 2011). So what are the prospects and limitations of this steadily growing relationship?

Prospects and Limitations

Strategic Convergence

The primary reason behind the growing Indo-US defence partnership is the fact that there are no sources of bilateral conflict between the two countries. Broadly speaking, the United States has a positive view of the rise of India. During his trip to India in later 2010, President Obama mentioned that the United States wanted to build 'a true strategic partnership' with India as India's rise as a 'global power' was 'in the best interests of both countries (India and the US), of the region, and the world' (*Hindustan Times* 2010). India's policymakers are also 'convinced' that 'US capital, technology, and goodwill are essential to India's continued rise as a global power' (National Intelligence Council 2008: 31). After all, Prime Minister Singh risked the survival of his government for the success of the Indo-US civil nuclear deal (*The Economist* 2008).[24] While there are a large number of areas of strategic convergence between New Delhi and Washington, the three most salient issues are the challenges posed by the phenomenal growth of Chinese power, religious fundamentalism and terrorism, and maritime security (in the IOR).[25]

Managing the Rise of China

After the end of the Cold War, the US-China-India triangle evolved from a US-China alignment against India, after the latter's 1998 nuclear tests, into an apparent Indo-US alignment to balance the rise of China during the Bush administration. However, it remains unclear whether the United States and India (whether individually or in tandem) are indeed pursuing a containment strategy vis-à-vis China. US-China cooperation against terrorism after September 11 as well as China's help in the ongoing nuclear crisis/stalemate on the Korean peninsula, not to mention the fact that China is America's largest trading partner, has led to some vacillation along competitor-partner spectrum in America's China policy (Qinghuo 2006: 23–36). However, the US-China relationship continues to remain very fragile as demonstrated by the complications related to American arms sales to Taiwan (Wolf and Blanchard 2010), Obama's meeting with the Dalai Lama (Buckley and Eckert 2010), and the cyber-attack originating from China on the American internet company Google (BBC News 2010). The United States also remains concerned with China's rapid military modernization and its increasingly aggressive behaviour in East Asia (*The Guardian* 2011; Alford 2010).

India is also wary about the rapid expansion of Chinese military power, as well as China's toughening stance on the border issue as well as its changing position on Kashmir (Malik 2010: 6–9). India is very concerned about the presence of Chinese soldiers in the Gilgit-Baltistan region of Pakistan—an area that New Delhi regards to be a part of the Indian state of Jammu and Kashmir (J&K).[26] Prime Minister Singh has also expressed concerns with Chinese assertiveness in its relations with India. Addressing an audience at the Council of Foreign Relations in the United States in late 2009, Singh spoke of 'assertiveness on the Chinese part' and added that 'he did not fully understand the reasons for it' (IBN Live 2009). According to a former American diplomat and China specialist Susan Shirk, while 'China has been trying to prevent clashes with neighbors', this strategy 'seems to have changed with India recently'.[27] In fact, so concerned is India about the rise of Chinese military power that Indian military planners are beginning to prepare for the possibility of a two-front war with China and Pakistan.

Given China's troubled relations with the United States and India, Chinese analysts have warily noted the dramatic transformation in Indo-US military and security relations. In fact, some Chinese analysts have even begun to refer to India as America's 'quasi-ally' (Ma 2006: 52). Chinese analysts believe that America is trying to 'reset the global balance of power' through its civil nuclear deal with India by building India 'as a counterweight to the mighty China' (Ding 2007: 12). There are also concerns in China that the growing Indo-US military partnership may lead India into playing a military role to share some of America's defence burdens given that it now finds itself overstretched in two wars (*Global Times* 2009). More importantly, a former Chinese Ambassador to India has warned that given China's 'friendly relations' with Pakistan, 'there might be changes in the situation that will be unfavorable to India' should an 'alliance' aimed at China emerge between India and the United States (Ruisheng 2008: 28).

In spite of all these developments—including a discernible pro-American tilt in Indian foreign policy in recent years—there seems to be little possibility that India will join any US-led grouping to contain the rise of China. Given its long-cherished quest for strategic autonomy, India will prefer to deal with a rising China on its own terms and as an independent pole in the emerging world order. In a more practical sense, India will remain cautious of being drawn into such an alignment because of its geographic contiguity with China. On its part, the United States does not (yet) see any wisdom in pursuing a policy of containment towards China given the level of economic interdependence between the two countries. Washington also needs Beijing's support in managing a growing number of international challenges from nuclear proliferation to climate change. However, it is not lost on any of these three countries—India, the United States, and China—that that close cooperation between the two democracies constitutes a viable hedging strategy against any Chinese belligerence in the future (Ganguly and Pardesi 2010: 65–78).

Counterterrorism Cooperation

Counterterrorism cooperation between India and the US can be traced back to at least 1981, even as it was for the most part 'a closely guarded and deniable secret' until January 2000 (Raman 2006: 160).[28] From 1981–2000, Indo-US counterterrorism cooperation went through peaks and troughs but cooperation was essentially on operational and tactical issues as fundamental differences existed between the Indian and American views on terrorism. While there has been a much greater understanding between the United States and India on issues related to terrorism after the 9/11 attacks, important perceptual differences between the two continue to exist, particularly those centred on the role of Pakistan.

In the aftermath of the 13 December 2001 attacks on the Indian Parliament by terrorists belonging to two Pakistan-based jihadi organizations—Lashkar-e-Taiba (LeT) and Jaish-e-Mohammed (JeM)—India responded with its largest-ever military mobilization along the Pakistan border since the 1971 Bangladesh War. While India's attempt at coercive diplomacy failed for a number of reasons (Ganguly and Kraig 2005: 290–324), India was unhappy about Washington's military and security cooperation with Islamabad as a reward for supporting US operations in Afghanistan (in spite of the growing evidence that links terrorism in India and beyond to sources in Pakistan). However, New Delhi welcomed the US designation of the LeT and the JeM as terrorist organizations. Similarly, while Washington expressed strong support for India in the aftermath of the dramatic November 2008 terror attacks in Mumbai/Bombay, security cooperation between the United States and

Pakistan has continued. This has caused much dismay in India even as the Indian leadership has restrained its criticism of this relationship in public.

It is also important to note that while India has provided important political and diplomatic support to America's global counterterror efforts, including the war in Afghanistan, India has not participated militarily in any US-led operations.[29] 'American officials describe India as an important *informal* ally in the global antiterror efforts' (Fair 2004: 1). Given the important role played by Pakistan in America's war efforts in Afghanistan, and as a consequence of Pakistan's sensitivities about the growing Indian influence in Afghanistan, the United States remains ambivalent about India's role there. Many American strategists share General Stanley McChrystal's view, according to whom, 'increasing Indian influence in Afghanistan is likely to exacerbate regional tensions and encourage Pakistani countermeasures in Afghanistan or India' even as 'Indian activities largely benefit the Afghan people' (McChrystal 2009: 2–11). These differences notwithstanding, the two sides are coordinating their policies in a number of areas. India is playing a significant role in the reconstruction of Afghanistan and has made contributions worth $1.2 billion to date (Lakshman 2010). While India has not deployed its military in support of US-led operations in Afghanistan, New Delhi has deployed a very small contingent of its paramilitary forces to protect Indian citizens working on reconstruction projects in Afghanistan (Mariet D'Souza 2006).

Like Afghanistan, India did not participate in America's military efforts in Iraq. While India was highly critical of any military action before the actual onset of hostilities in March 2003, India was surprisingly restrained in its official disapproval of the US-led invasion once the military operations began. Importantly, US officials were irritated with what they perceived as 'New Delhi's agnosticism' on 'Iraq's support for international terrorism' (Nayak 2006). Moreover, even after the United States expressed its desire for India's military participation in the stabilization process of Iraq in mid-2003, India chose not to send its troops there (even as India has been willing to partake in the humanitarian and economic efforts to rebuild war-torn Iraq). While India decided against contributing troops to a 'peacekeeping force' (Kifner 2003) in the US-led war in Iraq for complex reasons,[30] these factors only highlight the fact that practical Indo-US military cooperation faces severe limitations in the contexts of counter-terrorism as well as nation-building.

Maritime Security

As China and India rise economically, the IOR is emerging as a 'centre stage' for great power politics, and as another arena for the Sino-Indian rivalry (Kaplan 2009: 16–32). According to the Indian Ministry of Defence, India's geographic location at the 'top' of the Indian Ocean and its energy and trade links with countries that border the IOR and beyond 'impose an increasingly larger responsibility on India' to safeguard its 'strategic-economic' interests here (Ministry of Defence 2010: 2–3). While the IOR has not been a unified strategic region from the American perspective, the United States continues to remain the strongest naval power in the region, given its ability to project its military power across this region from its British-leased military base in Diego Garcia (Erickson, Ladwig III, and Mikolay 2010: 214–37). More importantly, both Indian and American strategic and military planners have identified the protection of the sea lanes of communication (SLOCs) in the IOR as the 'strongest area of strategic convergence' between the two countries (MacDonald 2002: xxi). In fact, the 2010 US Quadrennial Defence Review Report even goes on to state that as India's military capabilities continue to grow, it will 'contribute to Asia as a net provider of security in the Indian Ocean and beyond' (US Department of Defence 2010: 60).

While India and the United States continue to remain wary of China's growing naval power and presence in the IOR, the possibility of any contingency emerging that would involve a joint Indo-US military/naval response against China in this region remains remote in the short- to medium-term (Holmes, Winner, and Yoshihara 2009: 106–26). However, joint naval operations in terms of search and rescue missions and efforts to counter piracy, terrorism, drug trafficking, arms-smuggling, and responding jointly to natural disasters in the region remain areas of definite policy convergence (whether formal or informal).[31] In fact, when the Indian Navy updated its maritime doctrine in 2009, it specifically added that Indian maritime forces may undertake counterterrorism missions 'both independently and as cooperative endeavors with friendly foreign naval and coast guard forces'.[32]

However, for a number of reasons, including institutional factors, such cooperation has remained limited to the eastern IOR (or the Southeast Asian region) only.[33] Since the institutional cooperation with India falls under the US Pacific Command, Indo-US naval cooperation in the Persian Gulf region (including the Strait of Hormuz) has thus far remained limited (as this region falls under the purview of the US Central Command). The US Central Command has remained somewhat ambivalent of India's role in the Persian Gulf region because of Pakistani sensitivities.[34] The United States is also concerned with the Indo-Iranian cooperation (including naval cooperation) in this region (Fair 2007: 145–59). So even as India is interested in cooperating with the United States for the protection of the SLOCs in the IOR, such cooperation (while growing) is likely to remain geographically focused in the Southeast Asian region for the time being.[35]

Military-to-Military Relations

It is clear from the above discussion that even though India and the United States share many similar objectives, there exist only a limited number of areas of practical military cooperation between the two countries (at least for now). Even then, service-level cooperation in terms of joint military exercises and training is the fastest-growing dimension of their bilateral relationship. 'The United States now holds more military exercises with India than with any other country' (Armitage, Burns, and Fontaine 2010: 1–12). These military exercises have included all three services (the army, the navy, and the air force) as well as special operations forces from both sides, and have ranged from low-intensity operations in urban and jungle environments to battalion-level exercises, submarine warfare, and counterair missions.[36] In 2011, there were a total of 56 'cooperative events' across all services (US Department of Defence 2011).

There are many good reasons for such a wide-ranging military-to-military relationship between the two countries. To begin with, given their overlapping strategic objectives, it makes practical sense to hedge against future contingencies by cooperating to improve interoperability. However, and more importantly, given that each side excels in certain niche areas, such cooperation also helps with the enhancement of the capacities of a friendly partner. For example, India has sophisticated capabilities in high-altitude warfare, desert warfare, and jungle and urban operations—areas which are of great interest to the United States (Fair 2005). Similarly, India has much to learn from United States in terms of the developing and refining its doctrine, especially with the incorporation of high-technology systems and platforms. In fact, the United States has specifically stated that it is 'ready to discuss even more fundamental issues of defence transformation with India, including transformative systems in areas such as command and control, early warning and missile defence' (US Department of State 2005).

So even if avenues for practical military cooperation remain somewhat limited between India and the United States, cooperation with the highly-skilled professional military services of the other is likely to be mutually beneficial. However, institutional hurdles beset even this aspect of their relationship. The problems created by different US military commands that overlap the regions of strategic interest to India have already been discussed above. On the Indian side, the defence bureaucracy is ill-equipped to deal with the expansion in Indo-US military-to-military relations because India has never had the type of defence relationship that it now enjoys with the United States. Even the Indian link with the former Soviet Union was only 'centered on hardware, technical training, and logistical support; it did not encompass the broad array of exercises, exchanges, discussions, and military sales that the United States considers part of a normal defence relationship' (Gill 2006: 122). This problem is compounded by the fact that India lacks the equivalent of certain American institutions such as the US Special Operations Command. These institutional asymmetries are exacerbated by the Indian bureaucracy which makes it difficult for Indian military personnel to access their foreign counterparts.

Defence Trade

The passage of the Indo-US civil nuclear deal and the removal of Indian companies from the list of entities which were barred from dual-use high-technology exports have paved the way for closer Indo-US defence trade (and trade in dual-use technologies). For India, this was essentially a trust-building agreement. As a consequence, these changes, along with the overall positive momentum in Indo-US relations, have contributed to the purchase of high-profile US military hardware by India in recent years. In 2002, India purchased eight Raytheon radar systems from the United States. This was the first Indian arms deal with the United States in almost four decades (BBC News 2002). Since then India has purchased the USS Trenton (an amphibious transport dock), six *Sea King* helicopters, and six C-130J transport aircraft. However, all these deals were dwarfed in 2009 when India purchased eight Boeing P-8I *Poseidon* maritime patrol and reconnaissance aircraft for US$2.1 billion, thereby becoming the first international buyer to purchase this aircraft from the United States (Zee News 2009). In recent years, India has been on a massive arms buying spree as it rapidly modernizes its military to emerge as a major power in Asia (Cohen and Dasgupta 2010).

The United States clearly wants to be a part of India's multi-billion dollar arms bazaar and is making a strong bid for it (Bajaj and Timmons 2011). India was the third-largest buyer of American weapons in 2011 (Reuters 2011). While it is very likely that America's share will continue to grow in the Indian defence market in the years ahead, there exist strong political, structural, and institutional limits to its massive expansion. First and foremost, Indians continue to remain wary of the political implications of defence purchases from the United States. This wariness is not only a remnant of historical suspicions but also stems from the belief that the United States sells its defence hardware to gain political influence (Caverley 2007: 598–614).[37] Notably, India's current defence minister A.K. Antony is uncomfortable with the growing Indo-US defence relationship.[38] Second, Russia continues to remain India's single most important supplier of defence hardware. While India has come to rely on Israel for many military systems, Russia continues to be the source of India's most important weapons platforms, for example, the T-90S tanks and the Su-30 MKI fighter aircraft. In addition to this, India and Russia have also announced ambitious plans to jointly build a fifth-generation fighter aircraft (FGFA) as well a military transport plane (The Hindu 2010; The Economic Times 2010). Given the structural composition of the Indian military, the United States will not be able to displace Russia as the supplier of India's primary defence systems in the short- to medium-term.[39]

Third, American firms are likely to find India's defence offset policy very onerous to fulfill and will be thus deterred from entering the Indian arms market. At least one major Indian tender for attack and heavy-lift helicopters was canceled when several companies bidding for it withdrew after citing concerns with the country's offset policy (International Institute of Strategic Studies 2010: 353). Finally, the aim of India's offset policy is to build-up the country's defence-industrial base by moving towards a policy of 'self-reliance through coproduction' (Pardesi and Matthews 2007: 419–38). However, the United States has historically retained the plum role of prime contracting firms and systems integration tasks for American companies, thereby ensuring its dominance in the global defence industry even while trading and jointly producing with its partners and allies (Caverley 2007). Given that this is likely to limit the growth of India's defence-industrial base, negotiating contracts with the United States is likely to become a difficult and cumbersome task as the deals become more complex. Although it must be highlighted that India's ability to perform the task of systems integration and its ability to absorb high-end military technology remains limited (Cohen and Dasgupta 2010). However, as a consequence of all of these challenges, the Indo-US defence trade is not likely to experience any dramatic expansion even if India purchases certain big ticket items from the United States.

***

The Indo-US defence relationship is likely to grow steadily, albeit somewhat slowly, in the years ahead. The United States views India's rise as a positive and benign development in the international system. In turn, India itself views close relations with the United States as essential to its emergence as a major power in Asia. This chapter showed that such views stemmed from their largely overlapping grand strategic objectives—ensuring that China rises peacefully, confronting religious fundamentalism and terrorism, and managing the global commons in the maritime domain. However, there continue to remain important perceptual and institutional differences that limit this relationship from achieving its full potential and policy convergence despite shared grand strategic objectives.

The most important perceptual difference between the two countries centres on the role of Pakistan. While India views Pakistan as a source of terrorism, the United States sees it as an ally in its global war against terrorism.[40] On the other hand, maritime security in the IOR has emerged as the strongest area of practical military cooperation at the operational level between India and the United States. Their combined military operations are likely to be focused on non-traditional security threats stemming from piracy, smuggling, and arms trafficking. However, as a consequence of their different bureaucratic structures that deal with security in this region, Indo-US cooperation in the maritime domain will be focused primarily in the Southeast Asian region only for the time being. In spite of some perceptual and institutional hurdles, the two countries will continue to build on their already close military-to-military ties as a hedge against any unforeseen contingencies in the future, and to help enhance the capacities of their partner with whom they share common strategic objectives.

Notes

1. The Indian economy grew at an average rate of 6.3 per cent per annum between 1988 and 2006. See Panagariya 2008: 95–109. India has since maintained its high economic growth rate despite the current global financial crisis, and is projected to grow faster than 8 per cent per annum in the coming years. See The World Bank 2010.

2. For the logic behind India's policy of non-alignment, see Thomas 1979: 153–71.

3. However, India's massive poverty made it one of the largest recipients of American humanitarian assistance, especially in the 1950s and 1960s. On America's assistance to India during the food crisis of the mid-1960s, see Nayar and Paul 2003: 168–9.

4. On the estrangement of India and the United States during the Cold War, see Kux 1993.

5. However, Roosevelt's efforts came to naught in the face of strong opposition from his British allies who found themselves under attack in Europe as well as Asia. On this, see Kux 1993: 6–25.

6. On America's relations with Pakistan during the Cold War, see Kux 2001.

7. On Pakistan as a regional challenger to India's preferred regional order in South Asia, see Pardesi and Ganguly 2007: 134–8. On the role of the United States in India-Pakistan relations, see Cohen 1999: 189–205.

8. On the American support for India during the 1962 Sino-Indian War, see McMahon 1994: 272–304.

9. On this, see Harding 2004.

10. While this sentiment has certainly diminished in India since the end of the Cold War, and especially in the aftermath of the US-India Civil Nuclear Deal (which is discussed subsequently), it still lingers in certain quarters in New Delhi.

11. This decision was taken in spite of the fact that Indian military hardware was primarily of Western (European) origin heretofore, and even as its military doctrine was influenced by the West (due to the British colonial legacy).

12. For the full text of the treaty, see 'Treaty of Peace, Friendship, and Cooperation Between the Union of Soviet Socialist Republics and the Republic of India' 1971: 5.

13. On Pakistan's help in the American opening to China, see Kux 2001: 178–215.

14. The 1974 test may also have sent a signal to the former Soviet Union that India would retain its strategic autonomy in spite of the 1971 treaty. On an early view of India's nuclear programme, see Marwah 1977: 96–121.

15. See Sinha 1994: 63–70.

16. On Sino-Soviet rapprochement, see Garver 1989: 1136–52. Indira Gandhi sought to improve relations with the United States, an effort that resulted in the US-India Science and Technology Initiative in 1982 with US President Ronald Reagan that was extended under Prime Minister Rajiv Gandhi in 1985. See Marshal 1983: 694–5.

17. In the words of a then senior political leader (and later Prime Minister), Inder Kumar Gujral in 1992, 'It [non-alignment] is a mantra that we will have to keep on repeating, but frankly whom are you going to be non-aligned against?', quoted in Ganguly 2002: 379.

18. Due to domestic political considerations, India withdrew this support a day or so before the end of the hostilities against Iraq.

19. For the full text of this letter, see *The New York Times* 1998.

20. On these US-led multilateral sanctions and the suspension of Indo-US defence cooperation, see Bertsch, Gahlaut, and Srivastava (eds) 1999.

21. For details, see Talbott 2004 and Singh 2006.

22. On the Kargil Conflict, see *South Asia Monitor* 1999.

23. To be sure, there are certain quarters in India, such as the Indian communists, who remain deeply suspicious of the United States. However, this is a dwindling constituency.

24. The vigorous opposition of the Indian Left to a close partnership with the United States shows that it continues to remain deeply suspicious of America. However, as mentioned earlier, this is a declining trend in India today.

25. On these and other important issues, see Macdonald 2002.

26. A commentary in the *New York Times* had first revealed Chinese military presence in Gilgit-Baltistan. This was later confirmed by the Indian Army. See Harrison 2010; and Gupta 2010.

27. Quoted in Bagchi 2009.

28. The two countries established a Joint Working Group (JWG) in January 2000 to counter terrorism after high level talks in London between the then Indian Foreign Minister Jaswant Singh and the US Deputy Secretary of State Strobe Talbott.

29. The only exception to this is the Indian Navy's non-combat support to the United States in the Straits of Malacca.

30. On these issues, see Blarel and Pardesi 2010.

31. Perhaps the most notable naval cooperation between the Indian and the US navies in this regard was in response to the 2004 Indian Ocean tsunami. Their two navies jointly cooperated with the Japanese and Australian navies to help the affected countries in South and Southeast Asia.

32. Quoted in *The Military Balance* 2010: 336.

33. On Indo-US maritime cooperation in Southeast Asia, see Scher, Sawka, Radosh, and Strompf 2009: 35–42.

34. Institutionally, cooperation with Pakistan falls under the purview of the US Central Command. On this issue, see MacDonald 2002: xxviii–xxix. The US Africa Command which was created in 2007–8 is likely to complicate matters further.

35. However, it is noteworthy that India recently signed a defence pact (with provisions for maritime security) with the Persian Gulf state of Qatar. According to the agreement with Qatar, which is also home to a US naval base, India will provide assistance whenever Qatari assets need protection. The defence pact with Qatar reportedly includes the possibility of stationing Indian troops in that country. See Matthew 2008 and Raghuvanshi 2008.

36. For details, see Gill 2006: 113–30; and Fair 2005: 157–73.

37. For an argument that the United States gains international influence through its defence sales, see Jonathan D Caverley, "United States Hegemony and the New Economics of Defence," *Security Studies* Volume 16, Number 4 (2007), pp. 598-614.

38. While addressing a public function in 2010, Antony made the following statement—'I don't see any prospects of the Indian and US forces ever operating together'. Quoted in Unnithan 2011.

39. Interestingly, both Russian and American fighters failed to make it into the final shortlist of suppliers for advanced combat aircraft for the Indian Air Force. India has chosen to go ahead with European jets. At this point, India's decision is not entirely clear. See Lamont and Kazmin 2011.

40. However, there are some indications that the United States is beginning to take note of the problem of terrorism emanating from Pakistan. For example, Admiral Mike Mullen, the Chairman of the Joint Chiefs of Staff of the United States, recently accused Pakistan's Inter-Services Intelligence agency of having a 'long-standing relationship with the Haqqani network' which was targeting American troops (and those of US allies) in Afghanistan. See BBC News 2011.

References

Alford, Peter. 2010. 'US back in Asia to stay: Hillary Clinton', *The Australian*, 14 January.

Armitage, Richard, Nicholas Burns, and Richard Fontaine. 2010. 'Natural Allies: A Blueprint for the Future of U.S.–India Relations', *Center for a New American Security*. Available at http://www.cnas.org/files/documents/publications/CNAS_Natural%20Allies_ArmitageBurnsFontaine.pdf.

Bagchi, Indrani. 2009. 'Learning to Live with China', *The Times of India* (Crest), 3 October. Available at http://timesofindia.indiatimes.com/india/Learning-To-Live-With-China/articleshow/5083278.cms (accessed 14 February 2011).

Bajaj, Vikas and Heather Timmons. 2011. 'U.S. Delegation is Seeking Deals in India', *The New York Times*, 8 February.

Barnds, William J. 1972. *India, Pakistan, and the Great Powers*. New York: Praeger.

BBC News. 1999. 'Europe Embassy Strike "A Mistake"', 8 May. Available at http://news.bbc.co.uk/2/hi/europe/338557.stm (accessed 14 February 2011).

———. 2002. 'India signs "historic" US arms deal', 18 April. Available at http://news.bbc.co.uk/2/hi/business/1937313.stm (accessed 12 February 2011).

———. 2010. 'Google May Pull Out of China after Gmail Cyber Attack', 13 January. Available at http://news.bbc.co.uk/2/hi/business/8455712.stm (accessed 14 February 2011).

———. 2011. 'Mullen: Pakistan's ISI Spy Agency has "militant links"', 21 April. Available at http://www.bbc.co.uk/news/world-south-asia-13153538 (accessed 22 April 2011).

Bertsch, Gary K., Seema Gahlaut, and Anupam Srivastava (eds). 1999. *Engaging India: US Strategic Relations with the World's Largest Democracy*. New York: Routledge.

Blarel, Nicolas and Manjeet S. Pardesi. 2010. 'Indian Public Opinion and the War in Iraq', in Richard Sobel, Peter Furia, and Bethany Barratt (eds), *Public Opinion and International Intervention: Lessons from the Iraq War*, Washington: Potomac Books Inc.

Buckley, Chris and Paul Eckert. 2010. 'China warns against Obama-Dalai Lama meeting', Reuters, 3 February. Available at http://www.reuters.com/article/idUSTRE6120RR20100203 (accessed 14 February 2011).

Burns, John F. 1995. 'US-India Pact on Military Cooperation', *The New York Times*, 13 January.

Caverley, Jonathan D. 2007. 'United States Hegemony and the New Economics of Defence', *Security Studies*, 16 (4): 598–614.

CNN. 2001. 'U.S. Surveillance plane lands in China after collision with fighter', 1 April. Available at http://archives.cnn.com/2001/US/04/01/us.china.plane/ (accessed 14 February 2011).

Cohen, Stephen P. 1980. 'South Asia and U.S. Military Policy', in Lloyd I. Rudolph, and Susanne Hoeber Rudolph (eds), *The Regional Imperative*. New Delhi: Concept Publishing Company.

———. 1999. 'The United States, India, and Pakistan: Retrospect and Prospect', in Selig S. Harrison, Paul H. Kreisberg, and Dennis Kux (eds), *India and*

Pakistan: The First Fifty Years. Washington, DC: Woodrow Wilson Center Press and Cambridge: Cambridge University Press.

———. 2001. *India: Emerging Power.* Washington, D.C.: Brookings Institution Press.

Cohen, Stephen P. and Sunil Dasgupta. 2010. *Arming without Aiming.* Washington, D.C.: Brookings Institution Press.

Datta-Ray, Sunanda K. 1992a. 'In the Ashes of Nonalignment, a US-India Embrace', *International Herald Tribune*, 6 March.

———. 1992b. 'When "By Order" Says So, There's No Talking Back', *International Herald Tribune*, 28 October.

Ding, Ying. 2007. 'The Mounting Nuclear Imbalance', *Beijing Review*, 36: 12.

Embassy of India, Washington, D.C. 2005. India-US Global Democracy Initiative, 18 July. Available at http://www.indianembassy.org/press_release/2005/July/15.htm (accessed 14 February 2011).

———. 2005. 'New Framework for the US-India Defence Relationship', 28 June. Available at http://merln.ndu.edu/merln/mipal/reports/US_India_Defence_Framework.doc (accessed 14 February 2011).

———. 2010. 'Ambassador Meera Shankar Address at the George Washington University's Ambassadors Forum and the Distinguished Women in International Affairs Series', 12 October. Available at http://www.indianembassy.org/prdetail1615/address-by-ambassador-meera-shankar-at-the-george-washington-universityandrsquo%3Bs-elliott-school-of-international-affairsandrsquo%3B-ambassadors-forum-and-the-distinguished-women-in-international-affairs-series-andquot%3Bindo-u.s.-relations-%3A-an-evolving-partnershipandquot%3B (accessed 8 February 2011).

Erickson, Andrew S., Walter C. Ladwig III, and Justin D. Mikolay. 2010. 'Diego Garcia and the United States' Emerging Indian Ocean Strategy', *Asian Security*, 6 (3): 214–37.

Fair, C. Christine. 2004. *The Counterterror Coalitions: Cooperation with India and Pakistan.* Santa Monica, CA: RAND.

———. 2005. 'US-Indian Army-to-Army Relations: Prospects for Future Coalition Operations', *Asian Security*, 1 (2): 157–73.

———. 2007. 'India and Iran: New Delhi's Balancing Act', *The Washington Quarterly*, 30 (3): 145–59.

Feigenbaum, Evan A. 2010. 'India's Rise, America's Interest', *Foreign Affairs*, 89 (2): 76–91.

Foot, Rosemary. 2008. 'China and the Tiananmen bloodshed of June 1989', in Steve Smith, Amelia Hadfield, and Tim Dunne (eds), *Foreign Policy: Theories, Actors, Cases.* New York: Oxford University Press.

Ganguly, Sumit. 1999. 'India's Pathway to Pokhran II: The Prospects and Sources of New Delhi's Weapons Program', *International Security*, 23 (4): 148–77.

———. 2002. 'India's Alliances 2020', in Michael R. Chambers (ed.), *South Asia in 2020: Future Strategic Balances and Alliances*, p. 379 (endnote 6). Carlisle Barracks, PA: Strategic Studies Institute, US Army War College.

Ganguly, Sumit and Dinshaw Mistry. 2006. 'The Case for the US-India Nuclear Agreement', *World Policy Journal*, XXVIII (2): 11–19.

Ganguly, Sumit and Manjeet S. Pardesi. 2010. 'The Evolving US-China-India Triangular Relationship', *CLAWS Journal*, 65–78. Available at http://www.claws.in/CJ_Summer_2010_inside.pdf.

Ganguly, Sumit and Michael R. Kraig. 2005. 'The 2001-2002 Indo-Pakistani Crisis: Exposing the Limits of Coercive Diplomacy', *Security Studies*, 14 (2): 290–324.

Garver, John W. 1989. 'The "New Type" of Sino-Soviet Relations', *Asian Survey*, 29 (12): 1136–52.

———. 2001. *Protracted Contest: Sino-Indian Rivalry in the Twentieth Century*. Seattle: University of Washington Press.

———. 2002. 'The China-India-U.S. Triangle: Strategic Relations in the Post-Cold War Era', NBR Analysis, 13 (5): 26.

Gill, John H. 2006. 'US-India Military-to-Military Interaction: In the context of the larger relationship', in Sumit Ganguly, Brian Shoup, and Andrew Scobell (eds), *US-Indian Strategic Cooperation into the 21st Century: More than words*. New York: Routledge.

Gilpin, Robert. 1981. *War and Change in World Politics*. New York: Cambridge University Press.

Global Times (China). 2009. 'New Pact Puts Growing India-US Military Ties Under Spotlight', 21 July. Available at http://world.globaltimes.cn/americas/2009-07/449376.html (accessed 14 February 2011).

Gupta, Shishir. 2010. 'Army Passes Intel to Govt: PLA Men at Pass Linking PoK to China', *Indian Express*, 31 August.

Harding, Harry. 2004. 'The Evolution of the Strategic Triangle: China, India, and the United States', in Francine R. Frankel and Harry Harding (eds), *The India-China Relationship: Rivalry and Engagement*. New Delhi: Oxford University Press.

Harrison, Selig S. 2010. 'China's Discreet Hold on Pakistan's Northern Borderlands', *New York Times*, 26 August.

Hindustan Times. 2010. 'Obama Backs "India's Rise", But Promises Little', 3 November. Available at http://www.hindustantimes.com/specials/coverage/obamavisit/Obama-backs-India-s-rise-but-promises-little/india/SP-Article10-621730.aspx (accessed 11 February 2011).

Holmes, James R., Andrew C. Winner, and Toshi Yoshihara. 2009. *Indian Naval Strategy in the Twenty-First Century*. New York: Routledge.

IBN Live. 2009. 'I Don't Understand China's Assertiveness: PM', 24 November. Available at http://ibnlive.in.com/news/i-dont-understand-chinas-assertiveness-pm/105839-2.html (accessed 14 February 2011).

Kaplan, Robert D. 2009. 'Center Stage for the Twenty First Century', *Foreign Affairs*, 88 (2): 16–29.

Kapur, S. Paul and Sumit Ganguly. 2007. 'The Transformation of U.S.-India Relations: An Explanation for the Rapprochement and Prospects for the Future', *Asian Survey*, 47 (4): 643.

Kennedy, Paul. 1989. *The Rise and Fall of the Great Powers: Economic Change and Military Conflict from 1500 to 2000*. London: Fontana Press.

Kifner, John. 2003. 'After the War: Other Forces; India Decides Not to Send Troops to Iraq Now', *The New York Times*, 15 July.

Kohli, M.S. and Kenneth Conboy, 2002. *Spies in the Himalayas: Secret Missions and Perilous Climbs*. Lawrence: University Press of Kansas.

Kux, Dennis. 1993. India and the United States: Estranged Democracies 1941-1991. Washington, DC: National Defence University Press.

———. 2001. *The United States and Pakistan, 1947-2000: Disenchanted Allies*. Baltimore: The Johns Hopkins University Press.

———. 2002. 'India's Fine Balance', *Foreign Affairs*, 81 (3): 93–106.

Lakshman, Narayan. 2010. 'India Keeps Up Afghan Effort Despite Security Concerns', *The Hindu*, 18 December.

Lamont, James and Amy Kazmin. 2011. 'India Shuns US in $11 billion Fighter Deal', *Financial Times*, 28 April.

Macdonald, Juli A. 2002. 'Indo-US Military Relations: Expectations and Perceptions', a report from the Director, Net Assessment, Office of the Secretary of Defence, Ft. Belvoir: Defense Technical Information.

Ma, Jiali. 2006. 'The Posture of India's Rise', *Contemporary International Relations*, 7: 52.

Malik, Mohan. 2010. 'China Unveils "The Kashmir Card"', *China Brief*, 10 (19). Available at http://www.jamestown.org/single/?no_cache=1&tx_ttnews%5Bswords%5D=8fd5893941d69d0be3f378576261ae3e&tx_ttnews%5Bany_of_the_words%5D=beijing&tx_ttnews%5Btt_news%5D=36915&tx_ttnews%5BbackPid%5D=7&cHash=d5fbf6c8b0#.Ue8rotLfCvM (accessed 24 July 2013).

Mariet D'Souza, Shanthie, 2006. 'India's Role in Afghanistan: Need for Greater Engagement', *IDSA Strategic Comments*, 4 May. Available at http://www.idsa.in/idsastrategiccomments/IndiasRoleinAfghanistan_SMDSouza_040506 (accessed 14 February 2011).

Marshal, Eliot. 1983. 'US-India Project: Bold Plans, Few Dollars', *Science*, 220 (4598): 694–5.

Marwah, Onkar. 1977. 'India's Nuclear and Space Programs: Intent and Policy', *International Security*, 2 (2): 96–121.

Mastny, Vojtech. 2010. 'The Soviet Union's Partnership with India', *Journal of Cold War Studies*, 12 (3): 66, 71.

Matthew, Vinod. 2008. 'Security Pact with Qatar Gives India Gulf Toehold', *Indian Express*, 12 November.

McChrystal, Stanley. 2009. 'COMISAF's Initial Assessment', Headquarters, International Security Assistance Force, Kabul, Afghanistan, 30 August. Available at http://media.washingtonpost.com/wp-srv/politics/documents/Assessment_Redacted_092109.pdf (accessed 11 February 2011).

McMahon, Robert J. 1994. *The Cold War on the Periphery: The United States, India, and Pakistan*. New York: Columbia University Press.

Ministry of Defence, India. 2010. *Annual Report, 2009–2010*, pp. 2–3.

Mohan, C. Raja. 2006. *Impossible Allies: Nuclear India, United States, and the Global Order*. New Delhi: India Research Press.

Najib, Moska. 2011. 'Why India-US Defence Deals Have Become Big Business', BBC News, 7 February. Available at http://www.bbc.co.uk/news/world-south-asia-12381737 (accessed 10 February 2011).

National Intelligence Council. 2008. 'Global Trends 2025: A Transformed World', 31 November.

Nayak, Polly. 2006. 'Prospects for US-India Counterterrorism Cooperation: An American View', in Sumit Ganguly Brian Shoup, and Andrew Scobell, (eds), *US-Indian Strategic Cooperation into the 21st Century: More Than Words*. New York: Routledge, 137.

Nayar, Baldev Raj and T.V. Paul. 2003. *India in the World Order: Searching for Major-Power Status*. New York: Cambridge University Press.

Nehru, Jawaharlal. 2004. *The Discovery of India*. New Delhi : Penguin Books.

New York Times. 1956. 'Dulles Declares Neutrality Pose is an Obsolete Idea', 10 June.

Noorani, A.G. 1967. 'India's Quest for a Nuclear Guarantee', *Asian Survey*, 7 (7): 490–502.

Panagariya, Arvind. 2008. *India: The Emerging Giant*. New York: Oxford University Press.

Pardesi, Manjeet S. and Ron Matthews. 2007. 'India's Tortuous Road to Defence-Industrial Self-Reliance', *Defence & Security Analysis*, 23 (4): 419–38.

Pardesi, Manjeet S. and Sumit Ganguly. 2007. 'The Rise of India and the India-Pakistan Conflict', *The Fletcher Forum of World Affairs*, 31 (1): 134–8.

Qinghuo, Jia. 2006. 'One Administration, Two Voices: US China Policy During Bush's First Term', *International Relations of the Asia-Pacific*, 6 (1): 23–36.

Raghuvanshi, Vivek. 2008. 'India, Qatar Discuss Defence Cooperation', *Defence News*, 10 November.

Raman, Bahukutumbi. 2006. 'Indo-US Counterterrorism Cooperation: Past, Present, and Future', in Sumit Ganguly, Brian Shoup, and Andrew Scobell (eds), *US-Indian Strategic Cooperation into the 21st Century: More than words.* New York: Routledge.

Reuters. 2011. 'U.S. Foreign Arms Sales Reach $34.8 billion', 5 December. Available at http://www.reuters.com/article/2011/12/06/us-pentagon-weapons-idUSTRE7B500R20111206 (accessed 7 July 2012).

Rice, Condoleezza. 2000. 'Campaign 2000: Promoting National Interest', *Foreign Affairs*, 79 (1): 45–62.

Ross, Robert S. 2000. 'The 1995-1996 Taiwan Strait Confrontation: Coercion, Credibility, and Use of Force', *International Security*, 25 (2): 87–123.

Ruisheng, Cheng. 2008. 'Trend of India's Diplomatic Strategy', *China International Studies*, 1: 28.

Schaffer, Teresita. 2009. *India and the United States in the 21st Century: Reinventing Partnership.* Washington, D.C.: CSIS Press.

Scher, Robbert M., Andrew J. Sawka, Michael A. Radosh, and Kevin Strompf. 2009. 'Framework for Indo-US Cooperation in Southeast Asia', prepared for Director, Net Assessment, Office of the Secretary of Defence, pp. 35–42.

Singh, Jaswant. 2006. *In Service of Emergent India: A Call to Honor.* Bloomington: Indiana University Press.

Sinha, Ajoy. 1994. *Indo-US Relations: From the Emergence of Bangladesh to the Assassination of Indira Gandhi.* New Delhi: Janaki Prakashan.

South Asia Monitor. 1999. 'Kargil: What Does It Mean?', No. 12, 19 July.

Talbott, Strobe. 2004. *Engaging India: Diplomacy, Democracy, And the Bomb.* Washington, DC: Brookings Institution Press.

Tellis, Ashley J. 2006. 'The Evolution of US-Indian Ties: Missile Defence in an Emerging Strategic Relationship', *International Security*, 30 (4): 113–51.

Thakur, Ramesh. 1979. 'India's Vietnam Policy', *Asian Survey*, 19 (10): 957–76.

The Economic Times. 2010. 'India, Russia to Build Military Transport Planes', 10 September.

The Economist, 2008. 'India's Government Survives'. Available at http://www.economist.com/node/11779444 (accessed on 27 August 2013).

The Guardian. 2011. 'US Concerned Over China's Rapid Development of New Weapons', 9 January.

The Hindu. 2010. 'India, Russia Sign Deal for Fifth Generation Fighter Aircraft', 21 December.

The Indian Express. 1998. 'China is Enemy No. 1: George', 4 May.

———. 2009. 'India, US Agree on End User Monitoring Pact', 20 July.

The Military Balance 2010. James Hackett (ed.), 110 (1). London: Routledge for the International Institute for Strategic Studies. Available at http://www.

tandfonline.com/toc/tmib20/110/1#.Ue8tg9LfCvM (accessed on 1 August 2013).

The National Bureau of Asian Research. 2010. 'The U.S.-India Defence Relationship: An Update for President Obama's State Visit to India, November 2010', NBR Workshop Report. Available at http://www.nbr. org/downloads/pdfs/PSA/PR_US-India_Workshop.pdf (accessed 10 February 2011).

The New York Times. 1998.'Nuclear Anxiety: Indian's Letter to Clinton on the Nuclear Testing', 12 May.

The White House. 2002. The National Security Strategy of the United States of America. Available at http://www.globalsecurity.org/military/library/ policy/national/nss-020920.pdf (accessed 14 February 2011).

———. 2006. The National Security Strategy of the United States of America. Available at http://kms1.isn.ethz.ch/serviceengine/Files/ISN/15462/ ipublicationdocument_singledocument/c0eed63b-a497-4d07-9084-bfe1e22448af/en/nss2006.pdf (accessed 14 February 2011).

———. 2010. 'Press Gaggle on the President's Upcoming Trip to India', 27 October. Available at http://www.whitehouse.gov/the-press-office/2010/ 10/27/press-gaggle-presidents-upcoming-trip-india (accessed 8 February 2011).

The World Bank. 2010.'India Economic Update'; Available at http://siteresources. worldbank.org/INDIAEXTN/Resources/295583-1268190137195/ India_Economic_Update_June_23_2010.pdf (accessed 8 February 2011).

Thomas, Raju G.C. 1971.'Treaty of Peace, Friendship, and Cooperation Between the Union of Soviet Socialist Republics and the Republic of India', The Current Digest of the Soviet Press, 23 (32): 5.

———. 1979. 'Non-alignment and Indian Security: Nehru's Rationale and Legacy', Journal of Strategic Studies, 2 (2): 153–71.

Unnithan, Sandeep. 2010.'The ChiPak Threat', India Today. Available at http:// indiatoday.intoday.in/story/the-chipak-threat/1/117399.html (accessed 24 July 2013).

———. 2011. 'Lone Dissenter', India Today. Available at http://indiatoday. intoday.in/story/defence-minister-a-k-antony-reins-in-military-ties-with-the-us/1/134697.html (accessed 24 July 2013).

US Department of Defence. 2010. Quadrennial Defence Review Report, p. 60.

US Department of Defence. 2011. 'Report to the Congress on U.S.–India Security Cooperation'. Available at http://www.defence.gov/pubs/ pdfs/20111101_NDAA_Report_on_US_India_Security_Cooperation. pdf (accessed 7 July 2012).

US Department of State. 2005. *United States and India Successfully Complete Next Steps in Strategic Partnership*, 18 July. Available at http://merln.ndu.edu/ archivepdf/india/State/49721.pdf (accessed 14 February 2011).

———. 2005. 'Background Briefing by Administration Officials on US-South Asia Relations', 25 March. Available at http://www.fas.org/terrorism/at/ docs/2005/StatePressConfer25mar05.htm (accessed 7 September 2010).

US Embassy, New Delhi. n.d. 'Defence Relations: Shared Strategic Future'. Available at http://newdelhi.usembassy.gov/uploads/images/7tIuOzAx 8UV0mdK5nGCpJw/wwwfpppdef.pdf (accessed 14 February 2011).

Wolf, Jim and Ben Blanchard. 2010. 'US regrets China's response to arms sales', Reuters, 30 January. Available at http://www.reuters.com/article/ idUSTRE60T07W20100130 (accessed 14 February 2011).

Yashwant Raj. 2011. 'US Ends Export Controls for India, Lifts Ban on ISRO, DRDO', *Hindustan Times*, 25 January.

Zee News. 2009. 'India to buy Boeing P-8I Poseidon', 31 July. Available at http:// www.zeenews.com/news551686.html (accessed 12 February 2011).

9 Indo-Russian Defence Ties

An Overdependence Dilemma

P.L. Dash*

THE CENTRAL PROBLEM in Indo-Russian defence relations has been India's overdependence on Russia for the supply of weapons systems. Estimates suggest that the former Soviet Union was India's largest arms supplier to the tune of 70 per cent (Sergounin and Subbotin 1996: 23). US sources put the figure still higher—around 1991, when the Soviet Union disintegrated, 70 per cent of Army armaments, 80 per cent of Air Force armaments, and 85 per cent of Navy armaments of India were of Soviet origin (Conley 2000). In the post-Soviet years, although Russia was passing through the chaos of transition, sources suggest that 'Russia accounted for 77 per cent of India's arms imports during 2005–2009 followed by the UK (8 per cent) and Israel (5 per cent)'.[1] Russia today continues to exercise an influence of considerable magnitude on India's defence horizon thanks to the holdover from the Cold War.

In the post-1991 period, Indo-Russian defence relations have passed through four distinct phases—the inceptive phase of continuity amidst chaos (1991–95), the resumption phase of oscillation and reorientation on the part of both countries (1996–2000), and the resurgence phase of strengthening defence ties after the 10-year treaty of Strategic Partnership was signed in October 2000. The fourth phase began with Prime Minister Medvedev's visit to India in December 2010,

* The author is beholden to Professor Sunil Dasgupta for his valuable comments and to Air Marshal Pramod Mehra for sharing his practical insight.

when both countries decided to extend their military and technological cooperation up to 2020.

With India's emergence as a regional power and Russia's re-emergence in the global arms market under the Putin-Medvedev dispensation, the shape of things to come has rapidly changed, transforming the contours of Indo-Russian defence ties to a strategic partnership. What has strengthened these ties further is the rapid change in the India-Russia defence relationship in recent years. A cursory look at the past two decades elucidates that in 1991, Russian defence production was in chaos, while in 2012 Russia it is fairly stable and produces an array of modernized weapons. In 1992, India was not on the priority list of Russia in the Asian geopolitical matrix, but by now Russia has acknowledged its follies and reshaped its policy priorities. In the aftermath of the Soviet collapse, a westward-looking Boris Yeltsin and his foreign minister Andrei Kozyrev were Atlanticists, but for the past decade, the Putin-Medvedev tandem rule has been a pragmatic duumvirate looking at India as a partner in South Asia. In July 1993, Russia was browbeaten by the United States on the cryogenic engine issue.[2] Today, Russia has come entirely out of the American shadow. In 1991, India had just launched its economic liberalization process and her rise was as yet invisible; in 2012 India is Asia's third largest economy, next only to Japan and China. India's annual defence spending of $30 billion since 2010 has sought modernization and qualitative change in technology and military culture and transformed the image of its defence projections in the regional and global contexts.[3] As India looks ahead to modernizing its defence forces, in several key areas of weapon systems and military hardware, it remains tied to Russia for supply or co-production of weapon systems. This chapter seeks to take as contextual backdrop what was bequeathed from Soviet yesteryears as the main platform for India's military overdependence on Russia and analyse how both countries have shifted and shuffled their priorities in the last 20 years to focus on a few key areas of Indo-Russian defence cooperation. It also seeks to pinpoint the bottlenecks of lopsided military dependence and the implications for Indo-Russian defence ties for South Asia.

Lingering Legacy

India's defence industry has a double paradox. Before 1947 it had 16 well-established ordnance factories (OFs). Their number swelled to 40 through the years after independence. Its defence industries also include eight relatively autonomous defence public sector units (DPSUs) and 50 defence Research & Development (R&D) laboratories. Despite this, India remains a major importer of arms and weapon systems (Nugent 1991: 27–36). While this paradox continues even after 60 years of independence, there is another problem—its weapon systems are largely Soviet/Russian-made. Despite efforts at diversifying sources of procurement, India remains dependent on Russia because the indigenous military-industrial complex is not geared to meet the country's defence requirements. Although India decided to diversify her defence procurement basket in the 1980s, it is only in the past decade that signs of diversification have driven India to buy extensively from France, England, and the US in order to break Russia's monopoly over defence supply. Between 2007 and 2011, India's main defence acquisitions were 120 Sukhoi and 16 MiG fighter jets from Russia and 20 Anglo-French Jaguar fighters. India's biggest departure from the past pattern came when it opted in 2012 for the procurement of 126 multirole combat aircraft from French defence contractor Rafale in a deal worth $10 billion (Kumar 2012).

India's defence industry over the years has passed through two phases of development—between 1947 and 1962, it was buying off-the-shelf weapons from the UK and France. After the 1962 Chinese invasion, Nehru decided to set up a domestic arms industry through a combination of foreign imports and technology assistance—a policy that India continues to rely on even today. It is on the basis of this policy that the Soviet Union enhanced its presence in India's defence realm considerably. India in the 1960s was a country faced with tremendous difficulties. In this phase, the Soviet Union offered India help through direct offset arrangements of defence technology transfers, licensed production of weapon systems and sub-systems, local assemblage, and arms sales through loans with low interests. It also offered indirect offsets of barter trading with non-defence items like consumer goods, raw materials, and industrial products (Baskaran 2004: 218–19). The Soviet offers were unconditional and their terms were too alluring to resist.

By offering loans and military assistance with 'friendship price tags', the Soviets had their own geopolitical and strategic calculations. The Soviet leadership under Brezhnev decided to project India as a frontline partner in South Asia. Soviet leader Leonid Brezhnev came out with an Asian Collective Security Proposal that Indira Gandhi initially pooh-poohed, saying that it would 'accentuate superpower rivalry in the region' (Jain 2009: 112). But India's isolation vis-à-vis the emergence of a US-China-Pakistan axis in 1970–71 compelled it to sign the Indo-Soviet Treaty of Friendship (1971), thereby bringing the two together. The Treaty provided the legal framework for mutual military assistance in the event of an armed conflict. It stated—'...either Party being subjected to an attack or a threat thereof, the High Contracting Parties shall immediately enter into mutual consultations in order to remove such threat and to take appropriate effective measures to ensure peace and the security of their countries'.[4] The treaty was the culmination of a lingering legacy of mutual geopolitical dependence in a turbulent epoch and remained a guiding force for the ensuing 20 years of its validity until the Soviet collapse in 1991. Militarily and otherwise, it clearly demarcated that India was with the Soviet Union. As Brezhnev expressed it during a visit to New Delhi in October 1980, the Soviet Union remained India's 'reliable friend in good times and in hard times, in clear weather and in bad weather' (Donaldson 1980–81: 235).

Why Russia Dominates

India's overdependence on Russia for arms is central to the theme of Indo-Russian defence ties. The dye was cast in the early 1960s, when the Cold War divide pitted Russia against the US; and India against Pakistan. Each US arms deal with Pakistan produced a reciprocal Soviet offer to India, thereby extending the Russian presence in all three branches of the Indian armed forces, including its defence research establishments. India accepted Soviet military assistance as a sign of friendship that was in distinct contrast with the unfriendly response of the West. As Soviet dominance grew in intensity, it clearly distanced India from the US. While democratic India remained open to diversifying its weapons procurement, major Western arms producers were reluctant to sell India whatever it wanted. This caused India to view the US with caution as a potential arms supplier. As a result, the Russian dominance continued. Low upfront cost of weapons, Russia's readiness to share the latest military technology, India's geopolitical importance in South Asia, and India's readiness for military joint ventures and potential to absorb complex, modern weapon systems—all facilitated growing ties. Both countries invested time, money, energy, technology, and diplomacy in sustaining their bilateral ties.

Russia's strategic view of India's frontline position in South Asia weighed heavily in India's favour as a client state for arms supply. What Russia did to preserve its pre-eminence was to share its most advanced weapons systems with India as no other arms supplier did. These gestures were feasible due to the strong rapprochement between the political leadership of both countries irrespective of whether it was between Brezhnev and Indira Gandhi, Gorbachev and Rajiv Gandhi, or Putin with successive Indian Prime Ministers of different political persuasions. State-to-state dealings sans private sector participation strengthened Indo-Russian defence bonds because it was easy to handle complex arms deals at the state level. Such an arrangement was hypothetically feasible but practically impossible with the US, where different private producers provided different components of a single weapon system.

India has never done cost-benefit analyses of life cycle verses upfront cost of weapons it has bought from Russia. Even today, with the T-50 Fifth Generation Fighter (FGFA) deal, it is estimated that the price of the Russian T-50 would be less than $100 million each or just half the price of the Lockheed Martin F-22 (Kramnik 2010: 11). The Russian upfront cost was too tempting to resist. Price apart, reliability of Russian arms and credibility of Russian suppliers were two reasons why Russia dominated bilateral defence relations. Feathers were ruffled in New Delhi on two occasions when Russia dithered on commitments to supply India with cryogenic rocket engines and escalated the upfront price of re-cabling the carrier Gorshkov. However, these incidences have not dampened the bilateral spirit of defence cooperation as is evidenced by the transformation of ties from buyer-seller status to a strategic partnership.

Apex level corruption as a factor in bilateral Indo-Russian defence relations has never been a significant problem. Bofors-like scams in Indo-Russian defence deals were absent until Commodore Sukhjinder Singh, an Indian Navy Officer posted in Russia as production superintendent in 2005–7 to oversee the long Gorshkov refit, was 'honey trapped' by a Russian female for which he was ultimately sacked (Pandit 2011: 14). Sukhjinder's case was an eye opener to the Indian defence forces, but it had an insignificant impact on bilateral ties. As Prabhat Shukla, India's Ambassador to Russia, observed—'In substance there is no change in the intensity of our engagement' (Chengappa 2008: 58).

Two Soviet/Russian strategic considerations are relevant here. Russia had chosen two demographic heavyweights in Asia for rendering military assistance—first China and then India. This was a strategic objective to give Russia an edge over other competing powers in Asia. Realizing that this fundamental Russian approach was correct, Yeltsin did iron out the wrinkles in Indo-Russian bilateral relations during his maiden visit to India in January 1993, as did Putin with China during his first tenure. The Putin-Medvedev duumvirate is acutely aware of Russian interests vis-a-vis China and India. Russia has taken into account the huge demographic and economic prowess of contemporary China and India. It feels their pulse in Asian affairs and nurtures a desire to tether these countries to its defence supply system, which has been facing intense competition from other countries in recent years. Second, Russia feels that even if the arms recipients break away from the mainstay of Russian supply while forming future alliances with other powers, they cannot altogether eschew the Russian supply chain because they have been closely tied to the Russian weapon systems and have become dependent on it. India's defence inventory and arsenal remain primarily Russian, secondarily western, and tertiary indigenous. In this connection, China's successful deviation from the Russian arms market is interesting to observe. In the long run, for India too, when diversification is already under way, the present tethering arrangement is unlikely to be sustainable.

Shifting Sands

For Moscow, the immediate post-Soviet debates raised vital issues about arms supply and technology transfer on offset and barter arrangement to countries ranging from Angola to India and from Egypt to the Philippines. The Russian shift from an ideologically driven foreign and defence policy to a pragmatic one nonplussed the Russian military-industrial complex. 'Thousands of defence enterprises all across the Soviet Union met centrally determined production quotas and did not have any idea of costing, supply chains or market mechanism' (Sen 2011). With privatization replacing state monopoly, new norms began operating in defence relations from the mid-1990s. The Russian state abdicated its responsibility on the servicing of arms it had once supplied and the private sector was unprepared to take on those responsibilities. Consequently, a trust deficit emerged for India as spares stopped coming and past commitments were not met. By 1993, Russian military sales to India had plummeted to 45 per cent of their 1988 level (Blank 1993: 44). Thus, both sides were busy in a search for alternatives—Russia with how to shift from barter and India with how to free itself from over-dependence on Russia. Easy escape routes were not available to either.

In 1993, Russia faced a dire situation when the government refused to pay the defence industry for its earlier orders. 100 MiG fighters worth $2 billion were standing parked, unclaimed, and unpaid for at the MiG assembly plant near Moscow (Kogan 1994: 43–4). In 1995, the Russian Ministry of Defence paid only 1 per cent of its overall dues of 9 billion Roubles to the Sokol plant in Gorky, the producer and supplier of MiG 29s and 31s to India. As a result, by 1996, the company sacked 4,000 employees because it could not pay them salaries. By the fall of 1995, the debt of the Russian Ministry of Defence to the Nizhnyi Novgorod defence industry reached a huge figure of 42 billion Roubles. Victor Glukhikh, Chairman of the State Committee on Defence Production, revealed that by the end of 1993, the government owed the defence industry 8 trillion Roubles (*Komsomolskaya Pravda* 1994). It was estimated that by 1994, about 400 defence enterprises stopped all production, while some 1,200 plants were working part-time (*Segodnya* 1994). The years 1994 and 1995 were the worst for Russian defence industry. The situation was so dire that 15 years later, when this author in the summer of 2010 visited Bryansk—the city where SS missiles were once produced—the factory was lying idle and local experts at the Bryansk University averred that it could not be revived anytime soon.

While the Russian political leadership oscillated between the friendship price tag and the real price tag of defence products, Russia's defence industry was analysing the pros and cons of the age-old practice of barter and becoming highly critical of it. During the crisis phase of Russian transition under Yeltsin, the Russian defence bureaucracy aligned with politicians and favoured the Russian military-industrial complex to view that barter in defence trade ought to be removed. However, neither suggested any tangible way to salvage their sinking industry while wage arrears of employees continued to pile up and defence industry employees remained in jobs without salaries.

Meanwhile, India was running from pillar to post for defence spares. It went to innumerable locations in the post-Soviet space and Eastern Europe in search of spares—sometimes successfully, at others not so successfully. Eventually, Indian ambassador to Moscow Ronen Sen endeavoured to shift focus to persuading the Russian and Indian governments to restart production by way of India paying the salary of Russian workers in MiG spares production factories. The Russian workers, who had lobbied with their government in vain to modernize the MiG production facilities in order to meet the Indian demand, welcomed the idea and the Indian government readily approved it. But the Russian government was reluctant to accept Sen's approach, arguing that spare production facilities were of 1960s vintage, outdated and useless, and hence to be disbanded.

Finally, growing fears of workers' protests in MiG factories led the Russian government to agree to allow bilateral arrangement on spares productions, provided payments for it would be made to the Russian government in dollars. It was a clear indication of the friendship price tag disappearing and a pragmatic price tag replacing it. The arrangement worked well and revived spare supplies to India within a few months. But India knew that the days of mutually arranged Rupee-Rouble exchange were over and that a new era had dawned. Except India's past Russian debt of 36,000 crore rupees, it was agreed during Yeltsin's 1993 visit to India that the debt would be repaid in Indian merchandise; all other deals with Russia thereafter were on dollar parity.

A final touch to Russia's shifting gear defence policy was provided in 1996 by Yevgeny Primakov, an academic turned politician who revived Russia's Eurasian character in foreign, diplomatic, and defence policy. Primakov gave due importance to rising Asian powers like China and India and even suggested a possible triangular alliance between Russia, India, and China (Dash 1999: 1494–6). He advocated doing so when he was first the foreign minister and then prime minister of Russia. After Putin became the president in the spring of 2000, his pragmatic assessment of Russia's defence policy and his understanding of the importance of Russia's relations with traditional clients and friendly states in general, and India and China in particular, were the key drivers of Russian policy. After 2000, there has been no looking back and Indo-Russian relations in general and defence ties in particular have been looking up. It is therefore pertinent to examine major collaborations in bilateral defence ties in the past two decades in the three main branches of the defence forces—the Army, the Navy, and the Air Force—as well as the strategic relationship in dual-use areas like nuclear technology and space.

Major Military Transfers

Main Battle Tanks

Russia had begun producing T-series battle tanks since the Second World War and has been producing them for years in two cities—Omsk and Nizhny Tagil. India was one of the few countries using T-72s from the Soviet years as its main battle tanks (MBT). Other users included Cyprus, Venezuela, Algeria, Lebanon, Saudi Arabia, and Libya. In 1992, amidst post-Soviet chaos, the Russian Defence Ministry decided to merge the two tank-producing factories, but failed to implement the decision due to protests from workers. They were, however, given small orders to produce five to 15 tanks each. But each of them came out with innovative designs and models—T-80Us from Omsk and T-72BMs and T-72Bs from Nizhny Tagil—hoping for export orientation of their products. And this paid them dividends.

The T-90 is basically an improved hybrid model of the T-72BM with some added features of the T-80 series. It was developed by Kartsev-Venedictov Design Bureau at the Uralvagonzavod plant in Nizhny Tagil. The T-90 is a formidable battle tank whose performance history is impeccable as evidenced from battles in Chechnya. Mounted with powerful 2A 46M 125 mm smooth bore tank gun, it has an effective range of 100 metres to six kilometres and takes just 17.5 seconds to reach maximum range. The T-90s are further considered invincible in view of their 9 M1 19M Refleks anti-tank missiles. They are semi-automatic and laser guided and can penetrate up to 37 inches of steel armour as well as engage low-flying air targets. In the first go, India bought 310 T-90 tanks from Russia in 2001, of which 120 were delivered complete, 90 in semi-knocked down kits, and 100 in completely knocked down kits. India's choice fell on the T-90 for three reasons. First, the production of the indigenous Arjun was delayed and Pakistan was already procuring T-80UD tanks from Ukraine in 1995–97. Second, the T-90 was mechanically based on the T-72, which was already operational in the Indian Army (IA), thereby simplifying training and maintenance procedures for the T-90s. Third, the Russian Defence Ministry announced that the next model, the T-95, would not be coming out anytime soon, but that an extensively remodelled version of the T-90 would be the MBT in service until 2025. India's familiarity with Russian weapon systems made the newer systems attractive because it was easier to learn and train on them as well as maintain them at insignificant cost. Russia also offered better terms for purchase.

India signed the second contract with Russia for $800 million on 26 October 2006. This provided for 330 more T-90M 'Bhishma' MBTs to be manufactured by the Heavy Vehicles Factory at Avadi in Tamil Nadu. However, this was a contract with a difference. The M version was an improvement over the S version procured earlier, and this customized version has been developed with assistance not only from Russia, but from Israel and France to make it an invincible battle tank. The first batch of T-90M Bhishma was inducted into service on 24 August 2009.

The third contract was signed in December 2007 worth $1.23 billion for 347 upgraded T-90s. Many of these will be assembled at Avadi. The IA has plans to have 21 regiments of T-90s and 40 regiments of modified T-72s. The supply is in the pipeline since the end of 2009 (Korobeinikov 2009). The T-90s have become popular with the Indian Army because of their sophisticated capabilities, including a three-tiered protection system.

With a total of 620 tanks in operation, India has currently the largest number of T-90 MBTs anywhere in the world. In comparison, Russia operates only 400 of these tanks. With the addition of a further 1,000 T-90s to the IA by 2020 through local production, where India can carry out modifications as per its requirements, T-90s will remain the mainstay of the Army's defence in the near future.

Path-breaking MiGs

From the India-Pakistan war of 1965 to the Kargil conflict of 1999, the MiG-21 fighter jet supplied to India by the former Soviet Union dominated India's defence space as well as the combat aircraft list of the Indian Air Force (IAF). Artem Mikoyan and Mikhail Gurevich had designed a fighter aircraft in 1940—the MiG-1. Over the years, the MiG design bureau had churned out model after model of which four models have been famous worldwide—the MiG-21 (1960), the MiG-29, the MiG-31 (1983), and the MiG-35 (2007). For its shape and design, the Americans called the Mig-21 'fishbed', for its formidability the Russians named it 'Mongol', and for its strange shape, Polish soldiers called it 'Balalaika'—a Russian musical instrument to which it is similar in shape. The MiG-21 was designed for production in 1961 and the following year, India and the Soviet Union signed an agreement for their supply with provisions for full technology transfer and assemblage rights at the

Hindustan Aeronautics Limited (HAL) in India. The first supersonic jet to be inducted into the IAF, it was a light-weight jet with Mach 2 speed that combined interceptor and fighter characteristics in a single unit. Its sound technical characteristics, reliability, and operational simplicity put together made the MiGs superior to any other contemporary fighter jets; hence India's choice. By 1969, India had already obtained more than 120 MiG-21s and their number continued to rise over the years.

By offering India the MiGs, the Soviets were pursuing their goal of weaning India to their side in the Cold War divide, while Pakistan was firmly with the US and CENTO (Central Treaty Organization). In the thick of India's war with China in 1962, when Nehru was frantically pleading with US President John F. Kennedy to help the IAF, even take charge of the Indian sky in the north-east, his requests fell on deaf ears. In contrast, the Soviets came forward to help. The MiGs opened the door for other aircraft to follow, such as Kamov copters, Antonov and Ilyushin transporters, and Sukhoi jet fighters as and when required by India for its defence forces.

The MiG-21, however, fell into ignominy in India as a number of jets crashed owing to factors other than pilot error and earned the sobriquet of 'flying coffin'. During 1993–2002, more than 100 MiG fighters were lost to crashes (Menon 2011). The fighter jet has apparently exceeded its operational life and needs to be scrapped. Of the 976 MiGs inducted into the IAF since the 1960s, more than half have crashed (Menon 2011). While the newer MiG-29 and 31 have performed well, the MiG-21 has been vulnerable. The IAF's decision to go for refurbishing the jet with spares procured from non-Russian sources has enhanced the crash rate. Within nine plus months up to 7 October, six MiGs had crashed in 2011 (Menon 2011). Why was this aircraft persisted with for so long? One possible answer is that for over a decade in the 60s and 70s there was no competitor to the MiG-21. Also, as newer jets in the MiG series as well as competitors like the American F-16 appeared, the MiG-21 remained a preferred choice because of its much lower cost. The Indian government has decided to phase out the ageing fleet of MiG-21s and replace them with newer models.

Sukhoi Joint Venture

The IAF has for long been seeking a modern aircraft to suit its requirements. Though the French Mirage-2000H has been performing well, Russian

Sukhoi fighter jets have been chosen because they come cheap, and can be jointly produced in India with full technology transfer, which has put the Mirage on the backburner. India has signed several deals with Russia for procuring the Sukhoi MKI version, which is a long-range, heavy class air dominance fighter with a varied range of mission capabilities. The SU-27 began production in the former Soviet Union in 1982 as one of the world's most formidable fighter jets. The MKI version is India-specific just as the MKK is China-specific. Named after its designer Pavel Sukhoi, the 'MK' addition stands for Modernized Commercial while the 'I' denotes India. The Indian Defence Ministry views the Sukhoi as an unmatched fighter jet that can have no rival in the sky in the foreseeable future.

The first Sukhoi deal with Russia for 40 fighters with a price tag of $1462 million was inked on 30 November 1996, providing for delivery over a period of four years. The deal also incorporated setting up of a service support centre in India that would meet all requirements for repairs. Accordingly, the first delivery of eight Su-MKI came in 1997 followed by another eight in 1998 and a further 12 in the following two years. Of these fighters, 32 were to be subsequently developed into Su-MKIs with additional modernized fittings as per Indian requirements. The deliveries were on schedule. In the middle of the schedule, in September 1998, India decided to buy another 10 fighters with updated electronic warfare (EW) and precision guided munitions capability and updated radar and avionics. As India felt an increasing need for air force modernization and the Sukhois met expectations, it decided to embrace licensed production of 140 SU-30 MKI.

Thus, the third multi-billion dollar Sukhoi joint venture deal came about the time of Putin's maiden visit to India in October 2000. A memorandum of understanding was signed with the Russians followed by the formal deal in December 2000 in Irkutsk that incorporated technology transfer to India by a 'Deep License'. As per this deal, engines were to be produced at Koraput division of HAL, frames at Lucknow, avionics and electrical equipment at Hyderabad, and final assembly would be at Ozhar in Nasik. On an average, India planned to produce 14 fighters per year through this technology transfer and co-production arrangement. A joint production facility was thus firmly put in place.

As of 2007, India had requisitioned from Russia altogether a total of 230 Sukhoi combat aircraft in three major installments—first 50 in 1996, then 140 in 2000, and subsequently another 40 in 2007. The

Indian Air Force has in active operation 157 of them as of January 2013. In the modernization process of the Indian military, as demand for more airpower steadily grew and Sukhoi became popular, India signed another deal with Russia in December 2011 for acquisition of another 42 Sukhoi, thus taking the number of Sokhoi combat aircrafts in its fleet of fighter jets to 272. The upgrade and licensed production clauses were incorporated over the years, in the sway of mutual cooperation (*The Times of India* 2011).

The Sukhoi has made deep inroads into the IAF arsenal as is evident from the growing demand for it. India's collaboration with Russia in supply, assembly, and joint production of fighter jets far outpaces that with other countries. The MiGs and Sukhois are the fighter mainstay of IAF. In recent years, Russia has been putting greater emphasis on downsizing its military and capacity building of its armed forces. As a result, it has closed down many outdated production facilities, including those of the MiG-21 because they were units of the 1960s (Rumer 2007: 78). Therefore, MiG spares for the older version will increasingly be hard to come by, while for newer versions and Sukhois, Russia has assured uninterrupted supply as long as they fly in the IAF.

Supersonic BrahMos

In February, 1998 India and Russia signed an agreement for joint production of a cruise missile. The following year, in July 1999, when both countries finally decided the share holding pattern of their cruise missile joint venture to be 50.5 per cent Indian and 49.5 per cent Russian, little did anyone know that BrahMos would become a symbol of mutual synergy. Its name has been coined by both countries to connote a portmanteau from the names of two rivers—Brahmaputra in India and Moskva in Russia. The BrahMos marks a new era of bilateralism, a new spirit of cooperation in the defence-related strategic rocket realm. This also marks a paradigm shift in Russia's defence relations with India, transforming them from the buyer-seller platform to a sterling base of strategic partners. It began as a joint venture between Russia's NPO Mashinostroeyenia and India's Defence Research and Development Organisation (DRDO), which have formed the BrahMos Corporation of India under their joint aegis to produce the world's fastest supersonic and hypersonic cruise missiles. It helped boost India's missile programme, ushered in an era of rocket modernization, and made India the only country in the world to venture into the production of supersonic cruise missiles. India is privy to producing a supersonic cruise missile that carries warheads weighing 200–300 kilograms, travels three times faster than the speed of sound (nearly three and half times faster than the US Harpoon), and can attack surface targets effectively from an altitude as low as 10 meters (*The Times of India* 2010). A hypersonic version being test fired will have a speed of 5.26 Mach. Based on two-stage Russian missile propulsion mechanism and guidance system developed by India at the BrahMos corporation, the missile can be launched from virtually anywhere—from land, surface ships, submarines, and aircraft. The first stage is initially accelerated by a solid propellant rocket and the second stage by liquid-fuelled ramjet for sustained supersonic cruise. Since 2004, the missile has been launched from a variety of platforms to test its efficacy, including one from a mobile launcher in Pokhran Test Range of Rajasthan (www.india-defence.com).

The successful test firing of BrahMos on various platforms in various locales across India with proven capability of scaling mountain terrains and striking with precision from desert to sea has given the IA an edge over other armies in South Asia, thanks to partnership collaboration with Russia. BrahMos is perhaps the only collaborative joint venture with Russia without glitches. Its high speed provides a better target penetration capability than a subsonic Tomahawk. The missile is already in service with the IA and with the Indian Navy's Talwar and Shivalik-class frigates. The DRDO has affirmed that the air-launched version will be fitted into Sukhoi-MKI without any structural modification. It is planned that by 2012 all variants of BrahMos will be launched and inducted into operation. Due to worldwide interest in and demand for BrahMos, India and Russia intend to produce 1,000 missiles in the next few years, 50 per cent of which will be exported (www.9abc.net).

Air Craft Carrier

In 1995, when India sent a defence delegation to Russia to negotiate procurement of T-90 battle tanks, the delegation wanted to have a look at an aircraft carrier and was shown the Gorshkov. It is a gigantic ship with a displacement of 44,500 tons and can carry 30 MiG-29K fighter aircraft and 10 Kamov helicopters.[5] The tentative decision to purchase it was taken in February 2002, when Russian Deputy Premier Ilya Khlebanov visited India and had wide-ranging talks on Indo-Russian defence cooperation (*The Economic Times* 2002: 2). The deal was finally clinched on 20 January 2004 during the visit of Sergei Ivanov to New Delhi. It was then scheduled that Gorshkov would be renovated and would join the IN in four years time, by 2008.

However, suddenly, before Prime Minister Manmohan Singh's visit to Moscow in November 2007, the Kremlin shocked India by demanding a huge sum of $1.2 billion over and above the contract price. Initially, the delivery date was fixed to be August 2008, but this has been forwarded to 2013. Meanwhile, the Gorshkov has been rechristened as INS Vikramaditya and its re-cabling length enhanced from 700 kilometres to about 2,400 kilometres. It will enhance the intervention capability of the IN and help project force in the Indian Ocean. For further force projection, Russian officials accompanying Russian Defense Minister Sergei Ivanov hinted in 2004 that India might buy some 60 MiG-29s at a cost of $1.5 billion in phases, to be used from the Gorshkov platform.

Critics, however, look at Gorshkov differently. They consider it a decommissioned carrier rotting in the Russian yard, which India has retrieved. Despite all its merits, it is not worth the price India has paid for. An indigenous ship could have been the best solution to replace the ageing INS Viraat. Against this, it may be said that it fills an important gap as the production of an Air Defence Ship (ADS) or indigenous aircraft carrier has been greatly delayed. Analysts also raise queries about the very viability of the Gorshkov in view of its track record. In 1993, there was a major fire on the ship and in 1994 an explosion had torn through the engine room. Therefore, initially, the Russians had offered this ship gratis to India, provided India paid for refurbishment, modernization, and renovation as well as for the equipment that go into it. India was thus coaxed and trapped. A cost benefit analysis of two squadrons of MiG-29K and Kamov copters that would go into the carrier tells a tale of price exuberance for the Gorshkov. Naval sources revealed that the refurbishment cost was agreed on at $675 million. Subtracting this price from the total deal entails a figure far too high for the MiGs and helicopters and this is precisely why India had once threatened to buy naval fighters from another country (*The Economic Times* 2002: 2).

Besides, the timing of the deal was clashing with the core requirements of the Indian military. While the Indian basket of urgent need for negotiation and procurement was laden with three items—getting the long-range Tupolev-22 bombers, reconnaissance aircraft, and two nuclear submarines—the Russians insisted on striking the Gorshkov deal first before any other defence deal was clinched. The Indian Navy (IN), however, has its own arguments. It has argued that 9/11 had changed the strategic balance of power in the Indian Ocean. Maritime security has become an urgent need. INS Vikrant was decommissioned five years ago. The Hermes class INS Viraat, procured from Great Britain, is long overdue for decommissioning. A substitute carrier is essential, and the Gorshkov would be ideal for this purpose.

Submarines

Negotiations with the Soviets to build a nuclear-powered submarine indigenously in India began soon after 1971, when India felt threatened by the US 7th Fleet during the Indo-Pak war. Both countries continued talks for years for making Arihant ('destroyer of enemies') but kept them secret. Finally, Arihant emerged as a Navy project with Bhabha Atomic Research Centre (BARC) providing the reactor. The Navy designed the vessel, built its power plant, and did all the welding. Larsen and Toubro (L&T) built the hull of titanium steel at Hazira, Gujarat. Different parts of the vessel were made at Visakhapatnam, Mumbai, and Kalpakkam, and assemblage took place at a dry dock in Visakhapatnam. Arihant, still under development at the time of writing (summer 2012), will be India's first nuclear-powered submarine indigenously built with Russian help. It is expected to be inducted into the Indian Navy in 2013. It is a submarine of 6,000-tonne displacement that can fire K-15 ballistic missiles up to a range of 700 kilometres. Under the Advanced Technology Vessel (ATV) programme, a second Arihant-class nuclear submarine (to be named INS Aridaman) is under construction at the Shipbuilding Centre (SBC) in Visakhapatnam.

In addition, an agreement was signed in 2004 for the 10-year lease of a Russian-built nuclear powered submarine for $900 million. India inducted this Akula-II class K-152 Nerpa submarine into the IN in April 2012 and rechristened it INS Chakra (*Indian Express* 2012). A crew of around 70 people including 30 naval officers—all trained in Russia— operate the submarine. With a displacement of 8,140-tonnes and with a Russia-built nuclear reactor fitted in its core, Chakra can travel under water at a speed of around 30 knots and can dive to a depth of 600 metres with an endurance of 100 days. Possession of this sophisticated warship has put India into the league of only five nations—the US, Russia, the UK, France, and China—which operate nuclear submarines. The induction of Chakra provides the IN with an opportunity to train its personnel to operate nuclear-powered submarines in the future. The addition of Russian technology to the IN's capabilities is thus enhancing India's naval force projection to a significantly higher level.

Chinks in the Armour

Despite pervasive use of Russian weapons systems by Indian defence forces, Indo-Russian defence ties are not entirely trouble-free. The cryogenic engine supply is an example. When President Yeltsin visited India in January 1993, he had assured Prime Minister Narasimha Rao that Russia would not be dictated to by external pressure on the supply of cryogenic rocket engines to India (Conley 2001). However, subsequently, under intense US pressure, Russia backed out of the deal and ruffled Indian feathers, leading to a debate on the reliability of Russian commitment. In subsequent years, India stood its ground and developed and tested its own cryogenic engine technology.

However, the problem that persisted most in Indo-Russian defence relations was the nagging delivery delays from the Russian side. Russia dithered in commitments and took time for dispatch under one pretext or the other. If a definite delivery point was not mentioned in the deal, Russia interpreted the ambiguity in its favour and took its own time. Since a network of multiple agencies was involved in the delivery process (production centres, warehouses, port authorities, customs agencies, and so on), a coordinated approach ought to have been in place to take care of a smooth dispatch. But there were lacunae at each point which created unexpected roadblocks.

Second, after a deal was signed for delivery of a particular item, Russia came out with a series of subsequent modifications, sometimes insisting on selling a modified version of the equipment instead of the original one, stating that certain changes had been carried out, that addition of a certain spare would enhance the efficacy of the weapons system, and so on. Frequently, such deals cropped up as bilateral irritants, whether it was with regard to the Gorshkov or the manufacturing of the Fifth Generation Combat Aircraft.

Russia has been deviating from the norms for spares supply because it lacks commitment to quality maintenance. As per the agreements, India buys only new spare parts from Russia and not used or old ones. Some consignments of Sukhoi tires from Russia were found to be used ones.

Similarly, other spares were found to be used and unfit for use. There has been continuing disputation over the quality of spares. Sometimes, Russia has arranged for spares produced in post-Soviet countries on a swap deal over which it no longer exercises quality control. The MiG spares produced in Georgia in the past and supplied to India now is a good example. The increasing number of MiG crashes in the IAF increased India's concerns and prompted it to pressurize Russia regarding the quality of spares.

There is an inadequate supply mechanism between vendor Russia and buyer India. India is willing to sign defence deals directly with producers without the mediation of the state, but Russia does not allow those entities to enter into direct defence deals with a foreign country, thereby retaining state control over spares supplies. The Russian defence bureaucracy often delays supply through red tape. It is unwilling to give up its privileged position of control. Since defence deals between India and Russia are handled in the state sector without involvement of private players, these irritants are likely to continue until both countries allow private actors to play their competitive role in ensuring the quality of spares and timely delivery of supplies. In fact, not enough R&D has gone into replicating spares in India provided by foreign countries, including Russia. The Indian Ministry of Defence Production, as a state entity, is the consumer of what it produces at its 40 odd OFs. The department has avoided competition on the pretext of national security interest. The complacency of a government leviathan tends to incur high costs as a result of time lags, cost overruns, and technological backwardness. The upfront price advantage of a weapon system is neutralized by all these factors plus the problem of serviceability. Yet, India has retained its overall interest in Russian-made armaments. A good part of the reason lies in political-strategic considerations.

Strategic Drivers

Three Russian leaders—Evgeny Primakov, Vladimir Putin, and Dmirti Medvedev—have projected India in their strategic map of South Asia. While Primakov added the Eurasian direction to what was an excessively West-oriented foreign policy, Putin focussed on strategic Asia by bringing back India, China, Japan, and Korea to the heart of Russian foreign policy discourse. Medvedev followed Putin's course and brought India back to the centre stage of Russian defence and strategic policy. The drivers that facilitated the return of India to centrestage were economic and military. India's economic growth is the locomotive of its prominence. If yesterday it was buying weapons systems on long-term loan from Russia, today it is spending $30 billion dollars a year for defence and that too with a relatively low level of military spending at just 2 per cent of her GDP. At the same time, it is a nuclear power with a growing capability. If Western experts say that India has been 'arming without aiming', Russia has certainly aimed at arming India with clear strategic objectives. From the geopolitical vantage, Russia has acknowledged India to be its anchor in South Asia. With no other country of South Asia does Russia hold regular apex level meetings scheduled annually at the year end to take stock of progress in bilateral ties.

For India, the strength of the relationship is underlined by the fact that Russia has not only supplied India with advanced weapons systems, but allowed it to develop hybrids on the basis of technology transfer and licensed production, which other countries have been reluctant to do. Indo-Russian defence relations are also part of a wider strategic cooperation. Russia has helped India with the naval capacity to counter China's effort to establish a strategic position in the Indian Ocean; embarked on an ambitious programme to build 18 nuclear reactors across India; and developed an elaborate structure of scientific cooperation that encompasses a large number of laboratories in particle physics, space technology, and weather forecasting. India is also the only country in the world to which Russia has agreed to provide access to the military segment of its GLONASS satellite positioning system used for precision homing of guided missiles. Both countries are engaged in joint production of dual band GPS/GLONASS global positioning receivers for civilian and military use.

***

India and Russia have gradually moved away from a buyer-seller relationship towards a strategic partnership. As India's strategic priorities change, it inevitably seeks to become less dependent on Russia. Thus, it has diversified its sources, with the US and Israel emerging among the leading defence suppliers. Yet, the defence relationship with Russia remains strong despite numerous irritants. The bottom line is that India wants to remain strategically independent and thus has an enduring interest in buying arms from Russia. On its part, Moscow recognizes this and views India as a key player in the region. Also, as shown above, the terms of sale, incorporating technology transfer, and joint production of high-technology arms remain attractive, while India's familiarity with Russian equipment is an added factor. On the down side, this tendency towards dependence allows Russia to retain a strong hold on the Indian defence market. But for all its faults, Russia remains a top supplier. Though India, in the future, will continue to diversify its defence sources, Russia is likely to continue as a major weapons provider, though it will need to improve its associated services, particularly with regard to spares and maintenance, if it is not to allow its advantages to slip away.

For India, a degree of tension remains with respect to its overdependence on Russia. Former Indian ambassador to Moscow Ronen Sen put it succinctly while observing that—'India's dependence on Russia for defence supplies is greater today than with rest of the world combined. It is in fact greater than the dependence of most NATO countries on the US' (Sen 2011). On the other hand, there is a discernible paradigm shift in the contemporary Asian landscape that gives a new quality to India's defence relations with Russia—the emergence of India as a strategic partner not only of Russia, but of bigger players like the United States and China. India's trade with Russia is just a tenth of its trade with the United States and China. In years to come, Indo-Russian defence deals will undergo substantial change in tune with India's diversified trade and strategic partnerships. The leitmotif of Indo-Russian defence cooperation ought to be reducing dependence and promoting interdependence. Both countries have been gradually working in this direction. But India will not so easily shed its baggage of military dependence on Russia, and Russia cannot overlook India's strategic importance in South Asia as a geopolitical anchor. The process of change will likely remain a slow and prolonged one.

Notes

1. SIPRI Year Book 2010: 291. However, during Medvedev's December 2010 visit to New Delhi, it was announced that India's defence dependence on Russia was to the extent of 60 per cent—a considerable reduction compared with past announcements. Singh 2010.

2. A deal was signed between the Government of India and Glavkosmos of Russia on 18 January 1991 for $350 million for supply of cryogenic engine and

related technology. Two years later in 1993, the US protested the deal on the ground that it violated missile technology proliferation norms and pressured the Yeltsin administration to abandon the deal. Russia backtracked from the contract. For details, see the chapter on 'Strained Indo-Russian Relations', Conley 2000.

3. For a comparative picture of military spending, see Tellis and Wills 2005: 546. The figures cited are old and the annual defence budget of India since 2010 has been in the range of $30 plus billion. See Behera 2010.

4. For full text of the treaty, see Rao 1991: 482–4.

5. *The Indian Express*, 21 January 2004: 1, 7 (Mumbai). There is a discrepancy in the number of MiGs the Gorshkov can carry. The front page diagram says 30, while inside report says 20 MiGs. For further discrepancy of 28 MiGs, see *The Economic Times*, 21 January 2004, p. 2.

References

Baskaran, Angathevar. 2004. 'The Role of Offsets in India's Defence Procurement Policy', in Jurgen Brauer and J. Paul Dunne (eds), *Arms Trade and Economic Development: Theory, Policy and Cases in Arms Trade Offsets*. London and New York: Routledge.

Behera, Laxman K. 2010. 'Budgeting for India's Defence: An analysis of Defence Budget 2010-11 and the likely impact of the 13th Finance Commission on Future Defence Spending', IDSA Comment, 3 March. Available at http://www.idsa.in/idsacomments/BudgetingforIndiasDefence2010-11_lkbehera_030310 (accessed 13 July 2012).

Blank, Stephen J. 1993. *Challenging the New World Order: The Arms Transfer Policies of the Russian Republic*. Carlisle Barracks, PA: Strategic Studies Institute.

'BrahMos Cruise Missile: Vertical Launch Configuration Test Fired in Desert Conditions'. Available at http://www.india-defence.com/reports/4171 (accessed 13 July 2012).

Chengappa, Raj. 2008. 'The New Russia: What it Means for the World and India', *India Today*, 19 May, xxxiii (20): 58.

Conley, Jerome M. 2000. 'Indo-Russian Military and Nuclear Cooperation, Implications for US Security Interest', INSS Occasional Paper 31, Proliferation Series, Colorado: US Air Force Academy (see the Introduction).

———. 2001. *Indo-Russian Military and Nuclear Cooperation: Lessons and Options for US Policy in South Asia*. Lanham MD: Lexington Books.

Dash, P.L. 1999. 'Rise and Fall of Yevgeny Primakov', *Economic and Political Weekly*, XXXIV (24): 1494–6.

Donaldson, Robert H. 1980–81. 'The Soviet Union in South Asia: A Friend to Rely On?', *Journal of International Affairs*, 34 (2): 235.

'India agreed to sell BrahMos supersonic cruise missile Vietnam', 29 August 2011. Available at http://www.9abc.net/index.php/archives/2234 (accessed 13 July 2012).

Indian Express. 2012. 'Nuclear-powered submarine INS Chakra inducted into Navy', 4 April. Available at http://www.indianexpress.com/news/nuclearpowered-submarine-ins-chakra-inducted-into-navy/932455/0 (accessed 13 July 2012).

Jain, B.M. 2009. Global Power: India's Foreign Policy 1947-2006. London and New York: Lexington Books.

Kogan, E. 1994. 'The Russian Defence Industry: Trends, Difficulties and Obstacles', Asian Defence Journal, 10(94): 43–4.

Komsomolskaya Pravda. 1994. 27 April.

Korobeinikov, Dmitry. 2009. 'Indian Army Receives first T-90 tanks made under Russian License', RIA Novosti, 24 August. Available at www.Online en.beta.rian.ru/military-news,20090824/155910756/html (accessed 7 February 2010).

Kramnik, Ilya. 2010. 'The Fifth Generation is Here', New Theme, VII (1): 11.

Kumar, Hari. 2012. 'Why has India become the World's Top Arms Buyer?', The New York Times, 21 March. Available at www.India.blogs.nytimes.com/2012/03/21 (accessed 13 July 2012).

Menon, Jay. 2011. 'Indian MiG-21 Crashes; Sixth So Far This Year', Aviation Week, 7 October. Available at http://www.aviationweek.com/Article.aspx?id=/article-xml/awx_10_07_2011_p0-379394.xml (accessed 13 July 2012).

Nugent, Nicholas. 1991. 'The Defence Preparedness of India: Arming for Tomorrow', Military Technology, 15 (3): 27–36.

Pandit, Rajat. 2011. 'Navy Officer in Russian Honeytrap to be Sacked', Times of India (Mumbai), 1 April.

Rao, K. V. Krishna. 1991. Prepare or Perish: A Study of National Security. New Delhi: Lancer Publishers.

Rumer, Eugene B. 2007. 'Russian Foreign Policy beyond Putin', Adelphi Papers, No. 390. London: International Institute for Strategic Studies.

Segodnya. 1994. 18 October.

Sen, Ronen. 2011. 'India's Defence Cooperation with its Major Traditional and New Strategic Partners', Lecture delivered at the IDSA, New Delhi, 1 April. Available at http://www.idsa.in/keyspeeches/AmbassadorRonenSen (accessed 13 July 2012).

Sergounin, Alexander A. and Sergey V. Subbotin. 1996. 'Indo-Russian Military Cooperation: Russian perspective', Asian Profile, 24 (1): 23.

Singh, Harmeet Shah. 2010. 'India, Russia mark decade of strategic ties with Medvedev visit', CNN, 21 December. Available at http://articles.cnn.com/2010-12-21/world/india.medvedev.visit_1_nuclear-power-plants-rosoboronexport-new-delhi?_s=PM:WORLD (accessed 13 July 2012).

SIPRI Year Book. 2010. *Armaments, Disarmaments and Security*. Oxford: Oxford University Press.

Tellis, Ashley J. and Michael Wills. (2005).'Military Modernization in an Era of Uncertainty', Executive Summary, *Strategic Asia 2005–2006*, 546.

The Economic Times. 2002. 9 February.

———. 2011.'India, Russia Sign Deal for Another 42 Sukhoi Combat Planes', 16 December. Available at http://economictimes.indiatimes.com/news/politics/nation/india-russia-sign-deal-for-another-42-sukhoi-combat-planes/articleshow/11134934cms (accessed 17 December 2012).

The Times of India. 2010. 'BrahMos Test Fired, Creates World Record', 6 September.

———. 2011.'India and Russia Sign Deal for another 42 Sukhoi Combat Planes', 16 December.

10 Last Word

Military as a Stabilizer

PRAKASH MENON

THE WORLD'S ATTENTION has been drawn to the planned size of India's military modernization. In terms of costs, it is estimated to be $100 billion for the 12th Five-year Plan (2007–12) and $120 billion for the 13th Plan (2012–17) (Confederation of Indian Industry–Deloitte Report 2010; CII–KPMG Report 2010). This amounts to nearly 2.5 per cent of the Gross Domestic Product (GDP) with expenditure on defence decreasing in terms of percentage of GDP during the 13th Plan (Government of India 2009). The size and scale of India's military modernization, which is formidable, may be attributed primarily to the security dilemma, triggered by the scale of China's military modernization which may be primarily attributed to the conflation of Sino-US rivalry. Additionally, India's military growth arises from the tensions produced by Sino-Indian differences, the Sino-Pakistani nexus, and Indo-Pakistani disputes. China's military modernization has fuelled anxiety in Asia, in particular, and the world in general. In comparison, the reaction to India's military modernization has been different. Most countries perceive India as a huge arms market that provides commercial opportunities. The differentiated reaction stems from the fact that political ownership of arms matters more than the arms themselves. The world is concerned when North Korea or Iran acquires arms. Similarly, the nightmare scenario in Pakistan could be the ownership of nuclear weapons falling into the hands of religious radicals. The fact that India's acquiring of arms has a lesser impact in terms of raising security concerns with most Asian powers other than Pakistan provides the context within which India's military modernization needs to be understood. The nature of the reaction to India's military modernization can best be deciphered when viewed against India's record of using force for political purposes.

In these pages, India's military modernization is analysed at three broad levels. The first section contextualizes India's historical preferences with regard to the use of military force over the last six decades. The following section discuses India's emerging role at the regional and global level and the imperatives of the creation and fielding of Indian military capability. The subsequent section discusses the key elements of India's military modernization. The concluding section explicates the implications for future military modernization among the three services.

The Historical Context

Having achieved independence through a non-violent struggle, India has been reluctant to use force except as a last option when all other means for achieving justice have been exhausted. This doctrine has been reflected in all the occasions when India has used force. In the early period after independence, the newly created Indian Union used force to liberate Junagadh, a tiny princely state in Western India, where a Muslim minority leader remained recalcitrant despite the majority population wanting to accede to India. But force was used only after prolonged negotiations and all other means were exhausted. The situation was similar with the incorporation of Hyderabad in 1948 and later in Goa in 1961 against the Portuguese. Even when the tribal invaders swarmed into Jammu & Kashmir (J&K) in October 1947, India's action to rush troops was taken as a defensive measure to save the state from the Pakistani tribals, but only after having obtained the instrument of accession from the ruler of J&K. The Sino-Indian war of 1962, the Indo-Pakistani wars of 1965 and 1971, and the Kargil conflict of 1999 were all forced upon India with either China or Pakistan being the aggressor. In the popular imagination of most Pakistanis, India is considered to have been responsible for the breakup of Pakistan in 1971. But the fact is that Pakistan had unleashed genocide in East Pakistan, which resulted in several million refugees fleeing to India. The speedy withdrawal of Indian troops after the establishment of the Bangladesh Government headed by Mujibur Rehman provides ample indication of India's role in the war. The dispatch of an Indian Peace

Keeping Force (IPKF) to Sri Lanka in the 1980s was the aftermath of an agreement between the Sri Lankan Government and the Liberation Tigers of Tamil Eelam (LTTE). The swift dispatch of troops to the Maldives in November 1988 to save the government of President Maumoon Abdul Gayoom, then under threat from mercenaries, was undertaken at the request of the elected government of that country. Indian troops immediately withdrew once the mission was accomplished.

The Indian restraint displayed in the aftermath of the terrorist attack on Mumbai on 26 November 2008 perhaps personifies India's belief that force must be used only after all other means have been exhausted. It would not be too far off the mark to state that very few nations would have shown the restraint that India has shown in dealing with terrorism that emanates from Pakistani soil that is also abetted by elements of the Pakistan state. The fact that Indian political decision makers could display restraint despite the popular clamour for revenge is sufficient proof of political wisdom prevailing over strategic logic. India's rulers are convinced that force has utility, but its utility must be determined by the contextual vectors that produce a particular situation. The presence of nuclear weapons and the possibility of terrorists acts carried out with the aim of diverting the Pakistan armed forces eastwards to relieve pressure in the west were vectors that must have played a significant role in the political calculus that decided the Indian reaction to the Mumbai attack. Force, Indians believe, is certainly required to defend territory and interests. But force may not always be the appropriate instrument of statecraft.

Ever since independence, the Indian military has been and continues to be an apolitical institution. Whereas in every other country in the subcontinent and India's strategic neighbourhood the armed forces have been an impediment for democracy to flourish, the Indian armed forces have been a major stabilizing factor in laying and sustaining the foundations for India's democracy to flourish.

India's Emerging Role

It is often heard in international circles that as India emerges as an economic power with a concomitant growth of military power, it must assume greater responsibilities. Though not stated explicitly, there is always a hint that India must play a greater role in keeping order in the region, if not in the world. The problem with this prescription is the implicit notion that India will be part of a military alliance. The idea of India being part of a military grouping is anathema to the Indian political establishment. This proclivity rests on the belief that India would not like to be drawn into other nations' quarrels and the difficulty of deciding on whose side one needs to fight for justice to prevail. On the other hand, India is more at ease with the notion of strategic partnerships, wherein the partnership is issue-based and contextual. So India could partner America on nuclear proliferation and partner China on climate change or trade talks. The evolved Indian policy of contributing armed forces only under the banner of the United Nations is an expression of the Indian belief that force must be used only after political consent has been obtained from the United Nations. The appeal to India to shoulder responsibility commensurate with its growing economic power needs to recognize the principles that guide India with respect to the use of force. The international community should understand that India must be viewed not through their individual prisms and therefore in their own mould, but as a unique state entity in the international system. The uniqueness of India lies in the fact that India is a multi-cultural entity that is the most populous democracy in the world. India views use of force as a last resort and in its use, privileges the notion of justice over might and tolerance over intolerance as illustrated by its history post-independence. Moreover, India has never been part of a military alliance and probably shall never be except under the UN flag. India thus views itself as a stabilizing force in the world. So, the pertinent question to be asked is not what military capacities India is building, but what those capacities are meant for.

India is in the process of building its capacities in the realm of nuclear, regular, and irregular wars. The capacity it is building in the nuclear realm is guided by its nuclear doctrine, which espouses No First Use, Minimum Deterrence, and Civilian Control. Since survivability of the arsenal to a first strike is crucial to the effectiveness of the doctrine, India is in the process of developing a triad of mobile, land, air, and sea based weapons. While the land and air based components are operational, the sea based weapon resting on a nuclear-powered submarine is likely to be deployed operationally in the next few years. While not publicly known, India's arsenal is assumed to be small but sufficient to survive a first strike because of its mobility, which will be considerably enhanced with the deployment of nuclear-powered submarines. India's arsenal would be largely immune to any nuclear arms race due its crafting the size for survival. It has been made amply clear that India's nuclear arsenal serves only as a deterrent with emphasis being on no first use, with an ability for a retaliatory strike. This, it believes, should provide sufficient deterrence against states possessing nuclear weapons and inimical to it. The fact that there is complete civilian control over the arsenal is another major factor of stability.

In the realm of conventional or regular war, India's potential adversaries are both nuclear-armed. The presence of nuclear weapons undoubtedly imposes caution among political decision-makers, especially impacting the decision to go to war. But wars can be forced upon India under the shadow of nuclear weapons and therefore the challenge for Indian military planners has been to craft military strategies that minimize the chances of war slipping into the nuclear realm. This dilemma has obviously no easy solutions and is similar to the dilemma faced by the West and the Soviet Union during the Cold War. One of the main lessons from that confrontation was that the danger of escalation is not amenable to operational virtuosity as the battlefield has too many imponderables that go beyond the control of the opponents. The fog of war cannot be wished away and the danger of inadvertent nuclear exchange will be omnipresent. The situation is further compounded when there are dual-use arms. A conventionally armed missile could be mistaken to be nuclear-armed and a couple of conventional bursts could be reported initially as a nuclear strike. It would be prudent to assume that fear would be the predominant emotion prevailing amongst political decision-makers on both sides as also the public at large. Rational decision-making is unlikely in an atmosphere where fear is the predominant emotion and catastrophic mistakes are likely. All this complicates military planning, which leaves one no choice but to try and make plans and build capacities that cannot but be prisoner to the possibility of a nuclear exchange. There is no escape from war's structural condition that it is a duel between two opposing and independent wills whose reactions can never be assumed and is difficult to predict to any degree of accuracy. In these circumstances, what capacity for regular war is India building?

Elements of India's Military Modernization

Much of India's military modernization is replacement driven. For the Indian Army, Navy, and Air Force, much of their old equipment is being replaced as it has outlived its life and does not add fruitfully to the building of the country's war fighting capability. Replacement necessarily entails embracing as much cutting-edge technology as possible, which also means enhancing capability. But enhancement of capability must be viewed against a similar enhancement underway with the adversaries. The advantage gained in most areas would be marginal rather than overwhelming.

Army

In terms of conventional war fighting capability development of the army, the equipment deficiencies, especially in terms of state-of-the-art mechanized weapon platforms, artillery and air defence guns, and guided missile systems are glaring and indeed need to be addressed in the short to medium term. Some capability development measures have been taken, but they still fall short in holistically addressing operational effectiveness. For instance, India had negotiated a deal to acquire T-90S tanks to replace its ageing tank fleet in 2001. Subsequently, India began to assemble these tanks and has recently acquired another batch of T-90S tanks to assemble them within the country. But night blindness and platform serviceability have been a cause for worry, and these still need to be comprehensively addressed. Many experts argue that the artillery modernization plan has suffered acutely since the last major acquisition of 155 mm FH-77B howitzers from Bofors of Sweden in the mid-1980s. The government has after 27 years cleared a much delayed 145 M-777 ultra-light howitzers from the US in a direct government-to-government deal worth $647 million. The ANTPQ-37 Firefinder weapon locating radars procured from Raytheon in 2002 are grossly inadequate in numbers given the extent of our borders with China and Pakistan. They have also been beset with serviceability issues. The serviceability of the army air defence systems acquired from Russia in the mid-70s and the 80s has suffered significantly. The modernization of infantry weapon systems too needs attention. A network-centric information management system which synergizes the surveillance sensors and shooters over a seamless communication network is crucial. While there has been qualitative improvement in the static communications, the development of TAC3I systems is slow and tardy. Similarly, the integration of real-time satellite resolutions with networked platforms is yet to benefit the field commanders. Searcher and Heron unmanned aerial vehicles have been introduced into service since long, but these are too few in number to make any significant qualitative difference in real-time surveillance.

Air Force

Even as the Indian Air Force (IAF) pursues an ambitious war-fighting doctrine, its capability development continues to suffer for a variety of reasons. Prominent amongst these have been the fall in the number of frontline fighter squadrons, large-scale obsolescence of its fleet, high acquisition cost of replacement aircraft, and inordinate procurement delays. For instance, the collapse of the Soviet Union led to a drop in the number of air force squadrons from an all-time high of 45 squadrons to 42 squadrons. In 2009, the number of squadrons fell to 32, and some argue that the delay in new acquisitions could bring this figure down to 29. The MMRCA project mooted in 2000 has suffered from several delays and is likely to take a few years before the squadrons are operational. India's attempts at building a multi-role aircraft too have not been very encouraging. The Advanced Jet Trainer (AJT) project too has failed due to our inability to find a suitable engine for the aircraft, and consequently after several years of failure, the air force placed orders for the British Hawk trainer in the year 2000, and recently the government has accorded clearance for the purchase of the Pilatus PC-7 Mk-II from Switzerland. Similarly, the light combat aircraft (LCA) project conceived in the 80s continues to be plagued by time delays, insufficient budgeting, and poor performance. It is therefore no surprise that the air force tends to favour foreign acquisitions as against indigenized projects in pursuit of its readiness objectives. High dependence on foreign vendors too comes at a cost as these contractual obligations could affect the supply of critical spares, upgrades and their maintenance, and serviceability at crucial times.

Navy

Indian Navy's (IN) modernization plan formalized several decades back called for the development of a blue water navy. In the following decades, the navy has relentlessly pursued platform acquisitions in the form of destroyers, frigates, submarines, and maritime reconnaissance capabilities. Consequently, India's lone aircraft carrier is being kept operational awaiting the arrival of Vikramaditya from Russia. Some experts state that the IN is likely to have two aircraft carriers by 2015, and a third probably by 2020. In addition, the navy has acquired the INS Chakra this year from Russia with an indigenous nuclear submarine under manufacture in Vizag. There are Scorpene submarines being built in Indian shipyards. In addition, the navy has 23 destroyers and frigates as the major surface combatants which include five Rajput-class destroyers procured from the USSR during the 1980s, and three Talwar-class frigates from Russia more recently. Another class of destroyers, the modified Delhi-class, is under construction in India, and three ships of the Talwar-class are being built in Russia and are likely to be commissioned in the near future. Considering the capacity of Indian shipyards and the number of ships likely to be decommissioned in the future, the total number of major surface combatants in the destroyer and frigate class by 2020 should be about 29, a mere six more than the current holdings. As regards other smaller platforms, these would comprise 24 corvettes, 21 offshore patrol vessels (OPVs), and about 10 amphibious ships (LSTs). One amphibious transport dock (LPD) christened Jalashwa was bought from the US Navy in 2007 capable of transporting 1,000 troops and heavy loads. This totals to about 69 major and small sized sea going naval vessels.

Systemic Flaws

The foregoing analyses reveal that much of the military modernization underway among the three services is centred on sustaining the existing land, aerial, and sea war fighting capabilities. Whether this is good enough to meet the future military challenges or not is the question that needs to be addressed. Clearly, the Indian military establishment needs to break even with its long standing equipment deficiencies. Besides the timely budgetary allocations, there is need for a serious structural and systemic correction in the country's research development, production and acquisition procedures, and practices.

Over the years, India has established a defence industrial base (DIB) which now consists of 52 research laboratories and establishments under the Defence Research and Development Organization (DRDO), nine Defence Public Sector Undertakings (DPSUs), and 39 ordnance factories (OFs) under the administrative control of Department of Defence Production, Ministry of Defence. These entities together with a small but growing private sector are responsible for research, development, and production of various armaments primarily for the Indian defence forces. However, the overall efficiency of the DIB in terms of meeting the requirements of the armed forces is below optimal. This has resulted in India spending billions of dollars each year on arms import. According to some estimates, India has the dubious record of being among the top arms importers in the world, with a global share of 9 per cent between 2006 and 2010.

India will continue to remain dependent on foreign sources to meet bulk of its cutting edge needs of the defence forces. Indian efforts and utilization of its defence modernization resources is in effect subsidizing the military industry complex of other nations. India needs to redefine its structural processes and procedures to meet its defence needs. The heavy dependency on external sources not only adversely impacts India's conduct of sovereign foreign policy but is also contrary to the objective of self-reliance that the country had set before itself a long time ago. Way back in 1992, a committee under the chairmanship of the then Scientific Advisor to the Defence Minister, had visualized that self-reliance index, measured in terms of the percentage share of domestic content in total procurement expenditure, would progressively increase from then 30 per cent to 70 per cent by 2005. The target does not seem to have been achieved even today. Submitting to the Parliamentary Committee on Defence, the Secretary, DRDO, has recently observed that the index now hovers at 40–45 per cent.

To enhance self-reliance index, the Ministry of Defence (MoD) has initiated or contemplated various policy measures. In 2001, the government liberalized the defence industry, by allowing 100 per cent participation by Indian private sector and foreign direct investment (FDI) up to 26 per cent. The government has also created opportunities for the domestic enterprises to participate in defence contracts through the successive revision of is defence procurement procedures (DPP). In 2005, the MoD articulated an offset policy which has been elaborated and revised several times since. The policy intends to give a fillip to the domestic companies through mandatory investment by foreign companies winning defence contracts from the MoD. The DPP has also created categories such as 'Make' and 'Buy and Make (Indian)' which give exclusive rights to Indian companies to participate in arms contracts. Recently, the MoD has articulated the first ever defence production policy and a joint venture guidelines to facilitate more indigenous production. In addition, the DPP still retains the guidelines for selection of Raksha Udyog Ratnas (RUR) from among the private sector. The intention of the RUR is to create and nurture a select number of private companies which would assume the role of systems integrator.

Defence preparedness cannot be complete without a mature strategic vision that looks beyond the five-yearly Defence Minister's operational directive to services Chiefs. There is a need to have a long term vision for security of the country and define a role for the armed forces. This will enable them to build capacity and the capability to respond to the range of threats that beset India. A National Security doctrine is imperative to guide the services in developing its combat capability and force structure.

There is no mechanism in place for the government to receive essential single-point advice from the military, since summoning the three defence services Chiefs and seeking their views orally or in writing cannot give a holistic idea of defence preparedness. It also needs to be highlighted that the Indian armed forces are still struggling to produce a joint doctrine to achieve objectives by formulating strategies together. Individually the Army, the Air Force, and the Navy have evolved their own doctrines for achieving their service objectives but the three services jointly are yet to develop a comprehensive framework for synergizing their military power in combat. Future conflicts and operations demand a synergy between the three forces and evolution of a joint doctrine will be the first step in the right direction.

Balancing the Capability for Regular and Irregular Wars

India has unavoidably to be prepared to fight irregular wars. It has been engaged in such wars for almost the entire period of its existence since 1947. The Indian armed forces are presently engaged in irregular wars in the form of counter-insurgency in J&K in the north as well as in the north-eastern states. The central paramilitary forces are deployed to counter left-wing extremism in central India. The modernization process underway in the sphere of counter-insurgency is primarily aimed to harness the technological capability that can provide surgical firepower, improved mobility, better individual protection, effective surveillance, secure communications, explosive detection and neutralization, and improved intelligence inter alia. Doctrinally, India's counter-insurgency campaigns have not privileged fire power and have instead been extremely sensitive to people-friendly operations. Winning the hearts and minds of people has been the cornerstone of India's counter-insurgency doctrine.

The primary focus has been to attempt to mainstream the forces fighting the Indian state. The application of force is viewed as an instrument to create conditions for political settlement to prevail. The creation of the Rashtriya Rifles equipped and organized for counter-insurgency, populated by the army personnel on rotational basis, has been a highly successful experiment. The Rashtriya Rifles in its two decades of existence has performed commendably in J&K. More importantly, it has provided through its policy of two-year rotation, extensive experience in counter-insurgency operations to a significant number of personnel. This has also significantly enhanced Indian capability to deploy regular units in counterinsurgency after short reorientation training whenever required. The essence of the modernization of India's irregular war capability is human resource development coupled with technological upgrades that provide better protection, mobility, communications, intelligence, and surgical fire power.

India would prefer not to deploy its capabilities outside its boundaries in an expeditionary role. There is a growing voice amongst India's strategic community advocating the creation of expeditionary forces, but it has no serious traction in the political establishment. Hearing some of the debates of the strategic community in New Delhi, one notices the gulf between the political establishment and the majority of the strategic community regarding the use of force. In India, political wisdom has normally trumped strategic logic. Indian leaders realize that strategic logic is invariably a gamble that must be weighed against the issues at stake. India's political establishment is not easily swayed by the seduction of easy and quick victories that may be on offer. Such a political line of thinking has also provided the stabilizing element in India's strategic calculus.

***

India's military modernization is a natural accompaniment of its economic growth. Its direction and thrust is not to become the neighbourhood bully. The international community needs to avoid viewing India with the prisms of their own making. Instead they need to view India in the context of its cultural heritage that is derived from an ancient civilization. They need to understand the notions India holds regarding the use of force. They would therefore find that these notions are different from the concepts of power held dear by its leaders. They should expect that India's political behavior would be derived from its uniqueness—an India that will privilege notions of justice over might, good over evil, and tolerance over intolerance. Indians know that the best way to deal with the world is to treat it as *Vasudhaiva Kutumbakam.*[1] Like families, differences and clashes of interests are perennial to human existence. Differences are better settled through dialogue and consensus. Force has its use as an instrument of last resort and it must be applied knowing that it is a blunt instrument whose political impact is impossible to know *a priori* except as a gamble judged worthy by the issues at stake. It is in the embrace of such wisdom that India should be viewed as a stabilizing force in world affairs.

Note

1. *Vasudhaiva Kutumbakam* is a Sanskrit phrase that means 'the whole world is one family'.

References

Confederation of Indian Industry (CII)–KPMG Report. 2010. 'Opportunities in the Indian Defence Sector: An Overview'. Available at http://www.ciidefence. com/images/publication/pdf/Opportunities_IndianDefenceSector.pdf (accessed 17 May 2012).

CII–Deloitte Report. 2010. 'Prospects for Global Defence Export Industry in Indian Defence Market', pp. 5–6. Available at http://www.deloitte.com. br/publicacoes/2007/Prospects_for_global_defence_export_industry_ indian_defence_market.pdf (accessed 17 May 2012).

Government of India. 2009. Thirteenth Finance Commission Report.

Index

Editors and Contributors

Rajesh Basrur is Professor of International Relations, Coordinator of the South Asia Programme, and Coordinator of the Masters in International Relations Programme at the S. Rajaratnam School of International Studies (RSIS), Nanyang Technological University, Singapore. He has obtained MA and MPhil in History (University of Delhi) and MA and PhD in Political Science (University of Bombay). His work focuses on South Asian security, global nuclear politics, and international relations theory.

Richard A. Bitzinger is a Senior Fellow and Coordinator of the Military Transformations Programme at the S. Rajaratnam School of International Studies (RSIS), Nanyang Technological University, Singapore, where his work focuses on security and defense issues relating to the Asia-Pacific region, including military modernization and force transformation, regional defense industries and local armaments production, and weapons proliferation.

Ajaya Kumar Das is an Associate Research Fellow at the South Asia Programme of the S. Rajaratnam School of International Studies (RSIS), Nanyang Technological University, Singapore and a PhD candidate. His dissertation focuses on India's soft power relationship with the US. His research interests include international relations theory, international security, defence and strategic issues in Asia, India's foreign and security policy, India's traditional political ideas, and South Asian affairs.

P. L. Dash is Professor of International Relations and is currently ICCR India Chair at University of World Economy and Diplomacy, Tashkent, Uzbekistan. He was formerly Director, Centre for Central Eurasian Studies, University of Mumbai.

Gurmeet Kanwal, former Brigadier, is Adjunct Fellow, Wadhwani Chair in US–India Policy Studies, Centre for Strategic and International Studies (CSIS), Washington, D.C. He has authored several books and writes on nuclear deterrence and other national security issues.

Alma Lozano is a PhD researcher at the S. Rajaratnam School of International Studies (RSIS), Nanyang Technological University, Singapore. She has conducted extensive fieldwork research on international defence industrial dynamics in Europe and the US.

Ron Matthews is Professor of Defence Economics and Head of Graduate and Doctoral Studies at the S. Rajaratnam School of International Studies (RSIS), Nanyang Technological University, Singapore. He is also Chair in Defence Economics at Cranfield University, UK Defence Academy.

Pramod K Mehra, former Air Marshal, served the Indian Air Force for 40 years as a Combat pilot and Test pilot. He has been awarded the Param Vishisht Seva Medal (PVSM), Ati Vishisht Seva Medal (AVSM), Vayusena Medal (VM). He is presently a Distinguished Fellow with Centre for Air Power Studies, a think tank based in Delhi.

Prakash Menon, former Lieutenant General, is presently Military Adviser in India's National Security Council Secretariat. He was the Commandant of the prestigious National Defence College, New Delhi (2009–10). He has had varied operational experience that includes the Siachen Glacier and counter insurgency at various levels in Kashmir.

Anit Mukherjee is an Assistant Professor at Rajaratnam School of International Studies (RSIS), Nanyang Technological University, Singapore. He is currently preparing a book manuscript based on his dissertation examining civil-military relations in India.

Manjeet S. Pardesi is a Lecturer in International Relations at Victoria University of Wellington, New Zealand. He obtained his PhD in Political Science from Indiana University, Bloomington. His dissertation work focused on the initiation of strategic rivalries and their escalation to war. His research interests include causes of war, theories of foreign policymaking, international relations in world history, Asian security, and Indian foreign/security policy.

Bibhu Prasad Routray is a Singapore-based security analyst/consultant who has served in the National Security Council Secretariat, New Delhi. He specializes in decision-making, counter-terrorism, and force modernization in South Asia.

Ashok Sawhney, former Commodore, served the Indian Navy till 2008. He has held positions such as Director of Naval Operations, Naval Attache at Washington D.C., Fleet Operations Officer, and even taught at the Nigerian Naval College. His areas of interest include international relations and maritime affairs.